30

STUDIES IN MEDIAEVAL HISTORY

Edited by GEOFFREY BARRACLOUGH

Vol. VI

CROWN, COMMUNITY AND PARLIAMENT
IN THE LATER MIDDLE AGES

STUDIES IN MEDIAEVAL HISTORY

It is hoped that this Series, intended in the first place for students in the Universities, may help to bridge the gap between the tex-books and the learned monographs in which English and continental scholars of the present day are re-writing the story of the middle ages. Its object is less to furnish an outline of facts, than to introduce the student to major problems of interpretation.

CROWN, COMMUNITY AND PARLIAMENT
IN THE LATER MIDDLE AGES

STUDIES IN ENGLISH CONSTITUTIONAL
HISTORY

By

GAILLARD T. LAPSLEY

Edited by

HELEN M. CAM & GEOFFREY BARRACLOUGH

BASIL BLACKWELL : OXFORD

M CM LI

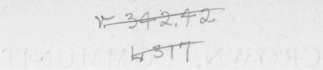

PRINTED IN GREAT BRITAIN
BY A. T. BROOME AND SON,
ST. CLEMENT'S, OXFORD

INTRODUCTION

CROWN, COMMUNITY AND PARLIAMENT IN THE LATER MIDDLE AGES

THIS selection of the more outstanding of Gaillard Lapsley's historical articles has been rendered post-humous by his death on August 17, 1949. Ill health had compelled him to entrust the editing of it to other hands, and it is thus possible for us to say some things of his work which might otherwise have gone unsaid here.

English mediaeval studies owe a long debt to G. T. Lapsley. He published only one book, *The County Palatine of Durham*,[1] which, although now half a century old, is still a model for the treatment of the great English franchises of the middle ages; but as a teacher and a contributor to learned reviews he exerted profound influence over the thought of generations of historical students, particularly the inter-war generation between 1919 and 1939.

Lapsley was born in New York City on November 14, 1871. After graduating at Harvard in 1893, he took up the study of law, a discipline which had lasting effects on his thought and technique, but soon abandoned it for history. Here ' his master ', as he loved to call him, was Charles Gross, the pioneer historian of mediaeval English boroughs and their gilds, whose encyclopaedic knowledge of English local historical publications is reflected in that bibliography of English mediae-val history which stands as a reproach and a challenge to the scholars of to-day. But when Lapsley came to England in 1904 and settled down to his lifelong work as Tutor of Trinity College, and as Lecturer and later University Reader in Constitutional History at Cambridge, the direction of his interests shifted. This can be attributed partly to his experience as a teacher but also, without doubt, to the stimulus of F. W. Maitland's ideas, the impact of which was heightened by active membership of Maitland's own university. Thenceforward, though he still

---

[1] Harvard Historical Studies, Vol. VIII (Cambridge, Mass., 1900).

found time for occasional excursions into other fields,[1] his thought and writing concentrated insensibly on the central theme of the mediaeval English parliament, and the problems inherent in the relationships on the one hand between the developing institution of parliament and the executive government, and on the other hand between the central parliamentary body and the local communities represented in it.[2] Not a little of this work was critical in character, some of it embodied in detailed reviews,[3] and not the least of its merits was the controversy it often provoked, which served to keep historical study alive, and caused ' us all ' (in Lapsley's own words) ' to test, examine, and very likely to revise our own views '.[4] In this acute analysis of minutiae, however, Lapsley never lost hold of the main thread : his criticism, far from being negative, was complementary to the constructive work of his own papers, designed as they were to build up a picture of what he once described as ' the Constitution *im Werden* '.[5] And as, over the course of a life's work, the detail was etched in, the view broadened, culminating in the most famous of all Lapsley's essays, the minute investigation of *The Parliamentary Title of Henry IV*, in which he, so to say, set the seal on his studies of fourteenth century government by undermining the foundations of Stubbs' ' Lancastrian Experiment '.

It may be said that Lapsley tackled with predilection the great crises in which the theory of the working precedents of the constitution was formulated ; and in this sense his paper on the revolution of 1399 is the natural sequel to his earlier articles on the Statute of York of 1322 and the crisis of 1341. Whoever studies as they deserve his contributions to the parliamentary history of the fourteenth century will emerge with a clearer view not only of the working of mediaeval govern-

[1] For example, his article ' The Flemings in Eastern England ', *E.H.R.* xxi (1906), 509 ff.

[2] This latter preoccupation led him at a later date to investigations into the history of the county courts ; cf. ' The Court, Record and Roll of the County in the Thirteenth Century ', *Law Quarterly Review,* ccii (1935), 299–325.

[3] For example, the important review of H. L. Gray's *The Influence of the Commons on Early Legislation, E.H.R.* xlviii (1933), 656–659 ; cf. also the critical article, ' Mr. Jolliffe's construction of early Constitutional History ', *History* xxiii (1938), 1–11.

[4] *E.H.R.* liii (1938), 704.　　　　　　　　　　[5] *Ibid.,* 702.

ment, but also of the political ideas, not to say the political theory, of the men who worked it. It is his strength—and in this he follows C. H. McIlwain and Fritz Kern, to whom he pays generous tribute—that he sees the most fruitful field for study where theory and practice converge; he eschews no less the technicalities of political mechanism studied for its own sake than the arid arguments of theoreticians withdrawn from the dust and heat of the political arena. 'Political speculation', he considered,[1] 'apart from the construction of Utopias, evidently consists of inferences from political experience.'

Lapsley's views of the mediaeval constitution were never coordinated into a single volume; 'we hold them back', he once said, 'not so much for want of faith in their validity as because we have not yet consolidated their defence'. Yet there is an obvious coherence in his major contributions to historical learning and interpretation, and it is the aim of this selection of essays to make available in one volume those articles which, both in their content and their interdependence, best illustrate his personal approach to constitutional history and the nature of his contribution to the advance of its study. They were written over a period of forty years, going back to the time when the author was a junior teacher at Harvard under Gross and extending to the time when he had laid down his Cambridge Readership, and was once more in the United States, severed by the barriers of war from his second academic home at Trinity. But they have all the characteristic mark of a single mind; all retain their value, independently and still more in association; and of some at least it may be said that, if they had not been written, the direction and even the rate of progress of our knowledge of the mediaeval constitution might have been different. They have left their mark on historical writing and historical thinking, and a brief appreciation of their importance is therefore in place.

The collection is introduced by the survey of recent advance in constitutional history written for the *Cambridge Historical Journal* in 1936 (Essay I)[2]. Were this merely a

---

[1] Below, p. 20.
[2] Below, pp. 1–33. Sections IV (The Church) and V (The Towns) have been omitted, as falling outside the range and framework of this volume.

critical bibliography of writings on mediaeval constitutional history from the beginning of the century to 1935 it might well be thought that, whatever its value when put together, it was scarcely worth preserving after a decade and a half of unflagging research and reinterpretation. But, in fact, it is more than this. Lapsley has in this article with great skill used the framework of a bibliography to sketch in outline his view of ' the theory of the mediaeval constitution and the nature of its principal organs and their relation to each other'; and it is therefore an almost indispensable key to his thought, linking together the more specialized essays which follow. In shape and content it reflects pretty closely the balance of Lapsley's main pre-occupation with the constitution—Parliament, Law and Constitutional Theory, and the Church—in that order; with a glance at the newer theme of administrative history. In his sketch of the transformation of parliamentary studies inaugurated by Maitland's edition of the Parliament Roll of 1305, Lapsley's own place in the process is naturally in the background. It is worth noting, therefore, that in 1915, before the publication of Pollard's *Evolution of Parliament*, or the opening of the series of articles on Parliament by Mr. Richardson and Dr. Sayles, Lapsley was insisting that round about 1341 ' no one thought of parliament as a whole ', and explanations were made not ' *to* parliament but to groups *in* parliament '.[1] Again, in the statement that ' Practice had, as so often before in England, outstripped theory ',[2] he was anticipating Mr. Galbraith's illuminating revision of Stubbs' famous dictum, ' Constitutional progress had outrun administrative order '.[3]

The influence of both Maitland and McIlwain is unmistakable; Lapsley is working along lines opened up by their books,[4] but doing so in his own way. Maitland's famous introduction to the parliament roll of 1305, ' a stronger solvent of orthodoxy than he perhaps intended or even realized,' was the flash of genius which touched off a new train of thought; but it was Lapsley who set himself the task of applying the insight

---

[1] Below, pp. 269, 270.   [2] Below, p. 262.

[3] Stubbs, C. H., III, 276. ' It would probably be truer ', Mr. Galbraith comments, ' to say that constitutional practice had outrun constitutional progress'; cf. *History* XXVI (1942), 233.

[4] Their key position is stressed by Lapsley himself below pp. 6–7.

' based on the records of a single parliament ' to the whole
field of parliamentary history, and testing in its light the
traditional doctrines of parliamentary government, just as
Lapsley was first in the field in the critical use of McIlwain's
brilliant generalisations. His method and his choice of subject
are his own; but he owes to the two great writers from either
Cambridge his approach to parliamentary history, in particular
his appreciation of the significance of the background of legal
thought against which political actions are played out. Legal
theory runs it close with institutional development in his
approach to parliamentary problems, and the concern with the
doctrine of fundamental, or rather inviolable law, natural to
one familiar with the American constitution, comes out
markedly in Essays V and VI. A legal discipline in examining
the character both of institutions and of political thinking
informs his work, and Essays VI, VII and VIII, dealing as they
do with a succession of fourteenth-century political crises that
led to the formulation of something like political theories are,
each in its own field, applications of this technique to the
problem of the relation of the functions and powers of the
Crown to the developing institution of parliament. No one
to-day will question the assertion that it is premature to speak
of a constitution in the fourteenth century ; that what we are
watching then is the accumulation of precedents in different
directions.[1] Perhaps the most pregnant passage in Essay V is
that which suggests that those who drafted the statute of 1322
sought to canalise political conflicts in parliaments, and that
the conflicts of 1327, 1340–1, 1376, 1388 and 1399 were played
out on a parliamentary stage ' as the Statute of York intended '.[2]
Nor should we be likely to deny that there was sometimes ' an
attempt to convert political aims into constitutional principles '.[3]
Nevertheless the need of an exact definition of terms when we
are dealing with the inchoate is as urgent when ideas are being
examined as when institutions are in question. The attempt to
define the functions and powers of the Crown in relation to
mediaeval law and custom may make the writer vulnerable,
but it is indispensable to the study of events like the crisis of

[1] Below, pp. 33, 262.   [2] Below, p. 200.
[3] Below, p. 259.

1341 or the deposition of Richard II, and no subsequent
writer can leave on one side Lapsley's handling of those
events. His interpretation of the revolution of 1399 can be said
to have held the field against all challengers hitherto; it is a
solid contribution to constitutional history. The far earlier
article on the crisis of 1341 has been not so much superseded as
supplemented by Tout's work—in particular by the brilliant
lecture on ' Conflicting tendencies in administrative history ',[1]
in which Tout brought out, as Lapsley had not done, the
significance of the part played by the civil service in the trials
of strength between king and baronage in the fourteenth
century. But Lapsley's discussion still retains its value because
he not only attempts to elucidate the political theories, both
formulated and unformulated, of the protagonists in the
struggle, but also adumbrates the theme he was to develop in
later essays—the ' sounding board ' function of a fourteenth-
century parliament. The ' anxious preoccupation with public
opinion ' evinced by the publication of political manifestoes,
as in 1341, relates also to the people collected on the occasion
of a parliament, whether suitors or members, or, as in 1399,
the London mob. They are a political source of ' moral
support ' not only in themselves but in their contacts with the
communities from which they came and to which they return.
In studying the history of representation, in particular, the
distinction between the political and constitutional aspect of
parliaments is, as Lapsley observes, hard to maintain.[2]

In Essays III and IV this line of inquiry is followed up,
and Lapsley shows himself a pupil of Maitland not only in his
legalistic but in his humanist approach to history, by translating
an institutional problem into the terms of the individual. The
consideration of the relation of the parliaments of 1339–41 to
public opinion led him to the investigation of the elections to
parliament under Edward II, and Essay IV tests the evidence
for the control of choice of the personnel of the Commons by
king or barons. The inquiry into personnel in its turn leads
to Essay III, with its study of the social status and administrative activities of the group from which the county members

---

[1] *B.J.R.L.* VIII (1924) ; cf. below, pp. 4 n. 1, 29–30.
[2] Below, p. 160 f.

were drawn in the thirteenth century. Such studies, as Lapsley was the first to recognise, must be multiplied many times before any safe generalisation on ' public opinion ' can be ventured on. Lapsley's essay of 1919 on ' The Knights of the Shire in the parliaments of Edward II ' has been the forerunner not only of many such specialised inquiries, but also of the more general project initiated by Lord Wedgwood, of which the first outcome was the Interim Report on Commons Personnel issued in 1932.[1] The essay on the ' Buzones ' has been and is being reinforced by the labours of other scholars. To those noted by Lapsley himself[2] should be added the more recent publications by A. L. Poole and N. Denholm-Young, together with writings recently published and shortly to be expected from R. F. Treharne, on the knightly class under Henry III.

The relations of Crown and Parliament, of Crown and Community, of Community and Parliament—these then have been the main themes of the essays here republished. Essay II, though concerned with the rights and powers of the Crown, is also an exercise in the technique of historical criticism. It is an application of Round's own methods to Round's dismissal of the story related by Hemingburgh of Earl Warenne's rusty sword and the history of the *quo warranto* proceedings. It is noteworthy that Lapsley's conclusions with regard to Edward I's policy would seem on the whole to be borne out by the latest treatment of the subject by T. F. T. Plucknett.[3]

The final study on ' The Problem of the North ' (Essay IX) also, to some extent, stands apart, and here again the work of other scholars, notably of Dr. Rachel Reid, has carried further the lines of investigation suggested by the young scholar of 1900. Yet the article forms a fitting epilogue to the consideration of the mediaeval Crown and Community in England. It is not only that the problem of the North bridges the whole mediaeval period from 1066 to 1537—that it has its roots in pre-Conquest conditions, and is intimately bound up with the neo-feudalism of the fifteenth century. More important is the fact that it brings the historian up against the seat and stronghold of those cruder political forces which came into play at

[1] Cf. below, p. 9.   [2] Below, p. 9 n. 4.
[3] T. F. T. Plucknett, *Legislation of Edward I* (1949), 35–50.

every turning point in English constitutional development. The
'problem of the North' is well worth consideration in the
present context precisely because it was not localized or isolated,
but impinged on the main current of English history at every
turn; the part played, for example, by the Percies in the
revolution of 1399 was already foreshadowed by the rôle of the
'northern barons' in 1214 and 1215. This rôle, of course, was
shared also by the Welsh Marches and the Welsh Marchers; it
was possible because the northern counties, like the western
marches, were never (in Lapsley's phrase) 'assimilated to the
rest of the kingdom' and to 'the general system of administration' there obtaining,[1] with the result that the lords marcher
exercised 'extraordinary powers',[2] which they were able to
bring to bear in the shaping of issues which we regard as
'constitutional'. Thus Lapsley's essay, although at first sight
remote from his main theme, is in fact closely interwoven with
it; and it still retains its value, alongside more recent work,[3]
as one of the studies which materially help to elucidate the
balance of law and politics in the fifteenth century. Lapsley's
main work stopped with the revolution of 1399; thereafter, he
said, 'the materials are lacking', 'the constitutional history . . .
remains to be written—or rather to be rewritten.'[4] In this
essay he looks forward beyond the turn of the fourteenth and
fifteenth centuries, when 'we are left . . . with two opposing
political theories each containing constitutional doctrines for
which some precedent might be cited',[5] to the Tudor settlement which, by killing 'political feudalism and dealing a mortal
blow to economic and social feudalism',[6] fundamentally altered
the political circumstances under which the mediaeval constitution had been painfully evolved.

This volume, which of necessity lacked the author's own
searching scrutiny, has now become not only a harvesting of his
work but a tribute to his memory. We have no doubt that,
had he been able to edit it himself, it would have been different
from what it is; not only might he have made exhaustive

---

[1] Below, pp. 375, 388. [2] Below, p. 387.
[3] Cf. H. M. Cam, 'The Decline and Fall of English Feudalism', *History*
xxv (1940), 216–233 ; K. B. McFarlane, *T.R.H.S.* xxvi (1944), 53–79.
[4] Below, p. 33. [5] Below, p. 33. [6] *History*, xxv, 233.

reference to subsequent publications, but it is probable that he would have wished to indicate, at many points, his reaction to more recent investigations and perhaps even to make a few substantive alterations in his text. We have not thought such things to be within our province. At a few points we have had the benefit of the author's own annotations which we have thankfully used ; in one case (Essay II) he specifically desired us, before his death, to add notes in accordance with directions which he gave us. Otherwise we have confined our editing largely to introducing uniformity of style and bringing bibliographical references up to date; far beyond that we have not deemed it wise to go. We have done our best without him; and that he should have been willing to entrust to us the responsibility of seeing his essays through the press, can only be a source of pride to those who have known him as a teacher, a colleague, and a dear and honoured friend.

It remains for us to acknowledge with grateful thanks the courtesy and sympathetic consideration of all those publishers and editors, who have so willingly permitted us to reprint from their pages the selection of essays which follows. The source of each of the nine essays is specified at the appropriate place, but we would also more generally extend our thanks to Messrs. Longmans, Green & Co., Ltd., to the Cambridge University Press, and to the editors of the *English* and *American Historical Reviews* and of the *Cambridge Historical Journal.* In accordance with the author's wishes, the essays (apart from the first which, it is hoped, may serve as an introduction) have been arranged in chronological order.

H.M.C.
G.B.

September, 1949.

ABBREVIATIONS

B.I.H.R.	Bulletin of the Institute of Historical Research.
B.J.R.L.	Bulletin of the John Rylands Library.
C.C.R.	Calendar of Close Rolls.
C.Ch.R.	Calendar of Charter Rolls.
C.F.R.	Calendar of Fine Rolls.
C.H.	Constitutional History.
C.P.R.	Calendar of Patent Rolls.
C.S.P.	Calendar of State Papers.
D.N.B.	Dictionary of National Biography.
E.E.T.S.	Early English Text Society.
E.H.R.	English Historical Review.
H.E.L.	History of English Law.
H.Z.	Historische Zeitschrift.
L.Q.R.	Law Quarterly Review.
R.H.S.	Royal Historical Society.
R.S.	Rolls Series..
S.S.	Selden Society.
T.R.H.S.	Transactions of the Royal Historical Society.
V.C.H.	Victoria County History.
Y.B.	Year Book.

CONTENTS

I

SOME RECENT ADVANCE IN ENGLISH CONSTITUTIONAL HISTORY (BEFORE 1485)[1]

I. INTRODUCTION

THE following notes were put together in response to a suggestion that workers in other fields might be interested to hear something of our problems and the solutions we are finding for them. I have addressed myself to such readers and have tried to avoid both the minute and the technical. An article that covered the whole ground could have been little more than a select bibliography, and what I thought was wanted in this case was an indication of what the books contained.[2] The selected topics have been chosen partly with reference to the amount and importance of the work that has recently been devoted to them, and partly because of their special relevance to the subject in hand. Thus much could have been said of the very interesting development of views as to origins and the pre-conquest period in general or of the important advances that have been made in the understanding of revenue, taxation and finance, but it will probably be agreed that these had to make way for such subjects as constitutional theory and parliament. Reasons for certain other obvious omissions will be given later.

Stubbs' great book[3] is still the point of departure for all constitutional research after 1066 ; and those who neglect it do so at their peril. Yet it is true that Stubbs' ' system ' has been completely rejected and a word must be said on this apparent

---

[1] Reprinted from *The Cambridge Historical Journal*, vol. v (1936), pp. 119–146. Sections iv (The Church) and v (The Towns), have been omitted, as falling outside the range and framework of the present volume.

[2] The best bibliography, a first-rate work in its day although the annual production has now outstripped it, is: Gross, C., *Sources and Literature of English History to* 1485, 2nd ed. revised, 1915. A new edition of this indispensable work is overdue. For publications from 1934 there are the volumes of *Writings on British History* (ed. A. T. Milne, 1937 seq.), and for the war years, L. B. Frewin, *Bibliography of Historical Writings*, 1940–1945 (Blackwell, 1947) ; cf. also the *Annual Bulletin of Historical Literature*, issued by the Historical Association from 1911 onwards.

[3] With the following remarks it is instructive to compare Helen Cam, ' Stubbs Seventy Years After', *Cambridge Hist. Journal* ix (1948), 129–147.

paradox. The truth is that *zwei Seelen wohnten in seiner Brust*, the one of a cautious, experienced scholar interpreting the evidence before him in the light of a prodigious documentation, and the other of an idealist strongly influenced by the Teutonic past created by German historians in response to Fichte's appeal. It would be hard to say that he ever formally contradicted himself, it would be harder to deny that he was able to offer simultaneous hospitality to notions that most people would regard as mutually exclusive.[1] A French scholar well versed in the sources of English medieval history has observed that Stubbs had ' a mystic conception of the origins of the English constitution ', and he might have added of its development as well.[2] M. Lefebvre, M. Petit-Dutaillis' co-editor of the French translation of Stubbs, speaks more strongly when he says :[3] ' There is no cohesion between his partial conclusions founded on the texts, and his general conception.' This is exactly the point, though the generalization may be thought too sweeping. If the system is gone the work of the scholar remains. The intuitions of an investigator whose memory is stored with evidence and whose imagination has been disciplined in the process of accumulating it cannot safely be rejected. Nor is their value destroyed or even impaired by the fact that the reasons alleged in support of them must sometimes be rejected, and this is so just because they are intuitions, not conclusions reached by a process of reasoning. Then, too, Stubbs had an acquaintance with the chronicles and biographies that gave him some such familiarity with the political movement and the personalities of his period as a modern publicist has with those of his own time. The importance of this equipment is nowadays less generally recognized than it deserves to be.[4]

[1] For an apt illustration of this point see Stubbs, *Historical Introductions to the Rolls Series*, ed. Hassall (Oxford U.P., 1902), 291.

[2] Petit-Dutaillis, Ch. in *Studies and Notes Supplementary to Stubbs' Constitutional History* III, 307–8, Manchester U.P., 1929. M. Petit-Dutaillis has since published a valuable study of the comparative development of French and English history, *La Monarchie Féodale en France et en Angleterre, X^e–XIIIe Siècle*, Paris, 1933, which may be read with interest and profit although, as far as English constitutional matters are concerned, with certain reserves. [3] *Studies and Notes*, 482, n. 2.

[4] But see Tout, T. F., ' The Study of mediaeval chronicles ' in *Collected Papers* III, i ff., Manchester U.P., 1934. A good example of the value of Stubbs' intuitions is afforded by the emphasis he laid on the quarrel between Henry II and Becket over the sheriffs' aid. Round had no diffi-

In two important respects, however, Stubbs' work has been supplemented and in consequence modified, and those are the history of law and of administration. It is not suggested that Stubbs was ignorant of what was to be known in his day of these two branches of history, but rather that he did not realize how much each had to contribute to his own subject. He considered that with the completion of the parliamentary structure in 1295 administrative history had no further bearing, and he did not anticipate what legal history could be made to yield in the hands of a genius. No one now is ignorant that the two disciplines are inseparable in the sense that they occupy a good deal of territory in common and even apart from that cannot do without each other. ' Pollock and Maitland ' and ' Holdsworth ' are as indispensable to constitutional as they are to legal historians, though each may use them in different ways and for different ends. The point need not be stressed, for Maitland's teaching has become part of the very texture of constitutional history, and Holdsworth's volumes are probably consulted as frequently by historians as they are by lawyers.

Maitland himself understood the value of administrative history and the need for exploiting the documents upon which it rests. No systematic attack was, however, made upon the problem until the late T. F. Tout devoted the best years of his life to it. He began his big book when he was 44, and died 30 years later before the concluding volumes had seen the light. The impact of Tout's work[1] on the investigation and teaching of constitutional history has been so considerable and so extens ve that what has to be said of it in general must take its place here rather than at a later stage. The work is based chiefly on the records which, since Stubbs' time, have been made relatively manageable by arrangement and calendaring. It is concerned mainly with the thirteenth and fourteenth centuries, but it brings together what can be said of the earlier

culty in showing that the payment involved was not danegeld and that Stubbs' argument that Becket was resisting a tax was inadmissible (Round, *Feudal England*, 497 ff.). What he could not or did not see was the importance of any resistance to autocracy on grounds of principle.

[1] Tout, T. F., *The Place of the Reign of Edward II in English History*, Manchester U.P., 1914 (2nd ed., revised by H. Johnstone, 1936). *Chapters in the Administrative History of Mediaeval England*, 6 vols., Manchester U.P., 1920–33. *Collected Papers*, 3 vols., Manchester U.P., 1932–4.

period. The real subject of the book is the wardrobe, but this
of course involves the other organs of the central government.
Tout cast his nets very wide and has necessarily written of other
subjects, such as parliament and the origin and nature of
peerage. The constitutional historian must thus consult him
at almost every turn. Here, as in the relation of constitutional
and legal history, there is much common ground and mutual
service but the ends differ. If we take Tout's work as a whole
we may venture upon two generalizations. He has called
attention to the working of an hitherto unrecognized factor in
the processes that went to the making of constitutional history.
This is the civil service, its development and the part it played
in the long struggle between the crown and baronage. These
Tout has used for the reinterpretation of constitutional history
in the thirteenth and even more in the fourteenth centuries.
He indicated the bearing of his work so far as the fourteenth
century is concerned in a lecture delivered in 1923 which is still
a valuable guide.[1] There is another side to the matter no less
important though he has emphasized it less directly. Writing
of the privy seal he refers to ' the perpetual effort [from John
to Henry VIII] to distinguish by a visible token between the
king as an official and the king in his personal capacity '.
' There are,' he continues, ' the equally unending struggles of
the king to extricate himself from the network of red tape
which choked his personal initiative and hedged his authority
by forms and routine which destroyed his individual will.' He
points to the history of the seals, all of which began as a means
of signifying the personal will of the king, and were one by
one ' officialized ' and so withdrawn from his control or else
ceased to exist.[2] But this is true of every organ of central
government, and the working out in the light of experience and
error of a departmental practice is the source of a good deal of
constitutional law. It has been well said that ' insensiblement
la fonction créa l'organe ',[3] and it might be added that in the
discharge of its function the organ in turn creates and imposes

---

[1] ' Some conflicting tendencies in English administrative history during
the fourteenth century ', *B.J.R.L.* VIII (1924), 82 ff., reprinted in *Collected
Papers*, III, 223 ff.   [2] *Chapters* V, 229.
[3] Viollet, P., *Histoire des Institutions Politiques de la France* III (1903),
296.

the law by which it lives. No doubt its only sanctions were expediency and custom, but they sufficed.

For present purposes we can scarcely go beyond these observations, though more detailed references to Tout's conclusions will be found in what follows. Those who wish for a more comprehensive view and have not the leisure to examine the whole work should turn to the admirable summaries provided by M. Lefebvre[1] and the general views which Tout gave in his occasional lectures[2] and the excellent index to which his last volume is devoted. The existence of these helps decided me to omit from the present survey such topics as the Council, Household, Chancery and Exchequer which would otherwise have demanded treatment.

With this general introduction we may turn to consider the first of the topics which we have selected for treatment.

II. PARLIAMENT

Stubbs' account of the early history of parliament resembles the opening chapters of the book of Genesis in two important respects—it describes an act of creation and it no longer commands general acceptance. When the notion that Edward I summoned the nation to a share in government by creating a parliament of estates, one of them based on a consciously evolved system of representation, was abandoned, it began to be seen that the origin of the institution like its nature was complex and must be sought in various quarters. If we attend to the nature of parliament at the end of the fourteenth century we observe that its normal business was threefold. In co-operation with the king it facilitated the process by which the community adjusted itself to its environment by redressing grievances and punishing misdeeds, whether as a supreme tribunal, by answer to petition, or (as was now becoming commoner) by legislation. It furnished the king with supplies, when it saw fit, by authorizing taxation which would not otherwise have been possible. It afforded the crown the opportunity of hearing and moulding public opinion. It was thus an organ

[1] In *Studies and Notes Supplementary to Stubbs' Constitutional History,* III. M. Lefebvre had seen only the first and second volumes of the completed work but he had used the fugitive publications in which Tout anticipated his most important conclusions.
[2] See *Collected Papers* III, 93–117, 191–276.

of government, but it had functions indispensable to the king which, in time, would enable it to exert a considerable influence on the course of public affairs. Such a body is obviously the outcome of much institutional history which has only slowly been traced and set in order. The first step was taken in Germany when Riess's little treatise on the English electoral law and his essay on the beginnings of the commons[1] taught people, among other things, to look at such matters from the point of view of the thirteenth rather than that of the seventeenth century. Eight years later Maitland published an edition of the parliament roll of 1305 with an introduction[2] which has proved a stronger solvent of orthodoxy than he perhaps intended or even realized. From a constitutional point of view this essay might be described as a comment on a now famous passage from *Fleta* specifically illustrated by the evidence of the roll of 1305. The king has his court in his council in his parliament in the presence of certain of his subjects (kinds or classes of them whom the anonymous author specifies), and his business there is to resolve the doubts of his judges, to provide new remedies for new wrongs as they appear and to render justice to all men according to their deserts. The personnel of the parliament of 1305 Maitland identifies from the roll: prelates, magnates, royal officials, judges and men learned in the law, knights and burgesses, but these latter are not mentioned in *Fleta*. He shows the period of their attendance and the work they do. He describes the elaborate machinery provided to deal with the mass of petitions submitted to the king, the important cases that are heard, the discussion of policy and indeed, the whole business of the session. The work is the work of a supreme tribunal, a royal council and a deliberative assembly, and those who appear to manage and direct the business are for the more part the king's officials. But when is

[1] Riess, L., *Geschichte des Wahlrechts zum englischen Parlament im Mittelalter*, Leipzig, 1885 ; ' Der Ursprung des englischen Unterhauses ', *H.Z.* LX (1888), I ff. A translation of Riess's volume, under the title *The History of the English electoral law in the Middle Ages*, was published by K. L. Wood-Legh in 1940.

[2] *Memoranda de Parliamento*, R.S., 1893. The permanent part of the introduction is incorporated in the volume of Maitland's *Selected Essays* (ed. Hazeltine, Lapsley and Winfield) published by the Cambridge University Press in 1936.

it a court, when a council and when a parliament ? It is hard to say, but it is pretty clear that its character of parliament does not depend on the presence of the ' commons '. We are left with the picture, based on the records of a single parliament and *Fleta's* generalization, of a court of three circles concentric about the king yet each sufficiently identified to have its own name and perhaps its own functions. It is not too much to say that upon this foundation the structure of our present knowledge of the beginnings of parliament has been slowly reared. Much, however, remained to be done, and in particular it was necessary to find further evidence for Maitland's generalization. The first step in this direction was marked by the appearance of Professor McIlwain's[1] *High Court of Parliament* in 1910. Professor McIlwain emphasized, perhaps he over-emphasized, the curial character of the institution. Institutionally it derived from the *curia regis*, itself in origin a feudal body. It became national with the progress of royal centralization, and eventually the remedies it gave were national too, for they took the form of statutes. But its function, in medieval theory, was to declare not to make the law, and in such circumstances the passage from a court making new law by judgment to a legislature making it by statute has somehow to be masked. But the distinction must at any rate be recognized in fact, and the institutional development of the law courts, the detachment of the judges from parliamentary work, and the fact that they were soon obliged to shape a doctrine of the force and interpretation of statutes,[2] hastened the process, although the old theory outlived the Middle Ages. In 1913 Professor Baldwin, in his book on the *King's Council*,[3] did for the conciliar aspect of parliament very much what Professor McIlwain had done for the curial. He marked the institutional differentiation of the council which by the end of the fourteenth century was attested by the oath,

---

[1] McIlwain, C. H., *The High Court of Parliament and its Supremacy* Yale U.P., New Haven, and Oxford U.P., 1910.

[2] See Plucknett, T. F. T., *Statutes and their Interpretation in the first half of the Fourteenth Century*, Cambridge U.P., 1922.

[3] Baldwin, J. F., *The King's Council in England during the Middle Ages*, Oxford U.P., 1913. With this should now be compared the relevant chapters in Wilkinson, B., *Studies in the Constitutional History of the Thirteenth and Fourteenth Centuries*, Manchester U.P., 1937.

the payment of salaries, and the existence of a corporate memory in the shape of minutes. He showed the varying proportion between the baronial and the curial elements of the council reflecting the political conditions of the reign. He confirmed Maitland's conjecture that in spite of the varying epithets applied by contemporaries to a body that fluctuated in composition but was constant in a function that can never be defined or restricted, that of advising the crown, there was one council and one only. In many cases in the fourteenth century it would be difficult to distinguish between the council and parliament[1] particularly as the persons summoned by writ to each were often the same. This confusion was partly avoided by the practice which arose about the middle of the century of issuing writs of summons to the council under the privy seal while the great seal was reserved for summonses to parliament. By the fifteenth century the distinction between the two bodies was clear enough.

During the last ten years Mr. Richardson and Professor Sayles have examined the whole ground again with interesting and important results. In a preliminary essay Mr. Richardson showed how the word parliament entered official language in the middle of the thirteenth century in connexion with the new terminal meetings of the king's court held for the purpose of giving such remedy and redress as could only be had by the exercise of the discretionary power that lay with the king.[2] In their view this and this alone, irrespective of the presence or absence of the commons or the business transacted, constitutes a parliament, though the word continued to be used more loosely by the chroniclers. The practice of representation increased, and the commons began to take on a certain political importance with the reaction of the magnates against the strong control imposed by Edward I, but throughout the fourteenth century, with increasing exceptions, the parliament was

---

[1] This has recently been discussed with reference to the exclusion of Archbishop Stratford from parliament in the spring of 1341 by B. Wilkinson, ' The protest of the Earls of Arundel and Surrey in the crisis of 1341 ', *E.H.R.*, xlvi (1931), 177 ff. See also Richardson, H. G. and Sayles, G. O., ' The parliaments of Edward III ', *B.I.H.R.* viii, 72 ff.

[2] See also Jolliffe, J.E.A., ' Some factors in the beginnings of parliament' *T.R.H.S.*, 4th ser. xxii (1940).

dominated by the council and its work directed and managed by the royal officials.[1]

On the side of the organization and personnel of parliament great advance has been made since the impulse given by Riess in the study of the electoral law in 1885. The ground covered has been surveyed by Pasquet in the English edition (revised by himself) of his little book first published in 1914[2] and in the Interim Report of the committee set up to direct the collective study of the subject.[3] The wide view that this body has taken suggests that even for the Middle Ages the bulk of the work remains to be done. What has been already accomplished, however, authorizes certain provisional generalizations. The balance of evidence is against the existence in the counties in the fourteenth century of any general reluctance to serve in parliament. The country gentlemen had undergone a long training in compulsory and unpaid public service, and in most if not all counties there was a group of them constantly active in local administration who took parliamentary representation as part of the day's work.[4] So it happened that many of them would have sat in several parliaments as knights for one or more counties and not infrequently as burgesses as well. Thus

[1] Richardson, H. G., ' The origins of parliament ', *T.R.H.S.*, 4th ser. XI (1928), 137 ff. Richardson, H. G. and Sayles, G. O., ' Early records of the English parliaments ', *B.I.H.R.* V, 129, VI, 71, 129 ; ' The parliaments of Edward III ', *ibid.* VIII, 65 ; IX, 1; ' The King's ministers in parliament, 1272–1377 ', *E.H.R.* XLVI (1931), 529; XLVII (1932), 194, 376; ' Parliamentary documents from formularies ', in *B.I.H.R.* XI, 147. Future investigation has been much facilitated by the critical study of the origin, nature and authority of the rolls of parliament to be found in the articles cited above and particularly by the learned authors' publication of a new collection of those rolls : *Rotuli Parliamentorum Anglie Hactenus Inediti MCCLXXIX–MCCCLXXIII* (R.H.S., Camden, Third Series LI) (1935). For a view of parliamentary development in the fourteenth century attributing much greater and earlier importance to the commons see the late Miss Clarke's book cited below 19, n. 1.

[2] Pasquet, D., *The Origin of the House of Commons*, translated by R. G. D. Laffan, with a Preface and Additional notes by G. Lapsley, Cambridge U.P., 1925.

[3] *Interim Report of the Committee on House of Commons Personnel and Politics*, 1264–1832, H.M. Stationery Office, 1932.

[4] Cf. White, A. B., *Self-Government at the King's Command*, Minneapolis, 1933—an excellent little book which does not appear to have attracted the attention that it merits. See also Cam, H. M., *The Hundred and the Hundred Rolls*, 1930 ; Edwards, J. G., ' The personnel of the commons in parliaments under Edward I and Edward II ', *Essays in Medieval History presented to T. F. Tout*, Manchester U.P., 1925 (followed by a controversy with A. F. Pollard in *History* XI, 15, 204) ; Lapsley, G., ' Knights of the

most parliaments in the fourteenth century would contain a reasonable percentage of experienced knights or burgesses. The Lancastrian statutes 1406-45, if we had no other evidence, would, as constituting a real code of electoral law, suggest that the choice of suitable persons to represent the counties was a matter of public concern just because election had become a matter of private interest. But we still need here much more detailed local study than we have as yet had. The most important contribution to the problem of borough representation has been made by Miss McKisack. It is, of course, common ground that the return to a writ of summons is by no means evidence of attendance, which must be sought for in the writs *de expensis*. But it now appears that the absence of these writs is not necessarily proof that the knights or burgesses summoned did not attend. Miss McKisack has shown that it was not unusual for town governments to make a private bargain with their elected representatives. She has also made it clear that some towns at least attached importance to representation, instructed their members during the session, and on their return asked for reports on what had taken place in parliament. On the other hand the problem of the selection and geographical distribution of the boroughs represented is no nearer solution than it was when Stubbs incorporated in a footnote a summary of Riess's exceedingly ingenious conjecture.[1]

As to the Speakership Mr. Richardson and Professor Sayles have made it highly probable that the function was at first

shire in the parliaments of Edward II ', *infra*, pp. 111–152, and ' Buzones', *infra*, pp. 63–110, Lewis, N. B., ' Re-election to parliament in the reign of Richard II ', *E.H.R.* xlviii (1933), 364 ; McKisack, M., *The Parliamentary Representation of the English Boroughs during the Middle Ages*, Oxford U.P., 1932 ; Muir, J. M., ' The personnel of parliament under Henry IV ', *B.I.H.R.* ii, 88 ; Tout, T. F., *Chapters* iii, 291–93 (an extensive and valuable note on the attendance of borough members) ; Wood-Legh, K. L., ' Sheriffs, lawyers, belted knights in the parliaments of Edward III ', *E.H.R.* xlvi (1931), 372 ; ' The knights' attendance in the parliaments of Edward III ', *ibid.* xlvii (1932), 398. I have cited only general works, though much has been done for single counties and boroughs, cf. *Interim Report*, 12–14, 49.

[1] Stubbs, *C.H.* iii (4th ed.), 465–6. Riess assumed that the boroughs wished to escape the burden and expense of representation, and that those succeeded in doing so which were able to interpose a bribeable official between themselves and the sheriff to whom the writ was addressed. This condition would be fulfilled in towns within hundreds or liberties. Riess's conclusions had been accepted by Gneist with certain reserves and Stubbs modified his text ' out of respect to Dr. Gneist's authority '.

discharged by a royal official until the commons began to elect one of themselves for that purpose.[1] A good deal of emphasis has been laid on the suggestion that the commons, though in attendance on parliament were somehow not part of it, since they retired to deliberate separately and can be described in a chronicle that appears to embody the report of an eyewitness as proceeding ' to parliament ' from the Westminster Chapter House where they had reached a decision.[2] It is, of course, true that the term ' Commons House ' or ' House of Commons ' is not used in a sense that is definitely institutional until the fifteenth century is half over.[3] But the real point is what you mean by parliament, and it may be suggested that from the moment that you have a statute, such as that of April 1340, providing that certain things can only be done by the consent of the lords spiritual and temporal and the commons (defined as the knights and burgesses) in parliament, any comprehensive definition of parliament must include the commons whether or no their discussions are carried on in the chamber where the king's ministers, the council, the prelates and the peers are sitting.[4]

It we turn from the commons to the two upper estates there is some notable progress to be recorded. The problem of the origin and nature of peerage in the Middle Ages was placed on solid historical grounds by the investigations of Round, Pike, Harcourt and Tout.[5] It is true that the ' vast legend ' of peerage law abides. It serves its practical purpose, and the historian may well take the old advice *guarda e passa*. At any rate the generally accepted historical view of the lay peerage as it existed at the end of the fourteenth century is that it represents

[1] Richardson, H. G. and Sayles, G. O., ' The king's ministers in parliament ', *E.R.H.* XLVII (1932), 377.

[2] Pollard, A. F., *The Evolution of Parliament*, 2nd ed., 1926, caps. IV and VI and XVI. *The Anonimalle Chronicle*, ed. Galbraith, V. H. (Manchester U.P., 1927), 79 ff.

[3] Pickthorn, *Early Tudor Government* (Cambridge U.P., 1934) I, 90–91. Chrimes, S. B., ' " House of Lords " and " House of Commons " in the fifteenth century ', *E.H.R.* XLIX (1934), 494 ff.

[4] I have selected only one of a number of available considerations to illustrate this point.

[5] Vernon Harcourt, L. W., *His Grace the Steward and Trial of Peers*, London, 1907. Pike, L. O., *Constitutional History of the House of Lords*, London, 1894. Round, J. H., *Peerage and Pedigree*, 2 vols. London, 1910. Tout, *Chapters*, vol. III.

the successful attempt of a powerful territorial aristocracy, materially secured by intermarriage, entail and primogeniture, to guard and perpetuate its political influence.[1] Its situation can hardly be called constitutional because, apart from the peerages created by patent, no one had a position defined and secured by law.[2] On the other hand, it must be recognized that in ordinary practice the king generally summoned the heads of the great houses or those who represented them by marriage with co-heiresses, and as far as is known the question of a right to a title and summons was never raised in the courts until the sixteenth century was well under way. This position appears to have been worked out in the course of the fourteenth century taking its origin in what has been described as the feudal reaction in the history of parliament.[3] This movement which begins under Edward II might, from another point of view, be called the adoption by the Lancastrian party of a constitutional policy in the sense of working through the council and parliament. In any case the term ' peer ' could be used to describe those who are habitually summoned to parliament by special writ. Then comes the claim that such peers, if serious charges were brought against them, should be tried only in parliament. This has its roots deep in the feudal past, and the trial of Mortimer in 1330 looks back to the case of Richard Marshall in 1233, and that again to the *judicium parium* of Magna Carta and the traditional practice of the feudal courts.[4] In 1341 an attempt was made to secure recognition of this by legislation, and although the statute was repealed the new doctrine of peerage seems to have been admitted in practice. By this time it was already possible to confer not only a title of honour but a peerage as well by letters patent (1340). The final establishment of judicial privilege, the multiplication of titles, the deter-

[1] For the stages of evolution see Stenton, F.M., ' The Changing Feudalism of the Middle Ages ', *History* xix (1935), 289 ff.

[2] The modern doctrine that a writ received and obeyed conferred a hereditary right was unknown, and even at the end of the fourteenth century ' peers of parliament ' were not necessarily barons sitting by hereditary custom, though probably this was more often the case than not. See Tout, *Chapters* iii, 136–9, 296 n.

[3] Richardson and Sayles, ' The king's ministers in parliament ', *E.H.R.* xlvii (1932), 194 and 377 ff.

[4] Stubbs, *C.H.* ii, 48–49.

mination of precedence and seniority followed in due course.[1]

The parliamentary position of the spiritual lords has long been a matter of controversy which is the more difficult as the evidence is ambiguous. The ecclesiastical tenants-in-chief, unlike their lay brothers, bore a double capacity, and if the constitutions of Clarendon affirmed that in their privileges and obligations they were *sicut barones caeteri*, their canonical disability to take part in a judgement of blood was still explicitly recognized. It has been held that they sat in parliament either by virtue of their official wisdom[2] or by reason of the baronies annexed to their sees or houses. The second of these views was strongly pressed by Pike[3] and has found pretty general acceptance. Miss Chew's recent book[4] has, however, put the whole matter in a new light. Six of the bishops, it appears, held by alms and therefore had no baronies at all. In spite of Archbishop Courtenay's claim in 1388 that clerics holding of the king by barony had a right to be summoned as peers of the realm, it appears that neither all the prelates holding in chief were summoned nor did all who were summoned hold in chief. These and other similar difficulties and anomalies present those who hold that the spiritual lords sit by feudal qualification alone with dilemmas which certainly make a re-examination of the whole question indispensable.

A word must be said of the subsidiary but difficult questions of procedure and privilege. The publication of *The Anonimalle*

[1] All this has been discussed from very different points of view by Professor Pollard in his *Evolution of Parliament*, 2nd ed., caps IV and V and Tout, *Chapters* III, 138 and 296, cf. Index, *s.v.* ' Peers '.

[2] Stubbs, *C.H.* III, 458–61. This is confined to the episcopate, but he considers that they were peers and not merely lords of parliament. If by peers you mean those who should be and are habitually summoned to parliament in the Middle Ages, this is of course the case. Archbishop Stratford could describe himself as ' par terrae major ' ; Birchington, in *Anglia Sacra* I, 28, cf. Anson, *Law and Custom of the Constitution* I (5th ed., 1922), 234–9.

[3] Pike, L. O., *Constitutional History of the House of Lords*, cap. IX. On his view the prelates were recognized as spiritual lords but ' so far as they were peers at all, were entitled to the name, only in virtue of their temporal possessions or baronies ' (p. 159).

[4] Chew, H. M., *English Ecclesiastical Tenants in Chief*, Oxford, 1932 We must go warily in these matters. The Bishop of Carlisle was one of the six bishops who held in alms and owed no military service to the king, yet when he was fined in 1263 before the Justices in Eyre the word ' baro ' was added to the record to indicate that he was to be amerced by the king in council. *Northumberland Pleas*, Newcastle-upon-Tyne Record Series II (1922), No. 704.

Chronicle[1] and Favent's account of the Parliament of 1388[2] have thrown much light on the ways of parliament in the last quarter of the fourteenth century. The satirical account of the motives and conduct of the commons in 1398 contained in Langland's ' Richard the Redeless ' has never been examined critically from this point of view and might yield important results under such treatment.[3] Dr. Gray's book[4] has thrown much light on the technical steps of legislation, successive readings, amendments and the relations of lords and commons. Professor Holdsworth's study suggests that the procedure of parliament was based on that of the law courts.[5] On the matter of privilege Dr. Wittke's little book[6] brings most of the cases together, and some of them have been discussed with more learning than he could command by Dr. Chrimes and Mr. Pickthorn.[7] Finally, the ghost of Haxey has been definitely laid by Tout.[8]

We may turn now to the political movement in the fourteenth century which enhanced the importance of parliament and helped to associate it definitely with the business of legislation and taxation. Tout[9] has shown how after the failure of

[1] *The Anonimalle Chronicle*, ed. Galbraith, V. H., Manchester U.P., 1927, contains an account of the Good Parliament taken from an unknown writer ' closely in touch with the events he is describing if not an eye-witness of at least part of them '.

[2] Favent, *Historia . . . de modo et forma Mirabilis Parliamenti . . . Anno Domini millesimo CCCLXXXVI*, ed. McKisack, M., *Camden Miscellany* XIV, R.H.S., 1926. In spite of the title it is, in fact, an account of the Merciless Parliament by an author who although a ' political propagandist ' is ' remarkably accurate in his relation of facts ' and may have been an eye-witness or received his information from one who was. The material furnished by these (and other) writers has been ably presented by Tout in ' The English parliament and public opinion ' in *Mélanges d'Histoire offerts à Henri Pirenne*, Brussels, 1926; reprinted in *Collected Papers* II, 173.

[3] Langland, *Works*, ed. Skeat, W. W., E.E.T.S. Pt. III, 500 ff. (Passus IV), 1875. Internal evidence restricts the date of the work to the first three weeks of September 1399.

[4] Gray, H. L., *The Influence of the Commons on Early Legislation*, Cambridge, Mass. 1932. See also *The Fane Fragment of the 1461 Lords' Journal*, ed. Dunham, W. H., Yale U.P., 1935.

[5] Holdsworth, Sir William, *The Influence of the Legal Profession on the Growth of the English Constitution*, Oxford U.P., 1924. Cf. his *History of English Law* II (3rd ed.), 429 ff.

[6] Wittke, C., *The History of English Parliamentary Privilege*, Ohio State University Studies, No. 6, 1921.

[7] Pickthorn, *Early Tudor Government* I, 108–14 ; Chrimes, S. B., *English Constitutional Ideas in the Fifteenth Century*, Cambridge U.P., 1936.

[8] *Chapters* IV, 17–19.

[9] *Place of Edward II* ; cf. also ' The English parliament and public opinion ', *Collected Papers* II, 173. Mr. Richardson and Professor Sayles, *loc. cit.*, emphasize the more general aspect of this feudal reaction in politics ; cf. above p. 12, n. 3.

the scheme framed by the Ordainers the magnates began a new policy. This was an attempt to exert their influence through the existing organs of government and particularly through the council, and in this struggle they tended more and more to make use of the parliament. He thought that parliament began to interest ' the man in the street ' at the time of the administrative and constitutional crises of 1340 and 1341. He has emphasized the rapid growth of this political side of parliament as illustrated in the crises of 1376 and 1388. The question of the development of constitutional theory in connexion with these crises and the even greater one of 1399 are discussed in another part of this article. Here we have to note that by the beginning of the fifteenth century the distinction between council and parliament was pretty clear,[1] and that the curial aspect of parliament was less conspicuous.

Meanwhile the activities which to-day we most associate with parliament were coming to the front. The standard accounts of the growth of that process of legislation, which is fairly reflected in the enacting clauses of the early Tudor statutes, have had to be modified in many respects.[2] We must take account of two movements ; one toward the recognition of the fact that law could and indeed must be made as well as declared, and another toward the development of a proper agency for accomplishing that purpose. As to the first of these it may be said that it was acted upon rather than understood, least of all in its implications. Still new law was being made by statute, and the courts by the end of the period had a working theory of statute law which included such important points as its general validity, the rules of interpretation and its relation to the royal prerogative.[3] In the history of the technique of legislation some old landmarks have been removed and others disfigured or obliterated. Dr. Gray has made it plain that the

[1] Baldwin, J. F., *The King's Council*, cap. XII. Pickthorn, K. W. M., *Early Tudor Government*, cap. II. Plucknett, T. F. T., ' The place of the council in the fifteenth century ', *T.R.H.S.*, 4th ser. I (1918), 157 ff.

[2] Cf. Barraclough, G., ' Law and Legislation in Medieval England ', *L.Q.R.* LVI (1940), 75–92.

[3] McIlwain, C. H., *Magna Carta Commemorative Essays*, 1917, 122 ; *The Growth of Political Thought in the West* (1932), caps. v and vi, e.g. 189 and see index. Pickthorn, K. W. M., *Early Tudor Government*, cap. v. Plucknett, T. F. T., *Statutes and their Interpretation*. Chrimes, S. B., *Constitutional Ideas*, cap. III.

movement from petition to bill has no significance in the history of medieval legislation originating with the commons.[1] The concession of 1414 by which the king is understood to have granted the principle that a petition shall not be altered in substance when it is turned into a statute, has been attributed by Dr. Gray to a particular cause which did not recur rather than to a general abuse. Following this lead Mr. Pickthorn and Dr. Chrimes regard the whole incident as of no great importance. Their reasons deserve careful consideration, but they have not convinced me that something like the concession of a second reading principle was not sought for and rather disingenuously granted. The upshot of the whole seems to be that at the end of the Middle Ages it was understood that in practice new law could be made in the sense of giving new rights or taking away existing ones, although the old theory of the ultimate supremacy of the law had still force enough to obscure the possibility of the legislative sovereignty of parliament. Further, the new law was made in a way which formally at least could be squared with the views of Bracton; for the king enacted the statute, employing for that purpose the power that he alone had, although he might not use it without the consent and authority of the lords spiritual and temporal and the commons in parliament assembled. Dr. Gray has worked out the process by which, beginning in the time of Edward II, matters of general or common interest which were to be embodied in a statute were assembled in a comprehensive petition by the commons. Eventually this took the form of a number of separate petitions presented collectively and became the normal way of initiating legislation. His valuable book is marred by some bad blunders and some not very happy inferences. In particular his argument as to the predominance of the commons in legislation in the Lancastrian period and the inferences to be made from it has found little acceptance. Finally we may cite a piece of critical and constructive work of a very different order, Mr. Richardson and Professor Sayles' essay on the Early Statutes.[2] They trace the beginnings of the practice of making law as need arose; the recognition in the

---

[1] Gray, H. L., *The Influence of the Commons on Early Legislation*, 177 ff.
[2] *Law Quarterly Review* L (1934), 201 and 540 ff.

fourteenth century of a statute as a royal command, subject to conformity with the law which the king was sworn to maintain and to certain formalities in promulgation and repeal. They suggest that a true distinction between statute and ordinance can only be made when it is recognized that normal legislation must pass through a normal and uniform course.

I had originally included in this survey a section dealing, among other things, with taxation. It had to be discarded for lack of space, but I wish here to refer to the works of Professors Mitchell and Willard who have made fairly clear the one the origin of national taxation by consent (feudal consent, as formulated in Magna Carta) and the other the working out, after more than a generation's experience of self-assessment, of the system of the taxation of moveables which was stereotyped in 1334 and lasted until the time of James I. To this must be added the latest work on the customs revenue which gives a lucid account of the origin of the system and its reorganization on the basis of the commodities taxed, together with an account of the diverse origins of the customs and the share of parliament in these and the subsequent control of them.[1] It may be said in general that the control of these matters which eventually came to parliament did so almost as a matter of necessity. I do not of course mean constitutional necessity enforced by contention for principle. It was rather that the crown and the treasury found that an aid could not be successfully raised on the old principle of the consent of the principal tenants-in-chief. They needed in practice the consent of the towns and counties as well, just as they were destined to find after long and costly experimentation that the wool trade could only be profitably controlled through the medium of parliament.[2] This at first, at any rate, was a matter of expediency, leaving open the question of the authority of parliament, even though

[1] Mitchell, S. K., *Studies in Taxation under John and Henry III*, Yale U.P., 1914. Willard, J. F., *Parliamentary Taxes on Personal Property, 1290–1334*, Cambridge, Mass., 1934. Gras, N. S. B., *The Early English Customs System*, Cambridge, Mass. and London, 1918.

[2] See Unwin, G., ' The estate of the merchants, 1336–1365 ', and Barnes, F. R., ' The taxation of wool, 1327–1348 ', both in *Finance and Trade under Edward III*, Manchester U.P., 1918. See also Wilkinson, B., *Studies in the Constitutional History of the Thirteenth and Fourteenth Centuries*, Manchester U.P., 1937, cap. III, and Power, E.E., *The Wool Trade in Medieval English History*, Oxford U.P., 1941, c. IV.

C

reinforced by representatives of the shires and some of the towns,[1] to impose a general tax. Mr. Edwards[2] has made an important contribution to the solution of this problem. He points out that the formula requiring knights and burgesses to be equipped with *plena potestas* to bind all and sundry of the communities which they represent was practically completed between 1268 and 1295. The writs from 1283 to 1297 demand full powers for every parliament with the exception of the one assembly (1283) in which no grant was made. He argues that the feudal theory of consent by the tenants-in-chief had broken down, and suggests that Stubbs' view that the commons were summoned in the first instance to consent to taxation has been too hastily discarded.[3] Looking forward he points out that you have in the knights and burgesses with full powers from the communities of the land a *societas societatum* well qualified to give that valid consent to taxation which cannot be derived from the curial theory of parliament because in a court there are no profits without a previous forfeiture. It is known, of course, that the authority of the king and parliament to impose taxation was indirectly (but quite effectively) sanctioned by the statutes of 1340. But even so there are a good many constitutional questions unanswered, some of which are discussed in works to which we have already referred.[4]

Before formulating some provisional generalizations a word must be said of a book that has attracted and deserved a good deal of attention. This is Professor Pollard's *Evolution of Parliament*. It will be understood that what I have to say of it refers exclusively to the parts treating of the Middle Ages.

[1] The principle, if any, upon which towns were selected for representation has not been ascertained. Whatever the tests were, they are not likely to have been applied consistently. There is an interesting discussion of the subject by the late J. F. Willard in his essay ' Taxation Boroughs and Parliamentary Boroughs, 1294–1336 ' in *Essays in Honour of James Tait*, Manchester U.P., 1933. He shows that in the period in question both the sheriffs and chief taxers, who were acting without instructions in the majority of cases, chose the same towns.

[2] ' The *Plena Potestas* of English parliamentary representatives ', *Oxford Essays in Medieval History presented to H. E. Salter*, Oxford U.P., 1934.

[3] See in this sense Stephenson, C., ' Taxation and Representation in the Middle Ages ', *Haskins Anniversary Essays* (1929), 291 ff., and McIlwain, C. H., *Cambridge Medieval History* VII (1932), 604–82.

[4] See Pickthorn, *Early Tudor Government*, particularly 21–9, and Chrimes, *Constitutional Ideas*, 152 ff.

These chapters contain the reaction of an acute and trained intelligence to some of the work that had been done on the history of parliament since the day when the teachings of Stubbs and Gneist were still unquestioned. Professor Pollard abounded in the sense of Maitland and McIlwain and used their doctrine to construct a system in which the importance of the medieval parliament lay not in what it was but in what it was destined to become in Protestant and Tudor England. Professor Pollard reacted so strongly against the system of Stubbs that he failed to see how much of it—the work of a trained and cautious medievalist saturated with a knowledge of the authorities—was of permanent value. Professor Pollard saw some of the most important points—the title of his book proves that—and formulated them brilliantly, provocatively and rashly. He dismisses as mythology much that had long ago been quietly set aside by those who were investigating and teaching the subject. The doctrine that he substituted, in so far as it was original with him, has been found in many cases to have put upon the available evidence a greater strain than it was capable of bearing. I may cite the case of his doctrine of peerage which has been dealt with faithfully by Tout, his notion that re-election of knights and burgesses was so unusual that the commons being without experience were incapable of continuity of mind or opinion which, in view of the evidence adduced by Mr. Edwards, Miss McKisack and Miss Wood-Legh, can scarcely be accepted. On the nature of the English parliamentary estates the last word has not been said (nor indeed many of the first), and probably cannot be until we reach surer ground in the matter of the *Modus Tenendi Parliamentum.*[1] That elusive pamphlet seems, in spite of his professed caution, to have tinctured Mr. Pollard's thinking about the subject to a greater extent than he was aware. At any rate some of the credentials which he attributed to it have not withstood the critical examination to which they have since been subjected. On the other hand, the literary skill, the spirit, the challenge and perhaps indeed the very recklessness of his book have

---

[1] This question is discussed at length in Miss M. V. Clarke's posthumous volume *Medieval Representation and Consent*, London, 1936. See also Professor Morris's essay, ' The Date of the Modus Tenendi Parliamentum '. *E.H.R.* XLIX (1934), 407 ff.

aroused attention in quarters that are habitually deaf to more cautious voices.

Where, then, do we stand ? Evidently parliament cannot be regarded as the centre of the struggle between the crown and the baronage in the fourteenth century, nor can we regard the Lancastrian period as an experiment in parliamentary government. On the other hand, we must not lose sight of the growing political and constitutional importance of a body which included the effective political elements of the country. As was said at the outset parliament must be consulted, and indeed had the last word, where taxation and in some degree legislation were concerned, it afforded an unique opportunity for colouring and moulding public opinion, and the measure of what could be done by means of it in an emergency had very likely never been taken. If it be objected that Fortescue, describing the government of England as he knew it, has next to nothing to say of parliament Fortescue himself supplies the answer. He was describing the government of England as he had observed it and as he thought it should be. In the normal government taxation and legislation were unusual, and in an ideal one the king should live of his own and the council would so effectively prepare legislation that parliament need scarcely do more than register it. The normal business of government lay with the king, his ministers, the council and the bureaucracy, and parliament was not concerned. But if a political crisis arose involving a struggle among the political forces in the community parliament was often drawn into the first line of interest. This was a practical matter. There was not much speculation as to the source and extent of parliamentary power, and such theories as were formulated were not pressed far.

III. LAW AND CONSTITUTIONAL THEORY

Political speculation, apart from the construction of Utopias, evidently consists of inferences from political experience. It can sometimes, therefore, supply the constitutional historian with the principles upon which public men were acting. But the method and a good deal of the material of medieval political speculation were, like the language in which it was expressed, international. This point is well illustrated by the case of John of Salisbury.[1] Therefore English constitutional historians have much to learn from Dr. Carlyle's volumes.[2] They provide abundant extracts from a very extensive series of writers classified by chronology and subject, and illustrate therefore the common stock from which English writers drew, though this is only one of a number of advantages which the work offers. Dr. Carlyle's generalizations must, in the case of England at any rate, be accepted with some reserve, but as he presents the evidence from which he has generalized the book is of permanent value.

The development in western Europe of a theory of kingship, deriving on the one hand from Teutonic notions of the sacral character and magical functions of the king and on the other from the church with its teaching of the divine sanction and moral responsibility attaching to the office, is perhaps the central fact of all constitutional history. ' L'état moderne n'est autre chose que le roi des derniers siècles.'[3] The cognate and indeed inseparable conception of a law discovered, not made, and, like the king who is its agent and interpreter, divinely sanctioned, is in England at least of equal importance. It would be difficult to point to a clearer and more learned treatment of these fundamental topics than those furnished by Professors Kern and McIlwain.[4] Then there is the need to determine the origin of the notion of a community, the *res publica* which comes to be identified with the *rex*, and to discover how and how

[1] See Webb, C. C. J., *John of Salisbury*, 1932. The preface gives the necessary bibliographical indications. Mr. Webb is the editor of John's most important speculative works. Mr. J. Dickinson has published a translation of certain parts of the *Policraticus* under the title *The States-man's Book of John of Salisbury*, New York, 1927 ; the introduction, which discusses medieval conceptions of kingship, appeared in part in *Speculum* I (1926), 309 ff.

[2] Carlyle, A. J., *A History of Medieval Political Theory in the West*, 6 vols., 1903–36, covering the period from the second to the end of the sixteenth century.

[3] Viollet, P., *Institutions Politiques de la France* II, 20.

[4] Kern, F., *Gottesgnadentum und Widerstandsrecht im früheren Mittel-alter*, Leipzig, 1914 ; ' Recht und Verfassung im Mittelalter ', *H.Z.* cxx (1919), I ff. (A translation of the preceding by S. B. Chrimes, entitled *Kingship and Law in the Middle Ages*, appeared in this series, vol. IV, in 1939). McIlwain, C. H., *The Growth of Political Thought in the West*, London, 1932 ; *The High Court of Parliament*, Yale U.P. and London, 1910 ; ' Magna Carta and the Common Law ' in *Magna Carta Commemoration Essays*, R.H.S., London, 1917.

soon it is differentiated from other groups or associations free or dependent, by the kind of distinction we make to-day between public and private law. This problem, as arising among the German peoples, was discussed in a vigorous and learned book, which has much to teach English readers, by the late Georg von Below.[1]

A narrower, but still an interesting and important aspect of kingship, is the reversion to primitive *Königszauber* in the claim to therapeutic powers first made by the second Capetian and imitated, as it now seems, by Henry I of England. In each case the motive was the same, the need to attest the ' blood right ' of a parvenu house. M. Bloch has worked out the whole history of the royal touch in a brilliant and soundly documented book.[2]

The study of questions of this order in the works of writers whose experience and observation was predominantly, and perhaps exclusively English, has been greatly facilitated by definitive editions of three important texts. What is known for convenience sake as the Oxford edition of the *Dialogus*[3] appeared in 1902. This treatise, although mostly concerned with financial administration, contains some independent political speculation.[4] In 1915 and 1922 Professor Woodbine published the first and second volumes of an edition of Bracton,[5] which, to describe his achievement comprehensively, already takes its place beside Liebermann's *Die Gesetze der Angelsachsen*. The first volume ' simply represents the work which had to be done to clear the way for a new text of the *De Legibus* '. The

[1] Below, G. von, *Der deutsche Staat des Mittelalters*, 2nd ed., Leipzig, 1925. The subject has long been vigorously and hotly debated by German scholars and a substantial part of Below's book is devoted to a summary of this controversy.

[2] Bloch, M., *Les Rois Thaumaturges* (Publications de la Faculté des Lettres de l'Université de Strasbourg, Fasc. 19), Strasbourg, 1924. Mr. J. C. Russell's study of ' The canonization of opposition to the king in Angevin England ' in *Haskins Anniversary Essays*, Boston, 1929, presents an interesting and relevant suggestion not very satisfactorily worked out.

[3] *De Necessariis Observantiis Scaccarii Dialogus*, ed. Hughes, A., Crump, C. G. and Johnson, C., Oxford, 1902.

[4] See Kirn, P., ' Die mittelalterliche Staatsverwaltung als geistesge-schichtliches Problem ', *Historische Vierteljahrschrift* XXVII (1932), 523. In §4 he deals with the *Dialogus*. He describes the author as a lively critic of the state about which he reasons by seeking the thought that lies behind the administrative arrangements he describes.

[5] *Bracton de Legibus et Consuetudinibus Angliae*, ed. G. H. Woodbine, Yale U.P. and Oxford U.P., VOL. I (1915), VOL. II (1922). A third volume was published in 1940.

second gives that portion of the text comprised in folios 1–159 of the first edition presented, as the editor says, ' as nearly as may be . . . as it finally left Bracton's hands '. He intends when this part of the task is completed ' to devote a whole book, if necessary, to commentary alone '. Meanwhile he has interrupted his work on Bracton to produce a much-needed and altogether admirable edition of his predecessor Glanvill.[1] This is furnished with notes illustrating the text by reference to recorded cases that are more or less contemporary. The importance of these editions for constitutional as well as legal history is too obvious to require comment. We note, however, that one of the first and for our purposes the most important results of the new Bracton is definitely to dismiss the famous *Addicio de Chartis* from the text, thereby depriving the doctrine which it expresses, that the king could be judged and coerced by the court of his barons if he contravened the law, of the authority previously claimed for it of a great and sober jurist.[2]

Here we have what from Magna Carta to the end of the Middle Ages, and indeed long after that, was the central problem of constitutional history, how to restrain a king who broke the law or, to put it in more general terms, how to convert a moral duty into an enforceable legal obligation. I propose therefore to draw attention to some recent contributions to the discussion of this problem in one or other of its aspects.

Dr. Ehrlich in the work just cited has covered the ground as far as the law is concerned up to 1377. He shows that nobody supposed that the king could not do wrong, consciously, unwittingly or through his agents. No action would lie against

[1] *Glanvill De Legibus et Consuetudinibus Regni Angliae*, Yale U.P. and Oxford U.P., 1932.

[2] The text is in Woodbine II, 110 ; see I, 330 ff., where he has described it as a not very distant echo of the troubles between Henry III and his barons and adds that the authority on which it rests is far too insufficient to allow us to regard Bracton as the author. The utmost that can be said for Bracton's authorship will be found in Ehrlich, L., *Proceedings against the Crown* (1216–1377), Oxford, 1921, 202 ff., and Kantorowicz, H., *Bractonian Problems* (1941) ; but on the latter, cf. Schulz, F., ' Bracton on Kingship ', *E.H.R.*, LX (1945), 175, and Lapsley, ' Bracton and the Authorship of the Addicio de Cartis ', *ibid.* LXII (1947), 1–19. The disputed passage crept into the text seemingly before 1290 when it was incorporated into *Fleta*, an anonymous law-book based on Bracton. In the time of Edward II it was developed in a sense unfavourable to royalty by a justice of assize in a gloss on Bracton. This has been worked out by Davies, J. C., *The Baronial Opposition to Edward II* (Cambridge U.P., 1918), 16.

him, but it was assumed that he wished to do right and would
correct a wrong if it were brought to his attention by petition.
Remedy might be given in various ways, one of which was to
authorize the courts to act. These simple principles had to be
adjusted to meet the development of a civil service working in
the king's name but often without his cognizance, and the
recognition of the fact that public interest might make it
desirable for the king to do what laws and customs forbade
the subject acting in his own interest to do. Dr. Ehrlich
describes the devices by which the common law tried to adjust
itself to these needs, and leaves off at the moment when the
new procedure of impeachment had been devised to meet one
of them.[1]

So much for the legal side. We may turn now to take
account, very briefly, of recent work on constitutional development. What for convenience sake I call ' constitutional ' must
be taken to refer to attempts to solve the problem without, or
following on, recourse to violence, whether by controlling
the king through new and essentially revolutionary bodies or
through his ministers and council by making them responsible
to parliament. It would be generally agreed that the question of
administrative reform was kept in the foreground as much and
as long as possible, and that when constitutional (I use the word
in its present sense) questions forced themselves upon men's
attention it was attempted to treat them in terms of private
law. Toward the end of the period men were feeling the need
of public law and constitutional theory, and this comes out
pretty clearly in the circumstances of Henry IV's accession.

Professor Powicke has interpreted Magna Carta in terms
which would make it a sincere attempt to obtain administrative
reform by securing from the king voluntary recognition of his
obligations under the coronation oath when he was absolved
by Langton in August 1213. The clumsy device of the committee of twenty-five set up at Runnymede was thus produced
by John's bad faith and the bitterness of the Civil War.[2] It

[1] See Clarke, M. V., ' The origin of impeachment ', *Oxford Essays in
Medieval History presented to H. E. Salter*, 164 ff., reprinted in *Fourteenth
Century Studies* (Oxford, 1927), 242–271, and Plucknett, T. F. T., in
T.R.H.S., 1942.

[2] Powicke, F. M., *Stephen Langton*, Oxford U.P., 1928 ; see also *Cambridge Medieval History* VI, 232 ff. Dr. Faith Thompson's *The First Century*

takes its place nevertheless as an advance from feudal individualism and the forerunner of the schemes of 1244, 1258 and 1311.

The best view of the constitutional movement from the accession of Henry III to the outbreak of the Barons' War is to be had in Tout's second volume, which shows in detail the political use made of the household organization first by the Poitevin officials and then by the king himself and the resulting exclusion of the magnates from what they considered their due share in the control of administration and the determination of policy. Professor Treharne[1] argues that this was the resumption and logical development of Henry II's policy, and Professor Jacob[2] has emphasized the deeper causes of an opposition that came from ' social groups now realizing themselves [and] finding a voice and to a limited extent a policy '.[3]

This brings us to the Barons' War, and here we shall again find Professor Jacob our guide. His book[4] is no doubt the most important recent contribution to the rewriting—which is now going on—of the history of those confused but significant years. His thesis is concisely stated in the sentence I have just quoted, and it is worked out in detail in the book under consideration. In the first of the two studies which compose it Professor Jacob is concerned with the effort of the new council to obtain trustworthy information in the localities and frame adequate legislation to correct the abuses that were revealed. He argues that the pressure which led at least to the partial application of their scheme came from the middle order of society who spoke through the ' bachelery ', not a chance group of rash young men[5] but a body with corporate interests

of *Magna Carta*, Minnesota U.P., 1925, is a real contribution to our knowledge of the history and influence of what may be called the Common Law Charter as distinguished from the dictated treaty of Runnymede. In this context it may be noticed that the direct constitutional importance of the Forest Law has been sensibly diminished by Miss Wright's proof that it did not (and indeed could not) exclude the Common Law within the area of the Forest, although it created new offences and restricted the exercise of proprietary rights. The study is a remarkable one and deserves attention. Wright, E. C., ' Common law in the thirteenth-century English Royal Forest ', *Speculum* III (1928), 166 ff.

[1] Treharne, R. F., *The Baronial Plan of Reform*, 1258–1263, Manchester U.P., 1932.

[2] Jacob, E. F., *Cambridge Medieval History* VI, cap. VIII.   [3] *Ibid*. 271.

[4] Jacob, E. F., *Studies in the Period of Baronial Reform and Rebellion*, 1258–1267, Oxford U.P., 1925.

[5] As Tout had argued, *Collected Papers* II, 277 ff.

and a definite policy drawn from the middle range of feudal society and attached to the *familia* or *societas* of some great noble. In the second study which is concerned with the Civil War and the restoration of order after Evesham he returns to the same theme and labours to identify the support given to Simon de Montfort in 1264 with the classes that had exerted pressure in 1259. The author's inferences are made from a mass of detail laboriously gathered from chancery inquisitions, curia regis and assize rolls, sheriffs' accounts and other fiscal records admirably digested and marshalled. Such evidence furnishes a wholesome correction to Matthew Paris, but you cannot, as Dr. Jacob observes, write the history of England from police court records.

A more general account of the period is provided in Professor Treharne's scholarly, spirited and eminently readable book which (it is a first volume) carries the story up to the Mise of Amiens. Professor Treharne (like Matthew Paris) is so much preoccupied with the immediate question of justice and reform that he scarcely comes to grips with the constitutional problem. It is true that the baronial opposition did not do so either and was content to accomplish some measure of reform by taking the government out of the king's hands and ruling without regard to his wishes. This may have been morally justifiable, but the theory of kingship on which St. Louis based his award at Amiens could not well be impugned. Simon's answer was to repudiate his oath, take up arms and endeavour, after an unsuccessful attempt at arbitration, to reconstruct the oligarchy upon the basis of a party reinforced by middle-class support. Constitutionally the upshot of the matter was to illustrate rather more clearly than had been done before the fact that the problem could not be solved by a revolution, however effective and however successful in accomplishing immediate administrative reform. Bracton had stated the law and recognized the difficulty. The arguments of the anonymous author of the *Song of Lewes*[1] are political rather than constitutional, for they do not recognize that you cannot submit

[1] He was a Franciscan friar who wrote soon after the battle. He gives a full and reasoned account of the baronial programme, but it cannot be made to square with Bracton's statement of the law. The best edition is that of C. L. Kingsford, Oxford U.P., 1890.

the king (as kingship was understood in thirteenth-century law and political theory) to a court of barons in any permanent constitutional arrangement. The king is the keystone of the arch, and if by denaturing his office you remove it the whole fabric comes tumbling about your ears.[1]

Throughout the troubled reign of Edward II the problem of controlling the king pressed for a solution. As before, the opposition put administrative reforms in the first rank, but new tendencies are observable.[2] The baronage began to show a definite political ambition, and from 1316 onward sought to realize it by securing a permanent position in the council, enlisting the support of representative parliaments and seeking to deprive the king of the control of the civil service which he exercised through the household. Again the attempt of the Ordainers to unify the administration of public revenue and withdraw the control of the privy seal from the king and the corresponding differentiation in the Statute of York (1322) between the estate of the king and the estate of the crown suggest that among politicians at any rate the distinction between the king and the crown was perfectly grasped.[3]

[1] A number of short but important studies of various aspects of this period should be noticed ; Jacob, E. F., ' The reign of Henry III ', *T.R.H.S.* 4th series x (1927), 21 ff. ; ' What were the Provisions of Oxford ', *History* IX (1925), 188 ff. ; ' The complaints of Henry III against the Baronial Council ', *E.H.R.* XLI (1926), 559 ff. Richardson, H. G., and Sayles, G. O., ' The Provisions of Oxford—a forgotten document and some comments ', *B.J.R.L.* XVII (1933), 291 ff. Powicke, F. M., ' Some observations on the Baronial Council, 1258–1260 ', *Essays Presented to T. F. Tout*, Manchester U.P., 1925. Denholm-Young, N., ' Robert Carpenter and the Provisions of Westminster ', *E.H.R.* L (1935), 22 ff. ; ' Documents of the Barons' War ', *E.H.R.* XLVIII (1933), 558 ff. (deals with the reconstruction of the government after the battle of Lewes). The classical study of Simon de Montfort published by M. Charles Bémont in 1884 was revised by the author and published in English (the translation was made by Professor Jacob) in 1930 (Oxford U.P.). The documents appended to the original edition were omitted and in some other aspects the venture proved less satisfactory than had been hoped. Treharne, R. F., ' The personal rule of Henry III and the Aims of the Baronial Reformers of 1258 ', *History* XVI (1932), 336 ff. Wilkinson, B., *Studies in the Constitutional History of the Thirteenth and Fourteenth Centuries*, cap. VI.

[2] Tout, *Place of Edward II* ; *Chapters*, vols. II and III. Richardson, H. G., and Sayles, G. O., ' The early records of the English parliaments ', *B.I.H.R.* VI, 71 ff. ; ' The King's ministers in parliament', Pt. II, *E.H.R.* XLVII (1932), 194 ff.

[3] The problem of the interest of the commons, if any, secured by the Statute of York in 1322 has long been the subject of a chronic controversy which has recently become acute. See Lapsley, G., ' The Commons and the Statute of York ', *E.H.R.* XXVIII (1913), 118 ff. and below, pp. 153 ff. Tout,

It is easy to overstate all this and to lose sight of its feudal character and background; but as a beginning it has its importance. There was moreover a disposition to face some of the theoretical difficulties of the problem. It has been customary to disparage Despenser's famous application of the doctrine of capacities to the king. But it is beginning to be clear that it was neither so novel nor used so inconsistently as has often been said. If the barons who invoked it to justify their expulsion of Gaveston used it later against Despenser himself they might be justified on the ground that action which was legally open to them collectively would, if taken individually, amount to accroachment of royal power. The incorporation of the *Addicio de Chartis* into *Fleta* and the gloss on it to which reference has already been made, would give some force to this suggestion.

Whatever theory the barons may have held of their right of constitutional resistance and whatever obligation they may have recognized to act collectively, were necessarily brought to the supreme test in the last act of the reign. It is clear that the managers of the revolution of 1326–27 made use of parliament, but the official form which they gave to the whole transaction represents it as a voluntary abdication of the king in favour of his son. The proceedings in parliament reported by the chroniclers appear in no official record. The problem had not been faced and there were probably good reasons of state for avoiding it. The whole episode deserves to be most carefully restudied. The late Miss Clarke devoted a most interesting and original essay to the subject, which she again treated in her posthumous book.[1] Her suggestion that the deputation

Place of Edward II, 150–1 ; Davies, J. C., *Baronial Opposition to Edward II*, 513 ff. ; Richardson, H. G., and Sayles, G. O., ' Early records of the English parliaments ', *B.I.H.R.* vi, 76 ; Johnstone, H., *Camb. Med. Hist.* vii, 425–6 ; Clarke, M. V., *Essays in honour of James Tait*, 29, 30, 42 ; McIlwain, C. H., *Growth of Political Thought in the West*, 377–8 ; Haskins, G. L., *The Statute of York and the Interest of the Commons*, Cambridge, Mass., 1935. Mr. Haskins argues that the position of the commons in parliament has been overrated and that this statute so far from securing to them a share in legislation represents a statement of autocratic royal power. It may reasonably be doubted whether this is the final word on the matter. A view emphasizing the importance of the commons will be found in Miss Clarke's book referred to above p. 19 n. 1.

[1] Clarke, M. V., ' Committees of estates and the deposition of Edward II ', *Essays in Honour of James Tait*, Manchester, 1933 ; see also *Medieval*

sent to the king to receive his abdication was consciously and in conformity with precedent given the shape of a committee of estates must be judged in the light of her whole argument and will depend in particular upon the validity of her reasons for assigning an early date to the *Modus Tenendi Parliamentum*. Meanwhile there is an inference as to constitutional theory that may reasonably be made from the whole episode. Those responsible for the revolution were unwilling either to do without parliament or to trust entirely to it. Edward II was deposed and Edward III acclaimed in a parliament that resolved to renounce homage and allegiance. But official documents ran in the name of Edward II until his abdication had been accepted by a parliamentary committee sent to him for this purpose, and not a word of all this appeared in the official version of the matter.[1]

It may perhaps be taken as characteristic of the English temperament to deal with the concrete case as it arises avoiding as far as possible reference to principles. But principles of some sort there must have been, and as the conflict of the fourteenth century proceeded it became increasingly difficult to conceal them. The constitutional and administrative struggle directly occasioned by the outbreak of the Hundred Years War produced at the outset measures and discussion of a very illuminating sort.[2] The famous crises of 1340–41 were really prepared by the publication in July 1338 of the Walton Ordinances. This document contained a series of administrative arrangements immediately required by the king's departure for the continent taking his household with him. They were intended ' to co-ordinate the several branches of the administration by vesting a severe executive control in the king and

Representation and Consent, cap. IX. Cf. Richardson, H. G., and Sayles, G. O., *Rotuli Parliamentorum Anglie Hactenus Inediti*, Camden Soc. 3rd series, LI (1935), 99–102. Tout's very brief notice of the matter will be found in *Chapters* III, 1–6.

[1] See below pp. 310–12.

[2] Below, pp. 231–72. See also Tout, *Chapters* III, 65–150 (other references up and down the volumes may readily be consulted by means of the excellent index). Hughes, D., *The Early Years of Edward III*, London U.P., 1915, Part. II, caps. VII–IX. Clarke, M. V., ' Forfeitures and treason in 1388 ', *T.R.H.S.* 4th series XIV (1931) ; ' The origin of impeachment ', *Oxford Essays . . . presented to H. E. Salter*, both reprinted in *Fourteenth Century Studies*, 114 ff. and 242 ff. Wilkinson, B., ' The protest of the Earls of Arundel and Surrey in the crisis of 1341 ', *E.H.R.* XLVI (1931), 177 ff.

his immediate advisers, supplemented in certain directions by the co-operation of the popular courts '.[1] Their effect would probably have been to make the household organization supreme, thereby reducing the great offices of state to ministries only in name.[2] They therefore express the view of the high curialist party. This unity of command was from the administrative point of view highly desirable, but politically and constitutionally it perpetuated the old tradition or rather the old aim of governing the country by the king's will and in his interest, like a private estate. As an administrative measure the scheme very early broke down, and it is not even clear that it was intended to be permanent. The principle it implied did not, however, pass unchallenged.

The intricate story of the administrative crisis of the autumn of 1340 and the constitutional crisis of the following spring is now better understood than ever it was before the publication of Tout's book, though there are still many dark places in it. For our purposes two points may be emphasized. In the first place the state papers (the word pamphlet would describe some of them better) exchanged by the king and Archbishop Stratford between November 1340 and April 1341 afford a reasoned statement of the Lancastrian view of constitutional government. Stratford argued that ministers are only responsible to the king collectively when there has been no departure from a policy framed in council and authorized by parliament. This statement of principle would obviously need to be qualified, but even in so condensed a form its implications are clear enough. But the opposition eventually, led by Stratford, wished to go further, and their ambitions found expression in the great statute of 1341 which the king accepted under political duress and subsequently repealed. The statute provided that the king's ministers and officers should be appointed by the consent of the magnates. They were required to take an oath in parliament ' to keep and maintain the points of the great charter '. During their term of office they were to be answerable in parliament to complaints of infringement of the charter made by individuals, and on the completion of their term they were to be again answerable in parliament for their conduct in office.

[1] Tout, *Chapters* III, 69 ff.   [2] *Ibid.*, 77–8.

Finally the statute sanctioned a law of peerage that restricted the trial of charges against peers for their conduct in office as well as out, to the baronage that had appointed them acting in full parliament. The privilege of peerage was in fact tacitly admitted after the repeal of the statute, but the full measure of ministerial responsibility, which would have made them completely dependent upon parliament, was withheld, although it remained an object of desire to the Lancastrian party.

The next step was taken in 1376 when a new method was employed to secure for parliament some means of control over the conduct of ministers in office. This was the procedure known as impeachment. It consisted of indictment by the commons and trial by the peers in parliament.[1] The doctrine of responsibility is not new though it is still a political and not a constitutional principle. The method which was adopted has however very important constitutional implications. The form of indictment instead of petition for remedy by way of grace which was all that the common law authorized in case of a wrong done by a royal official, attributed to the commons a right to demand, not merely to petition for, redress. Thus such proceedings in parliament were outside the common law, and the accused was thereby deprived of the rights guaranteed to him by cap. 39 of Magna Carta and the statutes founded upon its principle. These objections were recognized in 1376 when Latimer claimed trial by his peers and the right to answer only to charges made by particular persons who would be punished for failure to substantiate them, and again in 1387 by the judges who told the king that impeachment of royal officials was an act of treason.[2] The view of the judges obviously required an answer, and it received it in full measure in 1388.[3] The Lords Appellant were in power in virtue of what had been in fact a successful revolution. They were making use of a method of accusation older than impeachment and one in which the commons had no part. It had been intended that the trial should take place in the court

[1] Clarke, M. V., ' The origin of impeachment ', cited above p. 29, n. 2. What follows is a statement of Miss Clarke's contention in so far as it bears on the point I am trying to illustrate. The argument is to me convincing.

[2] The text is given in Lodge and Thornton, *English Constitutional Documents* (Cambridge U.P., 1935) 26, a very useful collection of fourteenth and fifteenth century texts.

[3] Clarke, M. V., ' Forfeiture and treason in 1388 '; cited above, p. 29, n. 2

of the constable and marshal until the king promised a parliamentary inquiry, when the venue was shifted. A technical question arose as to the form of the appeals, and a body of legal experts to whom it was referred declared that they were irregular. The lords observed that the case, since it involved the person of the king and the welfare of the kingdom, was a matter of state which it was for parliament alone to settle, and that in doing so it would be ruled by its own law and custom and by none other. The lower courts, indeed, they continued, are bound by rules of procedure, but they are only the executors of the customs of the kingdom and the law of the land which is made by the king in parliament.[1] Tout[2] observes that this ' declaration that parliament, as the law maker, could override the executive officers of the law, involved an assertion of the ultimate sovereignty of parliament '. It was obviously an answer to the judges' view of the subordination of parliament to the king by an assertion of the converse proposition. Against this must be put the facts that in dealing with Brember the Appellants had not the courage to go behind the existing statute by making a parliamentary declaration of treason and condemned him on common law grounds, and that their last act was to attempt to bind their successors by making it treason to attempt to reverse the acts of this parliament. Miss Clarke has emphasized these points in support of her suggestion that the party of the Appellants ' neither believed in nor understood their own declaration of parliamentary supremacy, since they failed to recognize that what one supreme parliament could do another could as easily undo '. It may be pointed out that a good part of the doctrine was tacitly conceded when the process of impeachment was admitted, and that faith is not necessarily embarrassed by holding two contradictory propositions at the same time. Elsewhere[3] reasons have been given for the suggestion that the Lancastrian leaders who managed the revolution of 1399 knew, understood and intended to act upon the doctrine in the sense that their original plan was to effect the change of dynasty by strictly parliamentary action. Their

---

[1] Lodge and Thornton, *op. cit.*, 156.   [2] *Chapters* III, 432.

[3] Below, pp. 317 ff. See also Galbraith, V. H., and Clarke, M. V., ' The deposition of Richard II ', *B.J.R.L.* XIV (1930), 24 ff. (reprinted in *Fourteenth Century Studies*, 53 ff.).

success may well be doubted, and it may further be argued that the determination of the succession by act of parliament in 1406 did not complete the defective parliamentary title of the House of Lancaster, nor indeed do more than settle the line of succession to a title the legitimate existence of which it recognized.[1] In any case it is not contended that the supremacy of parliament in this sense was ever generally admitted in medieval England. We are left, therefore, at the turn of the century with two opposing political theories each containing constitutional doctrines for which some precedents might be cited, though it is improbable that even the Lancastrians counted on a parliamentary title to the degree that Stubbs supposed. One constitutional rule, however, was established beyond question in 1399, and that is that the demise of the crown invalidated the writs under which parliament had been summoned and entailed its dissolution if it had actually been convened.[2]

No such brief survey of the development of constitutional theory as has here been attempted for the fourteenth century can be offered for the fifteenth. The materials are lacking, for the constitutional history of that period remains to be written —or rather to be rewritten, for it seems to be pretty well agreed that Stubbs' interpretation is inadmissible. A beginning has been made however, and we have Professor Plucknett's well-known essays,[3] and the discussion of Fortescue's views by Professor McIlwain,[4] Professor Jacob[5] and Dr. Chrimes,[6] while Dr. Chrimes in a work already frequently cited has analysed the constitutional ideas of the century, and Mr. Pickthorn's[7] powerful study of the theory and practice of government under Henry VII necessarily ranges wide over the fifteenth-century background.

[1] An argument in this sense will be found in Chrimes, S. B., *Constitutional Ideas in the Fifteenth Century*, 24–25.

[2] This point is discussed below, p. 336.

[3] Plucknett, T. F. T., ' The place of the council in the fifteenth century ', *T.R.H.S.*, 4th series, I (1918) ; ' The Lancastrian Constitution ' in *Tudor Studies*, ed. R. W. Seton-Watson, London, 1924.

[4] McIlwain, C. H., *Growth of Political Thought*, 354 ff.

[5] Jacob, E. F., ' Sir John Fortescue and the Law of Nature ', *B.J.R.L.*, XVIII (1934), No. 2.

[6] Chrimes, S. B., ' Sir John Fortescue and his theory of dominion ', *T.R.H.S.*, 4th series, XVII (1934).

[7] Pickthorn, K. W. M., *Early Tudor Government*, vol. I, Cambridge U.P., 1934.

D

JOHN DE WARENNE AND THE *QUO WARANTO* PROCEEDINGS IN 1279[1]

THE story of John de Warenne's rusty sword and the blustering speech with which he proffered it before the justices in eyre in the *quo waranto* proceedings in 1279 long held its place both in serious and popular accounts of Edward I's reign. It put, indeed, in dramatic, perhaps even in theatrical, form the essence of the struggle between the king's theory of sovereignty which was sound law and the barons' claims to hold their franchises by prescription which in a good many cases was sound history, as indeed the king was at length constrained to admit in the statutes of 1290.[2] Maitland apparently did not question the tale, and the extract from the chronicle in which it occurs held its place in eight successive editions of Stubbs' Charters. But the most eminent historical critic of the last generation entertained doubts, and when in 1910 Dr. Round published his work on Peerage and Pedigree, which was relished by the general public almost as much as it was valued by the learned world, it was found that the rusty sword, with many other tales of the Conquest, was dismissed from the canon of history. When, three years later, Professor Davis produced a ninth edition of Stubbs' Charters—a work no less valued by the world of scholarship than Dr. Round's, though it may be doubted whether it was much read for entertainment in other quarters —the well-known extract had silently disappeared.

Some apology, therefore, is required for re-opening the question, and it may be admitted at once that it is scarcely to be found in the historic value of the fact alleged. Its very appositeness, indeed, might be taken to militate against its truth. History, like the men and women who make it, abounds in *l'esprit de l'escalier*, and its apocrypha is full of the wise or pungent phrases that ought to have been uttered and the significant gestures that should have been made in critical moments of victory, defeat or the approach of death. From time to time some of these are rescued or partially rescued

[1] Reprinted from *The Cambridge Historical Journal* II (1927), 110–132.
[2] See note below, pp. 61–2, ff.

from the limbo to which they had been consigned, as witness
the story of the women of Weinsberg which German scholarship has of late done much to rehabilitate.[1] But the present
study proposes no such gallant adventure. Whether the tale is
true or false is not of very great importance. On the other
hand, the critical method which Dr. Round applied to its
scanty credentials raises some very interesting questions of the
use of evidence and historical argumentation and these, it is
thought, merit close scrutiny. It may well be worth our while,
therefore, to illustrate these questions by examining Dr.
Round's method.

The direct evidence for the story consists in a single document, a passage in one of the manuscripts of Hemingburgh's
chronicle. Familiar as it is, it may be convenient to the reader to
have it before him:

' Cito post inquietavit rex quosdam ex magnatibus terrae per
justiciarios suos, scire volens quo warranto tenerent terras, et si
non haberent bonum warrantum, seisivit statim terras illorum;
vocatusque est inter ceteros comes de Warenna coram justiciarios
regis, et, interrogatus quo warranto teneret, produxit in medium
gladium antiquum et eruginatum et ait: " Ecce, domini mei, ecce
warrantum meum. Antecessores enim mei cum Willelmo bastardo
venientes conquesti sunt terras suas gladio, et easdem gladio defen-
dam a quocunque eas occupare volente. Non enim rex per se terram
devicit et subjecit, sed progenitores nostri fuerunt cum eo participes
et coadjutores." Adhaeseruntque sibi et suae rationi caeteri magnates, et tumultuantes et impacati recesserunt. Rex autem cum
audiret talia, timuit sibi, et ab incepto errore conquievit.'[2]

Now Dr. Round is dissatisfied with this evidence in itself
and, apart from any objections that may arise from other
considerations, he points out that the tale is found in only one
manuscript of the chronicle and that it describes very inaccu-
rately the *quo waranto* proceedings. He blames the chronicler, in
particular, for saying that the king wished to know by what
warrant the magnates held their lands, which he immediately

---

[1] The problem is stated and the necessary references supplied by Mr.
A. L. Poole in the *Cambridge Medieval History* v, 349 n. 2.

[2] *Hemingburgh*, ed. Hamilton II, 6. The same, or a similar story, is told
of Gilbert de Clare by the Lanercost Chronicle, 168. [The records show
that he did in fact challenge Edward's proceedings, 1278–9, and suggest
that if there was any considerable opposition to them he, rather than
Warenne, was the leader. See Cam, *Liberties and Communities*, 178 f.]

seized if they did not produce good warrant; whereas, Dr. Round observes, ' the enquiry was essentially one as to franchises. Lastly ', he writes, ' Hemingburgh's statement that the king was alarmed by this incident and began to retrace his steps is not confirmed by what we know of the quo warranto proceedings '.[1] For these and other reasons he suggests that Hemingburgh's story, definite and elaborate though it is, is a mere invention based on John de Warenne's lawless and overbearing character.

Before coming to what is Dr. Round's main argument, it may be worth while to weigh again the considerations which lead him to disparage the testimony of the chronicle.

The chronicle of Walter of Hemingburgh appears to have extended in the first recension to the year 1297 and subsequently to have been continued to 1346 either by a continuator, possibly John of Tynemouth, or else wholly or in part by himself.[2] There are some eighteen manuscripts extant, of which the most ancient is Lansdowne 239. This belongs to the middle of the fourteenth century and is in substance a kind of second edition containing a good many corrections, additions and variations. It has been pointed out that this is by no means the best or even a very satisfactory MS. for the thirteenth-century part of the chronicle, but it is the only one which contains the story with which we are now dealing. The appearance of a fact once only in the MSS. of a chronicle so admittedly valuable and accurate and so widely diffused as Hemingburgh's inevitably suggests the doubt whether it formed part of the original chronicle, *i.e.* the portion of it extending to 1297, at all. It would be important, therefore, to discover if possible the origin of the story and the manner in which it found its way into the MS. of Hemingburgh. It appears that a copy of the first recension of Hemingburgh found its way to the scriptorium of the monastery of Abingdon where it became the basis of what is in effect a local chronicle extending to 1304. The author fitted into the framework supplied him by Hemingburgh's work the material available to his hand from a different quarter

---

[1] Round, *Peerage and Pedigree* I, 321–2.

[2] See Hardy, *Catalogue of Materials* (R. S.), III, 254 sqq. ; *Chronicon Walteri de Hemingburgh*, ed. Hamilton, Introd. vols. I and II ; Gross, *Sources and Literature of English History*, 2nd ed., No. 1788.

altogether. He must have done his work between 1304, when
his book ends, and the middle of the fourteenth century, when a
certain amount of his material was taken up into the new edition
of Hemingburgh preserved in the Lansdowne manuscript. The
Abingdon manuscript, written in a fourteenth-century hand,
is now in the Cambridge University Library. As long ago as
1844 those portions of it which are independent of Hemingburgh, and were therefore inserted by the Abingdon writer,
were printed by that prolific scholar J. O. Halliwell under the
title *Chronicle of the Monastery of Abingdon*.[1] It seems, therefore, that the story of Warenne's demonstration is independent
of Hemingburgh, and if it has not the measure of authority
that it would derive from inclusion in his chronicle it should
still not be disparaged because it is found only in an unsatisfactory manuscript of that work. We have to estimate its value
as coming from the Berkshire house of Abingdon, and one is
struck at once by the consideration that a Berkshire scriptorium
was likely to be better informed about the *faits divers* of Surrey
or Sussex than that of a distant northern house. What the
chronicler has to tell us in general is to a great extent gossip,
but he has something to say of public events as well and he
incorporates some documents. He seems to have been working
from a miscellaneous collection of material a reasonably long
time after the events which he records. Thus he says, *s.a.*
1291, something of Scottish affairs and adds *cujus rei seriem hic
duxi inserendam*, and again, *s.a.* 1296, *nunc ad ea quae circa
nostros sunt acta in Wasconia stilus se vertat*. Again, when he
foreshortens the years between the Statute of Gloucester and
the king's compromise in 1290 by representing the king as
giving way in alarm as a result of Warenne's demonstration,
he suggests that he was writing long enough after the events
which he recounts to see them dramatically. His sympathies
are clearly with the baronial party.[2] It appears, then, that
Hemingburgh has nothing to do with the story.

Now as to the two objections which Dr. Round makes to
the evidence in itself. To the first of these, that the chronicler
represents the king as giving way at once, we have already

---

[1] *Chronicle of the Monastery of Abingdon*, 1218–1304, ed. J. O. Halliwell,
1844 ; *Hemingburgh*, ed. Hamilton II, 6 n. ; Gross, *op. cit.* No. 1741.

[2] Cf. pp. 14, 15, 19.

suggested an answer. A writer of strong anti-royalist sympathies writing some time after 1290 and therefore aware that the barons had been able to make good their best grounded claim might very well lose his perspective. And this would be the more likely since the claim which the king conceded in terms in 1290 was in practice allowed in Warenne's case and in others by the king's attorneys in 1279. Thus the writer records two facts, the second amply established by official record. The first need not necessarily be untrue because the chronicler, writing at least fourteen years later than the second, asserts a causal connexion between the two and seeing them, so to say, foreshortened misses the twelve intervening years.[1]

Dr. Round's second objection is that the chronicler represented the *quo waranto* proceedings as directed against the barons' lands, whereas in fact it was not their lands but their franchises that were in question. Is this objection really fatal to the substantial truth of facts presented by a writer to whom we have no reason to attribute a technical or professional knowledge of the law ? Two considerations present themselves. In the first place, the connexion between land and franchise was close, how close perhaps no one in Edward I's time could well say. Clearly the doctrine of the king, that subjects could hold franchises only by direct grant from the crown, was resented as incompatible with the historical facts, and by 1290 the king had to admit that. But more than this, the writ *quo waranto* had been, and at the beginning of the fourteenth century could still be, used to recover land. This requires some explanation which, in view of Coke's warning to those historians who ' do meddle with any legal point or matter concerning the law ', must be offered with great diffidence and subject to correction by ' those that be learned and apprised in the laws of this realm.'[2] A generation before the Statute of Gloucester there

---

[1] This would also account for another difficulty to which Dr. Round has not referred. The chronicler states that other magnates associated themselves with Warenne and his contention and departed *tumultuantes et impacati*, whereas, however much they may have resented the proceedings they seem to have acknowledged the jurisdiction of the court and pleaded as Warenne himself did.

[2] Coke, *Second Institute*, 4th ed., 499. On what follows see also Reeves, *H.E.L.*, 3rd ed., I, 426 *sqq.*, II, 219 *sqq.* ; Pollock and Maitland, *H.E.L.*, 2nd ed., I 336–7, 572 ; II 521, 661 ; Holdsworth, *H.E.L.*, 3rd ed., I 88–9, 180, 229–30 ; *Statutes of the Realm* (Rec. Com.), I, 45 *sqq.* ; *Placita de Quo Warranto* (Rec. Com.), xvi.

was a common-law writ *quo waranto* which could be used either by the king or a subject.[1] Hubert de Burgh made use of this writ to recover lands that had been alienated by the king during his outlawry, after it had been reversed in 1234.[2] It was used in 1220 to settle a claim for dower between parties.[3] The king, too, could use the writ for land, as when in 1227 Stephen de Bendenges was summoned to show by what warrant he held the third part of the vill of Hyrteby.[4] Bracton explains that in many cases a mixed action will arise out of the writ. Normally, he says, if you obtain a writ *quo waranto* (it seems that the king's leave was necessary) it will not enable you to do more than force your adversary to disclose his title. The reason is that even though it may be proved that he has no right it does not follow that you are in better case until you have established your claim. If, however, something is added to the writ a double action may follow, one *in personam* in respect to your adversary and the other *in rem* in respect to your right to the land. That something would be the statement of your claim. It might be that the king had an interest in the land as escheat or ancient demesne or that you could not get seisin although you had previously succeeded in an action of novel disseisin.[5]

The common law writ was also used with respect to franchise by the king and, seemingly, by subjects with the king's leave. Thus the Bishop of Norwich was summoned to show by what warrant he claimed to take all the amercements in his liberty.[6] Then in 1231, when the Prior of Woodbridge was summoned to answer to the king by what warrant he had set up a market in Woodbridge to the injury of the king's market in Ipswich, it was the bailiffs of Ipswich *qui secuntur pro domino rege*, and Maitland draws attention to ' this use of the king's name by private litigants '.[7]

---

[1] See the references to the cases in Bracton's *Note Book*, I 185.

[2] *Ibid*. Plac. 1108, 1136, 1141.   [3] *Ibid*. Plac. 1390.

[4] *Ibid*. Plac. 241. In 27 Hen. III, the Bishop of Exeter is summoned to show by what warrant he claims to hold a manor in Sussex and half of another in Surrey. *Plac. Abbrev.* (Rec. Com.), 118 b. Similar cases are cited in the index, 568.

[5] Bracton (R. S.), fo. 284b, 285, 369b, 372b ; *Note Book*, Plac. 1175, 1181, 1358.   [6] *Ibid*. Plac. 391.

[7] *Ibid*. Plac. 578, cf. Plac. 1162. Cf. the case of Ballingham *v.* Burghill, *Y. B.* 6 *Ed. II. Pasch.* (S.S.), 78 *sqq.*, and Mr. Bolland's discussion of the point Maitland raised, Introd. pp. XX–XXI.

When the Hundred Rolls were complete, the Statute of Gloucester had been issued (1278) and the king was prepared to strike his blow, the writ of *quo waranto* was of course used for franchises as a prerogative writ on the king's behalf. Where the Hundred juries had reported *nesciunt quo waranto* it seems that a writ should be directed to the claimant. If, however, the report was *sine waranto*, then he had to answer without a writ under the general proclamation made by the justices itinerant. If in such cases he alleged that his ancestor had died seised, that point would be considered and referred to an inquest. If the verdict were favourable to the claimant and the king still wished to proceed, a writ of *quo waranto* would issue out of chancery.[1] In such cases, however, the king's attorney did not always continue the proceedings. This appears to be what happened in Warenne's case. He pleaded prescription, *quod ipse et antecessores sui a tempore a quo non extat memoria plene usi sunt omnibus libertatibus praedictis*, and asked for an enquiry *per patriam* whether he or his ancestors had usurped anything from the king. The jury sustained the allegation of the earl and *dictum est ei quod eat inde sine die*.[2]

But it is clear that after even 1278 the writ could still be used for the recovery of land apparently on the same terms as before. In 1283 the Abbot of Fécamp was impleaded by the king by a writ of *quo waranto pro manerio de Steninge quod est de antiquo dominico etc.*[3] Then there is the well-known case cited by Coke :

' where it is said in our chronicles that those writs . . . were for lands and tenements therein they are mistaken for . . . in the 31st year of his reign the king did bring a quo warranto against the lady of S. to know by what warrant she claimed to hold the manor of C. which . . . was ancient demesne; and there it was affirmed and not denied that this was the first writ that ever was seen to be brought for lands.' '[4]

There is a good deal here that needs explanation, in particular as to the origin of the prerogative writ and the grounds for the

---

[1] *Statutes of the Realm* (Rec. Com.) I, 45 sqq.

[2] *Plac. de Quo Warranto* (Rec. Com.), 745. [The distinction between seisin of an ancestor and *diutina seisina*, or immemorial tenure, was made clear in the case of Clare's claim to the two Kent hundreds in 1279, when he alleged seisin of his ancestor and it was found that his grandfather had acquired them wrongfully in the time of Henry III. *Ibid.* 337–8.]

[3] *Plac. Abbrev.*, 200.   [4] Coke, *Second Institute*, 495.

dictum quoted by Coke. The relevant point, however, is that the practice being such as we have seen, a monkish writer compiling a chronicle after 1304 may well be excused for supposing that the proceedings of 1279 were directed to land, partly because the writ could be used for that purpose and partly because a man untrained in law would not be likely to distinguish between advantages so closely related as the ownership of land and the possession of franchises appurtenant to the land.[1] The story may or may not be true, but if the evidence of the chronicler is to be rejected it ought not to be on the ground that he used the wrong terms in describing a technical matter of the law, particularly when the term would have been correct if applied to the same process used for another end.

If these considerations be allowed, Dr. Round's special objections to the evidence would appear to be removed and we should have to consider this extract from the Abingdon chronicler on its merits. At best, it is clear, it can have no greater force than any other literary evidence. If it is contradicted by or proves incompatible with the evidence of documents or official records, there is no question as to which will prevail. The testimony of the chronicler must be rejected. Otherwise we must enquire what means the writer had of knowing or knowing about the fact he records and then whether the story told is antecedently improbable, either from its nature or because it is incompatible with what is otherwise known of the character, temperament, interests or what not of any person or persons concerned in the transaction.

As to the first point, while the writer was obviously not an eye-witness and perhaps not even a contemporary of the event, it may none the less have reached the Abingdon scriptorium from one who was both. Neither this nor the other possibility that it was a bit of distorted gossip told by a credulous traveller or an indignant but muddle-headed adherent of one of the great earls can be ruled out at once. One knows that information from various sources and of unequal value found its way into the monastic scriptorium.

[1 The fact that the writ had been used for franchises for so long, and that protests had been made against it by ecclesiastics in 1257, makes this rather improbable. See, besides Cam, *Liberties and Communities*, 174 f., Jolliffe in *T.R.H.S.* 1940, 123–136 ; and Powicke, *Henry III and the Lord Edward*, 114 f.]

Let us turn, then, to the story itself and see whether it contains anything inherently improbable or contrary to what we know from other and better sources of John de Warenne. It can probably be shown that the chronicler's evidence is not open to an objection based on either of these grounds. Dr. Round refers to the earl's lawless and overbearing character, and no doubt he had in mind the well-known incident of a murderous attack which he delivered in the king's court on the two Zouches—his adversaries in a lawsuit which was going against him. The incident has a direct bearing on our argument. The circumstances have often been related in print and may be briefly restated presently. The nature and object of the legal proceedings which were so violently interrupted have not, I think, hitherto been known, and it may therefore be worth while to set down now information about them which has recently come to light, the more so as they arose directly out of the complicated business of the territorial settlement after the rebellion of 1264–65.[1] David de Ashby held lands in Northampton of Henry de Hastings, a well-known figure in what may perhaps be called the left wing of the baronial party. Ashby was unwilling to fight against the king, and when his lord put pressure on him to do so he and his wife fled to Lincolnshire and Hastings removed his goods to his own manor of Yardley and took his tenants' rents and fealty. At length Ashby, having nothing to live on, returned, discharged Hastings by charter of responsibility for what he had done and had his lands back. Hastings then renewed his pressure and, driven by force and fear, Ashby accompanied him to the battle of Lewes. In the spring of 1265, at the time of the proposed tournament between Gloucester and the younger Montforts,[2] Ashby supported Hastings very unwillingly and at length fled to his house at Ashby and remained there until Gloucester sent word to his steward Henry de Pudelicote that he should receive, on behalf of the earl, all those who wished to come into the king's party. Ashby then went to the steward and gave

---

[1] See Jacob, *Studies in the Period of Baronial Reform and Rebellion*, Pt. ii. Dr. Jacob observes (p. 149) that ' to penetrate to the mesne and smaller tenants is at times in the absence of records an impossible task.' The present case turns precisely on the situation of a mesne tenant.

[2] Ramsay, *Dawn of the Constitution*, p. 238, gives the references to the chronicles.

him horses, arms and money to be taken into the earl's protection and later, when the steward took sanctuary, fearing the violence of the barons, Ashby supported him and was actually with him for a period.[1]

After Evesham Ashby's lands were forfeited, presumably for the part he had borne in the battle of Lewes, and he died. In January 1266, by way of grace and favour, his widow was assigned a portion of these lands for her maintenance.[2] The lands had previously been granted by the king to Imbert or Humbert Guy who was a Gascon official.[3] Part of Hastings' forfeiture, including Yardley (of which Ashby's lands were held), had been granted to Warenne after Evesham.[4] At some date before 1267 it appears that part or all of Ashby's lands had passed to Alan la Zouche, for in that year the Patent Roll records the confirmation of a grant by Elias, son of Mosseus (*sic*), a Jew of London, to him of a yearly fee of £124 and a debt of £100 wherein David de Ashby was bound to the said Jew.[5] It seems probable that Zouche had bought out or otherwise disposed of the interest of Imbert Guy, for it appears in the record of Warenne's suit that before the inquest was taken Zouche came into court and stated that he first had entry into the manor by a certain Elias a Jew and afterwards by Imbert Guy and proffered the king's charters attesting this.

In the autumn of 1269, then, when the action began, matters stood thus. Alan la Zouche was in possession of the Ashby inheritance. The heiress Isabella was a ward of John de Warenne who stood in the place of her grandfather David's capital lord, Henry de Hastings, and her marriage would be a profitable business for him if the inheritance could be recovered. The simplest course appeared to be to appeal to the king's pardon to Gloucester's adherents,[6] and this was done by securing the earl's certification that Ashby and his son had been his supporters.

---

[1] These facts were established by the findings of an inquest in the course of Warenne's suit to which reference will be made presently.

[2] *C.P.R.* 1258–66, 529.

[3] *Ibid.* and *C.P.R.*, 1266–72, 47, 62.

[4] *C.P.R.* 1258–66, 540.

[5] *C.P.R.* 1266–72, 177.   The land appears to have passed from Ashby to Moses father of Elias. See Bridge, *History of Northamptonshire*, I 314.

[6] October 6, 1265 ; *Foedera* I, 464.

The surviving record[1] is not complete, but it illustrates well the part of the matter that is relevant to our argument, namely, the exasperation produced in Warenne by the delays and frustrations of a long and intricate lawsuit in which a valuable interest to which he considered himself entitled was at stake.

On the receipt of Gloucester's certificate in October 1269 the king had sent word to the justices that Isabella (a minor, daughter and heiress of Stephen, son of David de Ashby) was not to be disturbed. While this business was before the justices the king learned from letters patent of the Earl of Gloucester that the Ashbys had been neutral and given him no actual support, and the matter was drawn to the king's court apparently by *certiorari*.[2] The sheriff was directed to send an inquest *coram rege ubicunque fuerit* on November 18th. John de Warenne and Alan la Zouche appeared on the appointed day and put themselves on the inquest on the issue whether David de Ashby was an adherent of the Earl of Gloucester at any time before the battle of Evesham, but the business had to be postponed for want of recognitors. The sheriff was therefore directed to send a jury before the king *ubicunque* on January 20th. Warenne was aggrieved at the delay and at his request the king issued a special commission to certain justices to take the inquest locally at an earlier date.[3] This was done at Stony Stratford on December 20th and the inquest found that David was an adherent of the Earl of Gloucester before the battle of Evesham. Their report left open the question of whether David was a friend of the earl's steward or the earl himself and the date at which he had established the relation. Accordingly, the whole matter came before the king, again by *certiorari*, on February 15th, 1269–70, in order that these points might be determined. Warenne asked judgment on the earlier verdict and the jury, being questioned on the two

[1] Curia Regis Rolls, 193 (Mich. 53 and 54 Hen. III m. 28), 197 (Hil. 54 Hen. III m. 11). I am greatly indebted to Mr. W. H. B. Bird for skilful help in working out this matter.

[2] Cf. Jacob, *op. cit.* 201 *sqq.*, and particularly 205 and 213.

[3] The words of the record are ' Propter quod predictus comes sensit se gravatum propter prolixitatem diei. Ita quod ad instanciam predicti comitis mandavit dominus rex etc.' For the commission see *C.P.R.* 1266–72, 472.

points noted above, gave what must have been considered satisfactory answers. It was therefore judged that Isabella should recover seisin of the lands in question against Alan la Zouche without compensation. A postscript to the record adds that before the inquest was taken Alan disclosed the fact, which we have already noted, that he held the king's charters confirming his title acquired from Elias and Imbert Guy. What steps were subsequently taken I have not been able to discover, but it is pretty clear that Alan continued to defend his title on these grounds, seemingly with some success, and that Warenne was unable to get execution of the judgment he had obtained.

In the summer there followed the well-known incident before the king's justices at Westminster which is reported by the chroniclers and amply confirmed by official records. Warenne, anticipating defeat in a suit against Alan la Zouche involving what is variously described as a certain manor, and certain rights and lands,[1] entered Westminster Hall with his followers, created a great disturbance, delivered a murderous attack on the Zouches—father and son—and then fled to Reigate.[2]

Zouche appealed his assailant ' for a certain trespass and wounds inflicted on him in the king's hall at Westminster'. Meanwhile Warenne was besieged at Reigate by Edward, the king's son. The Earl of Gloucester and Henry of Almaine intervened and induced Warenne to submit and to undertake to clear himself and pay a fine at the king's discretion. He took an oath, supported by a considerable number of knights, *quod ex praecogitata malitia non perpetravit dictum facinus nec in contemptu domini regis;* a heavy fine, payable in annual instalments, was imposed on him and he was pardoned on August 4th.[3]

[1] These can scarcely have been anything but the Ashby inheritance.

[2] Wykes (R. S.), 233–5 ; *Flores Historiarum* (*R.S.*) III, 18 ; Ann. de Winton (R.S.) II, 108. Cf. Tout, *D.N.B.* LIX, 366 ; LXIII, 414–15 ; Malden, *V.C.H. Surrey* I, 347–8. There are a number of discrepancies as to date and some as to fact in these accounts. Wykes says that Alan was killed in court whereas it is clear that he did not die until after Warenne's pardon on August 4th. Mr. Malden must be mistaken in giving the year as 1268. As to the date of the incident, Wykes gives the Tuesday before the Nativity of St. John the Baptist, *i.e.* June 20th, and this is adopted by Professor Tout. (See also Powicke, *Henry III and the Lord Edward*, 584 f.).

[3] The pardon rehearsing these facts is printed from the Patent Roll in *Foedera* I, 485. The evidence of the chronicles is further confirmed by official documents, *e.g. C.P.R.* 1266–72, 438, 482. The *Flores* says ' Qui

Warenne's oath may have been taken in good faith; he may indeed have been moved by an outbreak of fury, but there can scarcely have been much respect for the king's court or the scrupulous and leisurely processes of the law to restrain him. He was a great prince, he had married the king's half-sister and had given the king important, if not consistent, support during the civil war and might well, in his own opinion, deserve some special consideration. Such consideration he had indeed received in November 1269 when the king had issued a special commission to the justices because he had professed himself aggrieved. Such a man would scarcely be overawed by the presence of the king's judges or a respect for the decorum of the court, least of all if his personal interests were compromised or his temper roused. Clearly in 1279 his interests were seriously compromised and it is not difficult to imagine that his temper was disturbed. Some demonstration such as that reported by the Abingdon chronicler might well have been expected.

But the argument from antecedent probability is in this case strengthened from another quarter. Warenne had something definite to gain by the violence and braggadocio attributed to him. In the *quo waranto* proceedings of 1279 the king's judges and pleaders took high legal ground asserting ' doctrines which would have destroyed a large half of the existing " liberties " '.[1] Among other things, they said that upon the conquest of England every jurisdiction was united to the crown. If this were so in fact the plea of prescription would not only be useless, it would be positively dangerous. If you produced no charter for the regalities you claimed to exercise it would be at least probable that your ancestor had usurped them. Now the words attributed to Warenne do in effect suggest a counter-argument. Admitting the principle—whatever may be said against it historically—he urges that the liberties enjoyed by those whose help made the conquest possible were an exception, that they were conquered not usurped. The fact that Warenne was descended only in the female line from the Warenne who

regi postmodum per purgationem et pecuniam satisfecit, parti laesae multa promittens, processu temporis parum donans,' *loc. cit.* The king was still receiving payments in respect of the fine in 1275 ; see *C.C.R.* 1272–9, 218.

[1] Pollock and Maitland, *H.E.L.*, 2nd ed. i, 572–3.

accompanied the Conqueror may perhaps have weakened the
force of the contention in his particular case, but the argument
itself was taken seriously enough to provide a counter-argument specially aimed at the clergy who put forward Anglo-
Saxon charters as their warrant. Maitland quotes the words
of Hugh Louther, one of the royal advocates, in 1292 :

' The Bishop cannot show that any of his predecessors came
with the Conqueror and obtained these liberties of [the] conquest
(*per conquestum*), for the Bishop and all his predecessors were, as
one may say, men of religion (*quasi religiosi, i.e.* in the same category
as professed monks) and they and their church were enfeoffed by
others, and therefore they cannot claim these franchises from time
immemorial.'

On this Maitland observes : ' these arguments about
liberties obtained by conquest afforded some ground for the
Earl of Warenne's famous assertion that his sword was his
warantus '.[1]

Now where it was open to grave doubt whether the court
would allow that user could ever beget title, anything that could
suggest and emphasize a claim to exceptional treatment might
help. A man who was in a position to do this by making a
scene, who was temperamentally capable of doing so and had
learned by experience that a court could be impressed in this
way, would not be likely to restrain himself. In the absence of
any definite evidence to the contrary (and that point we shall
have to consider next), there is room to suppose that having
drawn attention to his particular claim to consideration by
producing what in French political life is called an *incident*,
Warenne retired and allowed his attorney to enter the regular
plea of prescription. That, of course, was the plea entered,
and it will be seen that the words attributed to Warenne do not
necessarily constitute either a denial of the court's jurisdiction
or of the doctrine of regalities propounded by it. They put
forward rather an exception which the court was perhaps not
indisposed to consider. It is not as though he said : ' I will not
plead,' but rather : ' when I plead you should take the special
nature of my prescription into account.'

[1] *Plac. de Quo War.* 677 ; cited in Pollock and Maitland, *op. cit.* I,
573 n. [Cf. Sayles, *Select Cases before the Court of King's Bench* (S.S.) II, 142,
for the use of the same argument by the same advocate in 1293.]

It would seem, then, that the chronicler's story is not inherently improbable. On the contrary, it relates an act of which Warenne would have been capable at any time and one by which on this occasion he stood to gain very considerable advantage. Moreover, if the incident occurred at Guildford an account of it could readily have found its way to the Abingdon scriptorium and been noted there to be used later when the chronicle came to be compiled. So far, therefore, there would appear to be no good ground for rejecting the evidence.

Potuit, decuit—so far the argument from antecedent probability will take us, but before we may add *ergo fecit* we must consider whether any other and stronger argument stands in the way. This brings us to what appears to be the very heart of Dr. Round's contention.

' And yet it is he himself ' [*sc.* Mr. Malden], he writes, ' who has referred us to the legal record which proves that the earl appeared by his attorney before the justices in Surrey and made the prosaic answer of " prescription." Mr. Malden it is true seems to think that this was subsequent to the dramatic episode of ' De Warenne's rusty sword flung upon the council table '; but Hemingburgh, our only authority for the tale, distinctly assigns it not to a council, but to the earl's appearance before the justices [then follows a passage which will be cited and discussed later, showing that he pleaded prescription in Sussex when his right to free warren was challenged]. It appears that neither in Sussex nor in Surrey did the earl perform his celebrated sword trick before the King's Justices. In both counties he recognized their right to ask him *Quo waranto?* and advanced a peaceful plea. Are we to infer that Hemingburgh's story, definite and elaborate though it is, is a mere invention based on his lawless and overbearing character ? I find it difficult to escape from that remarkable conclusion ... Pitfalls are about the historian's path and, as I have always insisted, it is to the evidence of records he must look " as enabling the student both to amplify and to check such scanty knowledge as we now possess of the times to which they relate." Tested by record evidence Hemingburgh goes by the board.'[1]

Now the argument here set out would seem to be in effect a double one. In the first place, Dr. Round suggests that because it is established by record evidence that the earl

---

[1] *Peerage and Pedigree*, I, 320–2. The concluding passage in inverted commas is quoted by Dr. Round from the prefaces to his *Ancient Charters* and *Geoffrey de Mandeville*.

recognized the jurisdiction of the king's justices and pleaded before them by his attorney, therefore it follows that the incident did not occur. We have already seen some reasons why the incident need not have been incompatible with a subsequent plea of prescription and might indeed have done something to promote it. Further, it seems that in view of the procedure of the eyre it would have been quite possible for Warenne to have made his demonstration and retired leaving his attorney to safeguard his interests by entering the plea of prescription and asking for an inquest. It is pretty clear that Warenne came in under the general proclamation made on the first day of the eyre, alleged prescription and asked for an inquest. This course was definitely provided for in the Statute of Gloucester and was the practice in Edward II's time. The claim would be made on the first day of the eyre and the inquest would clearly have to be held later. The claim could be made in person, by attorney or by bailiff.[1] As has been said, we have not the returns of the Hundred Inquest in Surrey, but the forms in which the 1279 proceedings were begun throw a good deal of light on the nature of the material before the court. If the report of the jury had been *nesciunt quo waranto* a writ would issue and the record would begin A.B. *summonitus fuit respondere* or else C.D. *qui sequitur pro domino rege optulit se versus* A.B. If, on the other hand, the jury had reported *sine waranto* the record would be *presentatum fuit alias*. There was, however, a third possibility which can be illustrated from the neighbouring county of Sussex, where the Hundred jury reported that Nigel de Brock, Hugh de Buscy and others have the right of wreck in their lands *de antiqua tenura*.[2] In 1279, under the rubric *Libertates Nigelli de Brock et Hugonis de Buscy*, the record begins *Nigellus et Hugo clamant habere has libertates subscriptas*, and thereafter proceeds to the assertion that they and their ancestors have had and used them from time immemorial and have neither occupied nor usurped against the king.[3] Now, except for the circumstance that the earl appeared by attorney and that the words *has libertates subscriptas* are omitted, this is exactly the form in which the record of

---

[1] *Statutes of the Realm* (Rec. Com.) I, 46 ;　cf. Bolland, *Eyre of Kent* (S.S.) III, xxxiii.　[2] *Rot. Hundred.* II, 201.　[3] *Plac. de Quo War.* 754.

Warenne's claim before the justices in Surrey appears.[1] If, then, on the first day the earl appeared, threw down his rusty sword, delivered his tirade and retired, as we have suggested, it would be for his attorney to make the normal claim for the liberties by prescription. He could not indeed have made it otherwise, since if his principal was present he was *functus officio*.[2] When the earl had to plead before the justices in Sussex, where there is no question of an incident, he did so in person.[3]

The second and the more important part of Dr. Round's argument lies in the suggestion that because the incident is not recorded on the plea-roll it did not occur. It will be observed that the two arguments really hang together and can only be separated for purposes of analysis. Thus, when Dr. Round argues from the silence of the roll as to Warenne's sword, and its record of a peaceful plea, he appears to rely on the assumption that the incident and the regular plea were not both possible, because if the ' scene ' had taken place a record of it would have appeared on the roll. If it could be established that the record exhausts the whole transaction, and that whatever occurred must appear on it there would, of course, be nothing more to say. If it could even be shown that when brawling or acts of violence occurred in the king's court we might reasonably expect to find some note of them in the official record, the argument would be conclusive. The argument *e silentio* can be a powerful instrument, but its employment is attended with certain dangers unless the limitations to which it is subject are recognised. In criticizing Freeman's use of this argument Dr. Round has himself suggested the conditions in which it may properly be employed. Freeman had based certain assumptions on the silence of Domesday Book. Dr. Round described this as an error as great as it is common. Proceeding, he wrote :

' Like other inquests the Domesday Survey . . . was intended for a special purpose; special questions were asked and these questions were answered in the returns. So with the " Inquest of Sheriffs " in 1170; so also with the Inquest of Knights, if I may so term it, in 1166. In each case the questions asked are, practically known to us and in each they are entirely different. Therefore when Mr. Freeman writes—

[1] *Ibid.* 745.　　[2] Bolland, *op. cit.* I, xxxii.　　[3] *Plac. de Quo War.* 750–1.

The survey nowhere employs the feudal language which became familiar in the twelfth century. Compare, for instance, the records in the first volume of Hearne's *Liber Niger Scaccarii*. In this last we find something about knights' fees in every page. In Domesday there is not a word—
it is in no spirit of captious criticism, but from the necessity of demolishing the argument, that I liken it to basing conclusions on the fact that in the census returns we find something about population in every page, while in the return of owners of land there is not a word.'[1]

Dr. Round, of course, was writing with particular reference to Domesday and other surveys where the purpose of the enquiry can be established by the terms of reference to those who were commissioned to obtain the information. Thus if Domesday Book makes no mention of slaves in a given village we may be certain that there were none there because we know that the commissioners were instructed to enquire the number of slaves in every case. Perhaps the general principle may be fairly stated by saying that the silence of a document on any given point can only be used as an argument where it can be shown that there was a reasonable expectation that the matter would be mentioned. Let us see how this applies to the official records of the business transacted before the king's judges. The legal historians will tell us the purpose of the plea-rolls and what they should contain. Mr. Bolland writes :

' The plea rolls do indeed profess to give an account of what happened in the common bench at the trial of an action; but it is an account stringently edited, one from which everything which had not a material bearing on the determining judgment of the court or on the framing of the issue finally left to a jury was omitted. . . The record in the plea roll gives us a carefully drafted summary in Latin of the outcome of what was said and done in court thereby providing a permanent record of all that which it would be essentially necessary should be known to the justices if at any later time the court desires to certify itself as to what had been actually pleaded and determined during the hearing of any particular action.' [2]

' The record,' wrote L. O. Pike, ' was drawn up for the purpose of preserving an exact account of the proceedings . . . *but only in the form allowed by the court* '.[3]

---

[1] *Feudal England*, pp. 229–30. Freeman's words are quoted from *Norman Conquest* v, 465.

[2] *Y. B. 6 Edw. II* (S.S.), x–xi.

[3] *Harvard Law Review* VII, 266 (the italics are mine).

An important consequence of these facts is emphasized by Professor Holdsworth :

' Much pleading took place, and much argument thereon which never appeared on the roll. . . When we read the official record we think of a machine which automatically eliminates all the human dramatic element, and describes events and results in one impersonal, accurate, stereotyped form of words.'[1]

It is true that Mr. Richardson, the special advocate of the plea-rolls as a source of knowledge of the past, points out that they often give the facts of the case more fully and abundantly than do the Year Books.[2] But even he does not deny that the Year Books record certain occurrences in the court which do not appear on the rolls.

The particular roll with which we are concerned records the proceedings before the justices in eyre, but such rolls did not differ from those of the central courts in the matter of what was entered on them and what excluded. In his introduction to the eyre roll of Kent Mr. Bolland writes :

' Its records are as short and concise as possible. Nothing but the material facts are chronicled. There is no room for any such little story of the heroism or self-sacrifice of one single man, woman, or child, as often lights up the reports of our criminal courts of to-day.'[3]

Would there have been room for the story of a rusty sword displayed before the justices and a rhetorical speech addressed to them ? It is hard to believe—unless indeed the incident became a fact material to the case.

It is likely enough that brawling, acts of violence and other irregularities were not uncommon in the presence of the justices. We have seen an instance in Warenne's attack on the Zouches. Moreover, these things sometimes appear on the plea-rolls, but when they do it is because the attention of the court has been directed to them so that they form an essential part of the action. One or two instances may be offered by way of illustration. In November 1267 Robert de Fulham, a justice of the Jews, came to the Exchequer and complained to

---

[1] *H.E.L.* (3rd ed.) II, 538, 545. The point is abundantly illustrated from the Year Books in the pages which follow on this passage.

[2] ' Year Books and Plea Rolls as sources of Historical Information,' *T.R.H.S.*, 4th series v, 28 *sqq.* ; cf. Pike, *Harvard Law Review* VII, 266 *sqq.*

[3] *Eyre of Kent* (S.S.) I, lxxxii.

the Treasurer and Barons that as he was going into the king's hall at Westminster on business connected with his office a certain Robert de Colevill, sergeant-at-law, came and laid violent hands on him, dragging him by the breast; and he asked that amends be made him. Colevill was summoned before the Treasurer, Barons and two justices of Common Pleas then sitting at the Exchequer, admitted the charge and humiliated himself. He and his victim were then reconciled and the facts entered on the record.[1] A similar story is recorded on a plea-roll in 1294. During the trial of an issue there was some kind of pushing or scuffling between Hugh of Branteston who was pleading and Master Anthony of Bradele who wished to approach the bar. Anthony complained that Hugh's yeoman attacked him in the presence of the justices with opprobrious and vile words in contempt of the court of the king. The matter was submitted to a jury and the facts alleged in the complaint became part of the official record.[2] Mr. Richardson, in the article cited above, gives two relevant cases. In 1346, in the presence of the Justices of both Benches, William Daunay was taken in the hall of pleas at Westminster by the marshal of the king's bench on suspicion of cutting the purse of Thomas Simon, with which crime he was charged by popular clamour. Thomas would not prosecute, but Roger de Blaykeston came forward and said that William had been charged before the justices of gaol delivery at Carlisle with divers felonies, and that he was delivered to the custody of the Bishop of Carlisle as a clerk convict and had escaped from prison without making any purgation. Roger asked that William might remain in the custody of the marshal until the court should be more fully informed. Eventually, as no one prosecuted, he was released on giving an undertaking to stand his trial if anyone wished to proceed against him. The second case, which came up by the presentment of a Middlesex jury, involved the charge of picking pockets in the great hall at Westminster. One of the accused was discharged and the other sent back to prison and eventually liberated.[3] Finally, it may be worth while citing a curious

---

[1] Madox, *Exchequer* I, 236. The record is printed in the footnote.

[2] The extract from the roll is printed by Mr. Turner in *Y.B. 4 Edw. II* (S.S.), lxiii *sqq.*

[3] Richardson, *op. cit.*, 40, 41.

case from a Year Book of 1341. John de Manby was indicted for the death of Adam de Copandale, and it appeared that he was a clerk convict who had been outlawed. The question arose of the validity of his canonical purgation which had been accomplished in the court of the Archbishop of York during the vacancy of the see. The purgation had been certified by the Chapter as guardian of the spiritualities, while the Dean was absent from the country. Objection was taken to this as irregular. Eventually the outlawry was reversed, but John de Manby remained until the court should be more fully certified of his purgation.

' And afterwards the court said how formerly there was a dispute in the hall there and a brawl and amongst others this John de Manby was taken, and he put himself, etc., and it was found that he drew his sword in aid of the others who did the wrong, but that he did not strike ; wherefore as to him, for that matter it was proper that he should remain also.'[1]

This, of course, differs from the preceding cases in coming from the report and not the record. But since John de Manby ' was taken and put himself on the assize ' he must have been accused and the facts here set out would be material and would therefore appear on the record.

Two points are to be noted in connexion with these cases as relevant to our purpose. In the first place, brawling, turbulence and acts of wrong or violence certainly occurred in the courts in the thirteenth and fourteenth centuries and were probably not uncommon. In the second place, where an account of such things appears on the official record, it is because they have been made the subject of an accusation with which the court had to deal. Unless, then, a case or cases of this sort where there was no accusation can be shown to have been entered on the record, it will remain at least probable that the court roll would take no account of such a mild irregularity as that attributed to the earl in the chronicler's account. In view of this and of the established fact that a great deal went on in court which was never entered on the roll, it seems that before

---

[1] *Y. B.* 15 *Edw. III* (R.S.), 270–5. Cf. Pike, *History of Crime in England* I, 257 for other instances of brawling ; also *Cal. Inq. Misc.* II, No. 2098, p. 527 ; a case of violence ' whereby the King's court was disturbed and destroyed for the day ' (1314).

the argument *e silentio* may be legitimately used in the case we are examining a presumption ought to be raised that we might reasonably expect to find the alleged incident recorded on the roll. It is submitted that, as things stand, there is a presumption to the contrary.

Finally, we must consider a part of Dr. Round's argument, the bearing of which it is not easy to discern. Here is the paragraph in which he sets it out :

' And no one, it would seem, has observed that we have also the earl's answer to the *Quo waranto* enquiry in Sussex. His abuse of his franchises and hunting privileges in his Conquest lordship of Lewes was such that ' Sir Robert Aguylon ' petitioned Parliament for redress stating that the earl could show no title to their exercise. His hare-preserving was a pest to his neighbours, urged this vassal of the earl, whose manor of Perching nestled at the very foot of the South Downs. At the midsummer eyre of the year 1279 the earl " was questioned before the justices itinerant in Sussex by what authority he claimed free warren in Worth and divers other lordships in Sussex; he pleaded that his ancestors, on the loss of Normandy and their own lands there, had compensation for the same by the grant of other lands here in England, with this privilege; that they and their heirs should have free warren in those and all other their lands . . . *in regard of their surname*, " De Warenna " which plea was then allowed. . . .'[1]

' But what are we to say of the amazing story actually told to the justices and apparently accepted by them as confirming the earl's claim ? In the true Bulstrode spirit he alleged that his ancestors were granted free warren " in regard of their surname *de Warenna* ! " Now the origin of their name is known. The Varenne is a tributary of the Arques which flows into the sea at Dieppe; and on it stood Varenne, now Bellencombre, where there is still seen the mighty moated mound which is the typical stronghold of a conquest lord. That they should have been granted free-warren because they took their name from Varenne is obviously a ludicrous story, and when we realize that the earl told it only some seventy years after the alleged grant, it throws light on the real value of those " family traditions " on which Conquest and other tales all too often rest .'[2]

Before examining this matter in connexion with the main issue it will be desirable to get the facts as clearly as possible

---

[1] Dugdale, *Baronage* I, 79, from the original plea-roll. The italics are Dr. Round's.

[2] *Peerage and Pedigree* I, 320–3. Dr. Round describes this as ludicrous. Is it not possible that it was intended to be, *i.e.* that there was a deliberate pun on Warenne's name ?

before us. On turning to the Hundred Rolls we find that in
1274 the jury presented that the earl's father and the earl himself had appropriated chaces and warrens throughout the whole
barony of Lewes and in the lands and tenements of Robert
Aguylon and of others who held of the fee of the said earl
where the earl has no warren nor by right ought to have any.
They went on to explain that he had endeavoured to prevent
Robert and others hunting with dogs in places where such
hunting had been customary from ancient times and that he had
infringed on rights of which the king was seised.[1]

Robert de Aguylon's petition to parliament is assigned to
the sixth year of Edward I, so that it must have been dealt
with either in July or August or October 1278.[2] The petition
refers to and indeed would seem to be based on the return of
the Hundred jury. For answer, the petitioner was directed to
proceed by means of a writ out of chancery. Presumably this
means either that a writ of *quo waranto* would be issued on
behalf of the king against the earl or that Robert would be
allowed to obtain and make use of such a writ himself. The
manner in which the plea was begun in the summer of 1279
would suggest the former. The words ' the earl of Surrey was
summoned to be here at this day to show by what warrant he
claims to have free warren etc.,' were those regularly employed
when the Hundred jury had reported *nesciunt quo waranto*,
but the plea brought forward by the king's attorney was that
contained in the part of the 1274 return which we have already
quoted. That amounts to a return of *sine waranto* which would
require the earl to claim his franchise under the general proclamation and without an original writ. A possible explanation
of this difficulty may be found in the fact that the jury began by
saying that the Earl of Surrey holds in chief of the lord king the
whole rape of Lewes from the time of the conquest of England
and that there are nine hundreds in this rape which the said
earl holds by what warrant they know not.[3] Whether that be
so or not, the plea put forward by the earl was not quite what
Dugdale represented it to be. He cites, it is true, the original
roll, but he does not quote it in full, and there was the less

[1] *Rot. Hundred.* II, 209 a.   [2] *Rot. Parl.* I, 6 b.
[3] *Rot. Hundred.* II, 208 b.

need to vouch him as the full record is available in print in the *Placita de Quo Warranto*.[1] Turning to that authoritative record, we find that the earl pleaded in the first instance that his father had held the barony of Lewes with free warren and other liberties annexed, in chief of King Henry who accepted his homage, that his father died seised, and that the king held the barony during the seventeen years of John's minority and on his coming of age restored it to him with all the annexed liberties including warren and chace. Further, that the king had taken his homage for the barony and appurtenances and that the present king had done the same. This was his warrant and he asked judgment that King Edward ought to warrant him.

Afterwards (octave of St. Martin, *i.e.* November 18), at Chichester the earl came and asked whether the king claimed anything in certain parks of his at Worth and other places. The king's attorney replied that at present the king claimed nothing in them. With regard to the other places where the king claimed the aforesaid warrens and chaces (*i.e.* the liberties and places specified in the proceedings in the previous June) the earl then told the story repeated by Dugdale. This was done seemingly to show that his ancestors had had these liberties before the accession of Henry III as well as the manner in which they had acquired them, and this latter point is stated in terms. It was agreed to refer the matter to an inquest. What the real issue was appears from the terms of their verdict. They said on oath that William de Warenne, Earl of Surrey, father of the present earl, before King Henry, father of our lord king who now is, was crowned King of England, had all the aforesaid liberties, warren and chace as appurtenant to the honour and barony of Lewes. They excepted certain vills in the king's list as belonging to the fees of other lords. In these they said the earl neither has nor claims to have warren. Finally, they said that neither William nor John had usurped or occupied anything against King Henry or King Edward. It was adjudged, therefore, that the lord king should take nothing by his writ.

It appears, then, that the question which was decided was as to the rights possessed and exercised by the earl's ancestors and not the manner in which the earl alleged those rights to

[1] *Plac. de Quo War.*, 750–1.

have been acquired. All they say on that point is that there has been no usurpation. It would appear, then, that Dugdale was mistaken in saying that the earl's plea in respect of the manner in which the lands and privileges were acquired ' was then allowed '. That question did not come before the jury. At any rate they gave no verdict on the point. Dr. Round asks what are we to make of the amazing story told to the justices and apparently accepted by them as confirming the earl's claim. The record, however, does not say that the justices accepted that part of the earl's story—on the contrary, it says that the judgment was based on the verdict which was as we have seen. How the judges may have been impressed by the story remains a matter of speculation ; the reason assigned for the judgment was that the earl's ancestor had been seised of the land and privileges and that there had been neither usurpation nor occupation against the crown.

The question then arises as to how this Sussex case serves Dr. Round's argument that the incident of the rusty sword is not attested by admissible evidence. Three ways suggest themselves. The first is that the Sussex case gives further support to the contention that the earl was prepared to admit the king's right to ask him by what warrant he held his franchises and to plead as to them before the king's justices. But that is not contested. Further, if that were the point to be established, could it not have been done more effectively by citing the printed edition of the rolls ? If, in the second place, Dr. Round wished to forestall the suggestion that the incident might actually have occurred in Sussex—his words ' it appears that neither in Sussex nor in Surrey did the earl perform his famous sword trick before the king's justices ' seem to point in that direction—it may be pointed out that the reasons for expecting or not expecting to find the incident recorded in the rolls are the same whether it is assigned to the sessions of the justices at Guildford or at Chichester. Finally, Dr. Round's words suggest that he cites the case as discrediting the historical value of ' family traditions ' in general. No doubt the general proposition would be accepted, but the particular application of it to this case would seem to be that the other ' family tradition ' contained in the words attributed to the earl, namely, that his ancestor came with William the Bastard and conquered his lands with the sword, is as unhistorical as that which asserted that his ancestor received a grant of free warren in respect of his surname. But it will scarcely be seriously denied, in view of the positive evidence to the contrary, that the original Warenne came with the Conqueror and that the earl was descended from him in the female line and had inherited his English lands from his grandmother, the Warenne heiress whom Henry II had married to his own illegitimate brother. It is hard to see, therefore, how Dr. Round's case can be strengthened by reference to the proceedings before the justices in Sussex.

Let us see, then, how the whole matter stands. It appears that our knowledge of the alleged episode is derived from material available in the Abingdon scriptorium and inserted in what was in effect a small Abingdon chronicle based on a copy of Hemingburgh not earlier than 1304. The writer's slip in saying that the proceedings in 1279 were directed against the baron's lands is understandable on the grounds that there is no reason to suppose him to have been a lawyer—quite the contrary indeed—and that the writ *quo waranto* was actually used in connexion with land both before and after the proceedings of 1279. His second mis-statement, that the king withdrew from his position at once is not untrue in substance but only in overlooking the time that elapsed between the original proceedings and the king's compromise. It appears, further, that the earl was by temperament and position a man who might be expected to brawl, and that he had actually created a scene in the presence of the justices on a previous occasion and, further, that he had a very substantial reason for doing on this occasion much the sort of thing that the chronicler attributes to him. As to the argument drawn from the silence of the record, it has been seen that much went on in court in the course of an orderly and normal action which was never entered nor intended to be entered on the rolls and that although brawling and violence were probably not uncommon in the presence of the justices, when an account of them appears on the rolls it is because they have been made the basis of formal accusations brought against those who took part in

them. In view of these considerations it is suggested that the
argument *e silentio* is not admissible in this case. Finally, it
has been suggested that the conclusions which Dr. Round
appears to draw from the Sussex evidence either do not help
his case or else prove too much.

It does not necessarily follow that we ought to accept the
story as told by the Abingdon chronicler, but it is difficult to
resist the conclusion that it ought not to be rejected on the
grounds which Dr. Round has up to the present given for
doing so.

Note. This study was written before I had the advantage of
seeing Miss Cam's valuable article ' The Quo Waranto Proceedings
under Edward I ' (*History* xi, 143–148; reprinted 1943 in *Liberties
and Communities*, pp. 173–182, with documents). Miss Cam argues
that neither the policy nor the use of the writ was new, that the story
about Warenne cannot be accepted as it stands and that it is doubtful
whether the statute of 1290 does represent any departure from
Edward's original intentions. As to the first of these points it will be
seen that my argument lies in the same direction, the second does
not affect my contention that the story ought not to be rejected on
the grounds alleged by Dr. Round. As to the third I cannot quite
agree with Miss Cam. She relies mainly on a very interesting and
apparently hitherto unnoticed piece of evidence—a ruling made
by the judges of the two benches in 1279 on a point referred to them
by the justices in eyre. The judges lay down the principle that every
liberty is royal and belongs to the crown or to him who has sufficient
warrant either by charter or from time immemorial. Now where the
Hundred jury had reported *sine waranto* and prescription was
pleaded and established by inquest it was still open to the king to
bring a writ of *de quo waranto* if he wished (see above p. 41). He
probably would not do so but his right was reserved and as is stated
in the first statute of 1290 the judges had to know his pleasure in
each case before giving judgment. The subject therefore had no
security that his plea would avail until the king bound himself as
Coke says (2nd Institute, p. 495) in this particular of his prerogative
quod nullum tempus occurrit regi, by the statutes of 1290. In like
manner no one could be certain until that time how long a period
of user would be regarded as time immemorial. Finally the first
statute expressly extends the concession to all subjects *tam uiri
religiosi quam alii*, while before the statutes the clergy were not
allowed to plead prescription (see above p. 48). For these reasons
I still think, with all deference to Miss Cam's learned and skilful
argument, that the statutes of 1290 constitute a retreat from the
king's original position.

This would seem to be confirmed by a document published in 1931. In 1298 the king enquired about a certain ordinance 'de quo warranto' alleged to have been made in the Easter parliament of 1290. Gilbert de Rothbury sent a copy and added that it seemed to the justices and to himself that all pleas of quo waranto ought to be pleaded and terminated before the justices itinerant. *Et bonum est quod rex teneat graciam concessam et promissionem factam populo. Hoc est avisamentum nostrum.* As the quo warranto proceedings were from the beginning before the justices itinerant, the last words would seem to refer to the concession of 1290. Cf. *E.H.R.* XLVI (1931), 541 n.[1]

[1] [See, for a further discussion of this passage, G. O. Sayles, *Select Cases before the Court of King's Bench* II, lviii. In relation to the case in question in 1298, it would seem that the significant *gracia concessa* was that cases should be not merely heard but terminated in the eyre. The king's letter and the justices' reply, whilst clearly indicating that a real concession had been made in 1290, hardly support the chronicler's implication that it had been made in an atmosphere of crisis; in such circumstances it would be unlikely for Edward to have forgotten what he had granted, as his order to the justices of April 20th, 1299, declares. See *C.C.R.*, 1296–1302, 247. Cf. also T. F. T. Plucknett *Legislation of Edward I* (1949), 35–50].

III

BUZONES[1]

I

THE mysterious personages called by Bracton *buzones* in a passage that has often attracted the attention of legal historians have never been quite satisfactorily fitted into the scheme of English legal, constitutional, or administrative history. Meanwhile, Bracton's words, which seem to be of general application, and therefore, to contemplate something that might properly be called an institution, remain hanging in the air. They are, indeed, not quite completely isolated, as we shall see presently, but they leave us with the problem why Bracton should have embodied the term in his book unless a corresponding reality was to be found in most, if not all, of the English counties, whether it was called by the same name or not. It is to this problem that the present study is in the first instance addressed. A solution cannot be expected without a careful study of the appropriate evidence in all the English counties; something may be gained, however, if the problem can be related to a larger question of constitutional history and a *prima facie* case made for seeking its solution in a particular direction. If this attempt meets with any success, it will have the additional advantage of enabling us to classify what has hitherto been a practically isolated text or even, as I hope to show in a later study, two of them. This would be the more gratifying as the dry bones of historical material, in the absence no doubt of the prophetic voice, do not always come together bone to his bone. The larger question of constitutional history to which I hope to refer this question of the *buzones* is that of the election of the representative knights of the shire before the beginning of the Lancastrian legislation on the subject, and the other isolated text which will demand our consideration is the well-known petition of Matthew de Crauthorn, alleging that, although he had been elected for the county of Devon in 1319, the sheriff had returned some one else.[2]

[1] Reprinted from *The English Historical Review* XLVII (1932), pp. 177–193, 545–567.

[2] Stubbs, *C.H.* III (4th ed.), 435. [It should be noted, however, that the author never had the opportunity to complete the 'later study' centring around Matthew of Crauthorn, to which he here refers].

We may turn now to the *buzones*, and here it will be convenient to have the text before us. It occurs in that section of the book which stands under the general heading *De Placitis Coronae*.[1] This opens with a series of instructions to the justices as to how to proceed on their eyre. When the writs under which they act have been read, one of their number is advised to deliver an address explaining the purpose of the eyre.[2] Then follow the words which concern us :

> Quibus propositis, debent iustitiarii se transferre in aliquem locum secretum, et vocatis ad se quatuor vel sex vel pluribus de maioribus de comitatu, qui dicuntur buzones[3] comitatus et ad quorum nutum dependent[4] vota aliorum, et sic inter se tractatum habeant iustitiarii ad invicem, et ostendant qualiter a domino rege et consilio suo sit provisum, quod omnes tam milites quam alii qui sunt quindecim annorum et amplius, iurare debent quod utlagatos robbatores et burgatores non receptabunt, nec eis consentient nec eorum receptatoribus.

Then follow detailed directions for the detection and arrest of such persons, for the raising of the hue and cry and its management in appropriate cases, for the arrest of those suspected of purchasing provisions for the use of criminals at large, and for the enforcement of regulations with regard to hosting. The text then proceeds ' convocentur postmodum servientes et ballivi hundredorum, etc.,' for the purpose of electing the juries of presentment.

Two points attract our attention at the outset. In or at the time of a special meeting of the county court which had been deliberately made as representative as possible of all the elements of the community, the judges may count on finding a definite group of influential persons from whom they are to choose a certain number. Upon these in private conclave they are to impose certain special responsibilities in connexion with the policing of the county. This work is largely administrative,

---

[1] Bracton, *De Legibus*, etc., fo. 115 b, ed. Woodbine II, 327.

[2] Cf. H. M. Cam, ' On the Material available in the Eyre Rolls ', *B.I.H.R.* III, 152.

[3] Professor Woodbine notes and rejects the following alternative readings ' busones, barones, burgatores, butores ' ; the last of which occurs in one, and all the others in two manuscripts, while five agree on the form in the text.

[4] Three manuscripts give ' initium dependeant '. The other variants do not affect our point.

and from the end of the twelfth century had been often entrusted to appointed or elected knights of the shire. The persons to whom the judges are to explain the king's pleasure in this respect are evidently not merely the *maiores de comitatu*, but a special class among them designated by a special name. They would appear, therefore, to have something like an official, or at least an officially recognized, position, and this is the second point to be noticed. The suggestion receives some corroboration from the fact that, when the judges have delivered their instructions to the *buzones* of the county, they are to inform the officials of the hundreds of the duties that fall to them. Finally, it should be noted that Bracton evidently expected that *buzones* (or at any rate a definite body of persons corresponding in influence and position to those whom Bracton knew as *buzones*) would be found in every county to which the judges came. So much as least seems to be established by the text. The problem that remains is a double one. We have to ask first what is the derivation and original meaning of the word *buzo*, and then what was the composition and what the function of the group of persons to whom Bracton applied it. Before proceeding to the discussion of these problems we must marshal all the available evidence. It was said just now that Bracton's text was not quite isolated, and indeed the word *buzo* used clearly in the sense which Bracton gives it occurs in a Gloucester case with which he may well have been familiar. The word occurs in another sense, however, in certain thirteenth-century texts, and it appears pretty early to have been adopted as a surname in various parts of England. These texts and some examples of the surname form the remainder of the evidence which we have to consider.

The Gloucestershire case was heard before the king's judges at Westminster in February 1212, and has long been known from the condensed version which appears in the *Abbreviatio Placitorum*.[1] As will be shown presently, there is nothing unique or even unusual about the case itself except that it officially describes certain persons as *buzones*. For this reason, and because it is, as far as I know, the only record which does

---

[1] Curia Regis Roll, No. 54, m. 20 d, now printed in *Curia Regis Rolls* VI, 228–231 ; *Abbrev. Plac.* p. 85 a.

F

so, it is desirable that we should have the facts before us. By
way of introduction it may be said that this was a real action
begun by writ of right in a feudal court, transferred to the
county court of Gloucester, and thence removed on a suggestion
of false judgement to the king's court, where what had been
done in the county court was rehearsed and re-examined, the
judgement annulled and a new one given. The record opens :
' Willelmus de Parco, Hugo Mustel et Elias Kokerel missi pro
comitatu Gloucestrie ad faciendum recordum de loquela que
fuit in comitatu . . . recordantur.'[1] And this is the story that
they told. William de Eston brought a writ of right against the
prior of Ware in respect to a carucate of land in Willicot
in the court of the earl of Winchester,[2] where, as he alleged,
there was a default of justice. He then came to the county
court of Gloucester, where the default was proved and the prior
summoned to defend his right at the next session of the court.
At that sessions the prior neither came nor essoined himself,
and the court, being satisfied that the summons had been duly
made, ordered the land to be taken into the king's hand and
the case to be adjourned. At the next session both parties
appeared and the prior was allowed to replevy his land. Plead-
ings were heard on both sides, the prior asked for and obtained
a view of the land, was given a day, and appointed an attorney.
At the given day the attorney essoined himself, but as the
essoiner neither awaited judgement nor appointed any one
to represent him, the court held that the prior had made default
and directed the land to be taken again into the king's hand and
another day to be given to William. At the appointed day he
appeared, claimed record of the prior's default and asked for
judgement, which was awarded him, and obtained seisin.

Thus the county spoke through its three representatives.
The king's court then heard the prior's story, which was a very
different one, and was supported by evidence of a character
most damaging to those who had conducted or taken part in
the proceedings in the county court. He denied that he had
ever been summoned to answer William's plea, but added that,

[1] The record of the county was normally, whether in civil or criminal
cases, borne before the king's judges by four persons. See *infra*, p. 69.
[2] Saher de Quency who as lord of the manor of Ware was patron of the
priory. See *infra*, p. 71.

having been given to understand that the land had been taken into the king's hand, he had approached the sheriff within fifteen days, and sought to replevy it. He was told to come to the next session of the county court. There he was told that the record showed that he had made default. He denied both default and neglect (*supersisa*), asserted that he had not been summoned, and sought to replevy the land as he had done before. The sheriff testified that he had made his application within the proper time and the land was restored to him. William then brought his writ of right, and the prior submitted that he was not bound to answer without a summons; and because the court was not full, the case was adjourned. As the prior could not attend the next session, he appointed one of his clerks as attorney, who essoined himself, and obtained a day by means of the essoiner whom he had commissioned to act for him. The attorney came at the appointed day with his record (*cum libro suo*) to warrant his essoin, and then was told by the court that the essoin was not allowed because his agent had departed before judgement had been given or a day appointed, and thus the prior lost his seisin. On this version of what had happened he put forward two alternative pleas. First, that the record made by the county was either deliberately or carelessly inaccurate in stating that he asked for a view, which he had never done, and this he offered to prove by two responsible persons who had been present at the proceedings. Alternatively, he offered either to prove by means of a champion who had been present at the proceedings that the record should be as he alleged, or to deny by the same means that it was as the county had recorded it. This brought the prior to what was really the substance of his case, and at his instance the court summoned two royal officials, who had been concerned with the case when it was before the county court. These were Joseph Marsh, the king's official (*serviens regis*), in whose bailiwick the land lay, and Walter de Banbury, king's clerk who kept the roll of the pleas of the county. Joseph denied that he had ever summoned the prior, or taken his land into the king's hand, or given seisin to William de Eston, or that he had ever received orders to do these things. He further stated that he had said all this in the county court, and the knights sent on behalf of the county confirmed this. Walter testified that the steps taken by the prior were as he had described, and were so recorded in his roll after the session of the county court where the essoin was warranted. He and the clerk who wrote the roll then went to London on business of the king and the sheriff, leaving the roll with Richard, the priest of the castle. On his return from London, hearing what had occurred, he recovered and inspected the roll and found that it had been tampered with, as at the place where the essoin was recorded certain words altering the sense had been written between the lines in another hand.[1] He told the priest that the roll had been corrupted while in his keeping, informed the sheriff, and afterwards brought the whole matter before the county court. This last point was confirmed by the knights sent on behalf of the county.

The king's court then took account of the fact that the knights had neither produced the writ by which the plea was begun nor the summoners who were instructed to summon the prior, nor in their record had they stated that the prior was summoned after the taking of the land. They must also have remarked on the irregularity of the county being represented by three instead of four knights, because the record proceeds : ' Gilbert Martel who ought to have been the fourth knight came and said that he had not been present at the making of any judgement and knew nothing of the matter.'

Having regard, therefore, to the evidence produced by the prior and the procedural irregularities observed by the court it was held that the county failed at every point (*omnia eis defecerunt*), and a fine was imposed on them for false judgement. So far, although the story is disgraceful enough, there is nothing unusual about the case, but now follow the words that make it unique.

Milites de comitatu qui consueti sunt interesse falsis judiciis et sunt buzones judiciorum arestentur, scilicet Willelmus de Parco, Elias Kokerel qui presentes sunt, et committuntur vicecomiti . . .[2]

---

[1] ' Per manum alterius quam essonium scriptum fuit facta fuit litera interlinaria ante hoc verbum : " affidavit," scilicet haec interlinaria : " nec venit nec ".' The record, therefore, was made to say that the prior's attorney had neither come nor given sureties.

[2] Several words are here illegible, though one may be *habet*. They must refer, however, to the steps taken with regard to Hugh Mustel, the second of the knights who had been sent to represent the county. The lacuna is not noticed in *Plac. Abbrev.*

et Walterus de Aure et Phillippus de Bello Monte, alii buzones, capiantur et similiter Willelmus de Eston capiatur—et prior habeat seisinam suam et recuperet dampna sua.

Before we proceed to consider the problem presented by this text, something may be said of the case in what may be called its normal aspect. As we have seen, it reached the king's court on an allegation of false judgement. The appropriate procedure is described by Glanvill,[1] and the writ which he gives requires that the sheriff shall cause the record to be made in the county court and brought before the king or his justices by four knights who were present at the making of the record, and that both parties be properly summoned. It will be remembered, of course, that the assize of Clarendon had provided that in criminal accusations in certain circumstances the sheriff should bring before the justices two men of the locality *ad portandum recordationem comitatus et hundredi*.[2] The rule of sending four knights to speak for the county before the king's justices was regularly observed in the thirteenth century. They were there not merely to attest judicial proceedings, but to speak for the whole county in its corporate capacity, the community that was indistinguishable from its court, but could do wrong and suffer penalties. The county court, however, was not a court of record; therefore, whatever notes of its proceedings may have been kept had no probative authority until in a particular case the sheriff had been directed to have a record made.[3] The coroner's roll, which dealt with matters touching pleas of the Crown, was early regarded by the justices as having an official character which was entirely wanting to the sheriff's memoranda.[4] These were regularly kept, however, as

[1] Glanvill, bk. VIII, caps. 8, 9, 10, in G. Phillips, *Englische Reichs- und Rechtsgeschichte* II, 412–14.

[2] Ass. Clar., § 4, in Stubbs's *Charters* (9th ed.), 110 ; cf. Cam, *The Hundred*, 13.

[3] The roll, as we have seen, could be introduced as evidence where the record of the county had been challenged. The statement in the text involves a discussion of the questions recently raised by Professors Plucknett and Woodbine in the articles cited in the next note ; cf. G. T. Lapsley, 'The Court, Record and Roll of the County in the Thirteenth Century,' *L.Q.R.* LI (1935), 299–325.

[4] Pollock and Maitland, *H.E.L.* (2nd ed.) I, 536 f. ; II, 666 ; Cam, *op. cit.*, 115 ; W. A. Morris, *The Early English County Court*, 128–31. After 1275 the sheriff was bound by statute to keep a roll, but he must have done so much earlier ; cf. H. Jenkinson, ' Plea Rolls of the Medieval

the case before us shows. Walter, the king's clerk, had the rolls
of the pleas of the county, he had a clerk under him, and the
various steps in the proceedings were noted as they occurred.
Unluckily, the custody of the rolls was not so careful as to
exclude the possibility of corruption of the record. Such things
were not uncommon later in the century when the sheriff
tended to leave too free a hand to his clerks who dealt with
writs, had the custody of the rolls, and were accused of taking
bribes to falsify them.[1] Such interference with the course of
justice, this time on the part of the sheriff, is well illustrated
in a Somerset case a few years later than the Willicot case. This
came before the king's justices on a suggestion of false judgement, and the sheriff, having been directed by the knights sent
on behalf of the county, said that proceedings had been begun
by writ of right in the court of the late King John when he was
count of Mortain. When the case reached the county court,
the tenant pleaded a fine previously made in the franchise
court, to which it was objected that the fine was not made
before the king's justices. This objection, the knights said, the
sheriff maintained, and pressed the court to give judgement for
the demandant, because, as they alleged, he (*sc.* the sheriff)
was the *valettus* of the demandant's lord. The court resisted,
and all the suitors withdrew except two or three who remained
until the hour of vespers. These the sheriff exhorted to make
judgement fearlessly, undertaking to warrant them if they
would do so. The tenant being then in fear of personal injury
abandoned his fine, and sought to put himself on the assize,
but the sheriff would not allow this, declaring that the tenant
must stick to his chirograph. The suitors who were present
agreed, and proceeded to give judgement for the demandant
' without the assent or will of the county court '.[2] Where a
wrong of this sort had been alleged and the county was put on

County Court ', *Camb. Hist. Journal* I, 103, and *E.H.R.* XLIII, 21–33. Cf.
T. Plucknett, ' New Light on the Old County Court ', *Harvard Law Review*
XLII, 639 ; XLIII, 1111 ; G. E. Woodbine, ' County Court Rolls and County
Court Records ', *ibid.* XLIII, 1083 ff.

[1] Cam, *op. cit.*, 134–5.

[2] *Somersetshire Pleas*, ed. Sir C. E. H. Chadwyck-Healey (Somerset
Record Society, XI), No. 293 (9 Hen. III), 61 ff. An almost contemporary
case of a sheriff bullying, or attempting to bully, his court is in *Bracton's
Notebook*, No. 1730, discussed in Cam, *op. cit.*, 14–16.

its defence, the whole community would have to pay if wrong or carelessness were proved. We should expect, therefore, that it would choose to be represented at the king's court by men who were something more than the ordinary suitors, men of substance known in the community, and experienced in the business of the county court. It will be worth while to inquire how far this expectation was realized in the Willicot case by bringing together what can be known of those principally concerned in it.

We may dispose first of the tenant, the prior of Ware, with whom we shall not be concerned again, reserving what can be said of the demandant and the knights deputed to represent the county. The priory of Ware in Hertfordshire was a cell of the Norman house of Benedictines at St. Evroul, which had received extensive endowments in England after 1066. We first hear of the prior between 1203 and 1206, but the cell appears to have been founded by Margaret, countess of Winchester, sister and co-heiress of Robert Beaumont, earl of Leicester. The prior administered the English estates of the mother house and was treated in England as the owner of them. The patron was the lord of the manor of Ware who, after 1204, was Saher de Quency, earl of Winchester, and it was in his court, as we have seen, that the action against the prior originated.[1] The land lay in Willicot in Preston upon Stour, co. Gloucester, a member of the honour of Leicester. A share of the tithe here was granted to St. Évroul in 1176, and in 1204 Robert earl of Leicester added a hide of land in Willescote.[2]

The demandant was William de Eston, and in what can be said of him we must remember that, although he is not described as a *buzo*, he was ordered to be arrested like the other *buzones*. Obviously, he stood to gain more than any one else by the irregularities in the county court, and if we consider him as the promoter of them, it follows that he must have been able to exert very considerable pressure on the members of the court, and on the group of men called *buzones* from whom they selected four to represent them before the king's judges. It is

---

[1] Dugdale, *Monasticon* VI, Pt. II, p. 1049, referring to Tanner, *Notitia Monastica*, Herts. XXV; *V.C.H., Herts.* IV, 455–7.

[2] S. Rudder, *Gloucestershire*, 608; B. Atkyns, *ibid.*, 608–9; T. D. Fosbroke, *ibid.* II, 370–1; Round, *Cal. of Documents preserved in France*, 227, 229, 230.

important, therefore, to emphasize his relations with them and
to note their names, which were Walter de Aure, Philip de
Beaumont, Gilbert Martel, Elias Kokerell, Hugh Mustel, and
William de Parco. We shall consider them in that order when
we have disposed of the demandant.

William himself was a man of substance and influence in the
west country, with property in other parts of England.
Though his name occurs not infrequently in connexion with
administrative work in co. Gloucester, his chief interests appear
to have been in the neighbouring county of Somerset. His
name may have been taken from North Aston in co. Oxford.[1]
In 1201 he was holding land in three vills in Spaxton, co.
Somerset, which his wife Juliana had brought him, and they
had a son, another William, who was of age to act as attorney
for his mother in a suit brought against her in respect of these
holdings.[2] In the same year he had to defend his title to land
held by him at Cadbury in the Catsash Hundred of Somerset.[3]
In 1213 he appears to have been a knight in the same county,
as he appeared in person in response to the king's summons
of November of that year.[4] During the civil war he acted, it
would seem, first with the king, afterwards with the opposition,
for in January 1216 the sheriff of Somerset is notified that
William is to have seisin of the lands which had belonged to
Henry de Mudiford, unless they yield more than 20 marks a
year; while in September of the following year, under the
rubric *De Reversis*, the sheriff is notified that William, having
returned to the king's fealty and service, is to have seisin of the
lands in Blackmore which King John had granted to him.[5]

---

[1] He had territorial interests in North Aston. In 1200 he brought an
action against Robert de Eston for the vill of North Eston and his right
there which terminated in a fine, *Curia Regis Roll* i, 159, 216. The matter
seems to have dragged on, for in 1207 Robert de Eston gave the king 20s.
for leave to compound with William de Eston in respect of land in Eston
(North Aston, Oxf., in the index) (*ibid.* v, 285).

[2] *Curia Regis Rolls* ii, 90, 185 ; cf. iii, 42.

[3] *Ibid.* ii, 39 ; cf. W. Phelps, *History of Somerset* i, 391.

[4] *Rot. Lit. Claus.* (Rec. Comm.) I, 166a. The writ is in *Report on the
Dignity of a Peer*, App. i, 2.

[5] *Rot. Lit. Claus.* i, 245 b, 322 a. A connexion with Henry de Mudiford
and the Eston family may have persisted. In 9 Hen. III Henry and his
pledges, of whom Stephen de Eston was one, were in mercy for having failed
to prosecute an action of novel disseisin against Fawkes of Bréauté in respect
of these same lands (*Somerset Pleas*, ed. Chadwyck-Healey, No. 378, p. 86).

We have seen that he had land in Oxfordshire, and it is possible
that he also held in Wiltshire,[1] and in Kent he had in 1206 a
rent of 20s. in Ewell.[2] But outside the west country his chief
interests were in Norfolk. In 1203 his claim to a rent of
9s. 11d. in Tolthorpe or Thorpe Parva was met by the allegation
of bastardy. The matter was referred to the court of the bishop
of Norwich, where his legitimacy was established, and he later
recovered seisin before the justices.[3] In 1206 he was again in
litigation with regard to certain services in the same place
which he claimed against Alan le Peitevin and eventually
surrendered for a payment for 5 marks.[4] His chief lord in the
county was Robert de Mortimer, for the loss of whose swans
he and another had been held responsible in 1204.[5] A more
serious question arose in 1207, when Robert summoned a
number of his Norfolk tenants, including William, to show
cause why they had not furnished him with a reasonable aid for
his support in the king's service in Poitou as the lord king had
commanded. They all repudiated the obligation, and alleged
that they were not liable for any aid except in the three
appointed cases, and would not pay without the judgement of
the court. The case was heard before the king himself, and
the record concludes ' omnes sunt in misericordia pro defalta.'[6]

We must now take account of the evidence which shows
William engaged in the business of the county, sometimes in
association with the *buzones* of the Willicot case, in Gloucester,
Somerset and Dorset. In 1203 the county court of Gloucester
dispatched William and three others on an errand that, while it
must have been common enough, still required the services of
responsible people : this was ' ad videndum utrum infirmitas

---

[1] *Rotuli de Oblatis et Finibus* (Rec. Comm.), 535. There is some doubt
about this as his wife who was associated with him in obtaining a writ of
pone is named Agnes, but of course a second marriage was quite possible.

[2] *Curia Regis Roll* iv, 276.

[3] *Ibid.* ii, 291, 308–9.

[4] *Ibid.* iv, 193 ; v, 4.

[5] *Ibid.* iii, 162.

[6] Was this the scutage of the eighth year levied in connexion with the
campaign in Aquitaine or the gracious aid reluctantly granted by the
Oxford Council in February 1207 ? The former seems more probable,
for the aid was levied directly by the king's officers and was for ' a war to
be undertaken at some undertermined time in the future '. See Ramsay,
Revenues of the Kings of England i, 242–5 ; Mitchell, *Taxation under John
and Henry III*, 84–93.

qua Gaufridus de Cusintor essoniavit se, sit languor necne '.[1]
Some years later he was sent on a similar errand by the county
court of Somerset, and the record is worth noting because it
was Ralph de Aure who had essoined himself *de malo lecti*, but
the case was indefinitely delayed, because one of the four
knights sent to take the view would never act.[2] A like commission sent by the county court of Dorset, however, seems to have
acted promptly and effectively, and William and his associates
reported of the lady whom they had been sent to inspect
' quod infirmitas sua non fuit languor '.[3] At some uncertain
date the county court of Gloucester sent four knights, two of
whom were William de Eston and William de Parco, ' ad
faciendum recordum de duello vadiato . . . in comitatu Gloucestriae '.[4] Then in Somerset in 1207 William was one of the
four knights ' missi pro comitatu . . . ad faciendum recordum de
loquela ',[5] etc. In the same year he was one of the knights
elected to act on a grand assize in respect of land in Bourton-on-
the-Water in the county of Gloucester, and it should be noted
that one of the four electors was William de Parco, while
among the knights chosen were Gilbert Martel and Hugh
Mustel.[6] Again we find William acting as a surety for people
who had financial or other obligations to the Crown in the three
neighbouring counties. Thus in Gloucester he, with William
de Parco and Philip de Beaumont, was responsible for William
de Mara's standing to judgement in the king's court.[7] In 1221
he was one of the sureties for the appearance of the Earl
Marshal in connexion with a very shady looking murder case in
which one of the earl's men was involved.[8] In the same year
William and the Hundred of Berkeley were jointly responsible
for the chattels of a murderer who had taken to flight, and
William had to pay.[9] In Somerset in 1204 he was surety for a

[1] *Curia Regis Rolls* III, 46. The rules for this procedure and the appropriate writ are given in Glanvill, Bk. I, caps. 18 and 19, (Phillips, *op. cit*
343).
    [2] *Bracton's Notebook*, No. 922. Glanvill, *loc. cit.*, says that two knights
suffice for this purpose, though four must be appointed.
    [3] *Bracton's Notebook*, No. 923.
    [4] *Select Pleas of the Crown* (S.S.), I, no. 126, p. 80.
    [5] *Curia Regis Rolls* v, 45.   [6] *Ibid.* v, 14.
    [7] *Select Pleas of the Crown*, 81.
    [8] *Pleas of the Crown for the county of Gloucester*, ed. Maitland, 9, 10, 61.
    [9] *Ibid.*, 69, 126 ; cf. pp. 95, 106, 132, where in another hundred he made
himself responsible for ½ mark which one had agreed to pay ' ut possit esse
sub plegio standi recto '.

party to a real action who sought leave to compound,[1] and in
Dorset as early as 1200 he was appointed her attorney by
a lady who had been impleaded.[2]   If, as has been suggested
above and will be argued later, the *buzones* were a standing
group of country gentlemen active and influential in the affairs
of the county and its court, the evidence before us would point
to the inclusion of William in that group.   The fact that he was
not described as a *buzo* in the Willicot case may be because he
was a party to it or because of his discreditable conduct or both.
The order for his arrest with the other *buzones* points to his
being one himself.

We turn now to those persons who in the Willicot case bore
the record of the county before the king's justices and were
officially described as *buzones*.   Walter de Aure is a relatively
dim figure, but there is enough information about him to enable
us to situate him as a person of condition and some property in
the county of Gloucester.   Awre itself is in the Hundred of
Blidisloe and appears to have been held first of the king, then to
have passed to the earl of Salisbury, and then early in the reign
of Henry III through the Marshals to the earl of Gloucester.[3]
It is said that the manor of Awre came to Walter in 1204 ; while
this may be true, there seems to have been an older connexion
between his family and this place, for as early as 1191 Walter,
son of Walter Blount (Blundus), was drawing xx*s*. annually
from the place.[4]   Beside what he held in Awre he had a profitable
interest in the salt pans at King's Barton near the city of
Gloucester, and was concerned with the exploitation of the
iron in the Forest of Dean.   King John had allowed him to use a

---

[1] *Curia Regis Rolls* III, 195.

[2] *Ibid.* I, 118, 124.

[3] *Book of Fees* (R.S.) I, 51.   Aure was *terra Normannorum* held by Walter
at farm for *l* xxx (*Rot. Lit. Claus.* I, 365 b, 376, 1218).   The king has transferred to the earl of Salisbury what he had in the vill, and Walter is to pay
the farm to him and the men of the place are to be obedient and responsible
to Walter (*Cal. of Inquisitions Post Mortem* (R.S.) I, 156–7)(this is the
summary of the Gloucester inheritance made in 46 Hen. III).   Aure with
the Hundred of Blidesloe and the advowson of a moiety of the church were
held of the earl of Gloucester, cf. *Cal. of the Charter Rolls* (R.S.) I, 174.
Richard Marshal, earl of Pembroke, had a grant of the hundred in 17 Hen.
III.

[4] S. Rudder, *Gloucestershire*, 246 ; R. Atkyns, *ibid.*, 235 ; Fosbroke,
ibid. II, 184 ; *Pipe Roll, 3 Ric. I*, 92 ; *ibid., ann.* 4, 285 ; *ann.* 5, 113 ; *ann.*
6, 231.

movable forge there, and when these were prohibited by Henry III, an exception was made in favour of Walter.[1] This concession and an earlier one by which he had the privilege of not being impleaded for any free tenement except before the king or his chief justice suggest that he was a person of standing and influence.[2] In 1207 he was one of those appointed to assess the aid in Oxfordshire.[3] He died sometime in 1211, for in that year he had licence for his forge in the Forest of Dean, and before it was over his son and heir, another Walter, was made responsible to the king for the chattels of a murderer and the price of a horse from which a boy had accidentally fallen and killed himself.[4]

Philip de Beaumont has already come before us as associated with William de Eston and William de Parco, in Gloucester county business of uncertain date, and in 1221 he was acting as a surety for the defendant in an appeal of rape originating in that county.[5] It seems reasonable to assume, therefore, that he was a landholder in that county, though I cannot produce any direct evidence of it. In Somerset in 1201 he was holding of Walter de Cantilupe whom he was prepared to serve as a champion in the course of a real action.[6] In 1207 he was involved in a similar case which suggests that he was holding in Dorset as well. The tenant in this action alleged a fine made between his grandfather and the father of the demandant in 3 Hen. II, and offered to prove it by the body of a certain free man of his, Philip de Beaumont, who was present at the transaction.[7]

[1] *Historia et cartularium Monasterii S. Petri Gloucestria* (R.S.) ii, 143–5 ; *Rot. Lit. Claus.* i, 464 a ; Rudder, *op. cit.*, 29 ; Bigland, *Gloucester Collections* i, 459–60.

[2] *Rot. Pat.*, 5 *John* (Rec. Comm.), p. 41 ; Madox, *Exchequer* i, 118 n

[3] *Rot. Pat.*, 8 *John* (Rec. Comm.), p. 72 b.

[4] *Pleas of the Crown for the County of Gloucester*, ed. Maitland, 91, 92, 131. All these in the Hundred of Blidesloe ; cf. *Inquisitiones Post Mortem for Gloucestershire* (ed. Madge) iv, 47.

[5] Above, p. 74 ; *Gloucester Pleas*, 29.

[6] *Curia Regis Roll* ii, 29. In 1206 William de Cantilupe was directed to transfer the son of Walter de Aure, whom the king had caused to be arrested, to William Marshal, who had made himself responsible for him; cf. *Rot. Pat.*, 7 *John* (Rec. Comm.), p. 60.

[7] *Curia Regis Roll* v, 46–7. There are certain difficulties here. The man named in the offer of proof is Philip de Bello Campo, not de Bello Monte, but when the issue was ready for trial an addition to the record written in the margin notes ' campiones Philippus de Bello Monte ', etc. The editor

In Devonshire in 1222 he held the Hundred of Shirewell at farm from the king, and appears to have held land in those parts as well.[1] He must have died very soon after this, for two years later the younger Philip de Beaumont, who seems to have been a nephew, sued his stepmother who had got her dower out of Shirewell during his minority, although his father had not been seised of it when he married her.[2] As an illustration of the position and interests of the family it may be mentioned that the younger Philip, who came of age in 1224, had, as heir of his uncle Thomas, a reversionary interest in certain lands in Golder and Clare in the county of Oxford.[3]

Elias de Cokerel[4] was holding at Cotes Cokerel in Gloucestershire as early as 1207, when Walter de Sherbourne began an action against him which was intended to have led to a fine, but was not pursued. This Walter married Alicia de Cokerel, who after his death in 1210 was associated with William de Cokerel in a gift of land to the prior and monks of Bradenstock in Wiltshire.[5] We get, therefore, the suggestion that the family of Cokerel was of some standing and held land in more than one county. Their principal holding was no doubt Cotes, to which they had given their name. This consisted of half a knight's fee in the Kiftsgate Hundred which Elias seems to have held of

or at least the compiler of the index assumed that Bello Campo was a slip for Bello Monte. Supposing that he was ten years old in 3 Hen. II, he would be sixty in 1207, which would seem to be a ripe age for a champion, but we know that he was ready to act in that capacity in 1201, and in 1208 he and the demandant's champion had given sureties and a day had been appointed when they were to appear armed (*ibid.* v, 149).

[1] *Bracton's Notebook*, No. 197. This was an action against the abbot of Ford for suits at the court of the Hundred of Shirewell, in which Philip alleges that his uncle held the hundred of which he himself is now *firmarius regis*, and that it came to him eventually by way of inheritance. There is some difficulty about the date of his death. In 1221 Philip was one of the pledges for a man accused of rape, who did not appear and was therefore in mercy, and the roll adds ' Philippus obiit ' (*Pleas of the Crown for the County of Gloucester*, 29). The name of Philip as pledge is struck out in both manuscripts, so that it is possible and even likely that another Philip was intended. See on such a possibility Maitland, Introd. xlv–xlvii.

[2] *Bracton's Notebook*, No. 977. The younger Philip's Devonshire interest continued (*Pipe Roll*, 14 Hen. III, 21).

[3] *Bracton's Notebook*, No. 566 ; Jeayes, *Catalogue of Muniments at Berkeley Castle*, No. 172, p. 60.

[4] Kokerel in the record. I have altered the spelling in conformity with that of the place.

[5] *Curia Regis Roll* v, 9 ; *Calendar of Charter Rolls* (R.S.) I, 162 ; *Rot. Lit. Claus.* I, 377 b.

Ralph de Russell who was a tenant in chief.[1] Apart from the Willicot case, Elias has left little trace of his activity, but he was, of course, a knight, and we know that he was of sufficient weight in 1208 to be called on to witness a charter in respect of land at Rodmarton in Gloucester, and that in the same county in 1221 he was answerable for the payment of a fine incurred by another, presumably a neighbour, for a misdeed.[2] He was dead before 1235, when his widow was responsible for the payment due from his holding to the aid for marrying the king's sister.[3] This connexion with the Willicot case, however, has produced a document which for our purposes is particularly instructive. It will be remembered that at the end of the proceedings in the king's court certain *buzones* were ordered to be arrested, and that it was specially noted that Elias de Cokerel and William de Parco were present at the time. I know of no evidence that any of them except Cokerel actually suffered imprisonment, but it is clear that he did. He must have had interest at court, however, or contrived to make it, for in 1213 he fined with the king for 20 marks ' ut deliberetur de prisona domini regis in qua est pro quodam falso judicio delato coram justiciariis domini regis in comitatu Gloucestriae '. Henry de Braibroc was ordered to release Elias on receipt of the king's letters patent, Engelard de Cigoné having made himself responsible for the payment of 20 marks to the king and the delivery of certain lampreys which Elias had promised, presumably as a gratification, to the bishop of Winchester and Geoffrey Fitz Peter, earl of Essex.[4]

Gilbert Martél is perhaps the most obscure figure in our group. It will be remembered that his name does not appear until very nearly the end of the record, when we learn that he had been one of the four knights deputed to hear the record of the county. He took no part in doing so, however, because, as he said when he did appear before the justices, he was not present at the making of any judgement in the case and knew

---

[1] *Book of Fees* I, 439, 442; cf. *Landboc de . . . Winchelcumba* (ed. Royce) I, 237 ff. ; Fosbroke, *op. cit.* II, 289, 348.

[2] *Curia Regis Roll* v, 289; *Pleas of the Crown for the County of Gloucester*, 132.

[3] *Book of Fees, loc. cit.*

[4] *Rot. de Obl. et Fin.*, 470. None of the orders to Henry de Braibroc on the Patent Roll for 15 John refer to this matter.

nothing of it. As he was present in court and was not ordered to be arrested, it is to be presumed that, although he was a *buzo*, his story was accepted and he was discharged.[1] Something however, can be said of his position and activities which will serve to situate him socially and materially with the group of men with whom he appears in the record. He was a Gloucestershire knight, who had served the Crown in the troubles of 1193.[2] He married one of three sisters, who seem to have been co-heiresses in Gloucestershire, and as early as 1191 there was a dispute, about the distribution of the property among them, which dragged on for more than ten years.[3] He had interests at Kimble in Buckinghamshire, but it does not appear that they were extensive.[4] In Berkshire he was holding on a larger scale; he claimed to hold of the prior of Noyon at Coldharbour, and must have had tenants of his own, as an assize of mort d'ancestor was brought against him.[5] Finally, in 1201 we find him bringing an action to establish his claim to six virgates of land in Oxfordshire.[6]

If we ask about his share in county business, it will be remembered that in 1207 he had been associated with William de Eston and Hugh Mustel in a grand assize, and that William de Parco had been one of the four knights who elected them. There is evidence that he had been considered a suitable person for work of this kind earlier.[7] It is possible that he was one of a group of four acting on behalf of the county court of Gloucester in 1201, and it is clear that in 1215 he was one of such a group sent by the county court of Dorset to verify the illness of a lady who had essoined herself *de malo lecti*.[8]

[1] As the knights who actually bore the record and certain others as well were described as *buzones* in the record, it would appear at least likely that those who were sent to represent the county when it was charged with false judgement were drawn from the group of *buzones*. See above p. 71.

[2] *Pipe Roll*, 5 *Ric. I*, Glouc., p. 122 : a payment of arrears to him and three other knights in respect of their services *in exercitu de Windsor*. In 1196 he was party to a plea in Gloucester in which he obtained leave to compound (*Curia Regis Rolls* I, 24).

[3] *Pipe Roll*, 3 *Ric. I*, Glouc., pp. 98, 290 ; *ibid., ann.* 5, p. 127 ; *ann.* 6, p. 93 ; *Curia Regis Roll* II, 1.

[4] *Ibid.* I, 26, 27, 28. A rent-charge of 2s. in respect of a virgate in Kimble was involved. The matter had not been settled in 1204 (*ibid.* III, 147).

[5] *Ibid.* I, 215, 327 ; II, 12, 47–8 ; *ibid.* I, 97.

[6] *Curia Regis Roll* II, 2.

[7] Above p. 74 ; *Curia Regis Roll* II, 59, 148 ; III, 279.

[8] *Ibid.* II, 172 ; III, 344.

Hugh Mustel was a Gloucestershire knight whose interests, as far as the available evidence goes, appear to have been confined to that county. I cannot find where or of whom he held, but it is clear that between 1200 and 1222 he was of sufficient consequence to have acted as witness to a number of transactions, grants or confirmation of grants, in land.[1] In 1200 he is specifically described as a knight, and was acting as a recognitor in an assize of darrein presentment in respect to a Gloucestershire church.[2] Four years later he was again a recognitor in a like action in respect of another church in the county, and when the question was eventually referred to a grand assize, he was one of the twelve knights elected to constitute that body.[3] As we have seen, he acted in a grand assize in 1207 with William de Eston and Gilbert Martell, while William de Parco was one of the electors.[4]

William de Parco himself was a person of greater importance than any of the rest of the group in that he was not only a knight but one who held of the king and other important lords. He seems to have inherited from his father in 1194,[5] and after John's accession had grants of land in Gloucestershire at Briwern' and at King's Barton near Gloucester itself.[6] He was loyal to the king during the Civil War, and was rewarded in August of 1216 by a grant of the lands of Geoffrey de Marmion, who was in the king's prison, ' to sustain him in his service '. These lands were in Gloucestershire, and although Marmion was reconciled to the new government and regained possession of his lands in Oxfordshire in March 1217, it is not clear whether the Gloucester lands were restored to him or not.[7] In the city of Gloucester William held 22 *solidatae* of rent by the gift of the earl of Hereford.[8] In the county itself he held Bewper

---

[1] *Landboc* I, 159, 160, 168 (all these about 1200) ; W. H. Stevenson, *Cal. of Gloucester Records*, No. 110 (*c*. 1200), Nos. 150, 212 (*c*. 1220).

[2] *Curia Regis Roll* I, 315–16.   [3] *Ibid.* III, 216, 282.

[4] Above p. 74.

[5] *Pipe Roll*, 6 *Ric. I, Glouc.*, p. 4. The sheriff accounts for the farm of William de Parco's land for one quarter of the year.

[6] The holding in Briwern' is stated in the inquest to have been granted to Amaury's father William by King John (*Rot. Lit. Claus.* I, 417 a, 548 a ; cf. *Cart. S. Pet. Glouc.* III, 70 n). The holding at King's Barton consisted of one virgate (*ibid.* 69, 73).

[7] *Rot. Lit. Claus.* I, 283, 286 b ; *ibid.* 303 a. On Marmion see *Landboc* I, 155 and note.

[8] *Rot. Lit. Claus.* I, 266 a.

and lands in demesne and service at Hardwick of the abbot of Gloucester.[1] He had other lands in the county, for we find him granting a rent charge to St. Peter's, Gloucester, in 1220.[2] From the year 1196, when he witnessed a charter granting land to found a priory of St. Peter's, Gloucester,[3] until his death or entry into religion in 1220, we find him attesting documents of this kind in association with persons of importance in the county. For example, in 1210 William confirmed a grant of land made to the brethren of the Hospital of St. Bartholomew, Gloucester. Those who witnessed this document were all landowners in the county; one, Ralph Musard, was to act as sheriff for ten years (1215–25), and another, Ralph Wilton, to be constable of Bristol Castle for two (1224–6).[4] Again, we find him witnessing a grant of land made to Stephen de Segrave.[5]

In 1203 and 1204 he was engaged in some obscure transactions that involved recourse to Jewish money-lenders in Gloucester. In 1203 Geoffrey Fitz Peter was directed to discharge William of a debt, with usury of £7 which he owed to Helias the Jew of Gloucester. Whether this was the result of a royal favour or successful proceedings does not appear, but the next year another Jew had royal letters authorizing him to proceed against William and his brother to recover £8 with interest for which he held their bond.[6]

There is evidence that he was concerned with the business of the Gloucester county courts as early as 1200, when he was sent with three other knights to verify an essoin *de malo lecti*, and reported that the lady in question *languida est*.[7] Two years later he was one of the electors of a grand assize in respect of a knight's fee in Blaisdon, co. Gloucester.[8] We have already seen how he was associated in county business of this and other

[1] *Cart. S. Pet. Glouc.* I, 209, 336. Cf. *ibid.* II, 99, which records an exchange of land in Gloucestershire between William and Henry abbot of Gloucester.

[2] *Cart. S. Pet. Glouc.* I, 99 ; II, 29–30.   [3] *Ibid.* I, 288.

[4] Stevenson, *Calendar of Gloucester Records*, No. 125 ; *Cart. S. Peter, Glouc.* I, 99, 288 ; II, 29, 30 ; *Sel. Pleas of the Crown* (S.S.) I, 80.

[5] Jeayes, *Catalogue of Muniments at Berkeley Castle*, No. 208, p. 71 ; cf. Stevenson, *op. cit.*, No. 130.

[6] *Rot. de Liberate ac de Misis* (Rec. Comm.), 5 John, p. 73 ; *Rot. de Obl. et Fin.*, 6 John, p. 201.   [7] *Curia Regis Roll* I, 159.

[8] *Ibid.* II, 104–5 ; cf. p. 141. He was one of the knights elected to take the assize, but like a number of the others essoined himself when the appointed day came.

G

sorts, before the Willicot case, with William de Eston, Philip de Beaumont, Gilbert Martel, and Hugh Mustel.[1] He must have died or, more probably, entered religion in 1220, for although, as we have seen, he made a grant of land in that year, by April the sheriff of Gloucester was officially notified that William de Parco's land had been provisionally restored to Amaury, his son and heir.[2]

If we consider now what general impression is left on the mind by this mass of detail, I believe that it will be recognized as one that corresponds pretty well with Bracton's account of the *buzones*. The evidence, of course, is both fragmentary and incomplete, and the amount of it in any given case is the result rather of chance, the accident of carelessness, disputes, and the resulting litigation, marriage, inheritance, and relations with persons of importance, than the consideration and influence in the community enjoyed by the man in question. Still, when due allowance is made for all this, the very dearth of information is in itself instructive. We can see a group of men, obscure enough if measured by national consequence, but of weight in local affairs : rich men, or moderately so, for the most part dwelling peaceably in their habitations, and accustomed to work together in the administration of local affairs. They are men qualified by their lands and their knighthood to discharge these functions, and chosen it would seem rather than others equally qualified by reason of their taste and aptitude for such business. In that sense, and not as magnates or tenants-in-chief, they are properly described as *maiores de comitatu*, and if we ask whether indeed the *vota aliorum* depended on their nod, we shall find our answer in the disgraceful way in which the county court appears to have allowed its record to be falsified and its proceedings misrepresented before the king's justices under the influence of William de Eston and his friends in the Willicot case.[3] It is true that we hear nothing of those duties in con-

---

[1] Above, p. 74.

[2] *Rot. Lit. Claus.* I, 417 a. As he appears to have been a monk in St. Peter's Abbey, Gloucester, in 1223 (*Hist. et Cart. S. Pet., Glouc.* II, 29–30), it is more probable that he only suffered civil death by entering religion ; cf. Pollock and Maitland, *H.E.L.* I (2nd ed.), 434–5.

[3] The three knights who bore the record of the county before the king's justices could scarcely have done so without some previous commission or instruction from the county court, if only in the form of an understanding

nexion with the maintenance of the peace and the policing of the localities upon which Bracton lays so much emphasis, but it is equally true that these functions were notably developed in the years that lie between the Gloucester record and the composition of Bracton's book, and that in his time it was to men of the same class and qualifications as our Gloucestershire knights that such functions were being entrusted.[1]

II

If the two texts discussed above constituted the whole of our evidence, the task of formulating a generalization that would fit them into the texture of local government would be relatively simple. But even so the term *buzo* would remain to be accounted for and, as it happens, there is a certain amount of evidence bearing on that point which it is extremely difficult to bring into relation with the Gloucester record and Bracton's words. It will be convenient to have the texts before us.

We begin with the terms of the tenure of the manor of Bryanston in Dorset, which are known to us by an inquest taken in 1272 on the death of the holder and subsequent references in the course of proceedings in the king's court before the death of Edward I.[2]

Radulphus de Stopham tenuit de feodo comitis Winchester apud Bradeford vi. li. xiiij s. jv d. de redd. assis. per ann. et debuit invenire pro dicto manerio unum hominem peditem ad servicium domini Regis cum arcu et bosone per quadraginta dies ad custum dicti Radulphi pro omnibus serviciis.

Harl. MSS. 4120, fol. 11, 56 Hen. III.

with its leading members. In what I have said above I do not wish to prejudice the question of the relation of the county court to the roll of the pleas of the county ; cf. the article referred to above p. 69, n. 3.

[1] Cf. Cam, *The Hundred and the Hundred Rolls*, 16 : ' It was the knights who ran the local government . . . as suitors and controllers of the county court where their duties were steadily increasing as the century advanced.'

[2] These texts are given by Bolland, *Eyre Roll of Kent* (S.S.) I, xxviii–xxix. See also Hutchins, *History of Dorset* (1861) I, 248, where there is an extensive note on the word *buzon* drawn largely from Blount's *Ancient Tenures* (see Hazlitt's edition, 1874, pp. 45–6 and his note, p. 419). The second text is also given by Mr. G. J. Turner, *Select Pleas of the Forest* (S.S.), 137. In two inquisitions relating to the same manor but taken at a later date, which Mr. Turner also prints, the word *tribulus* is substituted for *buzo*. Mr. Turner gives reasons for rejecting the ordinary rendering of *tribulus* by caltrop and considers that ' the syllable *tri* seems to point to an arrow head with a triangular cross-section, that is to say a three-faced head '.

Radulphus de Stopham tenet manerium de Bryxaneston . . . per serianciam ad inueniendum domino regi quocienscunque contigerit ipsum habere exercitum in Angl' vel in Walliam unum garcionem differentem unum arcum sine corda et unum buzonem sine pennis.

Dorset Eyre Roll, 8 Edw. I.

Eva, filia et heres Radulphi de Stopham, cognovit tenere . . . per servicium inveniendi domino Regi in exercitu suo Wallie unum servientem peditem cum arcu sine chorda et buzone sine pennis.

Harl. MSS. 34, fo. 229, Mich. 30 Edw. I.

Then Britton[1] at the close of the thirteenth century has a passage which may well be based on a knowledge of this Bryanston serjeanty.

Petite serjauntie est service issaunt de tenement a fere a nous acun petit service, quant nous devoms chevacher en host . . . cum sount les services de nous porter en host . . . un broche ou un bozoun ou un arc saunt corde.

Next there is a forest inquest in the county of Hunts. in 1253.[2]

Quinque arcus de yf cum cordis quos tulerunt et tres walecthis et unum bosun traditi fuerunt Simoni de Copmanford.

Then in 1210–12 there is a Derbyshire serjeanty of which it is recorded :[3]

Willelmus de Gresle, Drakelowe per i arcum sine corda et faretram de Tutesbire et xii sagittas et i buzon.

Finally, we have another north-country text dating from the last years of the thirteenth century. This is the account roll submitted to the Exchequer by the builders of a royal galley at

[1] Britton, ed. Nichols, book III, ch. 3 ; cited by Bolland, *loc. cit.*

[2] Printed from the MS. by Bolland, *loc. cit.* The record is more fully given by Turner, *op. cit.*, 14, 79. Walectha (sagitta) is a Welsh arrow ; *ibid.*, 152.

[3] *Book of Fees* I, 228. There are several notices of this serjeanty which differ among themselves and sometimes appear to contradict each other both as to the situation of Drakelowe and the name of the tenant who held it in chief ; see *Book of Fees* I, 151, 223, *Red Book of the Exchequer* (R.S.) II, 566, 571. The difficulties are overcome by attending to the facts that Drakelowe was a member of the honour of Lancaster *extra Limam*, that is situated in another county, and that, although it was held in chief by the Gresleys in 1201, they were then mediatized by the transfer of their services to William de Ferrers, earl of Derby. See *Book of Fees* I, 63 ; *Rot. Chart.*, Rec. Com., p. 92 a ; Madan, F. ' The Gresleys of Draklow ' (*Wm. Salt. Arch. Soc. Coll.*), 1898, 33–4 ; Blomefield-Parkin, *Norfolk* x, 82 ; J. P. Yeatman, *Feudal History of the County of Derby*, § VII, ch. xi. 1. It should be noted that Buzun (al. Bussun, Buysson) occurs as a surname in Derbyshire in the first half of the thirteenth century, see H. Jeayes, *Descriptive Catalogue of Derbyshire Charters*, 1906, Nos. 1500–3, 1688.

Newcastle-on-Tyne in 23 Ed. I.[1] Our term occurs four times as follows :

In cclx clavis ferri videlicet spyking cum quinque buzonis ferri ad fundum Galee jungendum [p. 163].

In mercede Vttyng Fabri pro xxviii petris ferri fabricandis ad ligamina Gubernilis et Buzonis ad spurches[2] [p. 178].

In viii[to] petris ferri fabricandis ad Buzones [p. 179].

In xxv petris ferri emptis . . . ad Buzones [p. 187].

In Mr. Whitwell's glossary he defines *buzo* as bolt.[3]

There is an old French word *boujon* meaning bolt or arrow which appears in many alternative forms, and was not unusual in literary and poetical texts. It has a second sense, a rod of iron used to measure cloth, which is comparatively late, and indeed the earliest text which Godefroy can cite is from the Ordonnances of the Louvain Clothiers of 1325, and there are no others until the end of the fourteenth century (1381, 1382, 1398). At the same time (1325) and in the same document we have the derivative *boujonneur* defined as a member of the sworn body (*jurande*) of the clothiers who measured in cloth with the *boujon*, and in the fifteenth century (1410) this is used for the *jurez de mestiers*. A little later (1428) we have *boujonnier* for the workman who fashioned the shafts called *boujons*, and it is to be noted that this term came to be used as a proper name.[4]

Now in England, as we have seen the term *buzo* was used in the sense of arrow or bolt during the thirteenth century, but by the middle of the fourteenth it seems to have become unintelligible. It was exactly contemporary, therefore, with Bracton's use of the word in another sense. Moreover, a surname which has every appearance of being one of the many variants of this term occurs in English documents as early as the first half of the twelfth century and was pretty widely distributed over the country. Some illustrations of this may now be submitted,

---

[1] The document is printed by Mr. R. J. Whitwell with an introduction and translation by Mr. Charles Johnson in *Archaeologia Aeliana* (4th series) II, 142–88.

[2] Apparently wooden struts or spurs ; cf. Whitwell, *op. cit.*, Glossary.

[3] Trice Martin, who probably knew the Bryanston case either in Blount or Hutchison, gives it as the shaft of an arrow, *Record Interpreter*, Gloss. s.v. *buzo*.

[4] F. Godefroy, *Dictionnaire de l'ancienne langue française* I, 699 ff. The variants are very numerous ; a few should be noted as particularly relevant, *bouzon, boujun, bozun, bulzun, boucon*.

beginning, for reasons which will appear later, with the west country evidence.

In Gloucestershire in 1187 John Bouzon committed waste in the king's forest and had to pay two shillings, and nine years later he accounted for one mark *pro stulto dicto*.[1] In Dorset, Robert Buzun incurred a fine of 60 marks for a forest offence in 1176, which was not paid all at once.[2] In the same county in the year 1208 Simon Buzun was one of the knights composing the grand assize that was summoned to determine the right to the barony of Marshwood.[3] It may well have been this same Simon who was one of the knights elected for a grand assize taken in Somerset in 1201,[4] and in the same year and the same county we hear of William Bauzan, which the editor considers an alternative form of the name Buzun.[5] The name in this form occurs again in Somerset in 1205.[6] In Devonshire, in 1176, Reginald, son of William Bulzun, accounted for the old farm of the stannaries,[7] and three years later William was seeking to recover half a knight's fee in Luppeton.[8] Then, in 1203, we meet with Simon Buzun again when a plea of admeasurement of dower in Devon was brought against him and his wife Rose.[9] Then, in 1224, William Bozun and certain others who had been acting as commissioners or justices of assize were summoned to the king's court to make the record of an assize of novel disseisin, which had been taken before them by command of the king.[10] Perhaps it was his son, William Buzun junior, who in 1230 owed the king three marks for having a wardship

[1] *Pipe Roll, 33 Hen. II*, 139; *Chancellor's Roll, 8 Ric. I*, 106, both published by the Pipe Roll Society. The name appears on the Pipe Roll in the not uncommon form of Bulzun, but it seems that the forms of spelling in the Chancellor's Roll are in general more acceptable than those of the Pipe Roll proper, cf. C. Robinson, *Pipe Roll, 14 Hen. III*, pp. v, vi.

[2] *Pipe Roll. 22 Hen. II*, 160, where the name is Bulzun ; the Chancellor's Roll gives Buzun (*ibid., ann. 23*, p. 22).

[3] Pipe Roll, 10 John, printed in Madox, *Exchequer* i, 489–90 ; cf. p. 99 n.

[4] *Curia Regis Roll* ii, 65.

[5] *Ibid.*, 40.

[6] *Rotuli de Oblatis et Finibus* (Rec. Com.), 283.

[7] *Pipe Roll, 22 Hen. II*, 142. The farm was normally accounted for by the sheriff, but mines were occasionally farmed seaparately to private individuals. Cf. G. R. Lewis, *The Stannaries* (Harvard Economic Studies, iii), 34.

[8] *Pipe Roll, 29 Hen. II*, 117.

[9] *Curia Regis Rolls* ii, 181, 230 ; iii, 41. In one of these records Simon's name is spelt Bucun.

[10] *Bacton's Notebook*, No. 976.

and 25 marks *pro transgressionibus*.[1] Finally, we have the interesting evidence of Risdon, the Devonshire antiquary, whose book was written before 1640, although it was not published until the following century.

Bozunsele was the inheritance of Sir William Bozun in the time of king Henry the second . . . John Bozun had issue, Elizabeth, his daughter's heir . . . from whom the family of the Carews are descended.[2]

Thurleston . . . was Bozun's inheritance, and by a daughter of William Bozun came to Chiverston and so to the Courtenays.[3]

Okenbury was . . . the Bozen's inheritance.[4]

But the name was not confined to rural Devon, for the existence of Robert Bozoun in Exeter is attested in 1319.[5]

We may turn from the West Country to the occurrence of the name in other parts of England. Bozuns appear in Oxford, Nottingham, Leicester, Hampshire, Kent and Derbyshire.[6] Finally, it may be noticed that the name is prevalent in East Anglia. Thus, in Norfolk and Suffolk in 1181 Herbert Bulzun owed the king considerable sums *pro defalta*, and four years later Roger Buzun accounts for five marks for leave to compound.[7] In 1201 and 1205 we hear of two more Norfolk Buzuns, John and Ralph, the one appointed attorney for one of the parties in an action leading to a final concord, and the other a knight of the grand assize summoned to settle a claim to the advowson of the church of Stanford.[8]

Finally, there is no doubt that the heralds derived the name from the French *bodjon* in the sense of arrow or bolt, and if, as

---

[1] *Pipe Roll, 14 Hen. III,* 16, 21 ; cf. p. 30. The name is spelt Buszun on the Pipe Roll and Buzun on the Chancellor's Roll.

[2] J. Risdon, *The Chorographical Description or Survey of the County of Devon* (new ed., London, 1811), 168. In 1811 Bozunsele was the property of John Seale, *ibid.*, 381.

[3] *Ibid.*, 177.

[4] *Ibid.*, 183. The name does not occur in the list of the names of the Gentry of Devonshire . . . about the commencement of the seventeenth century, printed at p. 19 of the Additions.

[5] *Notes and Gleanings of Devonshire and Cornwall* v, 112, a series of extracts from the Exeter Muniments ; M. McKisack, *Representation of English Boroughs*, 92 n., 147.

[6] *Bracton's Notebook*, No. 798, a.d. 1233, Oxon. ; *Abbrev. Rot. Orig.* (Rec. Com.) I, 770, Nottingham temp. Ed. I ; *Curia Regis Rolls* I, 210, 305, Leicester ; *ibid.* IV, 239, Hants ; *ibid.* II, 118, Kent ; for Derbyshire, see above, p. 84, n. 3.

[7] *Pipe Roll, 27 Hen. II,* 89 ; *ann. 28,* p. 70 ; *ann. 31,* p. 38.

[8] *Curia Regis Rolls* II, 49 ; III, 83 ; III, 276.

we have seen reason to believe, that term was no longer current
by the middle of the fourteenth century, they or the families
to whose pride they ministered must have begun to do so
pretty early. In the chancel of the church of Chipping Camp-
den there is a monumental effigy to Thomas Smith, who died
in 1593 ; the armorial bearings on the pediment are those of
the families with which he was connected by birth or marriage.
His second wife was born Throgmorton and her maternal
grandmother was Goodith Boson. The arms attributed to the
Bosons are ' gules, 3 bird-bolts points downward, argent '.[1]
Hutchins, the historian of Dorset, commenting on the Bryanston serjeanty, with which we are already acquainted, remarks
on the connexion between the family name and the word *buson*,
and observes : ' This seems to have been a bird-bolt or bar-
bolt, such weapons being the arms of Herbert Bozon, a Norman,
to whom the Conqueror gave Wissingset in Norfolk ', and
points out that the same arms were borne by the Bozons of
Dorset.[2] Reference to Domesday disposes of this tale of the
Conquest, for which Spelman seemed to have been responsible,
but Herbert Bozon of Norfolk in the time of Stephen figures
as a benefactor of the priory of Castle Acre, and is probably
the founder of the family which, as we have seen, was distributed over other counties.[3]

Such, as far as I have been able to ascertain, is all the
evidence available, and it leaves us with the problem of finding
a solution that will account for the whole of it. Earlier com-
mentators, who took account of Bracton's text and the version
of the Gloucester record in the *Abbreviatio* only, once they
had rejected the alternative reading of *barones* for *buzones*

[1] *Trans. of the Bristol and Gloucester Arch. Soc.* xxv, 197 ; xxxii, 221–3.

[2] Hutchins, *Dorset* (1861) i, 248.

[3] On all this see the account of the Bozuns of Wissingset in Blomefield-
Parkin, *Norfolk* x, 81–6 ; Spelman, ' Icenia ' in *English Works* (1725), 150,
V.C.H., Norfolk ii, 101. The arms attributed to the Norfolk family differ
in some details from those given above, but they show the three boujons.
Blomefield considers that the Buzuns of Bedford and Devon were connected
with the Norfolk family, *op. cit.*, 82. Spelman suggests the connexion
between the name and the bolt. Cf. G. A. Carthew, *Hundred of Launditch*
i, 250–3 ; the author possessed a deed, anno 1 Hen. IV, to which there was
attached a seal bearing the Bozun family arms, 3 bird-bolts with a crescent
for difference. On the connexion between the surname which we have been
discussing and the term *buzo* and the OFr. *boujon* see Dr. Allen Mawer's
note below p. 109.

and the proposal to connect the word with the French *besoigne*, reached conclusions to which indeed we shall have to return, although, in so far as they leave the term unaccounted for, they are relevant to a part of the problem only.[1] More recently, however, two scholars, the late Mr. Bolland and Mr. A. Betts, have attacked the problem as a whole in the sense of recognizing that it presents a philological as well as an institutional question, and our next step, therefore, is to examine the explanations which they propose.

Mr. Bolland pointed out[2] that, with the exception of the Huntingdon forest inquest and the passage in Britton (he did not know either the Newcastle or the Derbyshire evidence nor did he take account of the occurrence of Buzon as a surname), the evidence comes from the west country. He suggested, with much probability, that Britton had the Bryanston inquest before him when he wrote, thereby removing one of two serious obstacles to his argument on the evidence before him. This, as Bracton was himself a west country man and the record which shows the *buzones* at work comes from Gloucestershire, would, he considered, situate the term in the west of England, although even there it would appear to have dropped out of use early in the fourteenth century. In order to reconcile the two senses of the word, the group of men referred to by Bracton and in the Gloucester case, and the weapon of the inquests, Bolland brings forward an ingenious argument. Its point of departure is the French word *boujon*, in its secondary sense of an iron rule for measuring cloth, and its derivative *boujonneur*, the cloth measurer, a man of position and influence

---

[1] The older ' literature ' of the subject, Spelman, Coke, Du Cange, &c., is referred to in A. Betts, ' Busones, a Study and a Suggestion ', *Juridical Review* XXVII (1915), 98–108. Maitland was at first inclined to connect the word with ' besoin ', but eventually rejected this without adopting any alternative explanation of the origin of the term ; see *Pleas of the Crown for the County of Gloucester*, xxiv–xxv; *H.E.L.* I (1st ed. p. 540; 2nd ed. p. 533). Sir Charles Chadwyck-Healey made a similar suggestion as to the origin of the word apparently in ignorance that Maitland had revised his opinion ; see *Somersetshire Pleas*, (Somerset Record Society, XI), xliv. Vinogradoff's suggestion, *English Society in the Eleventh Century*, 21, is not very helpful, and Professor Holdsworth, *H.E.L.* I (3rd ed.), 268, combines the views of Maitland and Bolland. Among literature published since this essay first appeared in 1932, it is sufficient to refer to C. T. Flower, *Curia Regis Rolls* VI, 525, and *Introduction to the Curia Regis Rolls* (S.S., 1944), 62.

[2] *Eyre Roll of Kent* I, xxvii–xxxi.

in general and in particular an official and a member of the
sworn body of the Clothiers' Gild. He points out that the
industry in question was common to northern France and
Flanders, where the *boujonneur* occurs, and to the English
west country to which, in his view, the *buzones* were confined. And so he reaches his conclusion, or rather his final
suggestion.

So, then, this word *boujonneur*, or in its Latinized form, *busones*,
may well have been adopted for a time from the technical language of
the principal industry of the neighbourhood into the colloquial
vernacular of the local hundredors to describe those who from their
social position or otherwise had acquired a predominant influence
in the counsels and over the decisions of the county court.[1]

Mr. Bolland's conclusion is just what is wanted. Unfortunately, however, the steps by which he reaches it are open to
objections which appear to me to be fatal to his argument. In
the first place *buzo* in what may be called its legal or official
sense occurs in English texts only twice. It is not heard of
after the middle of the thirteenth century, and the seemingly
related *boujon* or *buzon* which occurs last at the end of that
century had within fifty years become so unintelligible that it
was replaced by the Latin word *tribulus*. *Boujonneur*, from
which Bolland would derive Bracton's *buzones*, is attested first
in 1325, and continued in use throughout the middle ages.
The English term, therefore, was obsolete before the French
word from which it is to be derived had come into use. Yet
Bolland's argument would require both the office and the
name *boujonneur* to have been common in the west country
not only in Bracton's time but early enough to account for its
supposed derivative *buzo* being used officially in 1212. Again,
admitting Mr. Bolland's contention for the sake of argument,
we may object that a word in as general a use as he supposes
ought to occur in some such documents as those in which it is
found in France. Now the Southampton Gild ordinances ' are
perfectly French both in style and vocabulary . . . [and] except
for their chief official they retained the French titles for their

---

[1] It should be noted that Bolland thought it ' pretty certain ' that the
word was neither English nor Gaelic. On what grounds he based this
certainty we are not told. Also he does not attempt to account for the
occurrence of the word in Huntingdonshire.

officers '.[1] They had a sworn body, but they were styled *jureis*, and no word resembling *boujonneur* occurs in the text.[2] Again, in Bristol, where in the fourteenth century French was current, there were weavers and clothiers enough, but their craft ordinances show no trace of *boujon* or *boujonneur*, although foreign terms were not uncommon in these industries.[3] Evidence of this sort could readily be multiplied. If the terms had occurred in the west country to the extent required by Mr. Bolland's argument, we should have a right to expect to find them in some of the collections cited. As we do not, the argument *e silentio* is perfectly admissible.

In the second place the French word *boujon* in some of its variants, *e.g. buzo* and the name which appears to be derived from or at least cognate to it, were perfectly familiar throughout England in the late twelfth and early thirteenth centuries. It would appear, therefore, to be an unwarrantable multiplication of hypotheses to seek another derivation for the *buzo* of the records and Bracton. This objection is all the stronger since the word is not confined to the West Country as Bolland's argument requires, but occurs in Huntingdon, Derby, and Northumberland as well.[4]

[1] *The Oak Book of Southampton* (ed. P. Studer), i, xvi–xvii.

[2] *Ibid.*, Ordinances, 18, 44, 54, 75 ; see also the Glossary in vol. iii.

[3] *Little Red Book of Bristol* (ed. F. B. Bickley) ii, 2, 6, 40, 57, 71, 117, 123, 127 (note in particular ' quod nulla instrumenta textoris videlicet Webanlam de villis forinsecis venencia remaneant in Bristollia ') ; C. H. Mayo's *Records of Dorchester*, not such a promising quarter, also yields negative results. Bateson, *Borough Customs* (S.S., 1904–6) ii, beside the usual *index rerum*, gives, p. 215, a list of Rarer Words and Words with Glossarial Notes in the Text, in which we look in vain for *boujon* or *boujonneur* or anything like them. Even more significant is the silence of the *Anglo-Norman Custumal of Exeter* (ed. J. W. Schopp and R. C. Easterling, 1925) ; this was probably written between 1230 and 1257 and the glossary contains every Anglo-Norman word in the manuscript.

[4] Mr. Betts, *op. cit.*, raises an objection to Bolland's argument which does not appear to me to be well grounded. He points out (and in this, of course, he is perfectly right) that Bracton's words are of general import and applicable to what the judges would find throughout the kingdom and not in the west country only. This being so, a cant local term which the Gloucester scribe might admit to his roll could not be used by Bracton ' unless busones [*sic*] were generally known as such throughout the kingdom '. As the term does not occur in the *Notebook*, Bracton obviously knew that it was not in general use. What he says the judges may expect to find are the ' majores de comitatu ad quorum nutum dependent vota aliorum '. If he intercalates ' qui buzones dicuntur ', it may well have been because they were so called locally as we know they were in Gloucester. If the term were general and in any sense official, it ought to have appeared

We come now to Mr. Betts's system, which undertakes to explain the legal and official use of the term only, but recognizes the necessity of accounting for the term itself. Mr. Betts looks to Old Norse speech and law for the origin of the name *buzo* and its relevance to the functionaries who bore it. He begins with the Icelandic *bú* = house, *bua'* = to dwell, and *bui* = (1) neighbour, (2) neighbours acting judicially as jurors or dooms-men. He then draws attention to the duties of doomsmen in the English county courts in the thirteenth century, and observes that in Icelandic law neighbours (*bui*) were summoned to assess compensation for damages even in cases so important that they might lead to outlawry.[1] If Bracton represented the judges as consulting the *buzones*, ' this could only be for the purpose of assisting in the dispensation of justice.' They were *buzones comitatus*, and therefore neighbours, and their number varied ' probably according to the importance of the cases before them '. But further they were more than ordinary doomsmen, for they were charged with the duty of arresting evil-doers and handing them over to the sheriff. He cites the *Liber Albus*[2] for evidence of similar duties entrusted, in the absence of the proper officials, to the principal citizens of London. This power, he proceeds, would not be conferred lightly. In London only men of substance were permitted to exercise it, and ' it is certain that men of similar position would be selected in the county '. This is what Bracton meant by *majores de comitatu*, ' the class of estate-holders or principal men of the county '. In the Willicot case

certain *busones*[3] are to be arrested and other *busones* are to be taken in their place . . . all these were large estate or *bu* owners, otherwise they would not be of the greater men of the county, and it was natural

more than once in the abundant legal records with which Bracton was familiar. There are too many of these to suppose that the term was common in documents that have been lost. The alternative is to take Bracton's ' dicuntur ' in the sense of an apology for the introduction of a familiar though unofficial term used locally to describe what existed all over England.

[1] This part of the argument would have been strengthened by reference to E. Mayer, *Geschworenengericht und Inquisitionsprozess* (1916), 75, and the authorities cited there.

[2] Ed. Riley (R.S.), book III, pt. III, p. 388.

[3] Mr. Betts adopts this spelling throughout although it is contrary to that used in the Roll and Professor Woodbine's text of Bracton. We shall return to this point later.

that they and not the smaller fry should be arrested and imprisoned for false judgement. The court was aware of the kind of pressure likely to be applied to the small men by the great ones of that time, and it was just that the *busones* or great *bu* holders should bear the brunt, not so their fellow doomsmen who voted [*sic*] under their influence and who in practice were bound to follow their lead. They were *busones*, representative men or ring-leaders, and they were punished accordingly. If it were not their official designation the title was one by which they were usually known ... or Bracton would not have mentioned it.

Mr. Betts then proceeds to argue that the derivation of the Latin *buso* from some form or compound of *bu* is possible on philological grounds. The word *bu* was domesticated in England by the end of the thirteenth century, and the Danish settlements in South Wales and around the mouth of the Severn have left their mark in the shape of Scandinavian elements in west country Middle English texts.[1] *Bú* and *bui* are both related to the verb *bua* = to dwell; *bus*, the genitive of *bu*, is used to form compounds. What more natural than to suppose, he proceeds, that the word *buso* (*sic*) may be the Latinized form of the first element of some such compound meaning a householder, the owner of an estate, particularly when the Icelandic *bui*, a word of the same origin as *bu*, means neighbour or neighbour acting in a judicial capacity. Further support comes from the Old French *buze*, evidently connected with the Old Norse words mentioned above, which means habitation, village, residence.[2] This is taken as evidence that *bu* going into Latin would take an *s* or *z*, and leads to the conclusion that ' *busones* have come to us through the Normans who were themselves of Norse origin '.

We may begin by considering certain difficulties in connexion with the steps in each argument before considering the system as a whole. In the first place, Mr. Betts assumes that the *buzones* were exclusively, or at least primarily, doomsmen, judgement-finders. They were consulted by the judges, he says, and this could only be for the purpose of assisting in the

---

[1] He refers to *New Engl. Dict.*, s.v. ' Bu ', Ancren Riwle, Layamon's Brut, and Robert of Gloucester's Chronicle. But see Dr. Mawar's note below, p. 109.

[2] The reference is to Roquefort, *Glossaire de la Langue Romane* I (1808), 196, s.v. ' buze ', but see Dr. Mawer's note.

dispensation of justice; but Bracton does not say so. The duties he attributes to the *buzones* are the maintenance of the peace and the pursuit and apprehension of evil-doers. Moreover, the record of the Willicot case distinguishes between the functions of the doomsmen and the *buzones*, although it leaves room to suppose that the same persons might act in both capacities. 'Milites de comitatu qui consueti sunt interesse falsis judiciis et sunt buzones judiciorum', etc. The *et* gives the distinction. Now the *buzones* may be, and very likely are, doomsmen, but the two functions are not necessarily the same. It is true that the record uses the term *buzones judiciorum*, but it is not as judgement-finders that Bracton recommends the justices to consult with them. Bracton's words taken in connexion with the Willicot case suggest that, while the *buzones* were doomsmen, it was not on that account that they were so called, but because they represented the county when its judgement was impugned; as for other purposes they represented it at other times. Thus, when Mr. Betts writes, ' their number varied probably according to the importance of the cases before them ', he appears to assume that they were doomsmen appointed *ad hoc* by the justices. But the simplest explanation of Bracton's words is that from an already existing body of persons known as *buzones* the judges selected a certain number and charged them with the king's instructions as to the maintenance of the peace. The number chosen would naturally vary according to the area and population of the county to be policed.

Then in commenting on the Willicot case he writes, ' certain *busones* are to be arrested and other *busones* are to be taken in their place '. Now, I submit the words do not bear that interpretation. The judgement directs that the knights who represented the county and are *buzones* are to be arrested, namely Park and Cokerel, who are present in court; then follows a lacuna in which Mustel may be referred to, perhaps as having given surety, and then ' Walter de Aure et Phillipus de Bello-Monte, alii buzones, capiantur et similiter Willelmus de Eston capiatur '. *Capere* is regularly used for arrest,[1] and if, as Mr.

---

[1] E.g., Assize of Clarendon, §§ 2, 3, 4 ; Magna Carta, § 39 ; Stubbs, *Charters*, 9th ed., 170, 297. Maitland so translated it in the case in question *H.E.L.* I, 2nd ed., 553 and elsewhere, e.g. *Select Pleas of the Crown* (S.S.) xxv.

Betts supposes, it is used here to mean selected in the sense of being substituted for the discredited *buzones*, it would seemingly be necessary to include William de Eston, who was the villain of the piece, and would have been much more likely to be arrested than promoted. Moreover, the words *alii buzones* suggest that these two were *buzones* already (and therefore in some degree responsible for what had happened) and thus accords with what Bracton says, namely, that the judges are to summon already existing *buzones* for consultation before the eyre begins. Mr. Betts appears to assume, however, that they would be appointed by the judges *ad hoc*. Finally, Mr. Betts's contention quoted above that the *buzones* were the great land-holders, the county magnates in that sense, is directly traversed by what we have learned about the *buzones* in the Willicot case, who, as we have seen, were small country gentlemen with very modest holdings. Even if we assume that the derivation he suggests is open to no technical objections,[1] there is still a serious difficulty. If *buzo* is the Latin form of a term of Scandinavian origin, having the sense of neighbour acting in a judicial capacity, we should expect to find the word or some trace of it in the Danelaw or East Anglia, where Scandinavian influence was stronger than in any other part of England. Seemingly no such traces occur in those regions,[2] but we do find the French term *buzon* = arrow, shaft, or bolt and the surname which appears to be derived from it. Mr. Betts has thus obtained his result at the cost of ruling out all the evidence except the Willicot case and Bracton's text, in order to refer the term to a Scandinavian origin, and yet in those parts of England where the Scandinavian influence was strongest he has found no confirmation and is left with the rejected French evidence on his hands. Like Mr. Bolland he seems to have multiplied hypotheses if not wholly beyond need at least without warrant.

If then the learned and ingenious explanations of Mr. Bolland and Mr. Betts prove inadmissible, we must still recog-

---

[1] This assumption cannot, however, be made, as Dr. Mawer has shown in his note, below p. 109.

[2] It is worth noting that there does not seem to be any OE. personal name deriving from Bu, see E. Björkman, ' Nordische Personennamen in England ', and ' Zur englischen Namenkunde ', in *Studien zur englischen Philologie*, XXXVII, XLVII (Halle, 1910, 1912).

nize that each has made an important contribution to the discussion of the problem, Mr. Bolland by insisting that we must take account of all the evidence, Mr. Betts by pointing out that Bracton's words have a general bearing, and that the justices would find *buzones* (whether so called or not) in every county of the kingdom. Further, Mr. Betts, by identifying the *buzones* with the doomsmen of the county court, has raised a complicated question, or rather a series of questions. If it could be established that a body of doomsmen, distinguishable from, and superior in authority and function to, the rest of the suitors, existed in all or most of the county courts of England in the first half of the thirteenth century, a solution of the more important part of our problem might perhaps be found by identifying these doomsmen with the *buzones* of the Willicot case and Bracton's treatise. A suggestion of this sort has indeed been made since Mr. Betts wrote, and its possibilities must, therefore, be examined.

There was in the English county courts after the Conquest a body of persons whom it is convenient, and perhaps in certain cases admissible, to call doomsmen. They were the judgement-finders, *Urteilfinder*, and as such indispensable to the business of the court. The doctrine of Stubbs and Maitland, which still finds general acceptance, refuses to distinguish between the suitors, those who constitute the court by discharging their obligation, whether feudal or otherwise, of attendance, and those who, being present, actually render the judgement: the suitors were the judges, doomsmen and suitors were the same.[1] Recently, however, an older view has been revived by the suggestion that there might have been within the circle of the suitors a smaller group permanently and perhaps even hereditarily charged with the special duty of knowing the law and declaring it by giving judgement in cases as they arose, and it has been thought that Bracton might have had such a group in mind when he wrote his account of the *buzones*. Indeed, some words of Maitland, although he did not admit the distinction between suitors and doomsmen, pointed to a con-

---

[1] Stubbs, *C.H.* I (5th ed.), 426 ff. ; Maitland, *H.E.L.* I (2nd ed.), 85, 139, 144, 548–53, 592–4 ; *Coll. Papers* I, 458–66 ; Vinogradoff, *English Society in the Eleventh Century*, 5 ff. ; Liebermann, *Gesetze* II, ii, 565, 701–3.

nexion between *buzones* and those who, as suitors and doomsmen, were particularly active in the business of the county and
its court.[1] Mr. Betts's suggestion that the *buzones* were doomsmen but doomsmen of a special sort charged with certain
functions beyond that of giving judgement has already come
before us. He did not, however, appear to distinguish between
suitors and doomsmen. In 1925, however, Mr. Stewart-Brown
expressed the opinion that in the light of new evidence from
Cheshire which we shall have to consider presently the view of
Maitland and Stubbs would require to be modified,[2] and in this
Professor Plucknett concurred.[3] Mr. Sayles, writing of the
same Cheshire evidence, suggested that the doomsmen whose
existence as a selected group of suitors with a special responsibility in the Cheshire county court it attests might cast new light
' on the *judicatores comitatus* of our earliest pipe roll and the
mysterious *buzones* of Bracton '.[4]

The question is obviously a large and important one, but
only a part of it concerns the present study. Was there in the
English county courts in the twelfth and thirteenth centuries a
body of doomsmen officially distinguishable from the ordinary
suitors ? It must be put so because, as we have seen, Bracton
contemplated that *buzones* (however styled) would be at the
disposal of the judges in every county. If this question has to
be answered in the negative, then the attempt to explain the
term *buzones* as a local or cant name for a body of doomsmen
separated from the other suitors by their special functions and
constituting a normal and, indeed, a necessary part of every
county court must fail. Let us see how the matter stands, and
because the new evidence has in many if not all cases the
appearance of being the record of a survival, we may begin
with the period before the Conquest. Continental analogies

---

[1] Maitland, *op. cit.*, 552–3.
[2] *Calendar of County Court, City Court, and Eyre Rolls of Chester*, ed. R.
Stewart-Brown (Chetham Soc.), xxxii ff.
[3] *Harvard Law Review* XLII, 673 ff.
[4] *History* XIII (1929), 355. Professor Morris in 1926 expressed the view
that in certain counties the *buzones* were doomsmen in the sense of being
those who proposed judgements to the suitors who were already familiar
with the law ; he does not cite the theories mentioned in the text and
appears to be following Bolland ; cf. Morris, *Early English County Court*,
106. See also Adams, *Courts and Councils*, 131, n. 8, citing Brunner,
Forschungen, 242.

H

would lead us to expect to find in the communal court some
permanent official body like the Carolingian *scabini*, who were
appointed by the central government to find judgements which
in the regular courts would be confirmed by the whole body of
the suitors, and in the specially summoned ones would be valid
without confirmation. The connexion might even be sought in
the fact that such judgement-finders were often called *iudices*, a
term that occurs commonly in English documents before and
after the Conquest to describe judgement-finders.[1] It is true
that there is no specific Anglo-Saxon name for doomsmen,
but we must remember the existence of a strong Scandinavian
element and be careful ' not to slur over the fundamental dual-
ism of preconquestual England ' by overlooking the *lagmen*,
called in Latin *iudices*, of the Danish boroughs and their possible
or probable relation to the lawmen of the Scandinavian laws.[2]
The Anglo-Saxon evidence points to a group of judgement-
finders in the county court without affording information as to
its composition or numbers. But Dr. Liebermann thought that
there was nothing in the evidence incompatible with the view
that the body was made up from case to case and did not
consist of permanent officials. It differed, therefore, from the
Scandinavian institution of lawmen.[3] In the Anglo-Norman
period there is abundant evidence of *iudices* and *iuratores* in the
county courts, to whom the presiding officer or magistrate
must look for the judgement, and the pipe roll of 1130 shows
that, in the northern counties at least, some of them were
willing to pay handsomely to be relieved of their duties.[4] Now
there is evidence that in Cheshire and in Lancashire, in certain
local courts, a distinction was taken between *iudices* or *iudicatores*
and *sectatores*, that is between doomsmen and suitors, for there
is also evidence that *iudex* or *iudicator* would, in Lancashire at

[1] Brunner-Schwerin, *Deutsche Rechtsgeschichte* II, § 89 (pp. 295 ff.) ; an
abundant bibliography will be found at the beginning of the section.
[2] Vinogradoff, *English Society in the Eleventh Century*, 5 ff., and the
reference there cited ; Liebermann, *Gesetze der Angelsachsen* II, ii, 701-3.
But the lawmen represented the local or provincial community as against
the king and his officers and, although skilled in the law which they could
state and interpret if required, they do not themselves seem to have
exercised judicial functions ; see Mawer, *Camb. Med. Hist.* III, 333 ff.
[3] Liebermann, *loc. cit.*
[4] Cf. Stubbs, *loc. cit.*, and Pollock and Maitland, *loc. cit.*, and the
references given in both.

least,[1] be rendered doomsman. Of this evidence we must now take some account. First in importance is the group of judicial records originating in the palatine county of Chester in the second half of the thirteenth century. There was in this county court a clear distinction between doomsmen and suitors, *iudicatores* and *sectatores*. Thus, it was said in the course of an action in 1286 that, although the plea was before the justiciar, yet the decision really lay with the *iudicatores* of the county court.[2] Three years later in an action on a writ of entry the demandant was many times asked by the justiciar and the *iudicatores* if he wished to say anything before they gave judgement.[3] The county court contained the barons, knights, and other freemen of the county, and in 1259 *in pleno comitatu* they unanimously refused to accept a newly appointed custodian of the forests on the ground that it was part of ' the laws and customs used in the time of the earls ' that judgement on forest matters should only be given by the *iudicatores* before the justiciar.[4] The county was in the hands of the crown, and this was not the only occasion on which it invoked the local customs by which it was differentiated from the rest of England. In 1292, in reply to a writ of *certiorari* requiring a plea begun in the county court of Chester to be transferred to the king's court, the justiciar of Chester sent word that he had caused a record to be made before the *iudicatores* who were present, ' and because the *iudicatores* and *sectatores* claim that in such a case all the barons and their stewards and the *iudicatores* of the county ought to be summoned to hear the process and before they affix their seal to amend it if need be among themselves before the third meeting of the county court ', the report was delayed. For this privilege they invoked ancient use and custom, a claim which they were told would have to be proved before the king.[5] A case which arose in the city court of Chester in

---

[1] The word doomsman does not, I think, occur in the Chester evidence.
[2] Stewart-Brown, *op. cit.*, 60.
[3] *Ibid.*, 148. [4] *Ibid.*, 2.
[5] *Plac. Abbrev.*, 229, 287. It should be noted that this case, which brings out as clearly as possible both the distinction between the doomsmen and suitors in the county court of Chester and the difference between that court and the other county courts of England, was perfectly well known to Maitland when he formulated his view of doomsmen and suitors ; see *H.E.L.* i (2nd ed.), 551–2. It is true that he accepted evidence coming from

1293 affords some further illustration of the matter in hand. All pleas were adjourned for three weeks, because *iudicatores* and *sectatores* alike claimed that they should not be dealt with while the great fair held at the feast of St. John was in progress.[1]

Such, as far as I know, is the only direct evidence for the existence of a body of doomsmen separate from the suitors in an English county court. It should be noted, however, that the Chester county court bases its claim in respect to the doomsmen on ancient local custom, and it is obvious that conditions in Cheshire in the thirteenth century differed in many respects from those obtaining in other English counties. The Cheshire county court dealt with what elsewhere in England would be reserved for the king's court, and for this reason it would seem to be inadmissible to use the Cheshire evidence to supplement what we know of other county courts.[2] Professor Plucknett will not admit this limitation; he argues that the palatine organization was late, and that it does not follow that, because the Chester county court exercised additional powers, it was not still a county court, ' because enough is known of what the normal county did to make it possible in many cases to distinguish in Cheshire between county and palatine power '.[3] If, as appears to be the case, no normal county court made a distinction in kind between doomsmen and suitors, the argument that such a distinction should be made in the light of the Chester evidence is not convincing. It is not necessary, however, to regard the Chester doomsmen as part of the palatine organization; a survival of a local custom that did not take root (if it existed) in other parts of England, but found opportunity to do so in the special conditions of Cheshire, is not impossible.

Chester in the same way as illustrating the function of a doomsman, though his words, ' thus even in the presence of a royal justice the *doomsmen of Chester* decided questions of law ', suggest that it might not be so in other counties. (The italics in the quotation are mine.)

[1] Stewart-Brown, *op. cit.*, 182. I have dwelt only on the evidence which shows that in the Chester county court there was a body of doomsmen distinct from the other suitors. Mr. Stewart-Brown, in his learned introduction, pp. xxx–xxxviii, has brought together the evidence as to the doomsmen in the Chester documents and discussed it in the light of some other local records.

[2] Woodbine, *Harvard Law Review* XLIII, 1105 ; cf. Stewart-Brown, *op. cit.*, xvi–xviii.

[3] *Harvard Law Review* XLII, 643 ; XLIII, 1117.

We turn now to the Lancashire evidence. Persons bound to attend the wapentake courts and called *iudices* occur frequently in the records.[1] Thus, in 1324, five persons described as *iudices* pay different sums for respite of ' their suit of the common suit ' of the wapentake court of Lonsdale.[2] In 1326 ' the attorney of the *iudex* of Warton ' paid 6d. because he had departed from the wapentake court of Lonsdale *in dispectu curiae.*[3] Services of this kind were sometimes limited to cases where the gravity or difficulty of the matter made it desirable that the ordinary suitors should have some assistance.[4] *Iudicatores* occur also in connexion with local courts in Cheshire. At Over the abbot of Vale Royal had a tenant who was bound to provide a doomsman at the lord's court or make redemption, and at Weaverham there is a list of nine such bound to attend the manor court moot, but not all of whom are associated with some particular vill.[5] Evidence of this sort could be multiplied, but enough has been said to raise two questions which are of the first importance for our purpose. Did these persons attend the county court in their character as dooms-men ? Or to put it otherwise are we entitled to say that the county court of Lancashire, like that of Cheshire, contained doomsmen as well as suitors ?[6] Secondly, are we justified in rendering the words *iudex* and *iudicator* in the documents we have been considering by the term doomsman ?

As to the first question it may be admitted at once that persons who were described as *iudices* or *iudicatores* had in certain cases the tenurial obligation of discharging their lord's suit at the county court. In 1322 Richard de Molyneux held

[1] *Lancashire Court Rolls*, ed. Farrer (Lancs. and Ches. Rec. Soc., vol. XLI), 6, 9, 40, 45, 114–115, 117, 133, 134.

[2] *Ibid.*, 108.

[3] *Lancashire Court Rolls*, 137 ; cf. pp. 150–1, 154, 160–1. These and the references given above (note 1) refer to the wapentakes of Lonsdale, Salford, and Amounderness, and we shall see presently that there were *iudices* doing service at the wapentake court of West Derby.

[4] *Ibid.*, viii–xi ; cf. *Year Book, 15 Edw. III* (R.S.), 107 ff., with refer-ence to the court of Dalton in the barony of Ulverstone, Lancs.

[5] *Ledger Book of Vale Royal*, ed. Brownbill (Lancs. and Ches. Rec. Soc. LXVIII, 1914), 107–10 ; cf. Ormerod, *Cheshire* (ed. Helsby) II, 113–14 ; W.O. Ault, *Private Jurisdictions in England*, 252–66.

[6] ' The county court was attended by judges or doomsmen [and] by suitors, certain freeholders of the county required by their tenure to do suit, &c.' Farrer, *op. cit.*, vi, xv, xvii.

the manor of Sefton and one half of the manor of Downlitherland by certain services, and did suit at the county and wapentake courts[1] by the hands of William le Demande, his tenant
for the said manor. In respect of the other half of the manor
which he also held he did the like suit by the hands of Adam
and William le Demande.[2] In the same year Robert de Heppale
was holding certain manors in Leylandshire and also the
wapentake court of that district, and in lieu of all service Walter
le Demon (a tenant in one of his manors and in view of his name
presumably a *iudex* or *iudicator*) did suit at the county court of
Lancashire.[3] Then in 1265 Adam de Garston, who is not
described as *iudex* or *iudicator*, held of the earl of Derby, and
owed suit at the county court of Lancashire and the wapentake
court of West Derby.[4] A Lancashire lord, therefore, could get
his county court service done by one who was not apparently a
doomsman, and it would seem to follow that the court contained
suitors as well as doomsmen. This has been admitted, but it
remains to be shown that in the county court itself any distinction was made between the doomsmen and suitors. Where
doomsmen of the local courts did suit at the county court it
was on their lord's behalf, to do the service that was primarily
incumbent on him and could, therefore, have been discharged
by him in person. If the lord had gone himself, would he
have been a doomsman or a suitor ? Is there any evidence
that he was required to send in his place certain people who
were doomsmen ? I think that the probabilities point in the
other direction. There is no evidence that Adam de Garston
was a doomsman, and in the county court of Chester a distinction was taken between the barons and their stewards on the
one hand and the *iudicatores* on the other.[5] It is clear enough
that in the inferior courts the duty of providing a doomsman
(*iudex, iudicator*) was often a specific incident of tenure. Thus
in 1212 we find such a record as 'Adam de Bulling tenet
dimidiam carucatam in thainagio et reddit per annum x[s] et 1

---

[1] i.e. Lancashire and the wapentake of West Derby.
[2] *Lancashire Inquests*, ed. Farrer (Lancs. and Ches. Rec. Soc., LIV, 1907)
II, 79–80. It will be seen later that Demande = *iudex* or *iudicator* and
seems to be a form of doomsman.
[3] *Lancashire Inquests* II, 106–7.
[4] *Ibid.* I, 232.   [5] See above, p. 99.

iudicem de antiquo feffamento '.[1] Then in 1256 the duty of
providing a doomsman for the court of Widnes was by agreement assumed by the mesne lord of the holdings responsible.[2]
But no such condition is attached to the service of the county
court and this is further illustrated by a Westmorland fine in
1227, where it is agreed that the attendance of the lord's steward
or bailiff at the county court would acquit his tenants of any
duty in that respect, unless a question of afforcement of
judgement should arise, in which case they shall have certain
specified obligations of attendance.[3] Perhaps an answer to these
questions would be found if we had such *rotuli placitorum
comitatus* as have recently been forthcoming for other counties.[4]
But it is well to remember that, apart from the very special case
of Cheshire, these rolls make no distinction between suitors
and doomsmen. Meanwhile, it may be suggested that the
particular functions of the Lancashire doomsmen lay in the
local and feudal courts with which they were connected, and
consisted not merely in ordinary suit but in the afforcement of
the court when, as has been said already, matters of unusual
difficulty or gravity had to be dealt with. However that may be
—and we are not concerned here with accounting completely
for this very interesting Lancashire evidence—it would seem
that on the main point we must be satisfied with a negative
and perhaps a provisional conclusion. We are not yet entitled to
say that the Lancashire county court resembled that of Cheshire
in containing a body of *iudicatores* with functions differing
from, and more important than, those of the ordinary
suitors.

[1] *Book of Fees* I, 218. There are further illustrations of the point on the
same and the following page. The court at which the doomsman's services
were required was that of Newton ; see *Final Concords of the County of
Lancs.*, ed. Farrer (Lancs. and Ches. Rec. Soc. XLVI, 1903) II, 171.

[2] *Ibid.* I, 125–7—examples could be multiplied ; cf. *Ledger Book of
Vale Royal*, 107–10.

[3] *Lancs. Court Rolls*, x, xi. It seems very probable that one part, at
least, of the history of the doomsmen will be found in the study of this
matter of afforcement of judgement, as to which see Farrer, *Final Concords*,
xii–xiii. The case cited recalls the well-known passage in Leg. Hen. I ;
Stubbs, *Select Charters*, 124. It should be noted, however, that afforcement
of judgement was a contingent obligation, whereas in Cheshire the doomsmen are an integral part of the county court and can be mentioned as such
in connexion with barons and freemen (above, p. 99) ; they cannot, therefore, it would seem, be representing the barons or discharging their suits.

[4] See below, p. 104, n. 3.

If it be argued that the doomsmen of the Lancashire wapentake courts are survivals of what may once have existed in the court of that county, as it did in Cheshire, the question still remains whether it was ever to be found in the courts of other English counties, and the answer may perhaps be looked for in the reference to the *iudices et iudicatores* of Yorkshire in the pipe roll of 31 Henry I.[1] But even if we identify them with the Cheshire and Lancashire *iudicatores*, we shall have to remember that all our evidence would still come from regions that were subject to a considerable measure of Scandinavian influence,[2] and further we shall have to take account of the fact already mentioned, that in the county rolls at our disposal there is no evidence of doomsmen as distinguished from other suitors.[3] In these circumstances, it is submitted, the attempt to identify the *buzones* with such a body of doomsmen must fail, because, as we have seen, Bracton's words imply the existence of what he called *buzones* in every county to which the judges would come.

The word 'doomsmen' in the general sense of judge was used in English as early as 1200. It still survives and is current, of course, in a more specialized sense and in the form 'deemster' in the constitution of the Isle of Man.[4] It is to be noted, moreover, that it has given us the proper name 'Dempster',[5] and Liebermann thought that the Osbert Domesman who was a substantial burgess of Cambridge in the thirteenth century may have derived his surname from the lawmen of the Danish borough.[6] If we look for its use in the more special sense of judgement-finder in a court in which the presiding officer was

---

[1] *Pipe Roll, 31 Hen. I*, ed. Hunter (Rec. Com.), 34, 118 ; cf. Stubbs, *C.H.* I (5th ed.), 428–9. It may be suggested that the *quattuor iudices Insule* in Lincolnshire were not like the Yorkshire judges connected with the county but with some local court like the doomsmen of the wapentake of West Derby.

[2] See Mawer, *Camb. Med. Hist.* III, 333–6, and the relevant map.

[3] It is worth noting that two of the five counties for which we have such rolls, namely Beds. and Bucks., formed part of the Danelaw. The others are Berks., Cornwall, and Oxon. See Jenkinson, *Cambridge Historical Journal* I, 106 ; Morris, *The Early English County Court*, viii ; Jenkinson and Mills, *E.H.R.* XLIII, 21–32 ; Supplementary Stonor Letters, ed. Kingsford, *Camden Miscellany* XIII (1923) vi, 1 ; and *Rolls from the Office of the Sheriff of Beds. and Bucks.*, ed. Fowler (Beds. Hist. Rec. Soc.), 1929.

[4] *New Engl. Dict.* s.v. Doomsman and Deemster.   [5] *Ibid., loc. cit.*

[6] Maitland, *Township and Borough*, 162 ; Liebermann, *Gesetze* II, ii, 565.

a moderator only, we shall find a survival at least in a well-known Law Dictionary, which, however, restricts the term to the suitors in a feudal court.[1]

But we have evidence from Lancashire in the early fourteenth century that the office of *iudex* or *iudicator*, in two cases at least, had given to the family in which it was hereditary the surname of Demande or Demon. The lands in question lay in the hundred of West Derby and were held of the Molyneux, lords of Sefton.[2] We have seen that in 1322 Richard de Molyneux, lord of the manors of Sefton and Downlitherland, performed the suit that he owed at the county and wapentake courts by the hands of William le Demande and of Adam le Demande, his tenants for the two halves of the manor of Downlitherland.[3] The name Demon or Demande occurs as early as 1285[4] and is common enough in the early years of the next century,[5] and as early as 1246 we hear of William Judicator of Litherland.[6] Now in 1327 Richard, son of Adam the Judge, quit-claimed to Peter de Molyneux his right to an ox-gang in the vill of Litherland, and eight years later Richard le Demand granted to Richard de Molyneux one quarter of the manor. In 1335 Philip de Molyneux conveyed land to Richard, formerly judge, of Downlitherland.[7] This evidence seems to establish pretty clearly the fact that in certain Lancashire courts at least, the words *iudex* or *iudicator* would go into English as doomsman or some form of that word. The term, indeed, may at one time have been in general use for the judgement-finders in any court—Maitland thought so[8]—but it is submitted that the evidence before us will not suffice even to render probable the existence in the English county courts of a

---

[1] *Les Termes de la Ley.* Cited in *New Engl. Dict.* in the edition of 1708 ; it was first published, however, in 1527 and that edition does not contain the term in question, nor, I think, does it appear until after the edition of 1667.

[2] *V.C.H. Lancs.* III, 96 ; cf. *Book of Fees* I, 208–9.

[3] See above, p. 102.

[4] William Demon of Sefton incurs a fine, *Lancs. Assize Rolls*, ed. Parker (Lancs. and Ches. Rec. Soc. XLIX, 1905) II, 215.

[5] e.g. *Lancs. Inquests* I, 269, 281 (where the name occurs in 1288 and 1293), II, 22, 153 ; *Calendar of the Moore MSS.*, ed. Brownbill (Lancs. and Ches. Rec. Soc. LXVII, 1913), Nos. 826, 1184, 1185, 1218–20, 1222. Cf. *V.C.H. Lancs.* III, 96 n.

[6] *Lancs. Assize Rolls* I, 16.

[7] *V.C.H. Lancs., loc. cit.*, from manuscript collections.   [8] *H.E.L.* I, 85.

body of doomsmen distinct from and superior to the rest of the suitors. But a group of doomsmen in this sense is required, if the *buzones* are to be accounted for by the theories which we have been discussing.

III

An attempt must now be made to formulate the conclusions to which our investigation has led us. In the first place it would seem that the linguistic relation between the old French *boujon*, the *buzo* of the Latin and Anglo-French texts, and the widely distributed surname on the one hand and the *buzones* of the Willicot case and Bracton on the other can neither be denied nor demonstrated. To deny it would be to resort to an inadmissible coincidence. We should have to suppose that, on the one hand, an ordinary French technical term came into use in England when French was the language of the ruling classes and passed early into a surname, while, on the other, two examples of exactly the same form must either be left unaccounted for or else referred to a Scandinavian origin though never occurring in the regions of England where the Scandinavian influence was strongest. The evidence, I submit, establishes a presumption of linguistic connexion, and this is confirmed by Dr. Mawer, who considers that from an etymological point of view any suggestion connecting *buzones* with old French *boujon* is in order.[1] If, as is possible, the surname and Bracton's term have a common origin we are therefore to look for it in the bolt or arrow. There are various ways in which the name might have been derived from the thing, but that is not our problem, though we have to remember that ' the boundary-line between names and words is hardly real '.[2] The question is, why should an unofficial or only semi-official group of country gentlemen, active in judicial work and county administration, have been nicknamed bolt or arrow men ? Bracton himself suggests that the word was a nickname, for when he says that the *majores de comitati dicuntur buzones*, he appears to be using a bit of local slang or colloquialism for a thing which he knew to be general, although it had no official designation. The

---

[1] See below, p. 109.
[2] Weekley, *Etymological Dictionary*, vii.

ways of slang are often past finding out, for it is apt to depend like the humour which sometimes underlies it on the perception of a relation between apparently incongruous things. There are, however, simpler explanations, and we may remember that academic Esquire Bedells have for obvious reasons been disrespectfully described as poker-men. Now it has been suggested that the stringless bow and the featherless arrow (*buzo sine pennis*) of the Bryanston serjeanty may have been emblems of office,[1] and if one asks of what office, the passage from Britton in which he seems to be using the Bryanston case to illustrate the nature of petty serjeanty[2] would suggest that of the *servientes* in the feudal quota. It would not be unreasonable, therefore, to see an analogy between them and the *buzones* who rendered important services to the itinerant justices and the county courts, particularly if, as is not impossible, they received by way of warrant some such token as a rod or bolt. I put forward this guess, for it is scarcely more, not as a solution of the very old puzzle of the name of the *buzones*, but rather as limiting the field by indicating the quarter in which the solution must be sought.

Turning now from the name to the persons who bore it we have seen who and what they were in the one case where we can identify them. In functions they correspond well enough with the definitions framed by earlier writers ; Maitland thought of them as active business-loving men who led the county court and were its mouthpieces and would when the time came be justices of the peace.[3] This definition would treat the *buzones* as a group of country gentlemen actively concerned indeed with the business of the county court but having duties and capacities extending beyond it, men who from position, business capacity, and experience were influential in local affairs. The existence of such a group in any local community is antecedently probable, and I conceive that to-day any member of a Borough or County Council or an Academic

[1] Turner, *Select Pleas of the Forest*, 137. A suggestion looking in this direction was made to me independently by Dr. Previté-Orton.

[2] See above, p. 84.

[3] This definition is combined from the references given above, p. 89, n. 1, omitting ' those foremost men of the county ' in *Gloucester Pleas* and retaining the epithet ' business-loving ' which was dropped in the second edition of the *History of English Law*.

Senate could name without difficulty, if not without indiscretion, the *buzones* of his time. A strong central government committed as deeply as the Angevin government was to a policy of local self-agency would naturally take account of such a group when it came to select persons to do its work in the counties. Bracton's direction to the judges is proof of this. Such a body from whatever point of view it is observed shows itself as representative. If the county court is in the habit of selecting the same men to verify essoins or make a record and speak for the community when it is accused of wrong, it is more than likely that these are the men it will choose when the king sends for knights of the shire to speak with him of the affairs of the realm. Such a group of men on the other hand will naturally be treated as representatives of the county by the central government, and this becomes apparent in proportion as commissions for local administrative work begin to multiply. Some years ago an investigation of the parliamentary representation of five of the eastern counties in the reign of Edward II led me to the conclusion that in those counties, at least, there was a smallish group of gentlemen of moderate position and no national importance who were constantly occupied with local affairs and local administration, and were recognized by the central government, which put one task after another upon them, as particularly fitted for this work. Further, that it was from this group that knights sent to the king's parliaments were usually drawn, and that it was not uncommon for them to be returned several times so that the task of representing the county in the king's court was treated as just another aspect of the day's work to which they and their forbears had been accustomed.[1] One would be prepared to find a similar group in any other English county at that time. I suggest now that the existence of just such a group, chiefly occupied, it is true, with judicial and police work, in all counties in the thirteenth century is implied in Bracton's words. If this is the case, our inquiry will have resulted in fitting Bracton's *buzones* into the texture of English legal and administrative history at a point where it is beginning to be connected with the history of parliament.

[1] See below pp. 111–152.

ETYMOLOGICAL NOTE ON BUZONES[1]

From the etymological point of view, any suggestion connecting *buzones* with OFr. *boujon* is entirely in order. This becomes clear when we note that the earlier forms of that word, as recorded by Godefroy (*Dict. de l'anc. langue française* s.v.) are *bulzun, bouzun, bozon,* forms which agree with those of the surnames, found in ME. documents, which it is suggested may be identical with Bracton's word. Godefroy defines *boujon* as ' gros trait d'arbalète, assez semblable au matras, dont l'extremité se terminait par une tête ', the word being ultimately an augmentative derivative of Germanic *bult* (Mod. Ger. *bolz*), ' bolt ' (*v.* Diez, *Etym. Wb. der Roman. Spr.* s.v. *bolzone*). A weapon which could be thus described might well, in course of time, come to be used as a nickname, or even as a slang term, for an important official.

One would be justified in identifying the M.E. surnames *Bouzun, Buzun, Bulzun,* and even *Bozun,* with this word, but it is exceedingly doubtful if the form *Bauzan,* unless it be a sheer blunder, should be taken to be the same name.

One difficulty remains to be mentioned. In so far as the personal name *Bu(l)zun, Bo(u)zun* in ME. documents is of nickname origin, we should have expected, at least in the earliest examples, that we should have such forms as *John le Bouzun,* rather than *John Bouzun,* and the entire absence of such forms can hardly be explained unless we assume that already in France the word *bulzon, bouzon,* had come to be used as a regular second-name, suggesting that some such technical use of the word was already to be found on the Continent. Some few of the *Bozon* names might be explained as going back to the Frankish personal name *Boso,* but that would not account for the *Bulzun, Bouzun* names.

Mr. Betts's suggestions are etymologically unsound. He starts from the Scandinavian *bú,* ' household, estate ', and suggests that because certain Scandinavian words are found in Western and South-western ME. texts, this word also may well have existed in the West Country. Most of the ME. words which he cites are words of Scandinavian origin which had come to be used in ME. generally, and are no direct evidence of Scandinavian influence, and it is no longer believed that the *Ancren Riwle,* from which he quotes some words, is a purely south-western text. But even if all his words were correct, one could not admit the next stage in his argument, viz. that *buzo* is a Latinized form derived from a Scandinavian compound of *bú,* with *bú* in the genitive case *bús.* It is wholly impossible to believe that such genitival compounds were ever in use in the south-

---

[1] Dr. Allen Mawer, to whom I applied for help in dealing with the linguistic problems involved in this article, kindly prepared and placed at my disposal the following note. I gladly avail myself of this opportunity to thank him warmly for his generous act.

west, or that such compounds as existed in Icelandic (*v.* Cleasby-Vigfússon s.v. *bú*), could ever give rise to an official named *buzo.* He suggests that the allied *búi,* ' dweller, neighbour, juror ', might have developed a Latinized form *buso* as a name for a neighbour acting in a judicial capacity, but there is no parallel for such a formation. He tries to find support for it by quoting Roquefort, *Glossaire de la Langue Romane,* s.v. *buze,* where that term is rendered ' habitation, village, residence '. It is very difficult to know whence Roquefort got this word. There is no trace of it elsewhere. Possibly it is due to confusion with OFr. *busse, buce, bucze,* ' vessel ', which did develop a secondary sense ' small building ', but in any case it is impossible to derive an OFr. *buze* from OScand. *búi* on any known etymological principle.

It may be added that Mr. Betts's explanation would also leave entirely unexplained the ME. *bulzun,* if, as seems probable, that name is to be associated with *Buzo.*   A.M.

IV

KNIGHTS OF THE SHIRE IN THE PARLIAMENTS OF EDWARD II[1]

IN the history of the fourteenth century as it was taught and studied a generation ago, the chief place in the constitutional development of England was assigned to parliament. The struggle with the crown, the growth of the powers of the legislative, financial, and judicial authority of parliament were allowed to obscure the more difficult questions of the organization and character of the body itself. There was a tendency, indeed, to assume that once the model had been formed all subsequent parliaments would conform to it, and that it remained only for the knights of the shire to cast in their lot with the burgesses and organize themselves under a speaker, a process which was generally supposed to have been completed early in the fourteenth century.[2] Even in the cautious pages of Stubbs the works of the fourteenth century parliaments are often exhibited in the light reflected from the seventeenth century. Later writers have departed strongly and properly from this view, and the tendency now is to minimize the importance of parliament and bring forward the council and the administrative machinery as dominating the constitutional struggle of the period. I need scarcely refer to the studies of Professor Baldwin and Professor Tout, but it should be remembered that the reaction really began as long ago as 1885, with Dr. Ludwig Riess's remarkable and singularly neglected work.[3] Maitland, of course, knew Riess's book and apparently

---

[1] Reprinted from *The English Historical Review* XXXIV (1919), pp. 25–42, 152–171.

[2] See Stubbs, *C.H.* III (ed. 1890), 470 ; Dasent, *The Speakers of the House of Commons*, ch. ii ; Porritt, *Unreformed House of Commons* I, ch. xxi. Stubbs writes : ' The silence of records cannot be held to prove that an *organized assembly* like that of the commons could ever have dispensed with a recognized prolocutor or foreman. It can scarcely be doubted that Henry of Keighly, who in 1301 carried the petition of the parliament of Lincoln to the king, was in some such position '. But surely the words which we have italicized contain a *petitio principii*. To what extent, if at all, the commons were organized is precisely the question.

[3] For the relevant works of Baldwin, Tout and Riess, see above, pp. 3, 6, 7. Riess's book was published long after Stubbs wrote. In later editions he cited it in footnotes, e.g. iii, 472, but he does not seem to have allowed it to influence his text.

thought that he went too far, but I do not think that he ever expressed his whole view of the matter.[1]

It is possible that the study of the question may be advanced a little by considering first what the older writers meant and implied by the word parliament. Then for the same purpose it would be useful to distinguish between the methods and results of constitutional development, by which I mean the immediate purpose of the opposition and the crown, the attempt to restrict the prerogative, and the ultimate outcome of the measures taken to that end. On the first point it is quite clear that Stubbs meant by parliament an assembly which included the lords, spiritual and temporal, in conjunction with the representatives of the counties and certain towns. He implies, however, a solidarity in the whole body as opposed to the crown, a corporate consciousness and ideal, which it would perhaps be difficult to prove from contemporary evidence. To put it in another way, he suggests that the purpose of the struggle was to secure, not yet indeed parliamentary sovereignty, but a limited monarchy based on exclusive parliamentary control of taxation, co-operation in legislation, and some measure of control of the executive through the council and ministers. It appears now that to attribute such views and ideals to fourteenth-century statesmen and politicians would be to neglect the still strongly feudal atmosphere which they breathed and the powerful class-feeling which directed the lay and clerical magnates towards particularist rather than national ends; it would be further to exaggerate the solidarity and class-consciousness of the commons in national politics; and finally it would be to misread the political movement of the time.

This brings me to the second point I have mentioned, the immediate purpose of the opposition to the crown, as to which it will be enough to indicate the general results of recent study. What was wanted, it seems, was not the control of the crown through parliament, but rather to secure to the magnates as the ruling class that dominating share in the government which upon their feudal traditions they regarded as their right. This, in view of existing conditions, could best be done by obtaining control of the council and bringing the

[1] *Memoranda de Parliamento* (R.S., 1893), Introd., 75.

administrative machinery out of the king's own hands and into departments which could be directed by the council and would be strong enough to resist his arbitrary action. To deny to the barons a sincere desire for administrative reform, for orderly government secured by law, would be to do them an injustice and to neglect the evidence at our disposal. But the two aims of political ambition and reforming zeal are not incompatible. The true rôle of parliament in this programme has yet to be brought out. It may perhaps be put in this way : the word parliament may well have been understood as meaning a place and occasion, rather than a constitutional body. Where this second notion was present it would refer rather to the Magnum Concilium, in the first half of the fourteenth century, certainly, and it is that period which I have particularly in mind. Now a meeting of the Great Council at which representatives of the shires and towns were in attendance would furnish both an excellent place and a suitable occasion for registering acts or statutes which were intended to be permanent, for creating or influencing public opinion, for transacting in short any business that required to be done publicly and solemnly, or for which the country had to be prepared by means of preliminary statements. If something of this sort were the general attitude of the magnates in the early part of the century, it is easy to see how the repeated use of parliament in this sense could in time turn into something very different; how the commons, having moved towards or drifted into some form of corporate organization and having secured a pretty firm control of taxation, would become an important factor in the struggle between the king and the magnates.

I try to indicate only in the most general fashion a way in which the problem may be stated in order to fit in a small contribution to a small part of it. It is possible to bring together a good deal of minute, if not always very enlightening information about the county members, and an attempt is here made to look at Edward II's parliaments from this side. I have tried to make use of this material to illustrate two points : the position and importance of the knights of the shire in parliament, the sort of men who attended, with reference to their public life, and the place of parliamentary service in it. The present study

I

is only an experiment and as such I have limited myself to a group of five counties. The material consists of scattered references to obscure persons, and it only becomes illuminating by accumulation. Although much of that work had been done under Palgrave's direction, and the Digest of the Parliamentary Writs takes one a long way, it still leaves a good deal to be done. I have confined myself therefore to the five counties of Cambridgeshire, Huntingdonshire, Bedfordshire, Hertfordshire, and Essex, and have studied the lives of all the men who sat for these counties in any of Edward II's parliaments. The results can in many cases be most conveniently shown in tabular form, which I give in an appendix.[1] In this way it has been possible to indicate for each county the entire number of persons returned during the reign, the number who actually attended and the parliaments in which the county does not appear to have been represented. All these figures, of course, must be taken as approximate—thus under the last head there will be certain cases in which no returns are forthcoming, and others in which there are returns but no enrolments of writs *de expensis* and therefore, it may be assumed, no attendance.[2] Further points illustrated in these tables are the status of those returned, i.e. the numbers of freemen, knights, and tenants-in-chief respectively, the extent to which they were employed in local administration as local officers, such as sheriff and coroner, or by means of judicial or administrative commissions, and the number of attendances at parliament, and finally the number accused of crimes or serious offences.

When the material has been arranged in this way it appears, as one would expect, that within the large circle formed by those who were returned at one time or another during the course of the reign there was a smaller group of men who were returned and sat more than once, in some cases indeed repeatedly, and that these again are usually found to be particularly active in the work of local administration. As these may fairly be regarded as typical of the class from which the knights of the shire were drawn, I have set down in a series of notes what information I could gather about their situation, their families, and their activities. All this, of course, makes very dry

---

[1] Below, pp. 146–52.   [2] But see above, p. 10.

reading, and it seemed better therefore not to print these notes. Instead I hope to give in a later article a sort of survey of the business of local administration. It is not particularly instructive merely to be told that a knight of the shire for Cambridgeshire, for example, frequently acted as commissioner of array or conservator of the peace for his county. The information becomes a help toward understanding the day's work of the men we are considering when we have before us some account of the duties of the respective offices. Finally, I have ventured on some generalizations which must, however, naturally be taken as provisional in view of the very limited field from which the evidence on which they are based is drawn. In this way I have tried to determine whether any attempt was made to secure the return of members favourable to the political groups or leaders that happened to dominate public affairs when, for example, such important parliaments as those of 1318 and 1322 were summoned. Again, I have tried to get at the attitude of the knights of the shire toward the parliament by reference where it was possible to their work there, to the way in which they treated their returns, and to their public service in the way of local administration. This last subject I have illustrated in a summary fashion because parliamentary service seems to have been counted as part of it, and partly because it helps to make intelligible the daily life of the small country gentlemen with whom we are concerned. Some colour and contrast, characteristic enough of the period, are to be derived from the records of the misdeeds laid at the doors of many, I might even say most, of the men with whose lives we are concerned, and I have therefore given some account of these.

We may begin by asking whether any attempt was made to determine the political complexion of the county representation throughout the reign. As a convenient test we may examine the representation of our five counties in the parliaments which witnessed the confirmation of the ordinances, the triumph of Lancaster, the confirmation of the treaty of Leake, the banishment of the Despensers, the repeal of the ordinances. The following table gives the names of the members returned from the five counties to these parliaments, and the names of the sheriffs who presumably received and returned the writs. The names of those who did not attend and therefore received no allowance for expenses are noted, the names of those who sat for the first or only time are marked with an asterisk, and these we must examine carefully with a view to discovering whether their appearance is due to accident or political intention.

Parliament, August–October 1311 (*The Ordinances*)

*Thomas de Burgh *John de Lindhurst	Cambridgeshire	John de Swinford Sheriff
Richard de Stratford John Waldesheve	Huntingdonshire	
William de Walton John de Tany	Essex	Geoffrey de la Lee— Sheriff
Robert de Roos Walram de Rochford	Hertfordshire	
Walter de Molesworth Gerard de Braybrook	Bedfordshire	William Merree— Sheriff

Parliament, January–February 1316. (*Triumph of Lancaster*)

Baldwin de Stowe John de Swinford	Cambridgeshire	Ralf Giffard— Sheriff
Andrew le Moyne Roger de Cantilupe	Huntingdonshire	
Benedict de Cokefield John de la Lee	Essex	Richard de Perers— Sheriff
Richard de Perers Geoffrey de la Lee	Hertfordshire	
Peter de Loring Robert Dakeney	Bedfordshire	John de la Haye— Sheriff

Parliament, October–December 1318. (*Confirmation of the Treaty of Leake*)

Thomas de Burgh *Philip de Welle	Cambridgeshire	Ralf Giffard— Sheriff
John de Swinford John Waldeshef	Huntingdonshire	
*John de Lisle John de Enfield	Essex	Richard de Perers— Sheriff
Richard de Perers Geoffrey de la Lee	Hertfordshire	
John de Pakenham, jun. Ralf Fitz Richard	Bedfordshire	Roger de Tyryngham Sheriff

Parliament, July–August, 1321. (Banishment of the Despensers)

John de Creke / William Loveday	} Cambridgeshire	} Almeric la Zusche— Sheriff
William Moyne / Andrew le Moigne	} Huntingdonshire	
No returns, nor writs	Essex	} John de Doure— Sheriff
Richard de Perers / Geoffrey de la Lee	} Hertfordshire	
Ralf Fitz Richard / John Morteyn	} Bedfordshire	{ Ingelram Berenger— Sheriff

Parliament, May 1322. (Repeal of the Ordinances)

*John de Limbury / John de Cambridge	} Cambridgeshire	} Almeric la Zusche— Sheriff
Simon de Drayton / John de Swinford	} Huntingdonshire	
Thomas Gobion / Simon de Kynardesley	} Essex	} Nicholas de Engaine Sheriff
Richard de Perers / John de la Haye	} Hertfordshire	
John de Pakenham, jun. / John Morris	} Bedfordshire	{ Philip de Aylesbury Sheriff

We may begin with the Cambridgeshire members in 1311.
Both of them sit for the first time, Lindhurst never sat again, he
must have been a person of great obscurity, for the records
which furnish information, often so abundantly, about most of
the county members are silent about him. Burgh held land in
Suffolk of Henry de Percy and in Cambridgeshire of the earl of
Richmond, and he may have held of the king also, but this is
not so clear.[1] It looks, too, as though he were of the same family
as that Thomas de Burgh, king's clerk, who was one of the
royal escheators.[2] Percy seems to have been of the party of the
ordainers, but Richmond was one of the king's party.[3] If we
balance tenurial connexion, then, we shall think that Burgh
could scarcely have been the choice of either side. It looks
much more as though the return had been uninfluenced by
political considerations.

[1] *C.C.R.*, 1307–13, 133 ; *Feudal Aids* I, 142–3, 154–5.

[2] *C.C.R.*, 1318–23, 236 ; 1318–27, 128 ; *C.F.R.* III, 122 ; Tout, *Edward II*, 361, 363.

[3] Tout, *op. cit.*, 15 n., 94–5 ; Ramsay, *Genesis of Lancaster* I, 29.

Of the two members returned for Huntingdonshire in 1311 Waldesheve appears for the first time, but Stratford had been returned to the first parliament of the reign (Northampton, 1307). Both sat subsequently, Stratford twice and Waldesheve four times. Very little of the ordinary sort of evidence is forth-coming about Stratford, but one bit does shed a good deal of light on his connexion. In 1310 he is alleged to have been associated with Walter Langton, bishop of Lichfield, in certain acts of violence committed at Northampton.[1] Langton had been extremely obnoxious to the baronial opposition in the last years of Edward I. Edward II disgraced him a few months after his accession, but by 1311 he must have won his way back to royal favour, or at least have been striving for that, because the next year the king made him treasurer again.[2] An obscure country gentleman who in 1310 was associated, not greatly to his credit, with a disgraced bishop of the court party would scarcely have been selected by either side to represent its interests in 1311. John de Waldesheve seems to have been connected with Pembroke, in whose service he went abroad in 1313. But there is a connexion with the Clares and with Hotham which taken together seems to point back to Gaveston.[3] His return in 1311 then would scarcely have served the purpose of either side. Unlike Stratford he was a man of a good deal of prominence in local administrative work.

The sheriff who was responsible for the returns from Cambridgeshire and Huntingdonshire in August 1311 was John de Swinford, a country gentleman with lands in both counties, a tenant in chief in Cambridgeshire, who was concerned with local administration over a long period of years.[4] He sat at various times for both counties. It is hard to trace any political connexion for him in 1311, although he was an adherent of Mowbray in 1322.[5] With this fact in mind it might appear significant that he was appointed sheriff of the two counties in April 1311, and removed in the following November.[6] But

---

[1] *C.P.R.*, 1307–13, 260.   [2] Tout, *op. cit.*, 14, 28, 97.
[3] *C.P.R.*, 1313–17, 346, 577, 666 ; 1321–4, 148 ; 1313–18, 301 ; 1323–7, 259 ; cf. Tout, p. 95.
[4] *C.P.R.*, 1307–13, 527 ; *C.F.R.*, ii, 269, 271 ; *Cal. Inquis. P.M.* v, 263–4 ; vi, 105.   [5] *C.F.R.* iv, 23.
[6] *List of Sheriffs for England and Wales* (Public Record Office, *Lists and Indexes* ix, 1898), hereafter cited as *List of Sheriffs*.

there is evidence against this interpretation. John de Creke, whom he displaced and who succeeded him as sheriff, was connected with Badlesmere in 1313, and in 1311 had received the custody of the Bishop of Coventry's land.[1] There is, therefore, as much reason for regarding him as a Lancastrian as Swinford. Also the returns, as we have seen, are too indifferent to bear any strong political interpretation. Finally, another and simpler reason for Swinford's removal is the general investigation into the conduct of the sheriffs in office, which was undertaken late in 1311.[2]

With regard to the Essex representatives in 1311, William de Walton came of a family established on the borders of Essex and Cambridgeshire. They had land at Walton and Steeple Bumstead, and at Thaxted two manors held of the honour of Clare,[3] which suggests a tenurial connexion at least with the ordainers, of whom, of course, Gilbert of Gloucester was one. The fact that in 1311 William was appointed supervisor of array for Essex and Hertfordshire,[4] and that in 1313 he went abroad in the service of the earl of Pembroke,[5] may perhaps be taken as pointing in the same direction. Yet there is an indication that in 1322 he was on the losing side, for in that year some cattle which had belonged to him are described at the exchequer as 'rebel's beasts'.[6] John de Tany was keeper of the castle town of Chepstow from 1308 to 1310, and was acting in this capacity as deputy to the younger Despenser, who was, of course, at that time a Lancastrian.[7] He had a good deal of administrative work in Essex up to the time of his death in 1316.[8] Walton and Tany had been returned in 33 Edward I and Tany sat in 35 Edward I. They first appear in Edward II's parliament in the summer of 1311, and sat again in the autumn of that year, but never after that.

The two representatives of Hertfordshire in 1311 are rather dim figures. Neither of them had ever been returned before,

[1] *C.F.R.* II, 105, 169 ; *C.P.R.*, 1307–13, 567.
[2] *C.P.R.*, 1307–13, 327–9.
[3] Morant, *Essex* II, 348–9, 440, 540–1, 558.
[4] *Parliamentary Writs* (ed. Palgrave) II, i, 409.
[5] *C.P.R.*, 1307–13, 581.
[6] *C.C.R.*, 1323–6, 68. Some of the cattle belonged to the earl of Hereford
[7] *C.P.R.*, 1313–18, 68, 312.
[8] *Cal. Inquis. P.M.* VI, 455–6.

and Roos was not returned again except for the autumn meeting of 1311, which was a kind of prorogation, but Rochford sat in 1312 and 1315. Roos held land in Essex and in Hertfordshire of Humphry de Bohun which would give a tenurial connexion with one of the most vigorous leaders of the baronial opposition.[1] Rochford held land in Hertfordshire and Essex and Bedfordshire, but he held also in Yorkshire, and there his overlord was Henry de Percy, one of the party of the ordainers.[2]

Geoffrey de la Lee, the sheriff who was responsible for the returns we have been examining, was a tenant of Pembroke and Hereford, but I have not found any indication that he was a partisan.[3] Still, admitting that he was of the party of the ordainers, it might be argued that the returns for Essex and Hertfordshire in 1311 showed a political complexion and suggested that an effort had been made to secure members favourable to the reforming party. There is, I think, a simpler explanation. Hereford as earl of Essex was no doubt the dominating territorial influence in these counties, and this fact seems to have been recognized when in 1312 the barons charged him with the care of Essex and the eastern parts of England *ne aliquis tumultus fieret in populo*.[4] Further, if a definite attempt had been made to influence the returns it ought to have had some effect in Cambridgeshire and Huntingdonshire. But this, as we have seen, was far from being the case.

We may turn now to consider the members for Bedfordshire in 1311. Gerard de Braybrooke had lands in Bedfordshire and Buckinghamshire, acquired at Colneworth by marriage, and at Blounham, apparently by grant. The overlordship in the former case was in the family of Beauchamp, but there had been two partitions among co-heiresses, and the part of the original lordship represented by Ela de Beauchamp can have no political significance.[5] At Blounham, however, Gerard had one third of a knight's fee of John de Hastings, lord of Bergaveny, the

[1] Clutterbuck, *Hertfordshire* III, 169 ; *V.C.H.*, *Hertfordshire* II, 439 ; III, 319–20.

[2] *C.C.R.*, 1318–23, 636 ; 1323–7, 163 ; *C.P.R.*, 1313–17, 674 ; *Cal. Inquis. P.M.* V, 319 ; Tout, *op. cit.*, 95, 96 n.

[3] *V.C.H. Hertfordshire* III, 476–7, 482, 483.

[4] *Chron. Edw. I and II* (R.S.) I, 203–4.

[5] *C.C.R.*, 1323–7, 327 ; *Cal. Inquis. P.M.* VI, 390 ; *Parl. Writs* II, ii, 367, 372 ; *V.C.H. Bedfordshire* III, 12–14, 186.

claimant for the Scottish crown, who had served as seneschal of Gascony under Edward I and his son, and was related to both by marriage.[1] If we are to see any political character in this connexion it would obviously be royalist. Braybrooke had never been returned for Bedfordshire before, nor was he again, although he was still alive in 1324; but he had been returned for Buckinghamshire in 29 Edward I and 2 Edward II.[2]

Walter de Molesworth does not appear to have been returned before 1311, though he had been engaged in the ordinary judicial and administrative work of the county and was sheriff of Bedfordshire and Buckinghamshire in 1308-9.[3] He seems to have held in Buckinghamshire of the earl of Gloucester, and was employed as one of the keepers of the Clare lands after the earl's death.[4] He might, therefore, be considered a supporter of the ordainers, and his re-appointment as sheriff in 1312 would favour this view. But in that case the two members returned would have represented opposite sides in the great dispute, which would be extremely improbable if political considerations had influenced their choice. The sheriff who made the returns, William Merre, would seem to have been one of the ordinary administrative class—politically he seems to have been colourless, for he received local appointments from the king and ordainers alike.[5] He was never sheriff after 1311, nor can I find that he was ever returned to parliament.

Our results, therefore, as far as this parliament is concerned are negative. The knights seem to have been chosen from the group of country gentlemen accustomed to do the ordinary administrative work of the counties without regard to their previous parliamentary experience or their possible political or feudal connexions. This, indeed, is what we should have expected in view of the way in which the ordinances were carried through and the general attitude of the baronial party.

[1] *D.N.B.* xxv, 130 ; Tout, *Edward II*, 393-4.
[2] *Returns of Members* I, 13, 27-77 ; *Parl. Writs* I, i, 652, 654. He was infirm and sixty years of age at this time.
[3] *C.P.R.*, 1307-13, 270 ; Cole, *Records*, 188-9 ; *List of Sheriffs* ; *Parl. Writs* II, i, 409 ; ii, 75, 77.
[4] *C.C.R.*, 1313-18, 64, 129, 139 ; *C.F.R.*, II, 202 ; Lipscomb, *Buckinghamshire* III, 40.
[5] *C.P.R.*, 1307-13, 31, 92, 300, 327-9, 521, 536.

It remains to be seen whether this attitude in so far as it regarded the knights of the shires was modified at the moment of Lancaster's triumph in 1316.

In 1316 the sheriff of Cambridgeshire and Huntingdonshire was Ralf Giffard, of whom we can say little except that he was connected, though not very nearly, with men who at this time were holding with the middle party. He had land in a Devonshire hundred which was in the hands of Hugh de Courtenay, who became a member of the council when the middle party came into power in 1318.[1] In 1323 he was pardoned for his adherence to the rebels at the instance of one who had obtained his own pardon and restitution through the good offices of the younger Despenser, who, it will be remembered, had not joined the court party until 1318.[2]

Of the members returned for Cambridgeshire, one, Swinford, has already come before us in another capacity, when we saw some slight reason for connecting him with the Lancastrians.[3] He had sat for Huntingdonshire in 1302, 1305, and 1306–7, and he was to sit for that county again in 1318 and 1319. This raises a difficulty. If he was selected as a Lancastrian in 1316 he would scarcely have been returned in 1918 when Pembroke's party was in control of affairs. It is simpler to suppose that he was chosen without reference to his political views. This was the first and last time that he sat for Cambridgeshire, but he was a tenant-in-chief in the county and frequently employed in administrative work there.[4]

Baldwin de Stowe held Long Stowe in Cambridgeshire and lands in Huntingdonshire and Wiltshire as well.[5] He had been one of the conservators of the peace for the county and was often employed in raising troops there.[6] He had done more parliamentary work than was usual in these cases. He was returned three times in the later years of Edward I, in 1302, 1304 and 1306. He had been returned to Edward II's first

---

[1] *Feudal Aids* I, 380 ; Tout, *op. cit.*, 122 n. Courtenay was probably royalist in 1311 ; cf. Ramsay, *Genesis of Lancaster* I, 29.
[2] *C.P.R.*, 1321–4, 120, 236.   [3] Above, p. 118.
[4] *C.P.R.*, 1307–13, 527 ; *C. Inquis. P.M.* v, 263–4 ; *Feudal Aids* I, 152 ; *Parl. Writs* II, i, 168, 465.
[5] *Feudal Aids* I, 149, 157.   [6] *Parl. Writs* II, i, 465, 469 ; ii, 149.

parliament, but did not sit; in the spring and autumn of 1313, however, he attended at Westminster, and he sat again in the summer parliament of 1316. This was his last appearance. I can find no indication of any political connexion, but the inference from his attendance at parliament would be to associate him with the Lancastrians.

The members returned to parliament from Huntingdonshire in 1316 are dim figures indeed : of Andrew le Moigne I can find no trace, though William le Moigne, who may have been his brother, appears pretty frequently and seems to have been associated at one time with the elder Despenser.[1] But this point can scarcely count for much. Andrew sat again in the summer of 1321. Cantilupe is almost as obscure as le Moigne. His first and last appearance in parliament was in 1316. He was commissioned to raise troops in Huntingdonshire in this year.[2] He had land in Bedforshire, the overlordship of which was in the Beauchamp family, but in 1319 he was removed from the office of coroner of Huntingdonshire as being insufficiently qualified.[3] The result is again negative— the sheriff seems to have been associated with the middle party, one of the four members may be connected with the Lancastrians, but others were indifferent and two of them very obscure. In face of these facts it is surely impossible to suppose that the choice of these knights of the shire was made with any reference to the political situation of the moment.

We may turn now to Essex and Hertfordshire. The sheriff was Richard de Perers. The available facts illustrating the situation and career of this man throw so much light on the questions we are discussing that they deserve to be considered in some detail. They tend to show, to put the matter briefly at the outset, that Perers, who was a man of considerable local influence and importance, a strong partisan deeply involved in the political movement of his day, consistently treated the opportunity of attendance at parliament with contempt or at least indifference.

The family of Perers were established in the region of Cheshunt by the middle of the thirteenth century, and Richard's

---

[1] *C.P.R.*, 1307–13, 582.   [2] *C.F.R.*, ii, 297.
[3] *C.C.R.*, 1318–23, 72 ; *V.C.H.*, *Bedfordshire* ii, 251.

patrimony seems to have been Periers, a sub-manor of Cheshunt which was itself held of the honour of Richmond. In 1316 he acquired Knebworth from his mother-in-law, and, later, the manor of Cheshunt itself was committed to his keeping. There is evidence that he held land in other counties as well, Oxford-shire, Leicestershire, Cambridgeshire, Essex and Kent. A leaden seal bearing his name, and with some probability attri-buted to him, which was brought to light at Stevenage, would be further evidence of his substance and local importance.[1] From 1314 until the end of the reign he was pretty constantly engaged in administrative work in Hertfordshire and Essex. He was sheriff of the two counties from October 1314 until the end of November 1318, and again from November 1324 until September 1327. There is only one other case of the same man being reappointed sheriff of these counties in this reign, and he held office only for two terms of one year each.[2] In 1316 he was one of the knights appointed to perambulate the forests, in 1322 and in 1324 he was commissioned to array men-at-arms in Hertfordshire, and in 1325 he was inspector of levies in the same county. Between 1320 and 1326 he was four times com-missioned conservator of the peace in Hertfordshire.[3] It is a striking fact, however, that he seems never to have acted in any judicial capacity, nor even to have received those *ad hoc* commissions of oyer and terminer which were at once so frequent and so much disliked at this period. In common with many like him he was at least once accused of violence and turbulence.[4]

Politically his connexion seems to have been with the king's cousin, John of Brittany, earl of Richmond, known as one of the more royalist earls down to the closing years of the reign; no doubt the relation was at first tenurial, for Cheshunt was held of the honour of Richmond. But in 1322 Perers was going with the earl of Richmond to Scotland, and two years later he went abroad with him. On this occasion his letters of protection

[1] *C.C.R.*, 1318–23, 232, 236 ; *C.F.R.* III, 383 ; *C.Ch.R.*, III, 34, 37 ; *V.C.H.*, *Hertfordshire* III, 114, 451 ; *East Hertfordshire Arch. Soc. Trans.* III, 195–6.

[2] See *List of Sheriffs* ; on the changes of sheriffs at this time, cf. Tout, *op. cit.*, 201–2.

[3] *Parl. Writs* II, i, 167, 609, 662, 732 ; ii, 149, 168, 274, 282.

[4] *C.P.R.*, 1324–7, 136.

seem to have been issued at Richmond's direct request, an indication that Perers was something more than a mere ' follower's follower '.[1]

Richmond deserted his cousin and joined the queen in France in 1325,[2] and there are some curious indications that Perers followed his patron in his adherence to the party of revolution and was able to render them substantial service, and was duly rewarded. In 1325 Richard de Perers, described as ' knight of Essex ', was one of the mainpernors to the extent of £300 for his sister-in-law Ela, widow of the late James de Perers. This lady had been required to give security ' that she will not send or cause to be sent by herself or another any letter or token or by a messenger or otherwise within the realm or without, whereby scandal could arise to the king or his or any damage to the realm '. This undertaking with its reference to communications outside the realm points straight to the queen and Mortimer in France.[3] Nor would it be surprising to find that the widow of an Essex gentleman was furnishing them intelligence of their friends in England—we know that the gentry of Essex welcomed and supported the queen when she landed.[4] If Richard de Perers was able to cover this correspondence and thereby make its continuance possible, no doubt he had deserved well at the hands of the revolutionary party, and as sheriff of Essex and Hertfordshire, to say nothing of his position in the latter county, he was well able to render this service. To continue to do so effectively, of course, it was necessary that he should retain the confidence and favour of the king and of what was left of the court party. There is some evidence that he succeeded in doing so. In December 1325 he obtained leave to make an advantageous marriage.[5] In March 1326 he was among those commissioned to pursue

---

[1] *C.P.R.*, 1321–4, 189 ; 1324–7, 56.

[2] Ramsay, *op. cit.* I, 151.

[3] *C.F.R.* III, 295. The suggestion is corroborated by the fact that the lady's first husband, Griffin de la Pole, held land in the Welsh Marches ; cf. *ibid.* ii, 53, 54 ; *Rot. Parl.* i, 305–6, 355–6.

[4] Cf. Round, *V.C.H.*, Essex II, 213 ; Tout, *Political History*, 299.

[5] *C.P.R.* 1324–7, 200. The leave was conditional on the lady's willingness to enter into the arrangement, and the condition does not seem to have been fulfilled. She was a widow in 1325 and continued to describe herself as such until her death. See Clutterbuck, *Hertfordshire* II, 279–80, 288 ; III, 549–51.

and arrest the murderers of Sir Roger Bellers, one of the reforming courtiers who met his death in a private quarrel in January.[1] In the same month the manor of Cheshunt, of which his own patrimony was held, was committed to his custody for three years at the rate of £100 payable annually at the exchequer.[2] Then late in the year he received what we may perhaps regard as his reward from the revolutionary party. In December he was granted the custody of the manor of Ascote in Oxfordshire, forfeited by the elder Despenser, and it was worth noticing also, as an indication of the favour which he enjoyed under the new régime, that he was continued in his office of sheriff until the autumn after the king's deposition.[3]

We may now see how Perers treated the parliaments to which he was returned. In 1316, when he was sheriff of Essex and Hertfordshire, he returned himself for the latter county and attended the Lincoln parliament that saw the triumph of Lancaster. Two years later he again returned himself for Hertfordshire, to the parliament which after the treaty of Leake worked out the reforms of the moderate party. Perers's political connexion was, of course, with the group that had negotiated the treaty with Lancaster, for Richmond was one of them.[4] The parliament, it will be remembered, sat at York from Oct. 20th until Dec. 9th. Perers was in York on Sept. 22nd, on his way to Scotland with Hotham, bishop of Ely,[5] who, as is well known, bore an important part in the activities of the parliament,[6] and yet, as Perers obtained no writ *de expensis*, we must assume, failing evidence to the contrary, that he did not attend. Even supposing that he had gone to Scotland without his patron—which does not seem probable— neither he nor the chiefs of the party to which he belonged can have attached much importance to his presence at the meeting of the estates. In 1321 he was returned by another sheriff and attended the parliament held at Westminster in July and

---

[1] *C.P.R.*, 1324–7, 243 ; cf. Tout, *Edward II*, 201.

[2] *C.F.R.* III, 383. Cheshunt was held of the honour of Richmond, but the king had recently taken into his hand all the earl's English lands by reason of his 'contumacy and treasonable practices'. See the letter in Gale, *Registrum Honoris de Richmond*, 166–7.

[3] *C.F.R.* III, 427 ; *List of Sheriffs.*

[4] *Rot. Parl.* I, 453.

[5] *C.C.R.*, 1318–23, 15.

[6] Cole, *Records*, 3, 12.

August, in which the Despensers were exiled. The next spring he was returned to and attended at York the parliament which repealed the ordinances, but being returned again in the autumn of the same year he absented himself. In February 1324 he was returned to and attended the prorogued parliament held at Westminster, but in October of the same year he was returned and absented himself.[1] The inference from these facts seems irresistible : the political connexions of the particular knights chosen to represent a county and even perhaps their individual attendance were disregarded, or treated with indifference. Perers was clearly a strong partisan, and his services were employed and rewarded—but not his services in parliament.

The case of Benedict de Cokefield is in its way almost as instructive and interesting as that of Richard de Perers, because it gives some positive indications of what was wanted and expected of the country gentlemen who actually attended parliament. Benedict was a knight and tenant-in-chief, but his holding of the king was a small one,[2] and the names of the other lords from whom he held give no indication of a political connexion.[3] He was often employed on local administrative, and judicial work of one sort and another.[4] In 1316 he was returned for the first time and attended the parliament under our notice which sat at Lincoln in January and February.[5] The vexed question of the great Clare inheritance was considered at this meeting, and all the lands of the late earl were committed to the custody of three *probi homines*, of whom Benedict was one. The other two, another knight and a cleric, were not in attendance at the parliament.[6] He was commissioned to raise the troops provided by this parliament, and was

---

[1] *Parl. Writs* II, i, 242–3, 250, 258, 269, 301, 311, 314, 320.

[2] *C.C.R.*, 1313–18, 516 ; *C.Ch.R.* III, 41.

[3] *Cal. Inquis. P.M.* VI, 70 ; Morant, *Essex* I, 436, 453. The names of his overlords given by Morant are G. de Lay—possibly Geoffrey de la Lee, of whom something is said below, and cf. *V.C.H. Hertfordshire* III, 425, and R. de Burcher—possibly Robert de Bourchier, one of Cokefield's own class, whose father was a Justice of Common Pleas ; cf. *D.N.B.* VI, 11, 14 ; Tout, *Edward II*, 372.

[4] *C.P.R.*, 1313–17, 700 ; 1317–21, index *s.v.* ; 1321–4, 254, 309, 312, 384 ; *Parl. Writs* II, i, 168 ; ii, 103.

[5] *Parl. Writs* II. i, 158.

[6] *Rot. Parl.* I, 354 b ; *C.F.R.* II, 313 ; *Returns of Members* I, 50–1. The other knight was Richard de Rodney, whose name does not appear in the index to the *Returns*.

collector and assessor of a grant of a sixteenth made in the same year by a parliament at which he was not present.[1] At the direction of the parliament in which he sat certain knights were returned from the counties to attend upon the council and discuss the question of the forests, and certain of these again were subsequently appointed to carry out a perambulation in the course of the summer. Cokefield was returned for Essex and was one of those named to take part in the perambulation.[2] Now if we look for a political connexion in the case of Cokefield we might either suppose that as a feudal tenant in Essex he was of the party of Bohun, the dominant influence in that county, as we have seen, or in view of his selection as a custodian of the Clare lands that he had been an adherent of Gloucester. Bohun was, of course, a strong Lancastrian, and although Gloucester had been dead two years and had taken part with the ordainers in his lifetime, it is hard to believe that he would have been on Lancaster's side in 1316. But the facts of the present case offer a simpler explanation. Cokefield appears to have been a country gentleman accustomed to the routine of local administration, who came to parliament with other of his kind to hear new administrative arrangements discussed, possibly to assent to them and certainly to return home and help to execute them. There is no need, there is scarcely any room, to suppose that such men were concerned with questions of national politics.

Cokefield's colleague in the representation of Essex in 1316 was John de la Lee, a knight and tenant-in-chief who had served as coroner in Essex and sheriff of several counties.[3] If we are to discern a political connexion for him it will be Lancastrian. In 1314 we find him going abroad on the business of the earl and countess of Hereford, but as the favour of royal letters of protection was obtained for him through Archbishop Reynolds at the instance of the countess we can scarcely suppose him to have been a very strong partisan.[4] The fact that he was befriended by Badlesmere in 1318 may perhaps be

---

[1] *Parl. Writs* II. i, 465 and 168.
[2] *Ibid.* II. i, 161 ; *Report on the Dignity of a Peer* I. i, 276–7.
[3] *Parl. Writs* II, i. 589, 692 ; *C.P.R.*, 1313–17, 477 ; *C.C.R.*, 1318–23, 10 ; *C.F.R.* II, 352.
[4] *C.P.R.*, 1313–17, 113.

taken as a confirmation of this.[1] Still, any connexion with the Lancastrians ought, if we admit political motives, to have made him unacceptable to the sheriff who returned him. The same would be true of Geoffrey de la Lee, the fellow-member of Perers for Hertfordshire. We have seen that he held both of Pembroke and Hereford.[2] Perhaps, however, in view of the double connexion it would be safer to suppose him to be indifferent. Of Perers himself we have spoken at some length. Taking the facts of the Essex and Hertfordshire representation in this year together there can surely be no ground for supposing them to have been influenced by any political considerations.

We may pass now to the representation of Bedfordshire in 1316. John de la Haye had been sheriff since November 1314 and was to hold the office until the spring of 1318.[3] He seems to have come of an Essex family, though his land was in Hertfordshire, and he had been sheriff of the two counties in 1311.[4] His political associations, or at least his patrons, were royalist. In 1312 he obtained a grant of land in return for good services rendered to the king, and in 1311 he was one of those to whom the custody of the Templars' lands throughout England was committed.[5] His earliest patron, it is true, was Lord Latimer, a Lancastrian who was taken prisoner at Bannockburn,[6] but this was in 1309, and in 1312 Haye was commended to the king's favour by William de Melton.[7] Later he was protected by Roger de Waltham, who came into office in 1322, at the moment of the supreme triumph of the Despensers.[8] This connexion is worth noticing, as it helps to determine the social and political level of men of Haye's class. In the summer of 1322 Roger de Waltham obtained royal protection for a group of persons, presumably his retinue, who were accompanying him to Scotland; among these was John de Norwich, in whose service was John de la Haye.[9] He was therefore a

[1] *C.F.R.* II, 352.   [2] Above, p. 120.
[3] *List of Sheriffs*.
[4] *Ibid.*; Morant, *Essex* I, 85, 411 ; Clutterbuck, *Hertfordshire* I, 295 ; *V.C.H., Hertfordshire* II, 219, 222.
[5] *C.F.R.* II, 241 ; III, 116, 126 ; Cole, *Records*, 201 ; *C.P.R., 1307–13, 431–2.*
[6] *Ibid.*, 176 ; *ibid.*, 1317–20, 228 ; *D.N.B.* XXXII, 180.
[7] *C.P.R., 1307–20, 431–2* ; *D.N.B.*, XXXVII, 227 ; Tout, *Edward II,* 130.
[8] Tout, 160.   [9] *C.P.R., 1321–4,* 184, 186.

K

follower's follower in the train of a public official who was himself a man of little personal importance. Of the two members there is not a great deal to be said. Dakeney makes here his single appearance in parliament; he does not appear to have been returned for Bedfordshire or any other county before 1316, and he died in that year. He was holding in chief in Bedfordshire and Buckinghamshire, in the former county through his mother, who was a co-heiress of the Albinis.[1] He seems to have been a substantial country gentleman, but I can find no evidence that he had taken part in the administrative work of the county or had any political connexion. Loring, on the other hand, had attended four parliaments before 1316, and from 1315 onward was much occupied with administrative work.[2] He was himself a knight and came of a family that had been long established in Bedfordshire; the overlordship of their lands was in the barony of Bedford, at this time dissipated, so to say, among the co-heiresses of the Beauchamps.[3] It is impossible to see any trace of political influence in the return to a Lancastrian parliament of two substantial but obscure country gentlemen through the agency of a royalist sheriff.

In 1318, when Pembroke's party came into power, Ralf Giffard was still sheriff of Cambridgeshire and Huntingdonshire, and he, as we have seen, was probably connected with that party. The two members are shortly disposed of : we have found reason to suppose that Thomas de Burgh had patrons in both Lancastrian and royalist parties, and was probably politically indifferent.[4] Philip de Welle obtained no writ, and therefore presumably did not attend. He was not returned at any time before or after this. He was a knight and held land in Essex and in Cambridgeshire; he was holding of the king in respect to his wife's inheritance.[5] Turning to Huntingdonshire we meet with two names that are familiar to us : Swinford, we

---

[1] *C.C.R.*, 1313–18, 362 ; 1318–23, 185 ; *C.F.R.* ii, 76 ; *Cal. Inquis. P.M.* v, 134, 413 ; *V.C.H. Bedfordshire* ii, 321 ; Lipscomb, *Buckinghamshire* i, 133.

[2] *Parl. Writs* ii, i, 96, 99, 103, 115, 133, 140, 150, 465, 468, 470 ; *ibid.* ii, ii, 119, 125 ; *C.F.R.* iii, 316.

[3] *C.Ch.R.* iii, 287 ; *V.C.H. Bedfordshire* ii, 318 ; iii, 89, 345–6.

[4] Above, p. 117.

[5] *C.C.R.*, 1323–7, 390 ; *Parl. Writs* ii, i, 186, 445, 652 ; ii, 324.

saw ground for thinking, might have had some connexion with the Lancastrians, but it seemed more likely that he had no political bias, as he had sat in many parliaments of very different characters and appears to have been chiefly concerned with local business; Waldesheve, as we have seen, might have been either a royalist or an adherent of Pembroke. But there is scarcely room for supposing any political motive to have influenced the choice of four such men as these.[1]

The representation of Essex and Hertfordshire at the parliament of 1318 is very curious. Four persons were returned, one of them the sheriff himself, and one, John de Lisle, a man who was never returned before or after.[2] Geoffrey de la Lee, on the other hand, had been sheriff in 1311, and had sat for Hertfordshire before. He seems to have been no partisan, though his connexion with Pembroke and Hereford would have made him a very suitable choice at this time if political considerations had had weight.[3] John de Enfield was a knight, a tenant-in-chief, and a country gentleman of some importance in Essex and Middlesex.[4] His activities were of a wider range than those of most of the men we have to consider. He had commanded a group of the king's ships on an expedition to Scotland and taken part in the defence of the coast.[5] He was more than once employed as escort to foreigners who came to England, and acted in this capacity to the unlucky cardinals who were captured by Gilbert de Middleton, the Durham robber-baron.[6] He was charged with special police duties, as when he was directed to search for and arrest people passing themselves off as members of the king's household or those resorting to illegal tournaments.[7] At home he was employed on the more familiar and prosaic duties of levying troops, inspecting weights and measures, ditches and highways, and performing the many offices that fell to a conservator of the

---

[1] Above p. 118.

[2] He held of the king in Essex, apparently by grand serjeanty, the service being a chamberlainship of the exchequer ; cf. Morant, *Essex* ii, 588–9 ; Round, *The King's Serjeants*, 121 n.

[3] Above, p. 120.

[4] *Parl. Writs* II, i, 142, 150, 223, 229, 405, 451 ; ii, 171 ; *C.C.R.*, 1318–23, 482; *C.F.R.* II, 101 ; *Cal. Inquis. P.M.* v, 132; vi, 467; Morant, *Essex* I, 143.

[5] *C.R.P.*, 1307–13, 563.

[6] *Ibid.*, 578; 1371–21, 166, 201; Ramsay, *Genesis of Lancaster* I, 88, 104.

[7] *C.P.R.*, 1313–17, 534 ; 1317–21, 258 ; 1321–4, 300, 333.

peace.[1] His first appearance in parliament was in January 1315,[2] but there appears to be no trace of a political connexion of any sort.

But the striking fact about this case is that not one of the persons returned troubled himself to attend a parliament where the entire administrative system of the kingdom was to be remodelled. And this is even more striking in the case of Perers, who, as we have seen, was something of a royalist partisan and was actually in the north at the time the parliament was held. In view of his absence when the writs came down it is likely that the whole business was in the hands of his deputy, who may very well have suggested the names and secured the returns of people who were in the habit of doing work of that sort, including the sheriff himself who had been returned before. In this case another explanation would have to be found for the return of John de Lisle. At any rate the established facts, taken together with the earlier details we have been examining, go to support very strongly the view that the business of the knights of the shire in parliament was at this time quite unpolitical; though by this it is not intended to deny that their collective presence could and did have a political significance on certain occasions. That would be possible without attributing to them any important share in the proceedings of the assembly or taking into great account their individual political views—supposing any considerable number of them to have held views strongly or even at all.

The sheriff of Bedfordshire in 1318 was Roger de Tiringham, who was an old hand in the administrative and parliamentary work of the two counties. He had sat for Buckinghamshire as early as 1295, been conservator of the peace, assessor and collector of grants, and commissioner to hear complaints under the articles of Stamford.[3] He held land in Bedfordshire of the barony of Bedford, this, as we have seen, divided among co-heiresses and representing no political connexion.[4] The Buckinghamshire tenure is more illuminating; for there he

---

[1] *Parl. Writs* II, ii, 171 ; *C.P.R.*, 1324–7, 10 ; *C.F.R.* III, 314–15.
[2] *Parl. Writs* II, i, 142, 150.
[3] *Returns of Members* I, 4 ; *Parl. Writs* II, ii, 9, 12 ; i, 15 ; ii, 24 ; *C.P.R.*, 1307–13, 24, 31, 53, 249.
[4] *Feudal Aids* I, 16, 35 ; *V.C.H. Bedfordshire* III, 212.

held of John de Somery, who was appointed to the council in the parliament under consideration and fought for the king in 1322.[1] The political or feudal sympathies of the two members can also be pretty clearly discerned. Fitz-Richard held of Sir Robert Dakeney in Bedfordshire; he succeeded to his father's lands in 1318 and in that year obtained some valuable privileges from the king. At Boroughbridge he fought on the royalist side.[2] Pakenham[3] was one of the most important of the Bedfordshire country gentlemen. He and his father before him were pretty closely associated with Pembroke. They held of him in Suffolk and both had served him personally.[4] It is, of course, possible that these two men were chosen without reference to their political views or connexions or those of the sheriff who managed the election. But supposing the opposite to be the case, it would really help to establish our point by bringing out the vagueness and lack of purpose in the other elections we have been examining as contrasted with this one.

We come now to the parliament of 1321 which marked the break-up of the middle party and registered in the banishment of the Despensers the triumph of the Marchers and Lancaster. We may begin again with Cambridgeshire and Huntingdonshire. The sheriff was Almeric la Zusche, who was appointed in November 1320, and held office continuously for seven years. There is good reason for regarding him as a close adherent of Pembroke. He had gone abroad with the earl in 1313, and from 1315 until 1318 he was out of the country on Pembroke's business.[5] Pembroke's interests were, as we know, divided, and he had withdrawn from the county for good reasons unconnected with politics. We should expect, therefore, on this as well as on other grounds, to find the choice of members uninfluenced by political considerations. The

---

[1] *Feudal Aids* I, 82–3 ; *Cal. Inquis. P.M.* VI, 257; Lipscomb, *Buckinghamshire* IV, 277 ; Tout, *Edward II*, 130.

[2] *V.C.H. Bedfordshire* II, 321, 329–30, 346 ; *Parl. Writs* II, ii, 196 ff.

[3] The name has generally been written Pabenham, but Mr. W. H. Stevenson has corrected this ; see *C.C.R.* 1307–13, 508.

[4] *Cal. Inquis. P.M.* VI, 317, 332, 335, 339 ; *C.C.R.*, 1323–7, 267 ; *C.P.R.* 1307–13, 105 ; *C.F.R.* III, 113. The Pakenham holdings in Bedfordshire were of the barony of Bedford ; cf. *V.C.H. Bedfordshire* III, 771.

[5] *C.P.R.*, 1307–13, 581 ; 1313–17, 282, 672 ; 1317–21, 45, 104, 133, 217.

evidence at our disposal also points to this conclusion. John de Creke had been three times sheriff of the two counties and frequently charged with the work of local administration from the very beginning of the reign.[1] In 1311 he was acting as agent for Badlesmere in Bristol, and this is the only suggestion of any relation with the leaders of national politics.[2] He had sat once before in the autumn parliament of 1320. William Loveday is an obscure figure. This is his only appearance in parliament, and he seems not even to have been returned at any other time. He was a tenant-in-chief, but probably not on a large scale, for he was twice removed from the office of coroner as being insufficiently qualified.[3] This seems to have been his only venture in local administration in this county. The two members for Huntingdonshire have already come before us. William le Moigne appears frequently in the administration of the county from 1313 until the end of the reign,[4] and sat in parliament in 1315, 1321, 1324, 1325, and 1327.[5] In 1313 he went abroad on the king's service with the elder Despenser.[6] Of his brother we can say nothing. It can scarcely be said that the choice of these four was of a political character.

The case of Essex and Hertfordshire in this year is a conspicuous example of political indifference among the country gentlemen. The sheriff was John de Dover, a tenant-in-chief in Essex in a small way. He had been sheriff and conservator of the peace in 1319, and was a commissioner *de stratis et viis* in this year, but beyond these details I can find nothing about him.[7] No returns were made from Essex, and as no writs *de expensis* are enrolled the county must have been unrepresented. Hertfordshire was represented by Richard de Perers and Geoffrey de la Lee, the one, as we have seen, a royalist if he was anything, and the other seemingly indifferent, but both, of course, old hands at administrative and parliamentary work.

We turn now to Bedfordshire, where the sheriff was a figure somewhat out of the ordinary. His name, Ingelram Berenger,

[1] *List of Sheriffs* ; *Parl. Writs* II, i. 117, 164, 211 ; ii, 33, 103, 119.
[2] *C.P.R.*, 1307–13, 567 ; *C.F.R.* II, 169.
[3] *C.C.R.*, 1307–13, 109 ; 1313–18, 400 ; 1313–21, 160–1, 170 ; 1321–7, 452.
[4] *Parl. Writs* II, i, 177, 574, 598, 690, 732–3 ; ii, 73, 119, 288.
[5] *Ibid.* II, i, 140, 150, 238, 243, 300, 314, 336, 346, 356, 365.
[6] *C.P.R.*, 1307–13, 582.
[7] *Parl. Writs* II, i, 202 ; ii, 139, 171 ; Morant, *Essex* I, 72.

suggests a foreign origin, and his English lands were scattered over various counties, but chiefly in the west.[1] He held of Pembroke in Hampshire and Berkshire,[2] but the elder Despenser seems to have been his chief patron. He went abroad with him in 1309 and 1313, he acted as his attorney in 1319, and was one of the persons appointed to take his lands and goods into the king's hands in 1322.[3] Later in the same year he was granted certain privileges ' on the information of Robert de Baldock ', a further indication of his partisanship.[4] Under such influence we shall not be surprised to find that both members returned this year have royalist connexions. The case of Fitz-Richard we have already discussed.[5] John de Morteyn had sat in 1309 and 1313, and from 1316 onward becomes very active in local administration.[6] In July 1322 he had special protection to go to Scotland ' by the testimony of Roger de Waltham ', who came into office at the wardrobe when the Despensers returned to power.[7] Having regard to the sheriff this case may be taken as exceptional. But even so, when we consider the very small share taken by the commons in the proceedings of parliament it is hard to believe that much could have been expected from the return of members hostile to the dominating baronial influence. The case is chiefly interesting as suggesting the extent to which the sheriff was able to influence the election.

We come now to the parliament of 1322 which registered for the first time the constitutional importance of the commons. It will be of great consequence to ascertain whether the choice of members in our group of counties was in any way determined or influenced by the business that was to come before the parliament. The evidence from Cambridgeshire and Huntingdonshire seems to answer decisively in the negative : not one of the four members returned took the trouble to attend.

---

[1] *Cal. Inquis. P.M.* v, 226, 257, 391 ; vi, 126, 328 ; *C.P.R.*, 1307-13, 255-6, 511 ; 1313-17, 130.

[2] *Cal. Inquis. P.M.* vi, 328.

[3] *C.P.R.*, 1307-13, 191-3, 582 ; 1317-21, 262 ; 1321-4, 87.

[4] *Ibid.*, 1321-4, 88.

[5] Above, p. 133.

[6] *Parl. Writs* ii, i, 26, 35, 82, 92, 243, 279, 566, 607, 609 ; ii, 103, 125, 149, 231-2.

[7] Tout, *Edward II*, 160. Compare above, p. 129, on the connexion between Roger de Waltham and John de la Have.

This might perhaps be explained on the ground that they and the sheriff who managed the election sympathized with the defeated Lancastrians. But though the sheriff, Almeric la Zusche, had held office since 1320 and helped to return members to the parliament that banished the Despensers, we have seen good reason for regarding him as a close adherent of Pembroke, whose co-operation rendered possible the royalist victory of 1322. But what can be said of the men returned ? How account for their abstention on any ground except indifference ? If they were Lancastrians the reasons which moved them to seek or accept election should have carried them to parliament to do what they could for their cause. A like reasoning would apply if they were royalists, though, of course, if it could be shown that they were strong Lancastrians it might be argued that they sought election and then deliberately absented themselves in order to weaken *pro tanto* whatever support the government might hope to get from the presence of the knights of the shire. But it does not seem possible to show that they were Lancastrian; nor is it probable, if they had been, that they would have resorted to the sort of political service that has been suggested. John de Cambridge had sat in the autumn parliament in 1320, but from 1310 onward he was constantly occupied with the administration and particularly the judicial administration of the county. He was a judge before 1324, and eventually became a justice of common pleas.[1] There seems to be no trace of any political connexion or association with political leaders. The fact that in 1308 he was nominated attorney for Alice, countess of Oxford, widow of the fifth earl, can scarcely have had any bearing on the politics of Edward II's day.[2] John de Limbury did not sit, but he was returned and attended at the autumn parliament in this year.[3] From 1322 onward he was much concerned with the business of raising troops in the county, but I can find no other record of him.[4]

Turning to the members returned for Huntingdonshire we have the veteran John de Swinford, who we saw might just

---

[1] *Parl. Writs* II, i, 221, 229, 316 ; ii, 33, 79, 119, 188, 231 ; Foss, *Judges* III, 415 ; *D.B.N.* VIII, 447.
[2] *C.P.R.*, 1307–13, 38.
[3] *Parl. Writs* II, i, 248, 268, 278.
[4] *Ibid.*, 574, 609, 615, 628, 735, 739.

have been a Lancastrian, but was probably indifferent. Simon de Drayton had never sat before, but some facts about him are available which make it doubtful whether he can ever have been a very loyal partisan, though he was pretty clearly royalist at this time. In 1313 he received his pardon as an adherent of Lancaster in the troubles that culminated in Gaveston's death.[1] In 1317 he was granted certain privileges at the request of the queen.[2] In 1322 his bearings were entered on the Borough-bridge roll as one of those who fought for the king, and the next year he was sent abroad on the king's business on the recommendation of Robert de Baldock.[3] Finally, he was returned to and attended the parliament in which the king was deposed.[4] Such were the gentlemen of Cambridgeshire and Huntingdonshire who remained at home while the York parliament was undoing the work of the ordainers and formulating an important if obscure constitutional principle which closely touched their own order. We can scarcely doubt that they understood pretty clearly the degree to which the issue would be affected by their presence or absence.

The sheriff of Essex and Hertfordshire in 1322 was Nicholas de Engaine, a cadet of a family which may be called baronial since its head was commonly summoned in person at this time. They held of the earl marshal, the king's half-brother, which would imply a royalist connexion at this time. Nicholas himself had married a sister of John de Fauconberge, who was a Lancastrian.[5] In these circumstances we shall scarcely expect to find him a strong partisan on either side. Of the Essex members Thomas Gobion was a tenant of Hereford's and a strong Lancastrian who had come over to the court party in 1321 and had to be specially exempted from arrest in the next year.[6] He was clearly a partisan, and therefore the fact that

---

[1] *Parl. Writs* II, ii, 68.

[2] *C.P.R.*, 1317–21, 27.

[3] *Parl. Writs* II, ii, 197 ; *C.C.R.*, 1318–23, 715–16, 721 ; *C.P.R.*, 1321–4, 492.

[4] *Parl. Writs* II, i, 356, 365.

[5] *Cal. Inquis. P.M.* VI, 266 ; Morant, *Essex* II, 121, 217 ; Clutterbuck, *Hertfordshire* III, 177–8 ; Dugdale *Baronage* I, 446 ; II, 4; Ramsay, *Genesis of Lancaster*, I, 116.

[6] Morant, *Essex* I, 231, 234, 248 ; II, 96, 361 ; *C.P.R.*, 1317–21, 393; *C.F.R.* III, 192 ; *Parl. Writs* II, ii, 166 ; *C.C.R.*, 1317–23, 434 ; *C.P.R.*, 1321–4, 187.

this was his first appearance in parliament might be considered
significant. This view would be confirmed by what we know
about the other Essex member, Simon de Kinardesley. He
was now first returned to parliament, and I can find no information about him earlier than 1321, though after that he seems to
have been freely employed in local administrative work.[1] In
1322 he had special protection to go to Scotland with the earl of
Arundel, obtained on the earl's recommendation.[2] Now
Arundel had been a member of the middle party and an associate
of Badlesmere and came over to the court-party after the
incident at Leeds castle in the autumn of 1321.[3] In July 1322
Simon made himself answerable for the good behaviour
of an adherent of Lancaster's who was thereby released from
prison.[4] As we have seen, the two members for Hertfordshire
were strongly royalist at this time. They had both sat before
and were much concerned with local business, and their return
might be regarded as almost automatic if it were not for the
return of the Essex members, who were new men and certainly
appear to have been brought forward for a political purpose,
though the exact nature of that purpose may be open to doubt.

The sheriff of Bedfordshire and Buckinghamshire in the
spring of 1322 was Philip de Aylesbury. He held in Buckinghamshire both of the king and of the earl of Pembroke.[5] He
was sheriff in 1318–19 and again in 1325–7, and was returned for
Buckinghamshire in 1321 and 1323.[6] In 1323 he was selected
for some local judicial work by Robert de Baldock, and towards
the end of the reign seems to have stuck to the king's party.[7]
Sheriff and knight of the shire when Pembroke's party was in
power, and tenant of the earl, he may well have been associated
with the party that was supporting the king in 1322. Of the
two members returned, Pakenham we know to have been an
adherent of Pembroke. The same may be said of John Morris.
He had been a Lancastrian in the early part of the reign and
was pardoned for his share in the disturbances of 1312.[8] But in

[1] *C.C.R.*, 1318–23, 488 ; *Parl. Writs* II, i, 250, 258, 579, 581, 626.
[2] *C.P.R.*, 1321–4, 187.
[3] Cf. Tout, *Edward II*, 147.
[4] *Parl. Writs* II, ii, 212.
[5] *Feudal Aids* I, 104, 110 ; *Cal. Inquis. P.M.* VI, 328.
[6] *List of Sheriffs* ; *Returns of Members* I, 62, 69.
[7] *C.P.R.*, 1321–4, 318–19 ; 1324–7, 343–4.   [8] *Ibid.*, 1313–17, 25.

1322 he was going to Scotland with the earl of Pembroke, and from that year he begins to be employed in local administration.[1] In 1324 he was going abroad with Pembroke and had his protection by the testimony of the earl, and the next year he was abroad again with the widowed countess.[2] It must be admitted that these men were probably put forward because of their connexion with the party that was now in power. But as in the case of Hertfordshire and Essex we must make some reserve as to the part they were expected to play in parliament.

We may now formulate the results of our inquiry for purposes of comparison. It will be convenient to do this in summary form, distinguishing first the cases where some sort of political motive would appear admissible, secondly those of apparent indifference, and thirdly those of undeniable neglect. The first of these are not found in Cambridgeshire and Huntingdonshire, but in Hertfordshire and Essex in 1311 and 1322, and in Bedfordshire in 1318, 1321, and 1322. The second class is found in Cambridgeshire and Huntingdonshire in 1311, 1326, 1318 and 1321; in Hertfordshire and Essex in 1316; and in Bedfordshire in 1311 and 1316. The third appears in Cambridgeshire and Huntingdonshire in 1322, in Hertfordshire and Essex in 1318 and 1321, in Bedfordshire not at all.

The first point that emerges is the complete indifference of Cambridgeshire and Huntingdonshire, which should probably be explained on feudal rather than political grounds. The partition of the Honour of Huntingdon into three parts, one of them in the king's hands by forfeiture since 1306 and the others held by Richmond and Hastings respectively,[3] may well have meant that there was no dominating territorial influence in these counties. Without going into the question of feudal relations in the other counties it still seems safe to say that the existence of great political landlords like Pembroke and Hereford, while it may not have exercised any continuous or consistent influence, prevented the indifference that seems to

[1] *Ibid.,* 1321–4, 186; *Parl. Writs* ii, i, 574, 682, 684; ii, 250, 256, 274, 282.
[2] *C.P.R.,* 1321–4, 427 ; 1324–7, 200. There is some indication that he was in Pembroke's service as early as 1315 ; *ibid.,* 1313–17, 330, 506.
[3] On this see Miss Moore, *The Lands of the Scottish Kings in England,* 11–12.

have prevailed in Cambridgeshire and Huntingdonshire. The next point that strikes one is the question why if there were a true political motive at work it should have acted so capriciously ; why, for example, in Hertfordshire and Essex the parliament of 1316 should have been treated indifferently, and those of 1318 and 1321 positively neglected, if care had been taken to secure what were considered proper returns in 1311 and 1322. Several similar questions occur to any who take the trouble to consider the table we have printed.[1]

One conclusion seems clear. As far as these five counties are concerned, there is no consistent attempt to secure the return of members favourable to the particular group or party that happened to dominate any given parliament. On the other hand, there are certain cases that run contrary to this and seem to indicate a desire on the part of the great lords to secure the presence of their dependants among the commons at an important meeting of the parliament. This apparent contradiction may be resolved by examining very briefly the share of the commons in the proceedings of a parliamentary session. The examination must be brief, partly for want of material and partly because much of what can be said has already been said. If it should appear that the commons were wanted to register and ratify what was done by a great meeting of the king's council, then, while their collective presence would be of great importance, their individual view or the fact that some counties were not represented would be of little consequence. If this view be adopted it would still be necessary to explain why the magnates sometimes found it convenient to have their dependants returned. In other words, though we should be prepared to admit the presence of a political motive in some cases, we should attribute to the phrase a meaning different to that which it currently bears.

Some rough notion of the share of the commons in parliamentary business may be gained from an examination of the rolls of parliament. The incomplete and unsatisfactory nature of these documents has often been pointed out,[2] but they are all

---

[1] Below, pp. 146–52.
[2] Cf. Maitland, *Memoranda de Parliamento* (R. S.), Introd. ; Tout, *Edward II*, 90, 184–5.

we have and we must make the best of them. A considerable number of petitions are recorded as brought forward by the commons, or community of the land. The phrase varies a good deal, and in respect to one class of petitions needs careful scrutiny. Many of these petitions refer to the needs or interests of a single county. Thus the community (*comuneaute*) of Devonshire asks that their ex-sheriff, whose conduct in office is being investigated, may be attached in Somerset as he has nothing in Devonshire.[1] The form shows some variation, *les poures gentz de Devenschire, la gent del conte de Berk, les gentz de Cornewaille*,[2] but the meaning is determined by the contents of the petitions which refer to some local grievance that needs to be set right. These are most often complaints against abuses of their powers by the judges, sheriffs, coroners, and other officers; there are also requests for keeping roads and bridges in repair and complaints of the abuse of tolls, the privileges of the stannaries, or the inconvenient situation of a county gaol.[3]

There is another group of petitions which refer to matters of general rather than local interest. These are complaints of corrupt influence in the administration of justice, conspirators who corrupt assizes and inquests,[4] the release on bail of persons indicted of felony,[5] and the multiplication of special or *ad hoc* commissions of oyer and terminer which were used as instruments of oppression by great lords,[6] and the encroachments of the ecclesiastical courts upon secular jurisdiction.[7] Again, there are requests for the restraint of abuse and oppression on the part of sheriffs and other administrative officers. These, of course, are well known : the articles of Stamford, practically repeating the *articuli super cartas* in 1309;[8] the statute of Lincoln in 1315;[9] the *articuli cleri* of 1316,[10] and the request in 1318 for the removal of the existing sheriffs north of the Trent, and the substitution of persons who had never held the office before and were qualified by sufficient holdings in the counties which

[1] *Rot. Parl.* I, 289 ; cf. 291 (Lincoln), 293 (Suffolk).
[2] *Ibid.* I, 297, 300, 308.
[3] *Ibid.* I, 325, 293, 330, 314, 333, 324, 297, 312, 308, 300, 373.
[4] *Ibid.* I, 288, 289.   [5] *Ibid.* I, 372, 391.
[6] *Ibid.* I, 290.   [7] *Ibid.* I, 375.
[8] *Ibid.* I, 443–5.   [9] *Ibid.* I, 343.
[10] This, of course, is based on the Lincoln petition. It is printed in *Statutes of the Realm* I, 171, and *Letters from Northern Registers* (R.S.), 253 ff

they were to administer.[1] Then we get requests for the improvements of matters touching the economic life of the community. Tolls for crossing the Humber and passing from Dover to Witsand were represented as excessive.[2] The roads and bridges leading to London should be kept in repair.[3] Lead should not be exported nor pay weighing-toll (*tronagium*), and there should be a proper control in the use of the coket seal in London.[4] The system of re-farming bailiwicks at a rate higher than that assigned by the exchequer should be forbidden and a special grievance with regard to certain accounts in the wardrobe remedied.[5] Complaints are made of the inveterate disorder and violence of the times, ' felonies, trespasses, unlawful associations, and conspiracies leading to breaches of the peace in all counties '.[6] We must notice finally a request that petitions for the redress of grievances be no longer adjourned before the king or the chancellor in such wise that nothing comes of them. The share of the commons here is not clearly expressed, the form is *prient vos liges gentz*, but the rubric describes the petition as one of those granted ' de assensu prelatorum comitum baronum et aliorum in dicto parliamento tunc existentium '.[7] This was in November (octave of St. Martin), and as the commons remained until 5 December, as appears from the writs *de expensi*s, it may be supposed that they joined in this petition. Now it will be observed that with this exception all the petitions related to the general administration of the kingdom in such matters as justice, police, civil administration, finance, maintenance of communication, and so on. None of them imply or require the presence of the knights of the shire except as a matter of convenience; they might equally well have been drawn up in the counties and submitted by one of the prelates or magnates. With the single exception we have noted no questions touching policy, the form of government, or even the business of parlia-

---

[1] Cole, *Documents*, 6–7.
[2] *Ibid.*, 44 ; *Rot. Parl.* I, 291, 319.
[3] *Rot. Parl.* I, 308.   [4] Cole, *Documents*, 16, 36.
[5] *Ibid.*, 7, 42, 44.
[6] *Rot. Parl.* I, 371.
[7] *Ibid.* I, 430, but the date and provenance of the rubric are, of course, uncertain ; see Maitland, *Memoranda de Parliamento*, x–xii ; Cooper, *Public Records* II, 28–9.

ment are involved in the petitions which the commons present
or co-operate in presenting.

We may now ask how far the petitions we have been examining were the work of the commons themselves. According to
the form of words in which these documents describe themselves they may be arranged in three classes. The first class
will comprise those in which the share of the commons is
implied rather than expressed in such phrases as *la communaute
d'Engleterre*,[1] *communitas regni*,[2] *vos liges gentz*,[3] *communaute du
poeple de son roialme*.[4] The second class contains joint petitions
and those made by the magnates on the complaint of the
commons or people : the formula leaves this last point open to
some doubt; *les prelatz, contes et barons et tute la communalte du
roiame fesoint a notre seigneur le roi les requestes desoutz escrites*,[5]
or *prie la barnage od le commun poeple*,[6] are examples of the
form of what we have called joint petitions. Then we hear that
the king *par demonstrance* of the prelates, earls, barons, and
other magnates, *somons a cel parlement, et par grevouses pleintes
del pople*, understanding the evil to be remedied, has made a
statute *de l'assent des prelatz, contes et barons et les grantz avanditz
en son dit parlement*.[7] Neither of these cases, of course, necessarily
implies that the complaints of the people were made through or
by the knights and burgesses in parliament; but that seems the
most natural explanation, and it is hard to see how else they
could have been brought forward. It should be noted that the
words of the second case formally exclude the commons from
any share in the act of legislation. The formula of the third
class leaves us in no doubt as to the source of the petition, which
was met not by statute but by an order issued by the king in
council. It is as follows : ' in hoc parliamento inter ceteras
petitiones domino regi porrectas, quedam petitio per milites,
cives, et burgenses, pro comitatibus, civitatibus, et burgis regni
sui ibidem existentes liberata fuit, per quam suggesserunt,'[8]
&c. This is summarized in the marginal note as ' querela tocius
communitatis regni ', a phrase which throws some light on a

---

[1] *Rot. Parl.* I, 289, 299.
[2] *Ibid.*, 372, 375 ; Cole, *Documents*, 27, 36.
[3] *Rot. Parl.* I, 430.   [4] *Ibid.* I, 290.
[5] Cole, *Documents*, 6.   [6] *Ibid.*, 7.
[7] *Rot. Parl.* I, 343.   [8] *Ibid.* I, 371.

point we have just been noticing.[1] We must be careful, however, not to press these forms of words too far, nor to attach too much importance to them. It has been pointed out that the articles of Stamford are known to have been obtained by the baronial opposition, though they are described as submitted to the king by the community of the kingdom. The commons were present at the meeting in 1309 where these words were used, but they were not at Stamford where the concessions were actually made. In like manner there were no commons in the parliament in February 1310, in which the ordainers were appointed, although they were present the next autumn when the ordinances were confirmed. It is true that in the letters patent authorizing the election of the ordainers the permission is granted to the prelates, earls, barons, and commons of the kingdom, and that the king in confirming the ordinances describes them as made ' solunc la fourme de noz lettres '. We have good reason for saying that the parliament was still in session and the commons present when the ordinances were confirmed.[2]

Even from this brief review[3] it seems pretty clear that for whatever purpose the commons were wanted in parliament it was not to co-operate actively in any business of a political or constitutional nature. On the other hand, the famous words of the statute of York make it plain that for some purposes or at some times their presence was regarded as very important. I have advanced elsewhere a theory that the principle formulated in the statute of York was that no constitutional change was valid to which the commons had not given their consent.[4] It may be suggested now that their presence and tacit consent

---

[1] But see above, p. 142, n. 7 on the marginalia.

[2] See Tout, *Edward II*, 84, 87, 90–1 ; *Rot. Parl.* I, 281, 286, 443–5.

[3] A considerable volume of literature has subsequently been published on the subject of parliamentary petitions. In addition to the works of H. L. Gray, H. G. Richardson and G. O. Sayles, cited above, pp. 9, n. 1, and 14, n. 4, reference should be made to G. L. Haskins, ' Three early petitions of the Commonalty ', *Speculum* XII (1937), 314–318, and ' The petitions of representatives in the parliaments of Edward I ', *E.H.R.*, LIII (1938), 1–20; A. R. Myers, ' Parliamentary petitions in the fifteenth century ', *E.H.R.* LII (1937), 385–404, 590–613; D. Rayner, ' The forms and machinery of the " Commune Petition " in the fourteenth century ', *E.H.R.* LVI (1941), 198–233, 549–570.

[4] See *E.H.R.* XXVIII (1913), 118 ff., and below, pp. 153ff., Cf. Tout, *op. cit.*, 151 ; Stubbs, *Select Charters*, ed. Davis, p. 56 n.

would be considered highly desirable when important political or constitutional measures were taken, and this on two grounds, both of them practical rather than theoretical. In the first place, the presence of the commons would ratify the new measure in the sense of committing them and those whom they represented to approval of it whether their consent were necessary or not. This, of course, would be a step towards acknowledging the necessity of obtaining consent, though it would be far from conceding the principle. In the second place, the presence of the commons when new measures were discussed would necessarily help to form a favourable public opinion. For the men who heard the debates, even though they might have taken no part in them, would carry home with them abundant material for the discussion and explanation of the new measures. It is upon this ground that I venture to explain the care which the magnates seem occasionally to have shown in securing the return of members favourable to their projects—or at least to themselves. As a hostile public opinion could also be formed in the same way, the rule would explain the case (of which we have seen an instance) where care appears to have been taken to secure the return of members unfavourable to the schemes of the leaders who chanced to be in power.

The chief business of the representatives of the commons was, of course, to give their consent to extraordinary taxation and to facilitate the administration of the kingdom by furnishing the central government with information and acting as a check on the sheriffs and other officers who were charged with local administration. But these points have been so carefully worked out elsewhere that they need only be mentioned here.[1]

[1] Cf. the works of Riess and Pasquet, referred to above, pp. 6, 9.

APPENDIX

List of Knights returned during the reign of Edward II for Essex, Hertfordshire, Cambridgeshire, Huntingdonshire and Bedfordshire

ESSEX

Persons returned	. . . .	22
Received writs *de expensis*	. . . .	16

Returned but received no writs

John de Rivers Peter de Suthchertch	} October 1307	
John de Lisle *John de Enfield[1]	} October 1318	
John de Enfield Philip de Virly	} May 1219	
*John de Lyston	November 1322	
*John de Lyston	February 1324	
*Benedict de Cokefield	October 1324	
John de Broxbourne John Dyn	} January 1327	

Total	. .	9
Deduct those who received writs at other times	. .	3
		—
		6
Received writs but not returned		0
Parliaments for which no returns are found, March 1312, April 1314, July 1321		3
Parliaments at which no knights sat, October 1307, October 1318, May 1319, January 1327 . . .		4
Parliaments in which one knight only sat, November 1322, February 1324, October 1324		3
Persons who attended three parliaments[2] . . .		3

Nicholas de Barrington †William de Haningfield
†‡John de Enfield

Persons who attended two parliaments		5

†‡William de la Beche John de Tany
Robert de Hagham William de Walton
†John de Linton

Persons who attended one parliament		8

†‡Ralf Bigod †Thomas Gobion
†‡Benedict de Cokefield †Simon de Kinardesley
‡Jollanus de Durham †‡John de la Lee
†Walter Fitz Humphry †‡Richard de Rivers

---

[1] Those whose names are marked with an asterisk received writs *de expensis* at other times.

[2] Names marked † are knights; ‡ tenants-in-chief.

Members who were both knights and tenants-in-chief . . 6
Members who were knights only 5
Members who were tenants-in-chief only 1
Members who were neither 4
Knights of the shire holding any office or commission in the
    county 12
    Judicial commissions of any sort 6
    Offices such as sheriff, coroner, *conservator pacis*, &c. . 8
    Various administrative commissions 9
Persons appearing in all three lists 4

Benedict de Cokefield	John de Linton
Thomas Gobion	William de Walton

Persons appearing in two lists 3

John de Enfield	William de Haningfield
Robert de Hagham	

Persons appearing in one list 5

Nicholas de Barrington	Jollanus de Durham
Simon de Kinardesley	John de la Lee
John de Tany	

Knights of the shire charged with crimes or serious offences . 6

Nicholas de Barrington	Walter Fitz Humphry
Ralf Bigod	John de la Lee
John de Enfield	Richard de Rivers

HERTFORDSHIRE

Knights returned 11
Received writs *de expensis* 9
Returned but received no writs

*John de Aynel Gerard de Braybroke	} October 1307
Robert Baard *John de Somery of Bigrave	} July 1313
Robert Baard John de Somery of Bigrave	} September 1313
*Richard de Perers *Geoffrey de la Lee	} October 1318
*Richard de Perers *John de la Haye	} November 1322
*Richard de Perers *Richard de Montchensy	} October 1324

                       Total . . 8
Deduct those who received writs at other times . . 6
                                      — 2
Received writs but not returned 0

Parliaments for which no returns are found for Hertfordshire, March 1308, March 1312, November 1325 . . 3
Parliaments at which no knights sat for Hertfordshire, October 1307, July 1313, September 1313, October 1318, November, 1322, October 1324 6
Persons who attended seven parliaments 1
    †Geoffrey de la Lee
Persons who attended four parliaments 2
    †Richard de Perers
    †Walram de Rochford
Persons who attended three parliaments 2
    ‡John de la Haye
    †Richard de Montchensy
Persons who attended two parliaments 1
    †Robert de Roos
Persons who attended one parliament 3
    †John de Aynel   John de Sumery of Bigrave
    Ralf Montchensy
Members who were both knights and tenants-in-chief . . 0
Members who were knights only 6
Members who were tenants-in-chief only 2
Members who were neither 1
Knights of the shire holding any office or commission in the county 9
    Judicial commissions of any sort 4
    Offices such as sheriff, coroner, etc. 7
    Various administrative commissions 7
Persons appearing in all three lists 4
    John de Aynel   Geoffrey de la Lee
    John de la Haye   Ralf Montchensy
Persons appearing in two lists 2
    Richard de Perers   Robert de Roos
Persons appearing in one list 2
    Walram de Rochford   Richard Montchensy
Knights of the shire charged with crimes or serious offences . 2
    John de la Haye   Richard de Perers

CAMBRIDGESHIRE

Persons returned 21
Received writs *de expensis* 20
Returned but received no writs 4
    *Baldwin de Stowe   }October 1307
    Robert de Hastings
    Philip de Welle   October 1318
    Roger de Wateville   May 1319

*John de Limbury
*John de Cambridge } May 1322

John de la Haye
*John de Cambridge } October 1324

Received writs but not returned 2
    Thomas Clement
    John Bundre } October 1324

Parliaments to which no returns are found for Cambridgeshire,
    March 1307, February 1312, July 1313, April 1314,
    September 1314, May 1316, January 1318 . . 7

Parliaments at which no knights sat for Cambridgeshire, October
    1307, March 1308 2

Persons who attended four parliaments 2
    †Matthew de Bassingburn   Baldwin de Stowe

Persons who attended three parliaments 3
    †‡Thomas de Burgh   †John de Creke
    John de Cambridge

Persons who attended two parliaments 2
    ‡Baldwin de Colne   †‡John de Swinford

Persons who attended one parliament 13
    ‡Geoffrey de Bardeley   William de la Haye
    William de Boxworth   †Robert de Lacy
    John de Brescy   John de Limbury
    Simon de Bourn   John de Lindhurst
    John Bundre   ‡William Loveday
    Thomas Clement   Luke de Over
                  †‡Thomas de Scales

Members who were both knights and tenants-in-chief . . 3
Members who were knights only 3
Members who were tenants-in-chief only 3
Members who were neither 11
Knights of the shire holding any office or commission in the
    county 13
    Judicial commissions of any sort 5
    Offices such as sheriff, coroner, etc. 11
    Various administrative commissions 10
Persons appearing in all three lists 4
    Geoffrey de Bardeley   John de Creke
    Simon de Bourn   Thomas de Scales
Persons appearing in two lists 5
    Matthew de Bassingburn   Baldwin de Stowe
    John de Cambridge   John de Swinford
    Baldwin de Colne
Persons appearing in one list 4
    William de la Haye   William Loveday
    John de Limbury   Luke de Over

Knights of the shire charged with crime or serious offences . 5
    Matthew de Bassingburn   John de Cambridge
    Thomas de Burgh   John de Creke
                           William de la Haye

HUNTINGDONSHIRE

Persons returned 22
Received writs *de expensis* 18
Returned but received no writ

    *Richard de Stratford   }
    *John de Swinford   } October 1307

    Robert de Waterville   }
    *Richard de Stratford   } July 1312

    *Simon de Drayton   }
    *John de Swinford   } May 1322

    Roger de Chartres   }
    William Launcelyn   } October 1324

                        Total . 6
Less those who received writs at other times . . . 3
                                —
                                   3
Received writs but not returned 0
Parliaments for which no returns are found for Huntingdon-
    shire, March 1308, July 1313, April 1314 . . . 3
Parliaments at which no knights sat for Huntingdonshire,
    October 1307, July 1312, May 1322, October 1324 . 4
Persons who attended five parliaments 2
    †William le Moigne   John de Waldesheve
Persons who attended two parliaments 4
    Andrew le Moigne   Richard de Stratford
    John Morris   John de Swinford
Persons who attended one parliament 12
    William de Abbotsley   ‡William de Papworth
    Robert de Baieux   Roger de Cantilupe
    ‡Peter de Croft   ‡Simon de Drayton
    William de Ganet   †Peter de Saltmarsh
    Walter de la Huse   Henry de Tilly
    Hugo de Molesworth   William de Wassingley
Members who were both knights and tenants-in-chief . . 0
Members who were knights only 2
Members who were tenants-in-chief only 3
Members who were neither 12
Knights of the shire holding any office or commission in the
    county 8
    Judicial commissions of any sort 4
    Offices such as sheriff or coroner 5
    Various administrative commissions 8

Names of those appearing in all three lists 4
    Robert de Baieux   William de Papworth
    William le Moigne   John de Waldesheve
Names of those in two lists 1
    Henry de Tilly
Names of those in one list 3
    Roger de Cantilupe   Simon de Drayton
                         William de Wassingley
Knights of the shire charged with crimes or serious offences . 7
    Robert de Baieux   Richard de Stratford
    Simon de Drayton   Henry de Tilly
    William le Moigne   John de Waldesheve
    Peter de Saltmarsh

BEDFORDSHIRE

Persons returned 19
Received writs *de expensis* 20
Returned but received no writs
    John de Pakenham   } October 1307
    John Spigurnel

    *Gerard de Braybrook   } July 1312
    *Robert de Hotot   } May 1319

    John de Pakenham   October 1320

    *Robert de Hotot   } November 1322
    John de Sudbury

Received writs but not returned 0
Parliaments for which no returns are found for Bedfordshire,
    May 1316 1
Parliaments at which no knights sat for Bedfordshire, October
    1307, July 1316, November 1322 3
Parliaments at which one knight only sat for Bedfordshire, July
    1312, May 1919, October 1320 3
Persons who attended five parliaments 1
    †Peter de Loring
Persons who attended four parliaments 1
    †John de Morteyn
Persons who attended three parliaments 1
    ‡Walter de Molesworth
Persons who attended two parliaments 5
    †Hugh Bossard   †John Morris
    †Ralf Fitz-Richard   †‡John de Pakenham, jun.
    †David de Flitwick
Persons who attended one parliament 12
    ‡Roger de Bray   Henry de la Leghe
    †Gerard de Braybrooke   Roger Peyvre

‡Robert Dakeney   †Richard le Rous
Ralf de Goldington   †Nigel de Salford
†Walter de Holewell   †Thomas Spigurnel
†Robert de Hotot   ‡John de Wolaston

Members who were both knights and tenants-in-chief . . 1
Members who were knights only 12
Members who were tenants-in-chief only 4
Members who were neither 3
Knights of the shire holding any office or commission in the
    county 11
    Judicial commissions of any sort 4
    Offices such as sheriff, coroner, etc. 7
    Various administrative commissions 9
Persons appearing in all three lists 4
    Peter de Loring   John de Morteyn
    Walter de Molesworth   John de Pakenham, jun.
Persons appearing in two lists 1
    John Morris
Persons appearing in one list 6
    Robert Dakeney   Robert de Hotot
    David de Flitwick   Richard le Rous
    Walter de Holewell   Nigel de Salford
Knights of the shire charged with crimes or serious offences . 10
    Hugh Bossard   Walter de Molesworth
    Gerard de Braybrooke   John Morris
    Ralf Fitz Richard   John de Pakenham, jun.
    Robert de Hotot   Richard le Rous
    Henry de la Leghe   Thomas Spigurnel

V

THE INTERPRETATION OF THE STATUTE OF YORK [1]

I

AFTER the Lancastrian defeat at Boroughbridge (16 March 1322) and the execution of Earl Thomas three days later, Edward II was free as he had not been for twelve years to govern his kingdom without let or hindrance. The opposition, bent on administrative reform, political influence, and the realization of a theory of government radically different from that held by the king and his friends, was broken and scattered. The leaders of the middle party that coerced the king in 1318 had already rallied to his support. Parliament was summoned to meet at York on 2 May 1322. The writs were dated two days before the battle, and we can scarcely place any later the instructions which the king issued to his council in preparation for the meeting of parliament.[2] These show clearly that his first care was to free himself from the trammels of the hated ordinances which, since he had more than once consented to or confirmed them, had hampered his freedom of action and given the opposition a hold over him for the greater part of his reign.

The first item on the agenda was ' the statute on the repeal of the ordinances ', and the second was to provide for the perpetuation of such good points as they contained. Members of the council were invited to consider how the law could best be amended and, after discussion among themselves, to draft a scheme to provide remedies, by statute, if necessary, or if not by other suitable means, which would enable parliament to dispose of the matter as expeditiously as possible. The brief statute drafted by the council and enacted by the king in parliament closes with the following words :

> les choses qe serount a establir pur lestat de nostre seigneur le roi et de ses heirs, et pur lestat du roialme et du poeple, soient

---

[1] Reprinted from *The English Historical Review* LVI (1941), 22–49, 411–446.

[2] The text is printed in Davies, J. C., *The Baronial Opposition to Edward II*, 582–3, and Baldwin, J. F., *The King's Council*, 472.

tretes, accordees, establies en parlemenz par nostre seigneur le
roi et par lassent des prelatz, countes, et barouns, et la communalte du roialme, auxint come ad este acustume cea enarere.[1]

This text appears to have escaped the attention of the con-
troversialist historians and antiquarians of the seventeenth
century,[2] and to have made its appearance in English constitutional history in the first Report of the Lords' Committee on
the Dignity of a Peer (1819). The last clause of the statute is
there taken as declaring ' the constitutional law of the realm '
by confirming and securing what had previously been a matter
of custom and practice. The committee add that it ' extended
to all legislative purposes ', and that after its passage ' every
legislative act not accomplished in accordance with its term was
void '.[3] Hallam, Gneist, and Stubbs accepted this constitutional doctrine, though all three of them taking the text in its
historical setting saw difficulties and treated (it can scarcely be
said overcame) them characteristically.[4] Fortified by such
verba magistrorum the doctrine was accepted, repeated, or
developed by scholars who had occasion to refer to it until 1913.
In that year I drew attention to some of the serious difficulties
that stood in the way of a doctrine so comprehensive, and
proposed an interpretation of the statute which would restrict
the legislation contemplated in the disputed clause to matters
involving the royal prerogative.[5] This proposal, if it did not obtain general acceptance, served at least to concentrate attention
upon a difficult text which, to all appearances, had some light
to throw upon the history of parliament. The controversy so

[1] *Statutes of the Realm* (Rec. Com.) i, 189. The text, broken up into
numbered paragraphs for convenience of reference, is printed at the
end of this study ; the rubrics and arrangement do not quite correspond
to those in *Statutes* i, 189, but the text of course is the same. Two drafts of
this text, the first of which appears to be a preliminary version and the
second is unfinished, were recently brought to light by Mr. G. L. Haskins,
cf. *E.H.R.* lii, 74 ff.

[2] It is cited (under the wrong regnal year, 17 instead of 15, Ed. II) in
support of the general legislative power of parliament and its freedom of
debate in the second and greatly enlarged edition of Petyt's *Jus Parliamentorum*, revised and published after the author's death, London, 1739,
12, 13, 246.

[3] *Report on the Dignity of a Peer* i, 282–3.

[4] Hallam, *Middle Ages* iii, 232 ff. (ed. 1856) ; Gneist, *English Constitutional History* ii, 20–1 ; cf. his *Self Government* (ed. 1871), 28 ; Stubbs,
C.H. ii, §§ 225, 228.

[5] ' The Commons and the Statute of York,' *E.H.R.*, xxviii, 118 ff.

aroused still continues, and the interpretation of the statute
has moved in two directions, determined very naturally by the
respective writers' views of the history of parliament in general
and of its legislative function in particular. It has been widely
but not unanimously agreed that the statute cannot be regarded
as requiring the co-operation of a parliament of estates[1] in all
legislation, and it has begun to be understood that the success
of any positive interpretation of the statute will need an
exegesis of the text as a whole and in its parts and not of the
final clause alone. Within these limitations there has been a
tendency to regard the statute as associating parliament with
all ordinary legislation, while forbidding it to concern itself with
the prerogative. This view was formulated by Mr. J. C. Davies.[2]
He argued that it was intended to secure at once the personal
interests of ' the king and the wider rights of the people .'

The late Miss Clarke rated the constitutional position of
parliament after 1322 very high, higher perhaps than even
Stubbs did.[3] She considered that the statute ' was designed to

---

[1] I use this convenient phrase to denote a parliament to which representatives of the counties and some boroughs were summoned, and without
prejudice to the several controversial questions implied. I take it that a
parliament will be distinguished from a *tractatus* and a great council by the
form of the writ and the general or national character of the business
proposed. See Wilkinson, B., *Studies in the Constitutional History of the
Thirteenth and Fourteenth Centuries* (Manchester U.P., 1937), 25–54.

[2] *Op. cit.*, 512–18. The views of Mr. Davies are considered and criticized
in some detail in the course of the present study, but one of his arguments
which cannot conveniently be dealt with elsewhere must be noticed here.
It is to the effect that if the statute had been intended to authorize the
parliament of estates to deal with the prerogative, then when the king and
parliament in 1324 assigned the Templars' lands (previously forfeited by
feudal law) to the Hospital in deference to the papal order and by the
mutual assent of the ' earls, barons and noblemen ' and his regal authority,
he would have been obliged to associate the commons. This, however,
although they were available, he did not do. If the facts are examined it
will be found that the prerogative was not involved. In view of the pope's
action a conflict of law had arisen and the king had in an administrative
way surrendered his own forfeitures. The magnates had not done so, and
although they stood to gain materially by the king's action, morally they
had no standing ground, and the council, judges, and magnates in parliament with the king's authority liquidated the disreputable affair. *Statutes*,
i, 194 ; *Foedera* (Rec. Com.) II, i, 167–9, 236–7 ; Perkins, C., ' The Wealth
of the English Templars ', *American Hist. Review* xv, 525 ; Leys, A. M.,
' The Forfeiture of the Lands of the Templars in England ', *Oxford Essays
presented to H. E. Salter*, 155 ff. ; Tout, T. F., *Chapters in English Administrative History* ii, 338.

[3] Clarke, M. V., *Medieval Representation and Consent*, 138–9, 154–72,
176, 192–3, 196.

protect the monarchy in perpetuity from all limits imposed by subjects ' and to commit to a parliament of estates the discussion and settlement of matters of ' general legislation and administration '. She had convinced herself that the mysterious tract known as the *Modus Tenendi Parliamentum* could safely be treated as contemporary and semi-official evidence as to the nature and organization of parliament and the political views underlying moderate public opinion in 1322. Accordingly she derived from this *ignis fatuus* of parliamentary history the ideal which inspired the Statute of York. It is ' the joint and harmonious co-operation of all the orders of the realm, secured by insisting on common responsibility and applying the principle of representation or delegation within parliament itself '. This the statute did ' by guaranteeing the rights of the commons in parliament ', that is, it extended the familiar political device of committees of estates by including the lesser orders of the realm. Miss Clarke vouches the proceedings by which the crown passed in January 1327,[1] and illustrates the growing interest in representative parliaments by the increasing regularity of their summons after 1311, and by ' those pseudo- or counter-parliaments which met in the north between 1315 and 1321 '. She considers, therefore, that ' Edward II had come to understand that his own parliaments were less dangerous than baronial assemblies ', and although this may do more than justice to the king's statesmanship it is, I think, true of those who framed the Statute of York.

Miss Clarke's book raises some important points that will be discussed later; at present, therefore, we may turn to consider the opinions of certain scholars who have followed a very different direction. They consider that the statute is, from the point of view of constitutional history, the record of an act by which the court party in the moment of their victory undertook to secure the crown in the position it had had in the time of Edward I and to protect it effectually from such attacks as had been made upon it by the Ordainers. To do this the parliament of estates was explicitly forbidden to concern itself

---

[1] Miss Clarke's views on this matter are criticized below, pp. 195–8, 312, 336 ; and see also my notice of Miss Clarke's book in *The Cambridge Review* lviii, 237–8, where this point is further discussed.

in any way with the prerogative and to confine itself to voting
supplies, the only function by which it could render itself
serviceable to the king. This general view appears to have
originated with Professor McIlwain when he came to reconsider
Mr. Davies's interpretation of the statute which he had previously accepted without reserve.[1] Writing from the point of
view of political theory, he is concerned chiefly with the part
of the statute which he regards as a reaffirmation of the doctrine
of an inalienable prerogative deriving chiefly from the Mise of
Amiens and the Dictum de Kenilworth. Evidently if the
' global ' inalienability of the prerogative was generally accepted
and affirmed in the Statute of York the interpretation advanced
in this study would fall to the ground. This point is discussed
below. At this stage it suffices to notice Professor McIlwain's
exegesis of the text of the statute which may be stated in his
own words : ' The sentence[2] just quoted seems to make three
separate prescriptions : first, that no subjects of the king may
enact any provisions whatsoever which in any manner even
touch the king's *power* or *authority;* second, that they cannot
enact any valid ones *against* the king's estate (presumably such
as the provisions of the late ordinances touching the king's
wardrobe); third, that fiscal matters concerning the king and
the realm alike must be enacted by the king with the assent of
what later would be called the lords and commons in parliament. The first of these provisions has been obscured by the
supposed greater importance of the last, but it is with this first
provision alone that we are concerned here.'[3] Evidently this
is a statement made for clearness sake about the whole of a
matter with part of which only Professor McIlwain is directly

---

[1] See *Cambridge Medieval History* vii, 678–81, where Professor McIlwain
writes : ' The well-known statute of York provides that enactments
touching the estate of the whole realm . . . must have their (i.e. the
commons') participation ', and vouches in a footnote, ' the investigation
of Mr. Conway Davies ' ; and on a subsequent page, ' In 1322 it was established that common law as well as common grants needed the assent of
" all ", and a statute which enacted a common law required the assent of
" all " including the representatives as well as the lords '. This must have
been written some time before the publication in 1932 of the volume of
which it forms part. Professor McIlwain's later interpretation, referred to
above, will be found in *The Growth of Political Thought in the West* (London,
1932), 374–82.

[2] I.e. §§ 4 and 5 ; see below, p. 230.

[3] *Op. cit.*, 378.

concerned. It cannot, therefore, be considered arbitrary, nor, since he has not given his reasons, can it profitably be argued. Here it is enough to observe that no exegesis of the statute can be satisfactory that does not take account of all the special terms that it employs, e.g. ' royal power ', ' estate of the crown ', etc., and that the collective interpretation of those occurring in the last clause as ' fiscal matters concerning the king and the crown ' remains an *obiter dictum* until it is established by argument. It is, therefore, no disrespect to Professor McIlwain to refer to the second and third of the provisions which he finds in the statute as suggestions towards its interpretation. Certainly they have been treated as such by a scholar whose work now demands attention.

Mr. Haskins has devoted the whole of his little book[1] to the study of the statute in the light of Professor McIlwain's conjecture that the subject of clause v must be taken as ' fiscal matters concerning the king and the realm alike '. He regards the statute as ' an autocratic statement of royal power ' intended ' to preserve the customary rights of the king and people ' by enacting in permanent form what was already customary. ' This was the essence of medieval statutes and nothing new was intended by this one '.[2] To establish this position he marshals two groups of arguments. The first is directed to show the improbability, both antecedently and on the evidence, that the commons should have secured an important constitutional right by a grant from the crown in 1322. The second, by a critical examination of the text of the statute, seeks to show that so far from giving rights to the commons in parliament it expressly forbade that body as a whole to concern itself with the power and authority of the king and the crown. His exegesis is the first to reckon with the nature and dimensions of the problem, and in this respect sets a standard below which subsequent investigators will fall at their peril. He realizes that ' statutes at this time were drafted by men expert in the law who produced documents that were coherent and not disjointed ', and he accepts the resulting obligation to interpret

[1] Haskins, G. L., *The Statute of York and the Interest of the Commons* (Cambridge, Mass., 1935).
[2] *Op. cit.*, 111.

the statute from within its four corners;[1] and he accepts and develops Professor McIlwain's ' financial ' interpretation of the statute. All this is considered in some detail below.[2]

Dr. Birdsall[3] and Dr. Wilkinson[4] share with Professor McIlwain and Mr. Haskins the view that the statute forbade parliament to deal legislatively with the prerogative. The first is most interested in the inalienability of the prerogative, and the second in the place of the commons in parliament and the steps by which it had been attained up to the accession of Edward III. Their respective views are referred to and discussed below. Mr. Jolliffe[5] devotes an interesting passage to the statute, suggesting that it was intended to lay some responsibility on the commons for the determination (more perhaps for the consequences) of policy, ' *les busoignes le roi*, Scotland, Gascony, or the peace of the realm '. He emphasizes the growing recognition of the political consequence of the commons and its particular importance to the crown.

As to the view that the statute authorized the king in parliament to deal legislatively with the prerogative, it was accepted by Professor Tout in the first edition of his *Edward II* and retains its place in the second.[6] Professor Plucknett appears to be in general agreement with it,[7] and Professor Pollard allows that ' there is at least plausibility in the contention '.[8]

---

[1] I have reproduced here some sentences from a review of Mr. Haskins's book which I contributed to the *Law Quarterly Review* liii (1937), 159.

[2] M. Petit-Dutaillis has devoted a long review to Mr. Haskins's book ; see *Revue Historique* clxxix, 399–401. As he accepts Mr. Haskins's most important contentions it will be found that I have stated my reasons for dissenting from him in the course of the present study. His personal suggestions as to the genesis of the statute which he regards as ' a manifestation of the traditional ideas of the bureaucracy ', seem to me to rest on a failure to distinguish between the bureaucrat and the statesman and on his notion of the political role of the bureaucracy. There is a passage in an earlier book of M. Petit-Dutaillis which helps to explain his ideas on these subjects ; see *La Monarchie Féodale en France et en Angleterre*, Paris, 1933, 398–9.

[3] Birdsall, P., ' *Non Obstante*, a Study of the Dispensing Power of English Kings,' *Essays in Honor of Charles Howard McIlwain* (Harvard U.P. 1936), 37–77.

[4] Wilkinson, *Studies*, cap. ii.

[5] Jolliffe, J. E. A., *The Constitutional History of Medieval England* (London, 1937), 370–6.

[6] Tout, T. F., *The Place of Edward II in English History*, 2nd ed., 136 ; cf. Preface, xi.

[7] Plucknett, T. F. T., *A Concise History of the Common Law*, 2nd ed., 31.

[8] Pollard, A. F., *The Evolution of Parliament*, 2nd ed., 241–2.

Finally, we must consider the views of those writers who are unwilling to allow to the statute any constitutional importance. Mr. Richardson and Dr. Sayles write as follows : ' We should not ourselves attach any constitutional importance to the presence of the commons in the parliament of Edward II but we perceive . . . considerable political importance'; and they add that any constitutional interpretation of the Statute of York ' rests upon the assumption that *la communalte du roiaume* must mean the knights and burgesses assembled in parliament, and for that assumption we can find no warrant '. Further, they observe that the commons were summoned to give political support in the time of Edward I and Edward II, although their presence or absence did not affect either the functions or the legal authority of parliament. Under Edward II, they add, ' there is a greater admixture of politics—and perhaps therefore the more frequent presence of the commons '.[1] The question of the sense in which the statute uses the phrase *la communalte du roiaume* is discussed below, and need not detain us now. Whether the statute possessed constitutional importance or not will depend on the definition of the adjective, which is here taken to mean that which affects either the function or the legal authority of the parliament. Obviously the whole question which underlies such a concise definition, offered for purposes of lucidity in its context, cannot be discussed here. I must, however, draw attention to a difficulty which appears to me to have been overlooked. The remarkable advance in the functions and legal authority of parliament in the fourteenth century was not in any great measure the direct result of legislation, the effect of which in most cases was to create a precedent or corroborate an existing one. Where it did act directly, as in the attempt of parliament to control the king's ministers or bind its own successors, it failed or, as in the case of the statutes of April 1340, the commons had to fight for nearly a generation to secure in practice what the king had already granted in terms.[2] If we were to be strictly bound by the distinction between constitutional and political history made by Mr.

---

[1] Richardson, H. G., and Sayles, G., ' Early Records of the English Parliaments ', *B.I.H.R.*, vi, 76.
[2] Wilkinson, *Studies*, cap. iii.

Richardson and Dr. Sayles we might find that in practice the difference was lost sight of, and that such a text as we are discussing, cast out by their analytical fork, *tandem usque recurrit*. In this case the real question is whether the history of parliament in the fourteenth century confirms in any way the assumption that one makes as to the purpose of those who framed the statute. It is attempted here to show that such a correspondence exists, and that in the course of the fourteenth century matters touching the prerogative at issue between the crown and the opposition were, formally at any rate, discussed in parliament, and that this was the purpose of the statute. The effort to interpret it and to observe its consequences, whether direct or indirect, appears to me to be constitutional history.

Finally, there is the view of Professor Hilda Johnstone, who considers that ' the statute combines the assertion of liberty of royal action with the offer of orderly government ', and adds with regard to the interpretations of the disputed clause, that it is ' just possible that . . . [they are] a little too subtle and that all the Despensers meant to do was to follow up the clause in which they asserted the royal right with another in which they gave assurance that the crown intended to act in consultation with parliament '.[1] These views appear to rest on a scepticism which I think is unwarranted by the statute itself and what is known of its origin. It was drafted, for a clear purpose, by the king's council with more than seven weeks at their disposal for deliberation and the experimental drafting, of which there is evidence. The exegesis of this text is a distracting and arduous business, but it seems to me that the probability that it was intended to convey a definite meaning in language that is self-consistent (as the middle ages understood verbal self-consistency) is strong enough to require the attempt to be made. Hypotheses, indeed, must not be multiplied without necessity, but to avoid them where there is a possibility of their success is a counsel of despair. Professor Johnstone may have convinced herself that no exegesis is likely to be successful in this

---

[1] *Camb. Med. Hist.* vii, 424–5. M. Georges Lefébvre goes even further. He dismisses the statute as an ' emergency measure directed against the most troublesome barons and . . . powerless to modify in the slightest degree the situation of the commons in parliament ' ; *Studies Supplementary to Stubbs' Constitutional History* iii, 501–2.

M

case, but I think that she does scant justice to fourteenth-century statesmen and jurists by suggesting that the interpretations she was criticizing were too subtle.[1]

The controversy, if it has not solved the problem, has at any rate situated it in the main line of the political movement under Edward II and in relation to the institutional history of parliament, the development of its legislative function, and the political theory of the day. If after more than a quarter of a century I take the field again in the interest of my previous article it is because I still think that the solution of the problem lies in the direction in which it pointed. What follows is an attempt, made with deference and gratitude to my critics, to advance in that direction.

II

We come now to the problem of the exegesis of the statute itself. The principle upon which Mr. Haskins conducts his inquiry is one which will obtain general assent : we may give it in his own words :

> Statutes at this time were drafted by men expert in the law who produced documents which were coherent, not disjointed. The interpretation of sections should therefore proceed with reference to the whole. . . . A legal document must be interpreted from within its four corners. . . . The final proposition of the Statute of York can only be understood with reference to the previous one forbidding the enactment of provisions against the estate of the crown.[2]

With this sound rule and the author's extension of it to include the relation of the parts to one another we are in complete agreement.

---

[1] For the reasons given above I cannot attach much importance to G. B. Adams' dogmatic judgement of the statute as of no constitutional importance ; *Constitutional History of England* (London, 1920), 199.

[2] *Statute of York*, 98. We know that the business of framing a statute was confided to the council before Boroughbridge and that the form in which we have it is not the first draft. See above, pp. 153–4. In the council the work of drafting would be done by men of whom, or whose like, it had been said that they were ' trained in English and Roman (or at least canon) law, men who, when they gave a judgment or advised upon a decision, appreciated its legal or administrative consequences ' ; Richardson and Sayles, ' The King's Ministers in Parliament ', *E.H.R.* xlvi (1931), 550.

might appear to do, on a question of form cannot be conclusive
(which I should not admit), I may cite another difficulty deriving this time unmistakably from the substance of Mr. Haskins's
system. He holds that under the statute not even in parliament
may public prerogative be discussed or made the subject of any
enactment. Those who framed the statute enlisted the aid
of parliament to release the crown from the restrictions which
it had been forced to accept at the hands of the ordainers, and
they took pains to specify the elements which composed and
should in future compose it.[1] Mr. Haskins agrees that the
statute was intended to protect the prerogative, yet, on his
interpretation, it would preclude the king in parliament from
taking action designed to benefit it, as by way of restoration,
addition, peaceful settlement of disputes or otherwise except by
consenting to taxation. Is it likely that those who in framing
the statute made use of parliament should deliberately have
deprived the crown of recourse to the same support in future ?
Is it not rather probable that some other explanation of the
sense in which the statute uses the terms ' royal power ',
' estate of the king ', ' estate of the crown ', ' estate of the realm
and people ' respectively, must be sought for ?

Mr. Haskins's evidence does not appear to take him beyond
the fact that the word ' estate ' could bear the sense he requires
in more or less contemporary usage.[2] We must, therefore, consider his theory in relation to the statute itself and what we
know of its background. We observe first that in interpreting
section ii he appears to identify the ' royal power ' and ' seignurie reale ' with ' the estate of the crown ', which he describes
as blemished by the adverse legislation of the ordainers against
the household. The word ' blemished ' was applied by the
statute to the royal *seignurie*, which it clearly distinguishes

[1] For the business, that is to say, allotted to it in clause v. The question
whether the statute contemplated a parliament including the commons, as
to which Mr. Haskins and I do not differ, is discussed below.

[2] Mr. Haskins refers to the use of the word ' estate ' in the well-known
process of the exile of the Despensers in July 1321, *Statutes* i, 182 ff., particularly in the gravamina grouped under the third section of the preamble.
These, in his opinion, all refer to acts by which the pecuniary interests of
the crown were injured. I am prepared to argue that every one of them
refers rather to some form of accroachment on the royal power. I understand from Mr. Haskins, however, that without committing himself to that
view, he is not disposed to press his original argument.

from ' the estate of the crown '.[1] There is in the ordinances enough by which the royal power was injured quite apart from the king's revenue and property. Moreover, the distinction between ' the royal power ' and ' the estate of the crown ' (in Mr. Haskins's sense), which he throws overboard here, is vital to his system, because without it the absolute withdrawal of public prerogative from parliamentary discussion and action could not be maintained. Further, it will be noticed that the statute distinguishes between ' the estate of the king ' and ' the estate of the crown '. Either this distinction means something or else it is (to use Mr. Haskins's phrase) ' mere plethora of legal verbiage '. He appears to take that view, for he writes, ' by adverse legislation against the household the king's revenues had been diminished and the estate of the crown had been accordingly blemished '. ' Estate ' here, if we have understood Mr. Haskins, means revenue or property, and estate of the king or the crown means the same thing. Now we know that one purpose of the ordainers had been to enable the king ' to live of his own ', and that they sought to accomplish this by directing that the customs duties and all other issues of the kingdom should be paid to the exchequer and not to the wardrobe.[2] This clearly was the adverse legislation against the household to which Mr. Haskins refers. If these directions had been effectively carried out they must have resulted in a very considerable increase in the amount of money paid into the exchequer instead of the wardrobe. But there is nothing in the ordinances that would increase the total amount of revenue accruing to the king or collected on his behalf in any given year. It is perfectly true that the elimination of the Italian bankers, to whom Edward II had farmed the customs, by the provision that the revenue should be paid to natives must, had it been effective, have increased the total sum that reached the exchequer by the amount that the Italians had been in the habit of detaining. It would seem to follow, therefore, that the grievance referred to here is a loss not of revenue, but of the control and disbursement of it. It is hard to see

---

[1] ' . . . qe par les choses issint ordenees le poair real nostre dit seignur le roi feust restreynt en plusors choses contre devoir, en blemissement de sa seignurie reale et encountre lestat de la coronne.'

[2] Ordinances No. 8, *Rot. Parl.* i, 281-2.

how those who will not distinguish between 'the estate of the king' and 'the estate of the crown' can escape this difficulty.

But even if Mr. Haskins, sticking to his definition of 'estate' as revenue or property, were to adopt the distinction made in the ordinances and the statute and take 'the estate of the king' as meaning the revenue under his direct personal control and 'the estate of the crown' as meaning what was paid into and accounted for at the exchequer, he would still not be at the end of his difficulties. For he must show how the estate of the crown, which if it means revenue should be profited by the work of the ordainers, can properly be described in the statute as having suffered at their hands.[1]

But he must do more if his words which we have quoted mean what they appear to mean. He refers the passage in the statute, 'by the matters so ordained the royal power was restrained . . . to the blemishing of . . . [the] seigneurie . . . and against the estate of the crown', to the legislation against the household and concludes that 'the estate of the crown had been blemished' by the diminution of the royal revenue. But if the diminution of the royal revenue were all that was in question, it would seem that the injury could be healed and the welfare of the royal power promoted by a proportionate or greater increase of the revenue. Such an increase would, on Mr. Haskins's view, be open to parliament as a matter to be treated and established for 'the estate of the king' (since he does not distinguish between this and 'the estate of the crown') and 'the estate of the realm and the people'. But equally on Mr. Haskins's view such action, since it included discussion of, and legislation for, 'the royal power', which he takes to mean 'public prerogative', would in no circumstances be permissible even in parliament. It may be objected that this is a purely

---

[1] The only way, indeed, in which the revenue stood to lose under the ordinances was by the abolition of the new customs, and if apart from that the system could have been consistently applied over a long period it might well have resulted in producing a substantial increase in the resources at the disposal of the government. Thus, solely on *a priori* grounds, Mr. Haskins's interpretation is doubtful. If the ordainers did not diminish the king's revenue, however, they certainly attempted (possibly in the interests of economy) to restrict him in his disposition of it, and it is in that direction that the grievance of the court party is to be sought.

formal argument which does not touch the substance of Mr.
Haskins's contention that the king's friends, who drafted
the statute, aimed exclusively at re-establishing and maintaining
the royal power in its integrity, and would certainly never have
contemplated giving to a representative parliament any constitutional position in the government. The answer is that unless
we can reconcile the parts of the statute with each other we
cannot with any degree of security attribute to it a purpose more
exact or articulate than that of repealing the ordinances and
manifesting a desire to guard against a recurrence of the circumstances that had given birth to them.[1] It appears, then, when
we come to test Mr. Haskins's exegesis of the statute by asking
how it would work out in practice that the result is unsatisfactory, since at several important points it appears to be self-
contradictory, and to lead to conclusions that can scarcely be
squared with his thesis or even themselves be maintained.

Miss Clarke approaches the exegesis of the statute on the
assumption that ' its ambiguous phrasing was probably deliberate . . . it was not even clear whether grants of supply were
among the " matters to be established ", or whether the clerical
proctors were an integral part of the " commonalty of the
realm " '.[2] She observes that the clause which deals with the
royal power and the estate of the crown (i.e. clause 4) was
designed to protect the monarchy in perpetuity from all limits
imposed by subjects. The phrase ' estate of the crown ' was
(she argues) a new term which the draftsmen of the statute
took over from the opposition, by whom it had been used in
1308 to mark the distinction between the crown and person of
the king, and in 1321 as meaning the royal authority in general.
' In this sense it was taken up and applied in the Statute of
York, closely attached to the phrase " the royal power of our
lord and king and of his heirs ". Thus the hereditary and permanent prerogative of the crown was associated with the personal
authority of the king himself. A phrase, forged and popularized
by rebellion was adapted to express the inherent and sacrosanct
character of the monarch.'[3] Finally, she adopts the objection

---

[1] Although the dictum *privilegia statuti stricti sunt juris* is later by a
generation than the statute, the hypothesis we have adopted limits us to
some such rule of interpretation.

[2] *Op. cit.*, 139.   [3] *Op. cit.*, 156–7.

formulated by Mr. Davies, that clauses iv and v supplement each other, and concludes that it is impossible to suppose that what was specifically taken away in the one should be returned in the other.

I am at a loss to know what Miss Clarke actually meant by the words I have quoted. The word ' estate ' was currently used in several senses,[1] and the doctrine of capacities which had been known in England since the Conquest had been at any rate adumbrated in connexion with the crown on behalf of Edward I by his counsel in the *Quo Warranto* proceedings.[2] The distinction between the king and the crown was perfectly recognized and often made in official documents under Edward II, in such phrases as ' absque exheredatione et laesione coronae et regii juris nostri '; ' praejudicio . . . nobis et coronae ac regiae dignitatis nostrae '; ' in derogationem juris nostri aut coronae seu dignitatis nostrae regiae praejudicium.'[3] The words ' estate of the crown ' do not appear to associate the hereditary prerogative with the person of the king—that occurred ' when the estate of the crown descended '[4]—rather do they mark the distinction between two things different in their nature but inseparable except by death or cession, i.e. the person of the king and the estate of the crown. Finally, Miss Clarke does not appear to have recognized the problem presented by the fact that the statute uses five terms, ' seig- neurie reale ', ' royal power ', ' estate of the king ', ' estate of the crown ', and ' estate of the realm and people '; on the assumption that those who drafted it had a definite meaning to convey and did so in a document which is self-consistent these terms must be explained and reconciled. The senses in which the words are used in other texts may suggest or even authorize their interpretation in this context, but no one of them can impose itself. If the assumption proves to be unwarranted the interpretation suggested by Professor Johnstone is probably as far as we can safely go. At any rate it will not help much to

[1] Cf. Haskins, *Statute of York*, 87 ff.

[2] Davies, *op. cit.*, 22–8, citing *Placita de Quo Warranto* (Rec. Com.), 429–30. The term ' status regius ' there used by the tenant is pretty close to ' the estate of the king ' in the Statute of York.

[3] These are from royal letters addressed to the pope in 1310, 1311, and 1318 respectively, and will be found in *Foedera* (1727) iii, 204–5, 253, 838.

[4] *Statutes* i, 182.

suggest that the language is deliberately ambiguous unless you can resolve the ambiguity. When Miss Clarke does this it is with great ingenuity, but she does it in one case only.[1]

I must now expose myself to the risk from which others have not shrunk by offering an alternative solution. I suggest that any satisfactory exegesis must treat the statute as a whole, inspired by a positive intention which relates the parts to one another, and expressed in language admittedly difficult but neither intentionally ambiguous nor wanting in self-consistency. The statute appears to me to be based on the recognized and recurrent need to modify or adjust the prerogative in response to administrative requirements or political demands. Its subject evidently is the prerogative in its relation to parliament. It refers to the one as a whole and in its parts, and to the other as a normal organ of government contrasted with irregular and unauthorized groups. It consists of five chapters, each of which specifies an agent and the aspects of the prerogative upon which it has acted, or is either forbidden or empowered to act, in future. It will help to make the technical argument which must follow clearer if I begin by a summary of the statute intended to bring out the unity of its purpose and structure.[2]

In A the agent is the body of ordainers duly authorized and commissioned who have, however, acted *contre devoir*. In B the agent is any body of subjects, authorized or unauthorized, who make ordinances or provisions which have a specified effect. It is to be noted that there is an obvious antithesis between ordinances and provisions so made and the present act repudiating them made in a parliament by the king, prelates, earls, barons, and the commonalty of the realm and having, as we know from the preliminary instructions to the council, the character of a statute. Thus the provisions of the ordainers acting *contre devoir* are by implication classed with those made by the hostile committees set up *ab extra* in 1215 and 1258. In C we have a further antithesis between the authorized agent for the regulation of the questions with which the statute is concerned and the unauthorized agencies which have sometimes heretofore dealt with them. The one is the king in

[1] *Op. cit.*, 139.
[2] This is shown in the table in Appendix II.

parliament, and the other comprises subjects of the king acting by ' any power or commission whatsoever '. This must include such a legitimate royal commission as the ordainers were formally intended to constitute, and for that reason may be described as an act of self-limitation. This sweeping exclusion is contrasted with the clear definition of the authorized authority which the two clauses afford. The repeal is accorded and established in parliament by the king, prelates, earls, barons, and the whole community of the realm. Moreover, the text expressly contrasts the ordinances which are repealed and lose their name and force for ever, with the statutes and establishments duly made by the king and his ancestors before the said ordinances.[1] D presents the expected conclusion by specifying as sole agent for all future action in the matter the king in parliament, ' according as it hath been heretofore accustomed '. If we now consider the subjects of the prescribed legislation, we are confronted with a cluster of terms which require to be reduced to order and unity in relation to a whole of which they are parts. These terms occur in the groups shown on the table in the following order. In A, ' the estate of the household ' and ' the estate of the realm '; in B, ' the royal power ', the ' seigneurie reale ', and ' the estate of the crown '; in C, ' the royal power ', ' the estate of the king ', and ' the estate of the crown '; in D, ' the estate of the king ' and ' the estate of the realm and people '. Now let us begin by two assumptions which, although they will need to be supported by argument, are not in themselves unreasonable. The first is that the matter of which we are in search, the object, that is, of the positive and negative provisions of the statute, is contained as a whole and in its parts in the three terms shown in the table under C, i.e. ' the royal power ', the ' estate of the king ', and ' the estate of the crown '. Such an assumption would, indeed, appear to follow logically from the argument which we used against the view that the subject of the statute was the king's property or revenue. This was directed to show that the ordinances did not diminish and might eventually have increased the

---

[1] The first draft of the statute recently published by Mr. Haskins shows that this point was carefully considered and regarded as important. The antithesis of ordinance and statute regularly made is sharper in our text ; see *E.H.R.* lii, 74 ff.

resources of the king, and that his grievance can only be explained by supposing that the ordinances prevented him among other things from disposing of the revenue at his pleasure. Our second assumption is that the varying terms used in the different parts of the statute are not really disparate, and can be reduced to the unity which we have assumed for the three cited above. It is not, indeed, unreasonable to suppose that the statute should use different terms for the same thing, though our assumption as to its drafting would rule out the use of the same term for different things. This is so because the object to be specified (particularly when, as in this case, it is an abstraction) has numbers of aspects or relations, some of which may best be distinguished by different terms. The same term, however, used for two different objects would bring all the parts or aspects of two different wholes under a single exhaustive description which evidently cannot be true of both of them.

If, now, you consider the place of the king in the government, it will be evident that for all practical and most theoretical purposes the two are co-extensive, although in the nature of things the king is not punctually present at more than one place at one time, nor ever aware of everything that is being done in his name and by his authority at any given moment. This means that the king's will and authority have been to a great extent institutionalized without exhausting or even sounding his residual authority held in reserve for emergencies. The medieval king, though bearing a heavy moral responsibility, including respect for the subjective right of every subject, was above the positive law and within the very extensive sphere of administration supreme. Such supremacy, however, cannot be exercised by any individual because it is beyond the strength of his body and the time at his disposal.[1] The development of routine shows how large a part of the work may be delegated, and while common forms, such as the writs *de cursu*, reserve for the king's discretion all matters that could not be settled by reference to existing precedents and principles, they and the whole body of departmental rules and practice do, in fact, pretty effectively exclude the king's personal intervention. In no department, clearly, has this gone so far as in the judiciary,

[1] Cf. Bracton, fo. 108, ed. Woodbine ii, 306.

though the chancery and exchequer were well equipped for self-defence in this respect. The development of a parallel organization in the household through which the king's will could be more freely exerted, and the political turn that the rivalry of the two had taken, are now familiar matters. Then there was the exercise of the king's will in council as the practice was developed and articulated under Edward I in dealing with petitions. Briefly, the procedure was to meet as many cases as possible by authorizing the appropriate court or department, which would otherwise have been incapable of giving remedy, to deal with the matter, and that is in fact *ad hoc* delegation. On the other hand, there was a sense in which the royal power was inalienable, although it could be delegated in a very broad understanding of the word and up to a certain point restricted by acts of self-limitation.[1]

Naturally all this was familiar to the council which drafted the statute, and one would therefore expect to find them dealing with the restrictions that the ordainers had imposed on the free exercise of the royal power, and in particular on the king's control of the national and household administration. That, indeed, is what they do in the first clause. The ordainers had been authorized ' to ordain and establish the estate of the household of the king and the realm '. This brings us to the much disputed point of the sense we are to give to the word ' estate ' in the statute.[2] As contemporary use authorizes a number of alternatives we must look for a lead to the text of the ordinances and the statute itself. We have given some reasons for thinking that the sense of revenue or property proposed by Professor McIlwain and Mr. Haskins cannot successfully be fitted into the form or the substance of the statute and our own interpretation, so far as it has advanced, points to the sense of some part or aspect of the royal power. Now the purpose of the statute was to undo the work of the opposition and restore the king to a place in the government as advantageous as that on which he had entered at his accession. The council which drafted it must have been perfectly aware that the government

---

[1] The theory of an inalienable prerogative is discussed in detail below, pp. 200 ff.

[2] For a good general discussion, see Chrimes, *English Constitutional Ideas*, 81 ff.

could not be carried on without the discretionary power of the king freely exerted by him, and that the exercise of his authority had been hampered, in particular by forbidding the use of that power in certain contingencies,[1] and in general by depriving him of the control of the institutions through which his power was normally exerted. Their purpose would be achieved, therefore, if the king were in a position to act freely in the presence of the unforeseen by virtue of that undefined and in the nature of things indefinable reserve of authority which made him the mainspring of the government. He must be able to do what the situation required, and for that he must be in the free and unquestioned control of all the institutional machinery on and through which his will was accustomed to act. Such a state of things would exhibit the *esse* of kingship so situated as to constitute (in the view of the court party at any rate) the *bene esse*, not only of itself but of the realm committed to its charge. Now we know that the word ' estate ' in the fourteenth century was often used either in the sense of ' condition ' or ' welfare ', the one more characteristic of its Latin and the other of its French form.[2] Mr. Haskins, after making this point, recalls that the writs summoning the Welsh members to the parliament that passed our statute were asked to advise in matters touching the king and the *status* of his kingdom, and suggests that when the text of the statute uses *estat* with reference to the king, crown, and realm, its general sense of common profit or welfare must be particularly restricted to ' interest in lands, tenements, or other effects '. The antecedent probability, however, may be thought to point to the wider interpretation of ' estate ' in the sense of the *bene esse* of the king and crown respectively. We have seen that there is no need to regard such an application of the doctrine of capacities as an anachronism in the fourteenth century.[3] It is indeed implicit in the doctrine of the *Song of Lewes*, the *Addicio de Cartis*, and *Fleta*.[4] I do not, of course, suggest that the doctrine

---

[1] Thus § 9 of the ordinances forbade the king to declare war or go abroad ' without common assent of his baronage and that in parliament '.

[2] See Powicke, F.M., *T.R.H.S.*, 4th Series, xix, 10 ff.

[3] See above, p. 171.

[4] See *The Song of Lewes*, ed. Kingsford, ll. 445–50, 666–70, 804–11 (pp. 15, 22, 26) ; Bracton, ed. Woodbine i, 333 ; ii, 110 ; Ehrlich, *Proceedings against the Crown*, 202 ; Davies, *op. cit.*, 24–5 ; Tout, *Chapters* ii, 60, 210.

was official. Finally, it may be said that in so far as the distinction between the king and the crown was embodied in the institutions of the household and national government respectively its character is concrete rather than speculative.

The royal power, therefore, would appear to have presented itself to statesmen and politicians of the early fourteenth century under three aspects institutionally represented by the council, the household (wardrobe and chamber), and the national government (judiciary, treasury, and chancery). To the theoretical distinction between the direct exercise of the king's discretion by the king advised by his ministers, and its routine exercise in affairs of national government, with the household as a middle term in practice and theory, we have already referred. Now in practice what was essential for the maintenance of the royal power in its integrity—that restoration of it which it is agreed was to be the object of those who drafted the statute—was the complete control of the ministers who advised and might oppose him in council and at the departments, and the unquestioned right to determine policy by having the last word when a decision had to be taken. Discussion and trouble enough might arise over the other matters that the ordainers had handled, the organization of the household, the position of the privy seal, the regulation of the customs and so on, but such things were susceptible of compromise. The crown had many resources, and the court party in 1322 was not afraid of effective administrative reformers. The council that drafted our statute might have undone the arrangements made by the ordainers for the privy seal and wardrobe but, in spite of the general repeal, these seem to have remained.[1]

These considerations bring us back to the suggestion that the general subject of the statute is the royal power as defined in Bracton and the Mise of Amiens, as exercised by Edward I and as approved by the body of political doctrine that had been growing in the parties of opposition from the time of the Great Charter. This general subject is specifically defined as a whole and in its parts in clauses 3 and 4 of the statute as ' the royal power ', ' the estate of the king ', and ' the estate of the crown '. If this is what the framers of the statute meant it remains to

---

[1] Cf. Tout, *op. cit.* ii, 258, 304.

N

harmonize the terminology in various parts of the text and, if that can be achieved, to explain the unity and purpose of the whole document.

If we take the royal power to mean the ' ordinaria juris-dictio ',[1] the discretionary and residual authority of the king as the central will, we may define ' the estate of the king' as the *bene esse* of the king in relation to that part of his administration which looked to his person more than to his crown and was ordinarily carried on through the household organization. Where the estate of the king in this sense is ' unblemished ' he will freely control that organization and the financial and military resources which it held at his disposal. In like manner ' the estate of the crown ' will be the *bene esse* of the king in relation to that part of his administration which looked to his crown and realm rather than his person. When ' the estate of the crown ', in this sense, is normal the king directs the whole organization of the government freely, indeed, but only in the sense of the determination of general policy and with due respect for the constituted order and departmental practice. When these conditions are fulfilled the realm is at peace and prospers; contrariwise there is war. These definitions are inferences from the text of the statute, and their validity will be confirmed if it can be shown that they fit into or help to explain its five clauses and the coherence and unity of the whole which they constitute.

In clause 1 neither ' the royal power' nor ' the estate of the crown ' occur, and we hear only of ' the estate of the king's household and of his realm '. I suggest that the first of these is a more concrete and the second a more generalized form of the definition with which we are working. The ' estate of the king's household ' is the well-being or good order of that part of the royal power which functions through the chamber and ward-robe looked at from the point of view of the subject and there-fore thought of institutionally. In like manner ' the estate of the crown ' when looked at from the same point of view is the royal power and administration considered in its relation to

---

[1] Bracton, fos. 55 f., ed. Woodbine ii, 167. Bracton occasionally uses the word ' gubernaculum ' to distinguish the administrative authority of the king from his ' jurisdictio '.

the whole mass of the king's subjects, and may reasonably be described as the estate of the king's realm in this context. The text of the statute shows this, for the ordainers are said to have been commissioned to deal with the two parts of the subject ' to the honour and profit of the king and the profit of his people ', and the phrase recurs in the last clause as ' the estate of the realm and of the people '. The equivalence of these words and ' the estate of the crown ' may therefore be put as ' the same thing looked at, as it were, from below '.[1]

' The royal power ' does not appear in the first clause, nor could it properly do so because it was clearly not included in the terms of the reference to the ordainers. They were instructed to reform the institutions of household and national government with due consideration to the king's honour, profit, and responsibility under the coronation oath.[2] The meaning of the clause is clear enough : the ordainers had been warned to respect the integrity of the royal power, and their offence consisted in having ' restrained ' it. This point is developed in the second clause, which states that the ordinances restrained the royal power in several matters *contre devoir*, ' to the blemishing of his [i.e. the king's] royal *seigneurie* and against the estate of the crown '. It has been observed above that a medieval text may without loss of consistency use different terms to describe the same things, but when that is done in a document which *ex hypothesi* is self-consistent and carefully drafted there should be an assignable reason for the variation. The word *seigneurie* does not occur elsewhere in the statute. Its general sense is lordship, and the context of clause 2 suggests that it is to be distinguished, on the one hand, from the prerogative as a whole, and on the other, from that portion of it which is exercised through the departments of state, described here and elsewhere as ' the estate of the crown '. We should expect, therefore, to have found here ' the estate of the king ' rather than the unusual term ' seigneurie reale '. This, however, probably conveys more accurately what the draftsmen wished to express.

[1] *E.H.R.* xxviii, 123, n. 14. The words which I have quoted have been very properly criticized as confused and obscure ; I have now tried to put more lucidly what I had in mind in 1913.

[2] The coronation oath was often vouched in support of doctrines which it neither states nor appears to imply ; see below pp. 209 ff.

Clause 2 says that the restraints improperly imposed by the ordainers on the prerogative damaged the royal lordship and were contrary to the estate of the crown. Now what require emphasis here are those provisions of the ordinances which restricted or prevented the direct exercise of the king's will through the officers and institutions of his household; therefore to have said damaged or prejudiced ' the estate of the king ', although more formally consistent than ' royal lordship ', would have been far less specific. The real grievance was the restraint of the king's freedom of action and the resulting loss of the *bene esse* of the estates of the king and the crown, as understood and defined in the statute.

The terms which we are examining do not occur in the third clause, which is concerned exclusively with the repeal of the ordinances and the confirmation of all previous statutes and establishments duly made by royal authority before the said ordinances. In the fourth clause the terms recur in what, according to our hypothesis, is their normal sense and order. The clause is related to the one that follows by a sharp antithesis between the agencies described in each—the first, ' any body of the king's subjects acting by any power or authority whatsoever ', is as general as the second, the king in parliament, is specific, and yet the antithesis is unmistakable. It consists in the presence of the king in a constituted organ of government, the composition and procedure of which the statute defines for this purpose, and their respective assent to, and enactment of, the measures which after discussion have been agreed upon. On the other side must be included every sort of group which can be brought under the general definition, the twenty-five of the Runnymede Charter, the fifteen of the Provisions of Oxford, the Ordainers, and the pseudo-parliaments of Sherborne and Doncaster. These it will be seen had varying and in some cases technically valid authority, but for purposes of dealing with the royal power, the estate of the king and the estate of the crown, the statute incapacitates them and their like for the future.[1] In doing so it makes a distinction which

[1] The explanation offered above rests on a translation of the word ' sur ' (which occurs twice in the statute, each time in connexion with the royal power) not quite in agreement with the official translation given in the Statutes of the Realm. The word may be rendered either ' concerning ' or

we have already noticed between the whole of the prerogative, ' the royal power ', and those parts of it which may be described as institutionalized, ' the estate of the king ', and ' the estate of the crown '. This prepares the way for the discussion and adjustment of questions relating to the estate of the king and the crown and excludes a unilateral settlement of such matters; for a settlement by one of the parties to a dispute, though it may have the king's formal assent, lacks even the authority of an arbitral award since the king's interest cannot be supposed to have been duly considered. Such settlements are, therefore, ruled out and the proper form prescribed in clause v which secures that the king's interest shall be safeguarded by requiring his co-operation and consent. The sense of the clause then is dominated and determined by the antithesis between action by groups of subjects without the co-operation of the king and action by the king with the co-operation of parliament.

Turning now to the final clause, we observe that the term ' the royal power ' has wholly disappeared, that where we should expect the ' estate of the crown ' we have the ' estate of the realm and of the people ', and that the procedure which the clause prescribes is described as traditional, ' as it hath heretofore been accustomed '. There is a correspondence here with the first clause where there is no mention of ' the royal power ', and we have ' estate of the realm ' where we might have expected ' estate of the crown '. This point we have already discussed,[1] and for the reasons then given it is now suggested that the ' estate of the realm and of the people ' in clause v is just ' the estate of the realm ' which the ordainers were com-

' against '. In the official translation it appears in clause 2 as ' concerning ' and in clause 4 as ' against '. I have taken it as ' concerning ' in both contexts for two reasons. On the view of the drafting of the statute which is here assumed, a variation of this word would not occur without some special reason as in the case of the use of ' seigneurie reale ', where we might have expected ' estate of the crown ' in clause 2. There is no such reason apparent in clause 4, quite the contrary, indeed, for in the same sentence with ' sur ' there occurs the word ' contre ' which can only be rendered against. Moreover, there is a material as well as a formal consideration which suggests that ' concerning ' is a better translation in this context, for otherwise it might be argued that the irregular groups here referred to might legislate validly *for the advantage* of the estate of the king and the estate of the crown. This, as is argued in the text, is contrary to the manifest intention of the statute, and since the translation ' concerning ' which gives the required sense is legitimate it is contrary to its form as well.

[1] Above, p. 177.

missioned to reform to the profit of the king and his people, and that this again is that part of the king's government elsewhere described as ' the estate of the crown ' but here, regarded from the point of view of the governed, as ' the estate of the realm '. If this should prove acceptable there is a final difficulty to be overcome, and this arises out of the concluding words, ' according as it hath been heretofore accustomed '. It may well be objected that the matters which on our reading of the statute are comprised under the terms ' estate of the king ' and ' estate of the crown ' had not hitherto normally if at all been discussed and regulated by the king in parliament.

Bracton describes the method of ' legislation ', which he called the definition and approval of new law, in his day. It required the intention of the prince to legislate, the advice of his magnates, and formal enactment by royal authority after deliberation and discussion.[1] The words of the statute fulfil these conditions, and if they add that the process shall take place in parliament and substitute the assent of the prelates, earls, barons, and commonalty of the realm for the advice of the magnates, they may still find warrant in Bracton's text, for in treating the same subject in an earlier passage he derives the sanction of English laws from their due definition and approval by the royal authority ' de consilio et consensu magnatum et reipublicae communi sponsione ',[2] and further adds that the judgements of such cases as are dark, hard, and unprecedented shall be referred ' ad magnam curiam ut ibi per consilium curiae terminentur '.[3] Obviously Bracton's ' magna curia ' had taken a new name and new functions and contained new elements, but these develop without perverting Bracton's theory that the finding or making of law shall be deliberate, responsible, and co-operative, and that the law so declared or made shall be national and approved *more utentium*. If, as seems likely, Bracton meant no more than that by ' reipublicae communis sponsio ', the general interpretation of the statute for which I contend would still be unaffected. In 1322 there were a number of practical ways of accomplishing the purposes of legislation. One of these, though by no means the most usual, was enact-

---

[1] Bracton, fo. 107 (*a* and *b*), ed. Woodbine ii, 305.
[2] *Ibid*. fo. 1*a*., ed. Woodbine ii, 19.   [3] *Ibid*. fo. 1*b*, ed. Woodbine ii, 21.

ment by the king in a parliament comprising knights and burgesses. Another, generally associated with abnormal political conditions, may be roughly compared to a modern statutory commission; royal authority was remitted to an *ad hoc* body like the council of 1258 or the Ordainers themselves, to accomplish the desired changes. I suggest that the Statute of York prescribed the first of these two as the only proper method of dealing with certain matters and further explicitly forbade the second. It thus attracted these matters, hitherto treated somewhat irregularly, into the field of formal legislation, and in selecting a regular but infrequently used method for the purpose of settling disputes that were themselves likely to be infrequent, it conformed to established practice. The immediate aim of the statute may well have been political rather than constitutional, but having regard to the time and the questions involved, the line cannot be sharply drawn, and in any case constitutional matters often begin by being political ones. Now the questions at issue between the king and the magnates from 1215 until 1322 were largely political. The first settlement, though feudal in form, was in fact a dictated treaty imposed by successful rebels, and this factor was present in 1258, 1265, 1311, and 1318, though the civil war was sometimes no more than a threat or a memory. Further, after Runnymede the feudal form was abandoned in favour of a device which was essentially a confession of failure on the part of the king, who is forced to commit to a select body the right to make certain structural and functional changes in the régime and to give an undertaking not ' to perform the ordinary acts of sovereignty '[1] without their assent. Thus the arrangements embodied in the Provisions of Oxford and Westminster and in the Ordinances of 1311 are in form legislative acts issued in virtue of delegated royal authority and dealing largely with the prerogative, but in substance they are the implementation of dictated treaties. On the other hand, the proceedings after Lewes and at Leake are formal treaties, although they initiate change and reform. Parliament as the word was understood at the relevant dates was more or less

---

[1] Tout, *Place of Edward II*, 2nd ed., 110. The passage is in reference to the Treaty of Leake in 1318.

taken into account in every scheme. The draftsman of the statute, I suggest, understood the realities of these shifting precedents and reduced them to some degree of order by providing that in such cases the negotiations should take place in parliament and the result be given legislative form. Neither legislation in a parliament of estates nor the handling of the prerogative by legislation was new. It would follow that a statute defining the part of the prerogative susceptible of legislative treatment and prescribing one of several existing methods to effect it might claim with some show of justice *stare super vias antiquas*, and that the characteristic medieval dread of appearing to create a precedent would lead to such a claim being made.

Next we may observe that the omission of ' the royal power ' from clause 5 is as deliberate and significant as it was in the first, and it is its omission here and not the words of clause 6 that withdraw it from legislative treatment. The king's will is and must be free, but that freedom is subject to acts of self-limitation which in general are restricted to the institutions through which his will is ordinarily exerted. Such modifications had been within the scope of the ordainers by virtue of letters-patent, a method which the statute forbids. They are henceforth restricted to the king in parliament. Thus the chief purpose of the statute was to maintain the royal power in its essentials. That required some measure of protection both in theory and practice. The former was provided by the doctrine that changes in the control and organization of the central government must be accomplished by formal legislation—the latter consisted in calling to the support of the crown the parliament reinforced by the commons.

On this interpretation the statute shows a structural and material unity which depends on harmony and contrast. The subject is the sum of all the king's functions in government which the statute designates *le poair real*. The purpose of the statute is to maintain the essential independence of that power and to provide a means of avoiding such wars and other civil disputes as since 1215 had disturbed the country and threatened to compromise the integrity of the royal power. Its method is to distinguish between so much of that power as must be regarded as inviolable and the remainder which comprises proper subjects for concession and compromise by negotiation, and the free consent of the king. The distinction is a concrete one, and derives from the practice of the royal government by which much of the king's work is done by delegation to his household and ministers and the institutions of which they form part. The framers of the statute, recognizing that as all administrative authority derives from the king the royal power is indivisible, but also aware that in the exercise of so much of it as is delegated the king's freedom is practically restricted, treat the royal power under three aspects. There is the indefinable, discretionary authority which the king exercises when new decisions have to be taken, and this is as inexhaustible as the future, and carries a responsibility which cannot easily be delegated. As long as it is exercised directly it is inviolable, and it retains the name of *poair real* because although there is a difference both in kind and degree in the way in which the king functions in the three regions in which he administers, the administration itself and the power which animates it are but one. Thus the royal power consists in practice of three parts, (*a*) the royal power in the narrower sense determined by the fact that the king is acting directly although he will take advice before giving a decision or a judgement; (*b*) the estate of the king, his personal business (a good deal of which looks very public to modern eyes) which is transacted by household officials who resemble agents rather than ministers; (*c*) the estate of the crown, public business institutionalized in the courts and departments under the judges and ministers. In both (*a*) and (*b*) the king's will is restricted and hampered by departmental rules and practice, the elaborate and inflexible procedure of the courts and the wills and conveniences of the ministers and household officials. Theoretically the prerogative was immune from violence, and although it was often described as inalienable under the terms of the coronation oath, no such guarantee can be produced,[1] and acts of voluntary self-limitation within the field of delegated power were not uncommon. It was thought, however, that the king should retain general control of the institutions through which his will was expressed, and in

[1] See below, pp. 211–12 ff.

this consisted the *bene esse* of the king and the realm. Otherwise troubles and wars might follow. To prevent the recurrence of such attacks and disorders the statute defines what parts of the royal power may be discussed, where, and how. Finally, on our hypothesis it is possible to establish a unity and self-consistency in the language of the text which on a superficial view it appears to lack. We are not left with unexplained or redundant terms on our hands, nor are we obliged to attribute to the draftsmen, whose skill and common sense we have assumed, ' a plethora of legal verbiage '.[1]

III

It is evident that although the case for any interpretation of the statute requires an exegesis that will account reasonably for all the formal difficulties, exegesis alone will not suffice. Any interpretation must be fitted into the historical context of the action which the statute records and this involves the calculation of antecedent probability. The concrete question here is to estimate the view taken by contemporary statesmen and politicians of the parliament containing elected representatives as a factor in any political problem. The matter has been much discussed of late, and as to certain points I think there would be general agreement. The importance of parliament (with or without representatives) as a tribunal for the remedy of grievances and as a reinforced form of the king's council is well established. The increasing practice of reinforcing parliament by elected members is not denied. Representatives of the shires and towns came to be summoned first frequently and then regularly, and a determined, although ultimately unsuccessful, attempt was made to secure the attendance of elected representatives of the clergy. The crown had recognized that extraordinary taxation required the consent of those who were to be taxed, and it is likely that it felt the need of some means of manipulating public opinion and obtaining political support in times of domestic or international unsettlement. But it desired that parliament should be ' an

---

[1] Haskins, *op. cit.* 10. The case, indeed, would be worse than that, for ' legal verbiage ' is commonly justified by the need of definition and caution: without that it becomes wanton confusion.

instrument of government, not an organ of control '.[1] Under
Edward II the political movement had taken the form of what
has been aptly called a feudal reaction[2] which worked greatly to
the disadvantage of the king and made the magnates irresistible
as long as they could hold together. On the other hand, since
it was impossible to reconcile their territorial interests with
national interests, and since the influence of any one of them in
national affairs varied in direct ratio to the importance of his
territorial position, which under feudal conditions could rarely
be in quite stable equilibrium, the chances (even apart from the
risk of personal jealousies and antagonisms) of maintaining a
united front against the crown and the political aims of the
court party were small. In these circumstances one would
expect to find both crown and opposition seeking political
support and reinforcement wherever they might be found. A
representative parliament was a promising quarter, partly
because it drew into the struggle social classes of increasing
wealth and consequence. The value of the political support of
the country gentlemen and burgesses had begun to be recognized during the Barons' War, and was directly solicited by
Edward I on many occasions. Then the parliament, whether
containing representatives or not, was already recognized as
having a national character.[3] The increased tempo of parliamentary development between 1310 and 1322 on the one hand
and Lancaster's resort to irregular parliaments or *conciliabula*
on the other will be recalled in this connexion.[4]

[1] Petit-Dutaillis, *Studies Supplementary to Stubbs' Constitutional History*
iii, 331.

[2] *E.H.R.* xlvii, 397.

[3] This is reflected in the various forms of the writs of summons which
chancery was devising and the rubrics under which it classified them ; see
Wilkinson, *Studies*, 44–50.

[4] On the growing political importance of the commons in Edward II's
reign, see Tout, *Place of Edward II*, 2nd edn., 29–31, 79–82, 112, 136–7 ;
Chapters ii, 188–224 ; Wilkinson, *op. cit.*, cap. ii ; Richardson, H. G., and
Sayles, G. O., ' Early Records of the English Parliaments ', *B.I.H.R.* vi,
71–83. Miss Clarke emphasizes a text generally known as the Doncaster
Petition and taken to have been drawn up at, or in consequence of, the
Lancastrian meeting summoned to Doncaster for November 28th, 1321.
This is an attack on the Despensers who are accused of ' blemishing the
estate of the realm and the crown ' by encroachment on the royal power.
Miss Clarke thinks that the statute of York may have used the same form
of words in order to disallow ' the high claim of these pseudo-parliaments '.
Mr. Haskins, who has recently published the text, will not allow any causal
connexion between the petition and the statute, as it seems to me, on

The facts are not denied, and our task is, therefore, to try to fit the genesis of the statute into the background which they supply. We should note first the national and general character of the parliament (whether containing elected representatives or not) as distinguished from the great council or the *tractatus;* and second, the fact that the statute marks the antithesis between bodies or gatherings that are partial, irregular, unregulated, or even revolutionary, and the national parliament traditionally looked to for the provision of remedies and the solution of problems by the king in council. Then we may observe that the royal sovereignty and power which, presented under three aspects, is the subject of the statute has never yet been treated by parliament, though other groups or bodies had occasionally done so. Again, while the statute was in a sense an emergency measure, it was not drafted hastily. The victory of the king had been anticipated, arrangements for administrative reform were put in hand in February,[1] and before Boroughbridge the council had been charged with the business

insufficient grounds. He thinks that it would be necessary to prove that the statute used the words in the same sense as the petition and that its framer had in mind this ' indenture of a small number of northern barons belonging to a discredited party '. But this is surely an inadequate description of a document which Mr. Haskins agrees emanated from the Doncaster meeting and ' represents the formal deliberation of the party '. The Lancastrians, moreover, were so far from being discredited that the king thought it necessary formally to forbid 107 of the persons summoned, many of them the most important in the kingdom, to attend the meeting. Mr. Haskins sets the petition ' in the constitutional struggle of the reign . . . on the question of ' the king's prerogative. Part of that prerogative, as Mr. Haskins points out, was the king's exclusive right to summon meetings in which matters touching the estate of the crown were to be discussed, and to authorize such discussion in his presence or that of those of his council appointed by him ; *Foedera* (1727), iii, 867–8, 899–900. Mr. Haskins must have rendered this, ' his right alone as feudal overlord ', by an inadvertence; the text makes it clear that the king's right in this matter was not feudal. Inference is admissible and may be convincing where proof is impossible, and in this case where both the petition and the statute are concerned with the same subject and the statute refers explicitly to such assemblies as that at Doncaster it seems to me that Miss Clarke's inference cannot be dismissed, however one interprets the statute, on the grounds taken by Mr. Haskins. Clarke, *op. cit.* 164–6, and Haskins, *E.H.R.* liii, 480–2. Controversy has hitherto turned on what the statute may have done to promote or restrict ' the interest of the commons '. That I regard as a mistake ; the real importance of the statute was the proposal to facilitate negotiation between the crown and the baronage within a constituted organ of government which was steadily habituating itself to include elected representatives of the counties and parliamentary boroughs ; cf. Pollard, *op. cit.* 241–2.

[1] See the evidence in Tout, *Chapters* ii, 258–9.

of preserving what was of value in the ordinances and framing
a statute if it saw fit for matters of sufficient importance. The
council's chief task, however, was to restore and maintain the
prerogative, and on any long view that meant the provision
of some means of liquidating the recurrent disputes between
the crown and the magnates to replace those that had proved
little better than revolution in disguise. Is it credible that they
should have discharged their task by proposing that parliament should in no circumstances concern itself with the
royal power in any way but be content to vote supplies ? Did it
really need a statute treated, accorded, and established in parliament, to prevent parliament from doing what it had never yet
attempted ? And could such a statute be in any way regarded as
safeguarding the royal power in the sense of providing the
means of settling by negotiation and compromise some, at any
rate, of the questions which had been at issue between the
crown and the magnates since the rebellion against John ?
Conceivably such a solution might be adopted by a reactionary
and short-sighted council flushed with victory and intent only
on consolidating its fruits. But that was not the character of the
leading statesmen and administrators early in 1322. The
statute was carefully drafted by men who took a long view and
were not afraid of administrative reform, and we must bear that
in mind when we try to construe it.

Now this interpretation of the statute has been challenged in
advance on the ground that after Boroughbridge the royal
power was in no danger and the king had no need for precaution to safeguard it.[1] It is difficult to see how any Edwardian
statesman—least of all one with the political experience of the
younger Despenser—could have taken Mr. Davies's static view
of affairs in 1322. The crown, indeed, had triumphed, and was
proposing to realize its traditional policy and that fact alone
made the baronage an eventual source of danger. A statesman
must take long views, and a measure that aimed at settling
future disputes by negotiations in which the support of a new
political force, i.e. the commons, might be secured seems to me
neither contrary to antecedent probability in 1322 nor in its
essentials repugnant to political wisdom at any time. Miss

[1] Davies, *op. cit.*, 516.

Clarke, on the other hand, described this view as making of our text ' a statute to end rebellion by authorizing it ', and Mr. Haskins thought it inconceivable that the court party bent on re-establishing and maintaining the royal power could ever have contemplated the admission of a parliament of estates to a share in the discussion of such matters. There is truth in both of these objections and they require discussion though not, I venture to think, quite in the terms in which they are formulated. Miss Clarke writes that the conflicting claims of the monarch to the inviolability of the royal power and of the magnates to the indefeasible rights of their order ' cannot be forced into unison by the Statute of York, and no subtlety of interpretation [i.e. of the statute] will reconcile it with the deposition of Edward II '. It would be hard to specify the indefeasible rights of the baronage as an order in 1322 though one need be in no doubt as to their political aims. The question, surely, is not one of bringing conflicting political aims, and disputed rights into a sort of constitutional synthesis, but rather of providing a practical method by which the problems arising out of the conflict might as they presented themselves be adjusted after discussion and compromise. If one thinks in terms and uses the idiom of public law or political speculation, one may encounter difficulties that need not be felt in practice. Thus, Miss Clarke can write of the ' constitutional ' interpretation of the statute : ' we are asked to believe that when Edward II came to York " bringing rebellion broached upon his sword " he at once put forward legislation to insure the validity of " fundamental constitutional changes " in the future. In other words, a restoration parliament prescribed the method which later revolutions ought to follow .' In view, at once, of the unguarded language of my original article and the rigidity of some of Miss Clarke's own notions I think that the irony and the rhetoric of these two passages are not without warrant. If the restoration parliament, however, had happened to prescribe parliamentary negotiations and mutual compromise as the best method for avoiding revolutions because it so often rendered them unnecessary, I should accept Miss Clarke's gibe as illustrating my present position very happily. The fact is that all constitutional devices are in the last analysis substitutes for rebellion.

If, as has been alleged, the Tzarist régime was a despotism tempered by assassination, then the English constitution could, in the same spirit, be fairly described as an elaborate and until recent times not uniformly successful means of dispensing with assassination in public life. If the prerogative is inviolable and the rights of the baronage indefeasible, then you have an immovable object in the path of an irresistible force and are confounded by your own definition. If, on the other hand, it turns out that the area of actual inviolability of the prerogative diminishes in direct ratio to its permanent delegation and the degree to which it has been affected by acts of self-limitation, and if the baronage as an order has no rights except such as derive from tenure in chief, although wealth, influence, and custom have given them a position in public life for which they were already seeking legal security by political action, then the situation is transformed. There is room for a statute which canalizes that political activity just because compromise and concession are possible and political aims can be realised as rights more durably in that way than in any other. As for Mr. Haskins' suggestion, it does not take account of a point which has recently been developed;[1] the court party was in matters of institutional change and reform the party of progress and even of radical change, and it included the old middle party largely drawn from the ranks of the ordainers that had been responsible for the Treaty of Leake. The weakness of the Lancastrian programme, on the other hand, was its impracticability. It could neither get on with the king nor get on without him, and no scheme that separated the royal power from the person of the king could in the nature of things in medieval England be permanent.

Evidently the interpretation of the statute which I advance requires the assumption that the framers of the statute contemplated that parliament, acting under the authority of clause 5, would contain elected representatives of the shires and boroughs, and we must face the question of the sense in which we are to take the words ' commonalty of the realm ' in clauses 2 and 5 of the statute. Mr. Richardson and Dr. Sayles ' can find no warrant for the assumption that the phrase . . . must

[1] See Tout, *Chapters* ii, 189, 208–13, 245, 332, 337.

mean the knights and burgesses assembled in parliament'. They refer to the notion of the nation at large, which the lords occasionally claim to represent (notably in their letter to the pope in 1309), and also to a general body of suitors attending parliament, ' a body that claimed to represent the *communitas communis* or nation at large '.[1] They offer, in short, alternative contemporary meanings of the word, as did Mr. Davies whom they vouch. Now, in the case of a word that is currently used in several different senses, to say that there is no warrant for assuming that it must be used in a given sense in a given document is, I suggest, to state rather than to solve the problem. For one thing the contemporary sense of a word in another text is more often permissive than imperative in the case of the particular document under scrutiny, because the meaning must make sense in the context, and the possibility that the term is used in a new sense for the first time can never be wholly ruled out. The sense, therefore, will most often be determined by the rest of the document, and I suppose that what Mr. Richardson and Dr. Sayles mean is that they can find no warrant in the statute itself for supposing that the commonalty of the realm must be taken in the sense of the knights and burgesses. ' Must ' on the one hand is a strong word to use when so many questions have to be decided on the balance of probabilities, and on the other it is unlikely that anyone would assert that there was warrant for saying that the term must not be so used in the statute. It will be more profitable to ask what guidance is furnished by the text of the statute itself. There are two points to remark. We know that the statute was accorded and established by the king and the prelates, earls, barons, and whole commonalty of the realm ' at this parliament assembled ', and this is the method prescribed in the last clause for future use. We know also that the parliament of York in 1322 comprised duly elected knights of the shire and burgesses from England, and that a contingent of Welsh representatives and the elected proctors of the clergy were also summoned.[2] If we

---

[1] *B.I.H.R.* vi, 76–7 ; cf. Davies, *op. cit.*, 513.

[2] *Report on the Dignity of a Peer* i, 282–3 ; iii, 318–21 ; *Rot. Parl.* i, 456. In an official account of the midsummer parliament of 1321 to which the Lancastrians had at first refused to come, it is stated that they only arrived after the king had been holding his parliament for fifteen days, having

choose Mr. Richardson and Dr. Sayles's alternatives, we shall
have to suppose that the drafters of the statute, when they had
to enumerate the elements composing the parliament to which
the statute was submitted, specified either the community of
the nation at large, absent but represented by the lords, or the
whole body of suitors alternatively representing the nation. In
the first case the lords are counted twice, and in the second it
must be remembered that the suitors were not summoned
by writ and if they were in parliament were not of it. In both
cases the important elected element of the parliament which
had been summoned to advise and assent is not mentioned at
all. In these circumstances I submit that the balance of
probability points to the conclusion that the words commonalty
of the realm in the statute must be taken to mean the ' commons ',[1] and that this extends to such future parliaments as
may be concerned with the business allotted to them in the
last clause of the statute.

Mr. Haskins argues vigorously against the interpretation of
the statute in this sense. He thinks that both antecedent
probability and the available evidence are against the idea that
the king and his advisers at the moment of their triumph should
have assigned to the commons, by statute, such important
rights. On the one hand, he urges that the presence of the
commons was not essential to parliament, and when they are
there it is rather to receive directions than to co-operate in
government. The parliament was ' the handiwork and instrument ' of the king and his officials, and they were unlikely to
surrender any degree of control to the body of the commons
who were not, on their side, in a position to ask for such a
right. Then all probability is against new rights being given to

---

' caused to come before him prelates and other earls and barons, knights
of the shire and others who came for the commune of the realm ' ; *C.C.R.*,
1318–23, 545. In the order for the publication and enrolment of the statute
sent to the judges, they are informed that the ordinances which had been
ordained by certain prelates, earls, and barons have been examined in the
parliament at York by prelates, earls, barons, and the community of the
kingdom and by them and the king cancelled. Both texts in Clarke, *op.
cit.*, 170–1.

[1] *C.C.R.*, 1318–23, 139, 171–2. Miss Clarke has conjectured acutely and
with some reason, as I think, that in view of the dubious position of the
clerical proctors the phrase ' commonalty of the realm ' was adopted to
avoid reference to a controversy that was irrelevant to the main issue.

o

the commons by statute at a time when it was considered that the business of a statute was to declare or amend the existing law. Finally, Mr. Haskins argues that the statute had no effect or consequence that would corroborate such an interpretation, for, although the commons had some share in the deposition of Edward II, ' the proceedings in this revolutionary step were tentative and cautious ', and Edward III was justified in revoking the statute of 1341 ' because it was contrary . . . to the rights and prerogatives of the crown ', the inference being that such rights could not be limited by statute.

With much of this argument I am in agreement, because it is directed against the view that the statute associated the commons with all legislation or at any rate with so much of it as did not involve the prerogative. I cannot accept even the modified form of that view suggested by Mr. Davies and Miss Clarke, and I think that Mr. Haskins' argument increases the difficulty in doing so. Mr. Davies describes clause 5 as perpetuating the existing usage by securing to the ' people ' in parliament the right to take part in general legislation which had been recognized in practice by Edward I. To the first point the answer is broadly that it was not the regular practice under Edward I, who did not scruple to legislate without the participation or consent of the commons even in a parliament to which (as in 1290) they had been summoned, and that if Edward II's council had intended to make such a practice obligatory the statute did not have that effect.

The only positive evidence produced by Mr. Davies is the fact that provisions of the ordinances which were to be retained were ' in this very parliament established by the assent of the prelates, earls, and barons and the commonalty of the realm '. This, however, can prove no more than that the commons might still occasionally be asked to co-operate in legislation as they had been before. There is nothing in the Statute of York to exclude that. What Mr. Davies' point requires is evidence that the co-operation of the commons in general legislation after the statute rapidly became usual. But this would seem not to have been the case. It should be noted, moreover, that the act by which the king's ordinances were established and ordained was not technically a statute. It does not call itself that, and it was entered on the Close Roll while the Statute of York was entered on the statute roll. It will be remembered that the council had received authority to proceed, by statute or otherwise, at their discretion, and the Statute of York and the king's ordinances severally embody their recommendations.[1]

But in view of what we have learned since Mr. Davies wrote of the theory and practice of legislation in the fourteenth and fifteenth centuries, it must gravely be doubted whether those who drafted the statute could have understood, much less intended, the introduction of such a change.[2] Miss Clarke, writing later than Mr. Davies, like him argues (though on other grounds) that clause 5 was intended to commit to parliament all general legislation, and again, like him, fails to meet the objection that in that case the statute was a dead letter. She begins by an attack on the distinction between fundamental and ordinary law as lacking ' the warrant of contemporaries '. With that I agree, but I do not think that I used the term fundamental law in my earlier article.[3] What I mean is that people in the fourteenth century could recognize the difference in character and importance between concrete subjects of legislation without observing a distinction in kind. It requires no abstract theory and no subtlety to see, for example, that the legislative acts included under the name of the statute of Westminster I deal chiefly with procedure, and in general with ' the correction of

---

[1] *Rot. Parl.* i, 456 ; *C.C.R.*, 1318–23, 557 ; Davies, *op. cit.*, 515. It will be remembered that the distinction between a statute and other remedies was contemplated in the agenda sent to the council ; see above, p. 153.

[2] It is impossible to discuss the matter in detail within the limits of this study. I anticipated part of the objection to Mr. Davies' view in my original article, *E.H.R.* xxviii, 118 ff ; and the late G. B. Adams, in a private letter to me in 1913, summed it up in the words, ' it looks to me as if what the commons seem to gain in 1322, as far as general legislation is concerned, they have to gain over again under Edward III '. He would probably have put the date later now. See Plucknett, *Statutes and Their Interpretation*, 1–39 ; Gray, *The Influence of the Commons on Early Legislation*, cap. xii ; Pickthorn, *Early Tudor Government* i, caps. v, vi ; Richardson and Sayles, ' The Early Statutes ', *Law Quarterly Review*, l, 201–24, 540–71 ; Chrimes, *Constitutional Ideas in the Fifteenth Century*, cap. iii ; Hatschek, *Englische Verfassungsgeschichte*, 205.

[3] The words ' something in the nature of a *lex regia* ', might fairly be taken to imply that, although they were used, rashly no doubt, for illustration by analogy. Even speculation about the prerogative in the thirteenth and fourteenth centuries was apt to treat it concretely ; see below, pp. 200 ff.

many irregularities in the exercise of certain privileges and rights and for the better administration of justice both civil and criminal ',[1] and the classification of the statutes of Mortmain, Acton Burnell, and Shrewsbury is from this point of view even simpler. An enactment, therefore, that legislation concerning the estate of the king and of the realm should be effected only by the king in parliament need present no formal difficulty. But Miss Clarke presses a material as well as a formal objection, arguing that the concept of fundamental change was so alien to medieval statesmen that even the barons, trying to impose restraint upon the crown, invoke only the principle of *rex sub lege*. But surely this is to attribute to the barons the concept of fundamental law at the very moment that they are engaged in altering it ? The difficulty is avoided if one takes Miss Clarke's words literally and assigns to the reformers not the concept of fundamental law but the proposition that law is fundamental. This corresponds with medieval theory in regarding positive law as the sum of all subjective rights, fundamental because it is sanctioned by its correspondence with natural law and liable to change or amendment because that correspondence has to be maintained. It is true that this theory disregards a distinction in kind between public and private law, obvious to us, and silently made in practice in most growing political societies in the middle ages ; still the theory is well attested, it disposes of the formal difficulty and it sorts well with the empirical method characteristic of English constitutional development. On this view a very considerable degree of voluntary self-limitation on the part of the king was possible and did, as will be shown, actually take place. Returning to her contention that the disputed clause should be taken in the wider sense, ' as a reference to general legislation and administration ', Miss Clarke then considers the effect of the statute. The struggle between Edward II and the baronage, she writes, ' had endowed the parliament and estates with a new significance '. ' In great matters both legal and political the final decision must rest with parliament . . . summoned in due form by the king . . . it must include the commonalty of the realm . . . the king must enact but the common assent of the estates is essential

[1] Reeves, *History of English Laws*, 3rd edn. ii, 108.

to the validity of enactments . . . the sum of these opinions was expressed in the Statute of York . . . the principle . . . [there] stated was in some ways premature . . . and its full implications could be worked out only very slowly.'[1] The objections to this view raised by the considerations just now brought forward are not met in detail, though they appear to be felt by the qualification of the principle as premature. Then, if the final decision of ' political great matters ' must rest with parliament, it may deal with matters touching the estate of the king and of the crown and that it did so in 1341 is undeniable. It is not contended, of course, that the statute excluded the commons from such occasional participation by assent, in general legislation, as they had had under Edward I and continued to have in a slowly increasing degree as the importance of parliament and the commons' use of petitions grew in the course of the fourteenth century. That was not directly affected by the statute, and Miss Clarke's argument in this respect would appear to be *post hoc propter hoc*.

Mr. Haskins' positive argument[2] seems to me to be phrased in a way that corresponds but ill with the facts. It suggests a conflict between the crown and the commons over certain rights or privileges eagerly sought for by the commons and jealously withheld by the crown until at the moment of its triumph it concedes them without necessity and without explanation. Parliament, Mr. Haskins says, ' was not in a position to ask such a right '. The matter will show very differently, however, if one regards the statute not as conferring a right but as imposing a duty, not meeting a demand from the commons to enlarge their power but associating them with important and probably infrequent negotiations in a way that might make them available for the support of the crown. The king and his advisers may well have done this without in any way retreating from the view that the parliament was ' their handiwork and instrument ', if it was precisely to increase the efficiency and maintain their control of the instrument, that this new duty was imposed on the commons. This point may be developed in connexion with Mr. Haskins' argument as to the consequences of the statute, particularly when tested by

[1] Clarke, *op. cit.*, 172.   [2] See above, pp. 193–4.

reference to the crises of 1327 and 1341. The hypothesis with which I am working is that it was the policy of the framers of the statute to alter the conditions of the inveterate struggle between the crown and the barons by confining it as far as possible to parliament, which for that purpose should be authorized to deal with a certain part of the prerogative. This would avoid the dictated terms of a baronial committee by giving the king an active share in the negotiations, and would afford him the support of the commons or at least the opportunity of securing it. Moreover, it would make the whole matter a national rather than a class affair. The barons might be expected to acquiesce because they had something to gain as the king had something to concede, namely those acts of legitimate self-limitation which were consistent with the integrity of that part of the prerogative which was reckoned inalienable. Evidently such negotiation could never get as much as could be obtained by the direct action of a united baronage. On the other hand the chance of retaining what was secured by parliamentary discussion and statute was far greater than in any other case. Now such a device in its nature must contemplate a struggle between the crown and the baronage in which the court party might, indeed, be outnumbered, but was neither decimated nor divided. What could it have availed a fugitive king without a party against an opposition led by the queen consort and the heir-apparent ?[1] Again, what had those who aimed at nothing less than the cession of the crown, and were in a material position to secure it, to gain by parliamentary negotiation under the terms of a statute which safeguarded the royal power and sovereignty ? It could not extend to such a case. And, finally, the official records suggest that in 1327 no one knew or was prepared to speculate with any degree of confidence as to the extent of parliamentary powers when the issue was the crown itself. If parliament was allowed and even encouraged to depose the king and acclaim his son, no trace of these acts found its way to the parliament roll, and public documents ran in Edward II's name until, under intolerable pressure, he had gone through the form of a voluntary abdication. This was notified to the country as having been made

---

[1] See Stubbs, *Historical Introductions to the Rolls Series*, 516–19.

with the advice and consent of the magnates, and that was all.[1]

If we turn to the events of 1340–1 we see a very different picture. The king was in financial extremities and the administrative and financial arrangements which he had made before going abroad had in effect broken down. Stratford was reinstated as regent, and in December and January of 1339–40 in his attempt to secure supply was met with opposition from the commons who demanded concessions which, in his judgement, no minister could make on behalf of the king. What resulted when the king returned to England early in the year and the demands of parliament were formulated by a committee on which the commons were represented, was such an act of self-limitation (in the matter of taxation) as was contemplated by the interpretation of the Statute of York which is here advocated. In the background lurked the old opposition to the court policy of household government[2] beside the privilege of the peers and the clergy which had been endangered by the disorders of 1330 and 1340–1. When Stratford was able to reconstitute the Lancastrian party the old remedy of depriving the king of the choice and control of his ministers was again brought forward. This time, however, the whole struggle was carried on in parliament and the king was defeated.[3] His use of the prerogative to repeal the objectionable statute was as much in accord with the doctrine of 1322 as was the fact that the struggle was fought out in parliament. I cannot agree that the act belonged to the ' category of *coups d'etat* '[4] and, though the king was no doubt guilty of ' atrocious duplicity ',[5] it lay not in his repeal of the statute but rather in his failure to re-issue it without the objectionable provisions. If he had done so, it must have contained just such measures of self-limitation as were contemplated in 1322.

[1] Cf. Clarke, *op. cit.*, cap. ix ; below, pp. 310 ff.

[2] It is not certain that the Walton ordinances were intended to be permanent, but they suggested a policy of consolidating and extending the system of household government which was incompatible even with the moderate constitutionalism of the bureaucracy and the old middle party ; cf. Tout, *Chapters* iii, 69–150.

[3] Tout, *loc. cit.* ; Clarke, *Fourteenth Century Studies*, 126–37 ; below, pp. 231–72.

[4] Plucknett, *Statutes and their Interpretation*, 144.

[5] Stubbs, *C.H.* ii, 410.

In 1376 the conflict originated (formally at least) in the commons, and thereafter, until the accession of Henry IV, the struggle was made to centre in parliament, in which the procedural devices of appeal and impeachment were greatly extending the possibilities of political strife. Notwithstanding the lapse into civil war at the end of 1387 the issue was brought back to parliament early in 1388 when high constitutional doctrine was formulated to assert, rather rashly perhaps, the supreme authority of parliament. Ten years later, when events had come full circle round, it was in parliament again that Richard quit the score, and those who betrayed and discarded him in 1399 did all that was in their power to make it appear that they had parliamentary authority for their act. It is not contended that the outcome completely realized the calculation which is here attributed to the framers of the statute but only that, apart from the exceptional case of the rebellion of 1327, after 1322 the struggle between the crown and the magnates was carried on, formally at any rate, in parliament as, in our contention, the Statute of York intended should be done.

IV

Professor McIlwain, as we have seen,[1] regards the inalienability of the public prerogative as in some sense a fundamental law of the monarchy in England and France. It derives, in his view, from the absolute administrative authority of the king, which may be shared by none and is only limited by the proprietary rights of his subjects. On this doctrine, where the king had diminished the prerogative it would be his duty or that of his successor to resume the authority, privilege, or property that had been separated from the crown. Still Professor McIlwain agrees that there is evidence suggesting that the king could voluntarily abridge the rights of the crown but, while recognizing this as possible, he considers it very doubtful. Even the possibility seems to have disappeared in his conclusion which runs as follows : ' It seems then that the normal thought of Western Europe in the thirteenth century and afterwards— as much in England as elsewhere—placed the rights of the

[1] Above, pp. 157–8.

crown beyond even the "absolute" king's power to abridge or alienate : it certainly placed them out of the reach of any of the king's subjects or of any assembly of them '.[1] If this can be maintained the interpretation of the statute which is here contended for must fall to the ground; the point therefore demands careful examination.

Professor McIlwain is concerned with political thought but the context suggests that he takes the inalienability of the prerogative to be as much a matter of law as of political doctrine. Such a law could be enforced by the crown, and if evidence could be produced of an act of resumption under the single authority of such a law it would go a long way toward establishing its existence. In the cases known to me the king alleges some special fact, e.g. his own nonage, or the act of a *de facto* king whom he describes as ' an invader '. The case of the *quo warranto* proceedings under the statute of 1278 appears differently according to one's point of view.[2] The political theorist might argue that when Edward I recognized a charter of a predecessor alienating a regality he had *ipso facto* ranged it in the class of delegated not alienated rights. This would be no proof, however, that the king who granted the charter did not intend to alienate and have the authority to do so. The historian would be disposed to observe that although Edward I might treat the regality as delegated he could not take it back merely because it was theoretically inalienable, without a suggestion of abuse or non-user.[3] In the one case the importance lies in the theory to be inferred from a fictitious delegation, in the other in the fact that the day of private jurisdiction was practically over and delegation in the case of the professional judges was a reality. In these circumstances where, as is common, contradictory opinions exist at the same time it will be the business of the historian to determine which of them prevails at a given moment, for the views of the majority ordinarily represent what is, those of the minority what a certain number of people think ought to be. Practically speaking the distinction is

---

[1] McIlwain, *Political Thought*, 374–82.   [2] Cf. above, pp. 35–62.
[3] It might, indeed, be argued that the policy of the crown toward those franchise-holders whose only warrant was prescription (settled in the statute of 1290), showed that the king understood that in practice the doctrine could not be applied and that it would be wiser to avoid a discussion of it.

between law and politics. The prevailing view will in effect be the law (irrespective of the available means of enforcing it) or more accurately the accepted constitutional doctrine,[1] and in trying to ascertain or establish it we must scrutinize the origin and credentials of every text that presents itself with reference to this distinction. Accordingly we may classify the evidence cited by Professor McIlwain as official and unofficial. The process is legitimate, for it would be antecedently improbable either that those who drafted the statute should have disregarded the doctrine of such a text as the Mise of Amiens or felt themselves bound by the political views of the author of *Fleta*.

The leading official texts, earlier than 1322, will be found, I think, either to recognize formally the duty of the king to respect arrangements for self-limitation into which he has freely entered or to be compatible with this principle.[2] The Runnymede Charter grievously impaired the royal authority, but it was gained by violence and the two confirmations made in the name of the minor king omitted the controversial passages, reserving them for further consideration except, of course, the machinery for coercing the king which was never revived. Professor McIlwain[3] points out that Henry, when in 1223, having officially come of age, he was asked by the magnates to confirm the charters, refused. Matthew Paris reports that the king was acting on the advice of one of his counsellors, who argued that these liberties extorted by force ought not properly to be observed, and Archbishop Langton, the spokesman of the magnates, did not see fit to repudiate this doctrine. When, however, two years later the king confirmed the charters in a contractual form in return for an aid, Professor McIlwain observes that ' this is good constitutional doctrine ', and proceeds, ' no charter could bind the king in matters within his authority ', citing Bracton to the effect that there can be no adjudication concerning royal charters or the acts of kings. I should have supposed that the constitutional doctrine which he

---

[1] ' Which,' Maitland wrote, ' however well they may be obeyed, are no laws ' ; *H.E.L.* i, 525.

[2] It seems unnecessary to give references for the texts cited by Professor McIlwain and discussed here.

[3] *Op. cit.*, 374.

applauds was a double one providing that the king may not be forced to concede liberties (that is privileges) but was free to do so voluntarily as the result of a bargain. If that is so, surely the king's charters can bind the king in the only sense that he can be bound, by a self-assumed moral obligation ? The king's charter in this case concerned matters within his authority and was in fact an act of self-limitation accomplished with the warrant of good constitutional doctrine.[1] Therefore there would appear to be no objection to a grant of liberties by the king, though such a grant must not be extorted by violence. Professor McIlwain calls this good constitutional doctrine in 1223 and I find no evidence that it had ceased to be so in 1322. I venture to doubt whether the words of Bracton, which Professor McIlwain cites, are relevant. They occur in a section in which he is dealing *De Adquirendo Rerum Dominium*.[2] Bracton has been speaking of royal charters which are produced by one

---

[1] Professor McIlwain has now discussed this whole matter afresh in a volume entitled *Constitutionalism, Ancient and Modern* (revised ed., 1947). He attaches great importance to the distinction taken by Bracton in fo. 55 between the king's *jurisdictio* involving the proprietary rights of his subjects which he is bound to respect and his *gubernaculum* in the field of administration where he is absolute. It is on this basis that he affirms the inalienability of the prerogative. Obviously the matter cannot be discussed here, but I believe that he and I may be looking at two sides of the same shield. The difficulty is not merely to reconcile the divergence between theory and practice, but rather to formulate the theory precisely and to determine where the emphasis ought to be laid. As to the first, Professor McIlwain's view contemplates a rigid boundary line between such things as the king might alienate and such as he might not, while I have suggested that the boundary shifted in deference to the historical process. Edward I was scandalized at the bare suggestion that he should dismiss his treasurer ; Edward III and Richard II accepted the process of impeachment and its consequence (see below, p. 226). As to the second, Professor McIlwain's purpose required emphasis on the theoretical continuity of the doctrine of the inalienability of the prerogative, mine (as is worked out in the text) on the practical divergences from it. In regard to the passage above Professor McIlwain suggests that I have misunderstood him. He writes, ' the promises referred to procedures within the king's discretion but not necessarily dismembering his royal authority . . . or involving a diminution of it '. If it could be affirmed that it was not in the king's discretion to diminish or dismember his authority that would be different, but Professor McIlwain does not say that. It is evident that in practice the king could and did diminish his authority—the recognition of the palatinate of Durham before there was anything but feudal custom by which the crown could vindicate its authority there is a striking example of this. If under John there was at least one theorist who held that the king could not and should not do so, it must be remembered that the barons in framing the Runnymede Charter tacitly rejected that doctrine.

[2] Bracton, fos. 33*b*, 34*a*, ed. Woodbine ii, 108, 109.

or other of the parties to a civil action and would, were they private documents, fall to be tested by the criteria the courts commonly applied for this purpose. He does not say directly that they do not bind the king, only that they cannot be 'judged', i.e. questioned, and that if any doubt arises concerning them the matter must be referred to the interpretation of the king or the council. He has previously arranged royal charters in three classes according as they are granted to an individual, a number of individuals, or a group or community; obviously those referred to in the passage cited are the first and second class, while the Great Charter or similar documents belong to the third. Then, although true, it is somewhat misleading to say that no charter will bind the king. Since the machinery of the law cannot be set in motion against him by writ, no charter, contract, or obligation of any kind can be enforced against him.[1] But this is by no means to say that he is freed from the moral duty of discharging such obligations. It was, indeed, out of the attempt to bridge this gulf between a moral duty and a legal obligation, which the barons made in 1258, that there arose the most precise and authoritative definition of the nature and extent of the royal power which we possess. Professor McIlwain regards the Mise of Amiens, St. Louis's arbitral award (1264), corroborated by Urban IV's repudiation of the Provisions of Oxford, ' as strictly in accord with existing precedent and with the best and most generally accepted constitutional opinion in England and elsewhere '. ' The king was recognized to have of right " *plenam potestatem et liberum regimen* " in the words of St. Louis, and *liberum regimen*—" free government "—meant a rule unhampered by any outside restraint, and it meant nothing more.'[2] With this judgement, subject to one important reservation, I wholly agree. But surely it is impossible to maintain that St. Louis meant nothing more than a *liberum regimen* so defined, for he is careful to add that he is not to be

---

[1] Bracton, fo. 5*b*, p. 33 ; cf. Ehrlich, *Proceedings Against the Crown*, 113, 146–7, 243 ff. Here Ehrlich cites the well-known St. Albans case where a charter of Henry III, confirmed by two of his successors, which had the effect of ' restraining the common law from taking its course in the administration ', was pleaded and allowed. When it came before the council in chancery at the demand of the king's attorney it was annulled. Thus the king's conscience was successfully invoked to right the wrong which the undeniable authority of the king had done.   [2] McIlwain, *op. cit.*, 376.

understood as in any way disparaging already existing ' royal privileges, charters, liberties, statutes, and laudable customs of the kingdom of England '.[1] That is to say that the king in the free exercise of his royal power is none the less bound by the whole body of English law and custom and his own acts of voluntary self-limitation. This double restriction being freely accepted may perhaps not fall under the term ' outside restraint' (as to which there will be something to be said presently), but it does, I think, amount to something a good deal more than Professor McIlwain attributes to the words of St. Louis. They obviously refer among other things to the charters (that is the privileges) which ought not to be extorted from the king by force though they are constitutional when he concedes them voluntarily.[2]

A like reserve must be applied to Professor McIlwain's reading of the Dictum of Kenilworth[3] which he considers to have been inspired by Edward I. It declares, again in his words, the ' orthodox doctrine ' of ' absolute administrative authority ' and again, presumably, he would say ' that and nothing more '. It does, indeed, declare that doctrine in specific and unmistakable terms, but §§ 3 and 4 maintain no less explicitly the king's self-assumed obligations. The commissioners who drafted the settlement in § 3 urge the king to respect the liberties of the church and the charters of liberties and the forest which he is bound expressly and by his own oath to maintain and observe, and in § 4 they proceed to enforce the principle in stronger language : ' provideat etiam dominus rex quod concessiones quas fecit hactenus, spontaneus non coactus, observentur, et alia necessaria quae per suos ex ejus beneplacito sunt excogitata, stabiliat duratura '.[4]

[1] Stubbs, *Select Charters*, 397.

[2] Professor McIlwain takes exception to this. ' They are when they recognize private rights ', he writes, ' but does this teach the diminution of royal authority ' ? I think that it does, but he raises again the difficulty to which he has already referred (see above, p. 203, n. 1), the substance of which is best noted here. At all times during the middle ages there was a practical distinction between the parts of the prerogative that were and those that were not alienable, but the line was by no means stationary. Obviously St. Louis drew it at the appointment and control of ministers.

[3] Stubbs, *op. cit.*, 407–10.

[4] Professor McIlwain points out that ' they appeal only to his piety '. It is not, of course, contended that there was any other peaceful method of enforcing an obligation on the king ; but there were many obligations which he would find it unwise to neglect. Moreover, words such as ' provideat' or 'stabiliat' sound more like commands than appeals to royal piety.

Next to these two texts in importance and authority, if not indeed on the same footing with them, must come Bracton's treatise. From this Professor McIlwain quotes ' a significant statement to which historians have given scant attention '.[1] The keeping of the peace and the administration of justice, he says, ' cannot be separated from the crown *because they make the crown what it is* '. Those words are, indeed, significant, and the more so if they are read in their context and compared with a cognate and highly relevant passage in another part of the treatise. In the context two points attract attention. In the first place Bracton explains why the keeping of the peace and the administration of justice cannot be separated from the crown. These rights and this jurisdiction are in the king's hand, he says, ' ut populus sibi creditus in pace sileat et quiescat, et ne quis alium verberet, vulneret vel male contrectet ', and after several further illustrations he comes to the generalization that the king has the power, ' ut leges et constitutiones et assisas in regno suo provisas et approbatas et juratas ipse in propria persona sua observet et a subditis suis faciet observari '. Now it is obvious that these words answer in substance to the three *praecepta* of the coronation oath from the time of its introduction in the middle of the tenth century until its form was modified for Edward II's coronation,[2] and a later passage of the same section of Bracton's treatise confirms the resemblance. He says of these powers ' nullum, enim, tempus currit contra ipsum [*sc.* regem] in hoc casu cum probatione non egeat. Constare enim debet omnibus quod hujusmodi pertinent ad coronam, nisi sit aliquis qui docere poterit ex speciali gratia habita contrarium '.[3] It is no less obvious that these things are inseparable from the crown than that they belong to it, and the reason in both cases is obvious, for no man may be required to bear a responsibility unless he is assured both of the authority and the material force necessary for its discharge. Bracton

---

[1] *Op. cit.*, 381, citing Twiss's Bracton, lib. ii, cap. xxiv, fo. 55*b* (in Woodbine's edition, ii, 166–7). The passage quoted was, in fact, inserted in Professor Davis' edition of Stubbs' *Charters* (9th edn., p. 413) in 1913, and has long been commented on in lectures and private teaching in at least one university.

[2] See on this Wickham Legg, *English Coronation Records*, xxviii, xxxi 49 ; Schramm, P., *History of the English Coronation*, 179–203.

[3] Ed. Woodbine, p. 167.

recognized this in the opening words of his introduction, ' in rege qui recte regit necessaria sunt duo haec, arma videlicet et leges '.[1] Yet he can suggest in the words just cited that a case might be made for the alienation even of these prerogatives, and he is perfectly clear that the king has many other liberties and privileges which he may and does alienate. Further, even the inseparable prerogatives cannot be directly exercised by the king and must therefore be delegated, but this must always be done in such a way that ' ordinaria remaneat cum ipso rege'.[2] In a later passage he returns to this subject and contrasts the ' ordinaria jurisdictio ' of the king with the ' jurisdictio delegata ' of his judges.[3] Now ' ordinarius ' is a term of art in the civil and canon law and means in general one who exercises jurisdiction in his own right,[4] and Bracton's particular use of the term is explained in the well-known passage in which he recommends that cases which are without precedent or otherwise so hard that the judges cannot decide them should be referred ' usque ad magnam curiam ut ibi per consilium curiae terminentur ',[5] that is to say to the king in his court in his council. The reserved ' jurisdictio ordinaria ', therefore, would mean that residual and discretionary authority of the king without which a decision declaring new law or otherwise creating a precedent must not be taken.[6] This, in Bracton's view, is the inalienable prerogative for most of the work of justice, and police is done by officials on the king's behalf and secured to the crown by the theory of delegation. Then, although he is speaking of the administration of justice, what he has to say applies equally to the whole field of royal administration where the routine work at any rate must very early pass from the king's hands to those of his officials.

---

[1] *Op. cit.*, 19. This comes by way of Glanvill from the *Institutes* of Justinian ; see Glanvill, ed. Woodbine, 23, 124 ; cf. the Oxford edition of the *Dialogue*, 55, 163.

[2] Bracton, ed. Woodbine, 167.

[3] *Op cit.*, 340–7.

[4] *Op. cit.*, fos. 401, 402, 412, ed. Twiss (R.S.) vi, 161, 249 ; *Bracton and Azo*, ed. Maitland (S.S.), 199.

[5] Bracton, lib. I, cap. ii, ed. Woodbine, 21.

[6] This matter has been dealt with by Professor McIlwain in the book referred to above (p. 203, n. 1). Bracton will sometimes use *jurisdictio* in this sense and sometimes distinguish the king's administrative authority by the term *gubernatio* or *gubernaculum* ; cf. fo. 55.

We may now continue our examination of the more or less official texts cited by Professor McIlwain in support of his thesis. He refers to the seventh section of the Assize of Northampton[1] as evidence that the rights of the crown could not be abridged even by the king himself. The assize directs the itinerant justices to deal with ' omnes justitiae et rectitudines spectantes ad dominum regem et ad coronam suam per breve domini regis . . . de feodo dimidii militis et infra, nisi tam grandis sit querela, quod non possit deduci sine domino rege, vel talis quam justitiae ei reportent pro dubitatione sua.' Professor McIlwain's suggestion appears to be that the judges were to resume such rights of the king and his crown as they found in private hands. Such an act of general resumption had been made by Henry II on his accession, and it was based specifically on his refusal to recognize the acts of his predecessor.[2] There could, therefore, have been no contentious proceedings. But Henry was concerned with other business at Northampton, and the words of the text refer to the jurisdiction and in particular the procedure of the king's court which the itinerant justices are to make available in the counties through which they pass. What is involved seems to be the new criminal and civil procedure set up in the Assize of Clarendon extended at Northampton by the institution of the assize of *mort d'ancestor* and the stiffening of the sanctions applied to accused persons who are sent to the ordeal. This appears in the first place from the words of the chronicler who says that the council at Northampton was held ' de statutis regni ', and divided the kingdom into six circuits to be perambulated by eighteen justices, an arrangement that proved unsatisfactory, so that in 1178 a special committee of the king's court was set up to deal exclusively with common pleas (*clamores hominum*).[3] In the second place the section of the assize which Professor McIlwain vouches contemplates contentious proceedings under the king's writ involving the possession or ownership of land; now it is known that the king could and did deal with his manors

[1] Stubbs, *Charters*, 180.

[2] *William of Newburgh*, ii. c. 2, cited in Stubbs, *op. cit*, 152 : ' chartae invasoris juri legitimi principis praejudicium facere mimine debuerunt.'

[3] *Gesta Henrici Secundi* i, 107, 207, cited in Stubbs, *Charters*, 154, 155.

as he pleased,[1] and that the writ of *quo warranto* by which usurped or improperly alienated franchises could be recovered was not used for that purpose before the middle of Henry III's reign.[2] It is hard to find here any question of the recovery of alienated royal rights on the ground that they were inalienable, and it would seem therefore that the text is really irrelevant to Professor McIlwain's point.

Next we have a letter of Pope Gregory IX ' warning the English king that his coronation oath required him to recover all royal rights which had been alienated '. The letters (there are two), written in 1236 and 1238 respectively, are in fact concerned with the king's numerous grants of possessions, dignities, and other things to the magnates lay and clerical.[3] In the first letter he is absolved from the oath he has taken not to revoke these grants, because it is sinful in view of his duty in the matter defined in the coronation oath which required him ' jura, libertates et dignitates conservare regales '. In the second he is bluntly commanded to revoke the grants on the ground of the grave prejudice of the Roman Church to which the kingdom of England is known to belong. The letters thus constitute an ' ex parte ' statement with regard to a matter about which the writer was unlikely to have first-hand knowledge. Of course if there were any evidence that the coronation oath had ever contained a clause safe-guarding the prerogative the papal letters might corroborate it. But, as we shall see presently, the evidence points strongly in the opposite direction, although the view that it should be otherwise was held in certain quarters.

Next we have the communication which Edward I submitted to the magnates at the parliament of Lincoln in 1301, asking them to assume the responsibility of judging whether he could accept and execute the proposals for disafforestation contained in the perambulation submitted to him ' without blemishing his oath and without disinheriting the crown '.[4] It is not certain

---

[1] Pollock and Maitland, *H.E. L.* i, 335–7, 384.

[2] Cam. H. M., *History* xi, 144–5. On the Assize of Northampton in general, see Pollock and Maitland, *H.E.L.* i, 138, and Stubbs, *Historical Introductions to the Rolls Series*, 133.

[3] *Foedera* i. i, 229, 234, cited in McIlwain, *op. cit.*, 374, 379.

[4] *Parl. Writs* i, 104, no. 44.

P

that the oath referred to is the coronation oath,[1] although Professor McIlwain seems to assume that it is, much less that the coronation oath forbade alienation of the prerogative. It is important to read the passage in its context, which is the history of the struggle between the king and the magnates over the confirmation of the charters. At each crisis he had laboured to defend the prerogative against the obligation to observe the charter freely assumed by his father and recognized as binding in the Mise of Amiens and the Dictum of Kenilworth. In 1297 he safeguarded ' the ancient aids and prises due and accustomed ',[2] and in 1300 he only accepted the new points contained in the 'Articuli Super Cartas' subject to a clause saving ' le droit et la seignurie de sa couronne '.[3] In these circumstances the inference would be that Edward's words in 1301 constituted a move in a political struggle against the charters, an *ex parte* statement by way of an appeal to the political opinion held in some quarters that the coronation oath ought to and, perhaps by implication, did provide a safeguard for the prerogative. The constitutional principle, however, formulated in the Mise of Amiens, the Dictum of Kenilworth, and by Bracton, accepted the validity of acts of self-limitation and the coronation oath is silent. Indeed, until the changes made at the accession of Edward II, the substance of the oath consisted of the ' tria precepta ' which dated, it would seem, from the middle of the tenth century though probably with deep roots in the Anglo-Saxon and Teutonic past.[4] After the Conquest some additional undertakings were asked for by way of coronation charters from successive kings, but the oath was not changed although it was glossed by the chroniclers through whom it was transmitted. But in general the oath and its ' younger brothers ', the accession charters, did not go beyond the recognition that the king was under the law and was bound

---

[1] Stubbs, *C.H.* ii, 109, n. 2, treats as possible, and p. 147, n. 1, as probable, the view that Edward I's coronation oath contained a clause forbidding alienation of the prerogative. He was misled, as Blackstone may have been, by the spurious oath put into circulation (though not vouched for) by Machlinia, late in the fifteenth century ; see below, p. 212, n. 2.

[2] Stubbs, *Charters*, 491.   [3] *Statutes*, 141.

[4] Schramm, *op. cit.* 179 ff. ; cf. Liebermann, *Gesetze* ii, 562 ; Ward, P. L., ' The Coronation Ceremony in Mediaeval England ', *Speculum* xiv, 160–78.

in accordance with it to maintain the peace and defend the right of his subjects. The oath, itself, continued to be the ' tria precepta ' attested in the middle of the tenth century and twice quoted by Bracton with only slight verbal changes, and all probabilities point to this as the form of the oath taken by Edward I.[1] The important addition made in 1308 is silent on the subject of an inalienable prerogative. Still Professor McIlwain, relying on the texts already assembled, and some others which he cites later, including appeals to the coronation oath made by the king and the barons alike (and in contrary senses therefore) between 1311 and 1322, writes as follows : ' It is a curious fact calling for further investigation, that in no surviving contemporary form of the medieval English coronation oath is there to be found any provision touching the inalienability of regalian rights; and yet the statements just cited, and a number of others, seem to leave no doubt that in the thirteenth and fourteenth centuries at least, the English king at his coronation did take some kind of solemn engagement under oath not to dismember his realm nor to ' blemish ' the rights of his crown, possibly an addition to the regular oath somewhat analogous to the declarations against transsubstantiation, which English sovereigns made for two centuries in modern times '.[2] Now in view of the evidence before us the suggestion that some contemporary version of the formal coronation oath safeguarding the prerogative has not survived may, I submit, be definitely dismissed. As to the inference of ' a solemn engagement under oath ' which would presumably, on this view, have been taken regularly, in the thirteenth and fourteenth centuries, there is this much to be said. Mr. Richardson and Dr. Sayles have shown that in the early fourteenth century when both the official and liturgical parts of the coronation ceremonial were modified and re-shaped and the oath itself developed in a sense restrictive of the prerogative, that the rubrics contemplated the possibility of further modification at each coronation. That is to say they furnished an opportunity for a gloss or explanation by the archbishop of the tenor of the oath in a sense either agreed upon by the magnates

[1] See Schramm, *op. cit.* pp. 177–203 ; Richardson, H. G., and Sayles, G. O., *B.I.H.R.* xiii, 131, 136, and xv, 97.   [2] McIlwain, *op. cit.*, 379.

and the king or imposed by the former. The rubrics, of course, lacked the ' legislative authority' of the official coronation records, but Messrs. Richardson and Sayles think that they suggest an underlying political principle that there should be a fresh contract with each new sovereign.[1] It might, therefore, be argued that this principle was understood in the thirteenth century, if there were any evidence in support which outweighed such countervailing evidence as might be cited. Professor McIlwain, indeed, produces certain texts showing that in the course of the thirteenth century the view that the prerogative should be inalienable, or perhaps even that it was so, was held in certain quarters.

We must therefore consider the nature and authority of these texts. The first is an early thirteenth-century compilation in which, under the rubric ' quod sit officium regis' the anonymous author has put together the condition on which, in his opinion, the king should hold this office. He must swear that he will guard the lands, honours, and dignities of the crown and according to his ability recover such as have been dissipated or lost.[2] These are the strictly relevant words but there is much more as to the king's duties and obligations. This is worked out in some detail and is admittedly a piece of political theorizing—what the writer thought ought to be, not what was. We may ask, therefore, what authority he can claim and to what political group he may be assigned. He appears to have been a layman moderately educated and having access to the archives of London, which he used freely. On the other hand, he was a

---

[1] Richardson, H. G. and Sayles, G. O., ' Early Coronation Records ', *B.I.H.R.* xiii, 129–45 ; xiv, 1–9, 145–8 ; ' The Coronation of Edward I ', *ibid.* xv, 94–9 ; ' The Coronation of Edward II,' *ibid.* xvi, 1–11. See also Mr. Richardson's important studies, ' The English Coronation Oath ', *Trans. R.H. Soc.*, 4 ser., xxiii (1941), 129–58, and *Speculum* xxiv (1949), 44–75, and Wilkinson, B., ' The Coronation Oath of Edward II and the Statute of York ', *ibid.*, xix (1944), 445–69.

[2] The text is printed by Liebermann, *Gesetze* i, 635–7 ; for criticism and biographical notes see his *Ueber die Leges Anglorum Saeculo XIII Ineunte Londoniis Collectae*, Halle, 1894, particularly pp. 91–100. A form of coronation oath based on this and the oath of 1308 found its way into print at the end of the fifteenth century though without credentials. It was reprinted by Blackstone and Taylor and Stubbs conjectured that it might possibly or even probably have been the oath taken by Edward I. See Blackstone, *Commentaries*, bk. i, c. 6 ; Taylor, *The Glory of Regality*, 333–4 ; Stubbs, *C.H.* ii, 109 n., 157 n. ; Richardson and Sayles, *B.I.H.R.* xiii, 144–5 ; Schramm, *op. cit.*, 215.

man with strong political views which he promoted with evidence, when he could come by it, and with forgery when he could not. He had little sense of historical method or construction and none of the integrity of documents, for he did not scruple to introduce material of his own into the collection of laws which he used, in order to reinforce his own political and constitutional doctrine. He was an imperialist with a ' whig ' view of the crown which he wished to see strong but precluded from such despotism as John had exercised, by the obligation to associate the magnates with him in administration, ' omnia rite facere in regno et per judicium procerum regni '. Now he says that the king ought to swear publicly to observe all these things (including the words safe-guarding the prerogative cited above) before receiving the crown. This is scarcely the language of a man in whose life-time the reigning king has taken ' some kind of solemn engagement under oath not to dismember his realm or blemish his crown '.[1] The Londoner's text would appear to be rather an attempt to supplement or enlarge the existing coronation oath. Professor McIlwain calls the words significant, as indeed they are, as evidence that such views were held in certain quarters, but they cannot claim the authority of Bracton or the Dictum de Kenilworth. Liebermann[2] said of the author that ' he used alleged historical material for the promotion of a party programme like the modern political press ' and I think that the analogy is instructive.

[1] If such an oath had been taken by Richard I it would have been likely to leave some trace in the accounts of his coronation which are given at length in the chroniclers. If it had been administered for the first time to John or his successor the anonymous Londoner is likely to have known of it and to have framed his text accordingly. In the contrary case his words cannot prove more than is suggested above ; cf. Schramm, *op. cit.*, 69, 195–7.

[2] *Leges Anglorum*, 99. Mr. Haskins thinks that I disparage the evidential value of this tract unduly. He regards it, he writes, ' in much the same light as the *Mirror of Justices*. There too the writer has a strong bias, but he unconsciously reflects *prevailing* views '. It all turns on what you mean by prevailing. In this case two tests suggest themselves, one is contemporary practice and the other the use of the work by other writers. It will scarcely be argued that in the Londoner's time, the king could not and did not alienate any ' lands, dignities and honours of the crown ' or did associate the magnates with himself in the government of the kingdom. As to the second point Liebermann found that in the thirteenth century his work was used by several people who copied documents from it, one historian, one jurist, and practically no one else, *op. cit.*, 93.

Now it will be observed that in the matter of the ' absolute ' administrative authority of the crown the anonymous Londoner was as unorthodox as those who framed the ' Securitas Pacis ' of the Great Charter and the Provisions of Oxford and the anonymous authors of the Song of Lewes, the Addicio de Cartis and the book called *Fleta*[1]—valuable evidence for the growth of political thought but of little authority for the accepted doctrine of the crown in the thirteenth and early fourteenth centuries. Yet Professor McIlwain vouches the author of ' the important legal treatise passing under the name of Fleta ' in support of the doctrine of the inalienable prerogative in a passage which runs ' ancient manors or rights annexed to the crown the king shall not alienate, but every king is bound to restore to his crown those which have been alienated '.[2] This should be read in the light of another passage from the same book in which the author states the same principle in rather more detail and invokes authority for it as follows : ' secundum provisionem omnium regum christianorum, apud Montem Pessolonium anno regni regis Edwardi filii regis Henrici quarto, habitam '.[3] The meeting at Montpellier is no doubt legendary but the principle which in France, at any rate, was discrediting the feudal theory and practice that kingship and kingdom alike should be treated as the king's private property, was drawn from the Roman law. In the course of the fourteenth century it established the rule of the inalienability of the prerogative in France, and a suitable theory was provided when by the personification of the crown the title, prerogative and domain were lodged in it, and alienation by the personal act of the king became impossible.[4] But this distinction came slowly if, indeed, it can be said to have come at all in medieval England,[5] though between Maitland's extremes of antique family law and trusteeship for the nation there is, as he has shown, the practical distinction between the estate of the king and the

---

[1] Mc Ilwain, *op. cit.* 375–6.

[2] *Fleta* (1685), lib. i, cap. 8, p. 3 ; McIlwain, *op. cit.*, 380.

[3] *Fleta* (1647), lib. iii, cap. 6, cited in Schramm, *op. cit.*, 270.

[4] Esmein, *Cours Elémentaire d'Histoire du Droit Français* (4th edn.), 327–31, cited in Schramm, *op. cit.*, 270, from the 15th edition.

[5] Pollock and Maitland, *H.E.L.* i, 518 : ' The king who asserts a right to revoke the improvident grants of his ancestors is relying upon an antique rule of family law rather than upon any such doctrine as that kings are trustees of the nation.'

estate of the crown exemplified, as I have suggested, in the Statute of York.[1] Meanwhile, if we are to assess the bearing of the evidence of *Fleta* on our present problem, we must keep two facts in mind. In the first place the treatise appears to be without authority in the sense that the London compiler's evidence is without authority. Both are the views of private, irresponsible, and anonymous persons as to what in certain respects the law, or if you like, the accepted constitutional doctrine, should be. Moreover, these views cannot have been widely held for there is scanty evidence of the popularity that is attested either by surviving manuscripts (there is only one of *Fleta*) or citations in other works.[2] In the second place, what the author says in these passages of the king's power to alienate is, in a large measure, contrary to the established theory and practice of the thirteenth century.[3] Professor McIlwain further cites a passage from the late thirteenth century law-book called Britton as follows : ' kings also may not so alienate the rights of their crown or of their royalty as not to be revocable by their successors '.[4] This book, like *Fleta*, is founded on Bracton, but it has a greater authority, derived both from its originality and its popularity, attested by the considerable number of manuscripts which have survived. Britton's treatment of the subject is so like that in *Fleta* as to suggest either that he borrowed from that book or that both were following a common source. In any case the doctrine is unsupported by contemporary theory and practice. Maitland, commenting on the passage, speaks of the ' strong sentiment—it is rather a sentiment than a rule of law '—that the ancient demesne should not be given away, and that if it be given away some future king may resume it.[5]

[1] Pollock and Maitland, *H.E.L.*, i, 524–5.

[2] See Liebermann, *Leges Anglorum*, 95 ; Holdsworth, *H.E.L.* ii, 321–2 ; Ogg, D., *Johannis Seldeni ad Fletam Dissertatio* (Cambridge U.P., 1925) ; N. Denholm-Young, *Collected Papers* (1946), 69.

[3] Pollock and Maitland, *H.E.L.* i, 329–49, 383–406, 511–26. Commenting on the doctrine of *Fleta*, Maitland says, ' This is hardly a matter of law ; all the king's manors are the king's to give upon what terms he pleases ', *op. cit.*, 384.

[4] *Britton*, ed. Nichols, i, 221, cited in McIlwain, *op. cit.*, 380.

[5] Pollock and Maitland, *H.E.L.* i, 518. If the author of *Fleta* intended the words ' ancient manors ' to restrict the application of his rule to the ancient demesne, the passage would not be of much help to Professor McIlwain's contention.

If we come back, therefore, to Professor McIlwain's conjecture as to the king's oath not to dismember his realm nor blemish the right of his crown we may feel that the balance of probability is strongly against it. It is difficult to admit the existence of an oath, regularly taken, affirming a doctrine contrary to that of Bracton and the Dictum de Kenilworth and the attested practice of the time which has left no trace in any known text connected with the coronation. It is clear that throughout the thirteenth and early fourteenth centuries the doctrine of an inalienable prerogative was held among people of rather extreme views and sometimes invoked by more moderate men when it was to their interest to do so. Evidence, on the other hand, of a superior order and authority makes it pretty clear that it was open to the crown to limit itself within bounds, which must be stated in principle and not detail, by freely assumed obligations and that by these it was bound.[1] If, nevertheless, such an undertaking were given and confirmed by oath at the thirteenth-century coronations and had proved ineffective (as might be argued from the repetition of the point in *Fleta* and Britton), then it would be natural to look to the coronation of Edward II for some development of this political aim. Yet it would seem that the magnates on that occasion considered themselves free to make their own terms with the king and that they carefully re-shaped and developed the coronation order, and added a fourth clause to the oath.[2] If the supposed undertaking had been given for a century and was still ill-observed, what more natural than to incorporate it in the coronation oath or to introduce a rubric directing the archbishop to explain that the doctrine of the inalienability of the prerogative was implicit in the coronation oath itself ? As no such steps appear to have been taken, the argument *e silentio*

---

[1] Cf. *Foedera* (Rec. Com.) i, 419, for Henry III's undertaking to observe and secure the liberties contained in the two charters after he had been absolved from his oath to the barons in May 1262.

[2] Except for one point this work seems to have been done deliberately and at leisure and not, as Dr. Wilkinson suggested, in consequence of a baronial ultimatum threatening to make the coronation impossible. The postponement of the date originally fixed was due to the negotiations consequent on Archbishop Winchelsea's absence in Rome. See Wilkinson, *Essays in Honour of James Tait*, 405 ff. ; Schramm, *op. cit.*, 207 ; Richardson and Sayles, *B.I.H.R.* xiii, 129–45 ; Ward, P. L., *Speculum* xiv, 160–78 ; and the further literature cited above p. 212, n. 1.

is not only admissible but powerful, and it is reinforced by the frequent appeals made to the sense of the coronation oath from 1308 to 1327, of which it has been said that ' in these disputes the meaning of the coronation oath was tossed backwards and forwards between the parties '.[1] If the oath specifically imposed only the obligation to observe and maintain the laws and customs of the kingdom and those which might subsequently be made by legislative act, then on any particular point there was room for honest difference of opinion about the interpretation, and more than room for partisan invocation, of it. On the other hand, this would hardly have been the case if there had been a specific engagement under oath, say in the terms of the anonymous Londoner's formula, to preserve the integrity of the rights and endowment of the crown. It seems to me that Professor McIlwain's conjecture is inadmissible. This brings us back to his main contention that the complete inalienability of the prerogative is part of the accepted constitutional doctrine attested in Bracton, the Mise of Amiens and the Dictum de Kenilworth.[2]

This view is advocated even more strongly by Mr. Haskins, who cites some of the texts we have already discussed, appar-

[1] Cf. Schramm, *op. cit.*, 209.

[2] Two further points in Professor McIlwain's argument should be noticed here for completeness' sake. The first is his apparent omission to allow for the development in political and legal thinking that followed on the experience of the thirteenth and fourteenth centuries. The doctrine of an inalienable royal prerogative attested in Professor McIlwain's view under Henry II and formulated by the London compiler under John evidently rested on an implied theory of the state very different from that which animated the act of 1366 repudiating the papal tribute. There are differing views as to contemporary judgements of John's act in 1213, but however impolitic it may have been thought it can scarcely be argued that it was regarded as alienation or blemishing of the prerogative as it certainly was in 1366 ; see the discussion in Luchaire, *Innocent III* v, 214–34 ; Adams, G. B., *Magna Carta Commemoration Essays*, 28–45 ; McKechnie, *Magna Carta* (2nd edn), 29. Even the act of 1366 recognizes by implication that such a submission as John had made would be open to Edward III with the assent of parliament. The second point is the relevance of the continental analogies which Professor McIlwain cites to his doctrine of the inalienability of what may be called ' global ' prerogative which embraces endowment and excludes acts of free self-limitation. In most departments of English medieval history it will be found that against such analogies must be set large allowances for the conditions and the history of the country in which the text affording the analogy originated. The dangerous development of the appanage system in France towards the end of the thirteenth century, and the destitution of the empire as such in the fourteenth, are cases in point.

ently without noticing that the most authoritative of them contemplates acts of self-limitation by the king. To these he adds a new piece of evidence. ' Even the king can do nothing in restraint of the royal power ', he says,[1] relying on the words of the king's counsel in the case of Rev *v*. Badlesmere in 6 and 7 Edward II.[2] I venture to think that if Mr. Haskins had considered the whole case more attentively, including the record and the editor's observations in the introduction as well as the report, he would have rated the value of this evidence much lower than he has done. The point of the case, if I have taken it, is that the defendant, whose franchise included the right to impound for three days all distraints made by the sheriff in the hundred in which his liberty lay, claimed that no distraints could be made except in the presence of his bailiff. The king's counsel, Hartlepool, objected to the impounding of distraints on the ground that it would deprive people of their right to replevy them immediately and, further, that the claim in favour of the lord's bailiff ' would be in restraint of the king's power in his demesne land', i.e. impede on the normal functioning of the king's officials outside a liberty. It was in speaking to this point that he used the words on which Mr. Haskins relies, ' the king himself by his own grant cannot do aught in restraint of the royal power '. The first objection was met satisfactorily and the second submitted for judgement. The question at issue was whether the king could grant a franchise which deprived his subjects resident in the geldable of their common law right to replevy their distraints or cause distress to be levied on their behalf, without vexatious delay. The first point did not arise because it appeared that such replevin was promptly facilitated by the defendant. The second raised the whole question of the nature of the prerogative and its relation to the law. Hartlepool makes the point squarely in asserting ' quod illum clameum est in preiudicium domini regis et contra corone sue dignitatem, maxime cum nullus debeat alicui ballivo seu ministro domini regis in aliquo resistere nec in officio suo faciendo secundum legem et consuetudinem regni etc. contradicere '.[3] But pre-

---

[1] Haskins, *op. cit*, 84–92.
[2] *Year Books of Edward II, Eyre of Kent,* ed. Bolland (S.S.) iii, 169–73.
[3] *Op. cit.*, 170.

cisely this was done in respect of the residents in any of the numerous franchises of which the lord had the return of writs or similar liberties involving the exclusion of the king's officers. Such a prohibition of the ' introitus judicum ' would, as Mr. Bolland did not fail to point out in his introduction, ' have made the grant of any immunity at all impossible '. Evidently such a question could not be settled ' rege inconsulto ', and it was referred to parliament where it appears to have been shelved.[1] Meanwhile the recognized practice with regard to franchises continued to belie Hartlepool's contention.[2] His words used ' arguendo ' in a case that never went to judgement can scarcely be taken as strengthening Mr. Haskins' argument. Finally, it should be noticed that his emphasis on Innocent III's condemnation of Magna Carta as a ' regalis juris dispendium '[3] is really irrelevant, for it is not contended that the terms of the Runnymede Charter were compatible with the prerogative any more than those of the Provisions of Oxford. But it was not the Runnymede Charter that Henry III confirmed and to the observation of which he was bound by the Mise of Amiens and the Dictum of Kenilworth.

We have now to consider Mr. Birdsall's view to which reference was made above.[4] He argues that by his revocation of the statute of 1341 Edward III ' asserted that not even a statute may legally restrain the royal prerogative '. He cites in support of this the Statute of York and the practice of the royal judges who consistently allowed the king to dispense with statutes which restricted his freedom of action in the appointment of royal officials. Now while I agree that the appointment and control of the king's ministers was a part of the prerogative which, in fact, was protected from alienation by the nature of the administrative system and the instinct of self-preservation on the part of the crown, I do not think that Mr. Birdsall's

---

[1] *Op. cit.*, xxxiv, xxxv.

[2] See now Mr. Haskins' article, *E.H.R.* liii, 478 ff. If I understand him he would regard Hartlepool's words as evidence that the doctrine of an inalienable prerogative was known in England in the early fourteenth century. That is no doubt true and highly relevant to the history of political thought but much less so to that of the constitution. It may perhaps be said that as far as public life and the conduct of government went no one was prepared either to deny or affirm the doctrine, still less to allow it to embarrass the king.

[3] *Op. cit.*, 86.   [4] See above, p. 159.

argument will serve to establish his point. This, if I understand him, is that a statute freely enacted by the king in parliament in restraint of the prerogative would not be valid. Edward III in his repeal did, in fact, assert less than that and the practice of the judges implies, I suggest, the contrary. The king assigns two reasons for annulling the statute, the first that it contains articles expressly contrary to the laws of the kingdom and his own royal rights and prerogatives which he was bound by his oath to defend, and the second that it proceeded from his act and not his will.[1] As to the allegation that the laws of the kingdom make certain parts of the prerogative inalienable, i.e. the control of ministers and all that that implies, if by laws we are to understand custom and the accepted theory of kingship, this is true subject to the reserve (argued above) that the content of this custom and theory was not immutable. From this it would follow that, as has been said above, it could safely be formulated in principle only and not in detail. If, as is here contended, the king had the power of self-limitation the condition of self-preservation must be implied in justice both to his successor and to the administrative system of which he was an indispensable part, and I suppose that the nearest we can come to a medieval formula for this rule is the condition Bracton attaches to the king's power of delegation, ' quin ordinaria remaneat domino regi ', extending the implied ' jurisdictio ' to cover the whole field of administration. This, indeed, Bracton does for he says that secular jurisdiction belongs ' ad reges et principes qui defendunt regnum ' and that the king is the ' judex ordinarius '.[2] As to the assertion that the king is bound by his oath to defend the prerogative something must be added here to what we have already said on the subject. First the prerogative must be understood in the sense we have just given to it because the only parts of the statute to which the king and the judges took exception were those affecting the appointment and responsibility of ministers. Moreover, when in the Easter parliament of 1343, which repealed the statute, the commons returned to the charge

---

[1] The antithesis *de voluntate* . . . *de facto* in the text appears to make the insertion of the word ' dread ' in the official translation unnecessary and confusing ; *Statutes* i, 297. See below, p. 255.

[2] Bracton, fo. 55b, p. 167 ; cf. pp. 107, 304–5 ; and cf. *Bracton and Azo*, ed. Maitland, 199.

two of their petitions dealing with matters touching the prerogative, although not that part of it with which we are concerned, were favourably answered.[1] Then the oath can only
mean the coronation oath, and the form in which Edward III
had taken it contained the clause which required him to hold
and maintain the laws and lawful customs, ' les quiels la communaute de nostra roiaume aura esleu '.[2] Did the new clause
require him to enact the laws chosen by the community of
the realm ? The wishes of the ' community of the realm ' could
only reach the king by way of petition which, formally, at any
rate, he was free to refuse. But if, which appears unlikely, the
question was asked, it is in the highest degree improbable
that it should have been answered, and indeed the king himself
avoids the dangerous issue by the suggestion that the statute
was technically invalid because his consent had not been
voluntary. The statute, therefore, is inconclusive on the point
at issue. It was invalid because the king's consent was wanting.

Mr. Birdsall's argument, however, rests chiefly on the nature
and effect of the king's unquestioned power of dispensing with
statutes in any particular case by means of a *non obstante* clause,
and it turns on an ingenious and able treatment of two statutes
of Edward III forbidding the appointment of any man as sheriff
for more than one year. It is admitted that this is in restraint
of the prerogative, and that until statutory provision to the
contrary was made by Henry VI it could be dispensed by the
crown. For our purposes, therefore, it is unnecessary to follow
Mr. Birdsall in his analysis of the well-known discussion of the
matter in the Year Book of 2 Henry VII, because the point at
present at issue is only whether the fact that in the reign of
Edward III the king could dispense at his pleasure sustains Mr.
Birdsall's contention that at that time a statute in restraint of
the prerogative would be invalid, although it had been enacted
with the king's free consent. I have given some reasons for

[1] *Rot. Parl.* ii, 141, no. 35, invites the king to retain ' lands, rents and
escheats and other profits touching his crown and right '; no. 38 complains
that in certain franchises annexed to his crown which he has recently
granted out the lords' bailiffs are exploiting the inhabitants.

[2] Schramm, *op. cit.*, 211 ; Richardson and Sayles, *B.I.H.R.* xiii, 129–45;
xiv, 1–9, 145–8 ; xvi, 1–4 ; Ward, *Speculum* xiv, 160–78 ; Wilkinson,
Historical Essays in Honour of James Tait, 405 ff. ; and see above, p. 212,
n. 1.

thinking that Edward (or his advisers) did not hold that view. It may now be pointed out that until the king dispensed the statute was valid, otherwise the dispensation would have been superfluous, and when he dispensed it remained valid for everyone except the person or persons in whose favour the dispensation had been made. An instructive analogy is to be found in such statutes as that of Mortmain and the Staples which, although based on principles of justice and expediency, were freely dispensed and in many cases very properly so. It is no real objection that the statutes regarding the sheriffs fall into another class as involving the prerogative, partly for the general reasons set out above and partly because the prerogative in this as in other instances had already been restrained in the same way by the king's grant or recognition of life-shrievalties, to say nothing of the whole range of franchises from the palatinates down to the small liberty with the return of writs. In neither case is any wrong done to the king and ' volenti non fit injuria '.[1] I agree with Mr. Birdsall that the Statute of York conforms to the constitutional doctrine of the Mise of Amiens and intends to withdraw from legislative action that part of the prerogative which I have called the residual or discretionary authority of the king. This was exercised directly through his ministers, it was universal and not local, reserved and not delegated and, therefore, I suggest that the case of the sheriffs is not on all fours with that of the ministers.[2] As a result of this discussion it would appear that the doctrine of an inalienable prerogative which entitled if it did not actually require the king to revoke grants of land or franchise made by his predecessors or himself, and definitely bound him by a separate oath taken at the time of the coronation not himself to make any such grants can scarcely be maintained—at any rate in the terms in which Professor McIlwain formulated it.

---

[1] The maxim is cited by Maitland in discussing this subject, *Constitutional History*, 303. There will be no practical distinction between restraint of the prerogative by grant and by statute unless it should be argued that the king was bound to enact the laws which the community of the realm shall have chosen, and this, since nobody doubted his power to refuse a petition, was obviously not the case.

[2] The fact that before the century was out the king's ministers were liable to impeachment for their conduct in office aptly illustrates what was said above, that the custom or law which protected the reserved prerogative could only be formulated in principle.

I am far from denying that the accepted constitutional doctrine treated certain parts of the prerogative as inalienable and recoverable when accroachment or enforced alienation had occurred, but I still contend that clause 5 of the Statute of York contemplates the possibility of certain acts of self-limitation being made by the king in parliament. The apparent contradiction will disappear if we consider a little more closely what the king had to alienate. All that came to the heir to the throne ' when the estate of the crown descended ' may be arranged in two classes. First there is the king's administrative authority whether external or internal—the former will be looked at in one way when people are thinking in terms of feudalism, as in 1213 when John accepted papal suzerainty, and in another as in 1366 when king and parliament repudiated it. In any case a wanton dismemberment of the kingdom (John's act was not that for he retained the direct dominion) would, on grounds of common sense and self-interest, be so far removed from practical politics as scarcely to need formal prohibition. Alienation of the king's authority to his subjects, on the other hand, in the various forms which the immunity might take, so far from being prohibited was evidently a matter of everyday practice whether by way of acquiescence or direct grant. For two centuries after the Conquest it could be practically justified as indispensable administrative co-operation and thereafter fitted into a more developed scheme of things by a theory of delegation. It is at any rate undeniable that in the fourteenth century much royal authority was in private hands and administered either in virtue of producible royal grant or recognized prescriptive right.

The second class comprises lands, services, and the profitable incidents of feudal tenure, and these may be subdivided into the ancient demesne, the material endowment of the king as recorded in Domesday Book, and other lands subsequently acquired. Then there was a store of personal property, such as jewels, plate, furs, and such like ; and finally escheats, forfeitures, wardships, marriages, advowsons, casually or temporarily accruing to the king. In practice it is obvious that he was free to alienate any of these, and, indeed, he was limited only, if at all, by the feudal sentiment (hardening into custom)

which expected him to regrant escheats and forfeitures and
hoped that he would keep the ancient demesne intact.

Evidently there were political and material reasons which
would make it to the advantage of the king and the baronage
alike to maintain the alienation both of lands and liberties. The
king must secure and retain the political support of the more
powerful of the barons and they in turn must consolidate or
extend the material basis of such power. On the other hand, as
the demand for extraordinary taxation became more frequent
there was enough to be said against alienation to account for the
political views which were expressed in certain quarters in the
thirteenth century. Clearly it would be to the advantage of the
barons if the king could contrive to live of his own, or failing
that if they could secure from his necessities either administrative reform or the realization of their political ideals. In the
second alternative it would be to the king's advantage to be able
to meet their demands with a ' non possumus '. It is relevant
here to recall that definite acts of resumption were commonly
referred to a special reason and not to the constitutional
principle we are discussing. Edward I, when in 1301 he raised
the general principle of the restriction of the prerogative, asked
the magnates to judge whether what they asked was within his
competence. Although the question whether a king could bind
his successor may perhaps have been an open one, I doubt
whether a king would have attempted to revoke his own free
grants or those of his predecessors on the sole ground that they
had blemished the crown;[1] I make exception, of course, of that
part of the prerogative which it is agreed was inalienable. Resumption in one form or another was often a matter of policy,
but not I think of law in the sense that the king was entitled,
much less bound, to resort to it. When we turn from the
material resources of the king to the administration of the
kingdom in which he was absolute, it will be observed at once
that a large part of his authority had passed from his control to

---

[1] The king's counsel in the *Quo Warranto* proceedings in 1279, however,
could on occasion argue that he was bound to resume all rights unlawfully
detached from the crown ; *Placita de Quo Warranto* (Rec. Com.), 429–30.
This was a gift made by Edward I before he became king ; see Pollock
and Maitland, *H.E.L.* i, 524. The case, however, owing to the circumstances of the grant is not quite relevant.

that of the civil service and the judiciary, under a theory of delegation which by 1290 Edward had extended to cover the anomaly of the decaying feudal jurisdiction. No doubt the king could dismiss his judges and clerks, but he had lost or was losing the judicial functions that his predecessors had still occasionally discharged in person, and his power of dislocating the self-consistent development of the common law by ill-considered or capricious writs. Perhaps the growing body of departmental rules and practice in chancery and the exchequer was less able to protect itself than the common law, but it must have had very considerable powers of resistance. Nevertheless, the king remained the central will and exercised through his ministers and counsellors in the whole range of administration that final, discretionary power which in the judicial system under the name of ' jurisdictio ordinaria ' was reserved for him and his court. Here then we have the line beyond which the prerogative is inalienable—it lies at the frontier of delegation. Clearly the frontier will vary from time to time tending, with the advance of bureaucracy and the legislature, to restrict the king's discretion while acting in his name. What is permanent, however, is the fact that the king cannot exercise this power alone but will require the service of counsellors and ministers. Such agents are indispensable to him, but since their business is to enable the king to exercise his free will they must be his servants and his alone. This is not to say that a minister can be required to carry out a policy which is contrary to his advice and judgement —Stratford made that point in 1341[1]—none the less the minister is not bound to serve any master except his conscience.

V

In the foregoing discussion it has often been necessary to speak in terms of constitutional doctrine and political theory, but such language is only relatively appropriate to the very practical interpretation of the Statute of York which I have proposed. I conceive it to have been an act of long-sighted statesmanship that had taken the measure of the changing condition of government and political life and profited by a favourable moment to

[1] See below, pp. 264–5, where I have discussed this point and cited authorities.

Q

authorize a procedure that would enable the king to take advantage of them. It was not the fault of those who framed it if they were obliged to deal with problems that speculation has not yet solved, though the fact gives a permanent interest to the proceeding that it might otherwise have lacked. In the thirteenth century when, as Maitland said, ' the number of legal ideas is very small and public law had hardly an idea of its own ', what he called the notion of proprietary kingship sufficed for active political life.[1] It died hard both in theory and practice, and though, as we have seen, there was some radical speculation among the politicians, the opposition was chiefly concerned with questions of administrative reform and the realization of their political ambitions. Edward I, on whose behalf the lawyers could suggest that on occasion his prerogative would put him above the laws and customs of the kingdom,[2] was imbued with the proprietary view of his office. When he was asked by the parliament of Lincoln to dismiss his treasurer he indignantly replied that they might as well take his kingdom from him, and added that none of the lords would allow a third person to interfere with his choice and control of his servants.[3] Yet his grandson courteously heard the commons' criticism of his administration, and with the advice of the lords appointed a committee to inquire into the alleged grievances;[4] but the crown in each case embodied the central will and its discretionary power was unimpaired. In fact, the nature of that power would be determined in any generation by the amount and efficiency of the delegated authority. Thus the opposition of the thirteenth and early fourteenth centuries sought to secure administrative order and efficiency by violence, or the threat of violence, resulting in some measure of temporary oligarchy, and this was steadily and properly resisted by the crown. But as the fourteenth century advanced it was seen that there was an alternative course that we shall not be misunderstood in describing as constitutional because it was compatible with the king's administrative supremacy. For the opposition to criticize

---

[1] Pollock and Maitland, *H.E.L.* i, 526.
[2] *Rot. Parl.* i, 71.
[3] Rishanger, *Chronica*, ed. Riley (R.S.), 460 ; Brunne, *Metrical Chronicle* ii, 312 ; both cited in Ramsay, *Dawn of the Constitution*, 476–7.
[4] *The Anonimalle Chronicle*, 79–94 ; Tout, *Chapters* iii, 290–305.

the acts of a minister of the crown or even to ask for his removal was to submit the justice of their case to the king, as the individual did in the courts by a petition of right, and the crown was no more blemished by giving redress at the request of parliament than by authorizing its judges to do justice on the petition of a private suitor. Before the century was out impeachment had become a recognized means of criticizing the government, and the old turbulent method of appeal was forbidden by statute in 1399. But more can be said. From Runnymede to Boroughbridge every attempt of the magnates to impose their will upon the crown involved violence and generally civil war. In the period between Boroughbridge and Richard's betrayal at Conway the direct conflict between the crown and the magnates only once degenerated into civil war.[1] Yet during that period king and parliament negotiated and often compromised in the settlement of questions which touched the prerogative. If the proceedings of 1388 were ferocious and those of 1397 vindictive and neither directly fruitful from a constitutional point of view, it cannot be denied that both were in form parliamentary. The point I wish to make is that the Statute of York offered a substitute for violence and civil war which was effective as long as neither side pressed its advantage to the point of upsetting the equilibrium which Edward III's policy had shown to be possible,[2] and that both parties to the dispute continued to use the method until they reached the deadlock of 1397.

As to the constitutional importance of the statute, that will depend on how the word is defined. It did not, on the view here advanced, alter either the structure or the legal functions of parliament, although it defined and developed a subject with which it authorized parliament to deal legislatively. The intention of its framers appears to have been political rather than constitutional, if by that the formulation of new doctrines and principles of government be meant. On the other hand, although it was intended to charge parliament with new duties

---

[1] I have already made the exception of 1327 and should class Bolingbroke's invasion with Isabella's, as the one involved the question of the succession and the other of the dynasty, and neither, therefore, was susceptible of compromise.

[2] See this point well treated in Jolliffe, *Constitutional History*, 394 ff.

as an instrument of government, it contributed largely if unintentionally to its importance in the business of government. An enactment which deflected the current of political dispute from the camp to a constituted organ of a government is, I submit, constitutional in its effect whatever may have been the intention of its framers or the composition of the parliament which they contemplated.[1]

[1] Cf. Pollard, *Evolution of Parliament*, 2nd., 241–2. I put the point at its lowest but do not retreat from the position taken above that the statute contemplated a parliament of estates.

APPENDIX

I

THE REVOCATION OF THE NEW ORDINANCES, 1322

Statutes of the Realm, i, 189.

[§ 1] Come nostre seignur le roi Edward, fitz au roi Edward, le sezime jour de Marz lan de son regne tierce, al honur de Dieu et pur le bien de lui et de son roialme, eust grantez as prelatz countes et barons de son roialme queux peussent eslire certeines persones des prelatz countes et barons et des autres loiaux queux lour sembleraient suffissantz de appeller a eux, pur ordener et establir lestat del hostel nostre dit seignur le roi et de son roialme solonc droit et reson, et en tiele manere qe lour ordenances feussent faites al honur de Dieu et al honur et profit de seint eglise et al honur du dit roi et a son profit et au profit de son poeple solonc droit et reson et le serment qe nostre dit seignur le roi fist a son corounement : et lercevesqe de Caunterbirs, primat de tot Engleterre, evesqes countes et barons a ceo eslutz eussent fait ascunes ordenaunces qe comencent issint, Edward par la grace de Dieu roi Dengleterre, seignur Dirland, et ducs Daquitaigne, as tous ceux as queux cestes lettres vendrount, saluz. Sachez qe come le xvi me jour de Marz lan de nostre regne tierce al honur de Dieu &c., et finissent issint, Donne a Loundres le quint jour doctobre lan de nostre regne quint :

[§ 2] Les queles ordenaunces le dit nostre seignur le roi a son parlement a Everwyk a tres semeynes de Pask lan de son regne quinzisme par prelatz countes et barons, entre queux furent touz le pluz des ditz ordenours qi adoncs furent en vie, et par le commun du roialme ilœqes par son maundement assemblez, fist rehercer et examiner. Et pur ceo qe par cel examinement trove feust en dit parlement qe par les choses issint ordenees le poair real nostre dit seignur le roi feust restrynt en plusors choses countre devoir, en blemissement de sa seigneurie reale et encountre lestat de la coronne, et auxi pur ce qe en temps passe par tieles ordenances et purveaunces faites par les suggets sur le poair real des auncestres nostre seignur le roi, troubles et guerres sount avenuz en roialme, par quoi la terre ad este en peril :

[§ 3] Acorde est et establi au dit parlement par nostre seignur le roi et par les ditz prelatz countes et barons et tote la commune du roialme a cel parlement assemblez, qe totes les choses par les ditz ordenours ordenees et contenues en les dites ordenances desoremes pur le temps avenir cessent et perdent soun force vertu et effect a touz jours, les estatutz et establissementz faitz duement par nostre

seignur le roi et ses auncestres avaunt les dites ordenaunces demor-
auntz en lour force :

[§ 4] Et qe desore james en nul temps nule manere des ordenaunces ne purveaunces faites par les suggetz nostre seignur le roi ou
de ses heirs, par quele poair ou commission qe ceo soit, sur le poair
real de nostre seignur le roi ou de ses heirs, ou countre lestat nostre
dit seignur le roi ou de ses heirs, ou countre lestat de la coronne,
soient nulles et de nule manere de value ne de force :

[§ 5] Mes les choses qe serount a establir pur lestat de nostre
seignur le roi et de ses heirs, et pur lestat du roialme et du poeple,
soient tretes accordees establies en parlementz par nostre seignur le
roi et par lassent des prelatz countes et barons et la communalte du
roialme, auxint comes ad este acustume cea enarere.

II

ANALYSIS OF THE STATUTE OF YORK

A. (Statute § 1)

Agents . . The ordainers within their terms of reference.

Subjects . . 1. The estate of the household of the king.
2. The estate of the realm.

B. (Statute § 2)

Agents . . The ordainers acting *contre devoir*, or similar
groups of subjects previous to the ordainers.

Subjects . . 1. The royal power of the king.
2. *The seigneurie reale* of the king.
3. The estate of the crown.

C. (Statute §§ 3, 4)

Agents . . 1. The king in parliament.
2. Groups of subjects.

Subjects . . 1. The royal power.
2. The estate of the king.
3. The estate of the crown.

D. (Statute § 5)

Agent . . The king in parliament.
Subjects . . 1. The estate of the king.
2 The estate of the realm and of the people.

VI

ARCHBISHOP STRATFORD AND THE PARLIAMENTARY CRISIS OF 1341[1]

I

EDWARD III's angry dismissal of his ministers in December 1340, followed by his heated controversy with Archbishop Stratford, and the parliamentary crisis of the spring of 1341 form a group of events that have been dealt with so frequently and from so many points of view that some apology for bringing them forward again would seem to be required.[2]

The concessions which the king had been forced to make in 1340 had thrown him into almost complete dependence upon parliament for extraordinary supplies. The consciousness of this restriction may well have stimulated him in the pursuit of the policy which had become almost traditional with the Crown, of carrying on his government by means of persons wholly dependent upon himself and therefore amenable to his will. Opposition to this policy was perhaps the most consistent principle of the Lancastrian party, which insisted on the king's duty to govern by the help of his natural counsellors, the magnates.[3] It should be noted that if this principle had a constitutional future, it had also a feudal past. The fourteenth-century middle term was perhaps not far off oligarchy. Stratford, who with his brother had been responsible for the

[1] Reprinted from *The English Historical Review* xxx (1915), 6–18, 193–215.

[2] The subject was critically examined by L. O. Pike, *Constitutional History of the House of Lords* (1894), 186–98, where references to most of the older literature on the subject will be found. To these should perhaps be added Barnes, *Edward III* (1688), 211–35, for the sake of the documents which are given in full, although unfortunately in English. Mr. Pike's conclusions are modified and criticized in L. Vernon Harcourt, *His Grace the Steward and the Trial of Peers* (1907), 338–45. Stubbs's account is in the *Constitutional History* (3rd ed.) ii, 402–11. The general political histories are not very helpful; but reference may be made to Hook, *Archbishops of Canterbury* iv (1865), 2–79 (Longman's *Edward III* merely reproduces this); *D.N.B.* lv, 30; J. Mackinnon, *Edward III* (1900), 166–94; and Ramsay, *Genesis of Lancaster* (1913) i, 285–92. Since the publication of this article, the crisis has been examined afresh by D. Hughes, *The Early Years of Edward III* (1915), 100–181; Tout, *Chapters* iii, 126 ff.; Wilkinson, *E.H.R.* xlvi (1931), 177–193.

[3] See Baldwin, *King's Council*, ch. iv, particularly 74–83, 93–130.

administration since the fall of Mortimer,[1] was identified with this party, partly, it may be conjectured, owing to his legal training and partly to his position, to use his own words, as *par terrae maior.*[2]

Meanwhile the king, who was besieging Tournay, was hard pressed by his allies, who wished to be paid and were also desirous of raising the siege. It is not clear that the king would have retained their support if money had been forthcoming, although that is what he gave out. But it is fairly clear that the revenue of England did not suffice for a war carried on by hired allies. The treaty of Espléchin, concluded on 25 September, brought the campaign to an inglorious close and left the king in an embarrassing position. His crown was in pawn and he had no money to redeem it; he had apparently little chance of obtaining further supplies from parliament, or of getting the benefit of those which had already been granted. Who was responsible for this situation ?[3] As a matter of fact, it was probably due to economic inexperience and the king's unwisdom in organizing a subsidized coalition. We shall argue presently that as a matter of theory the question of who ought to assume the responsibility was still an open one. Meanwhile an excellent opportunity was given for attacking those who were in charge of the government at home.

We come here upon very evident traces of an intrigue. The chroniclers bear witness that it was openly reported in England that the king's failure was due to the dishonesty and neglect of his ministers. Knighton writes that the king made the truce of Espléchin because

non esset ei ministratum de pecunia de communibus regni Angliae illi hactenus concessa pro defectu ministrorum suorum in sua absentia.[4]

And Baker, writing of the ministers deposed in November, says:

Nec eos absolvit quousque sua melancolia concepta de pecunie detencione, quam ad obsidionem Torneacensem debuerant misisse, fuerat sedata.[5]

---

[1] Ramsay, *op. cit.* i, 286.   [2] Birchington, in *Anglia Sacra* i, 28.

[3] The king was already uneasy on this point ; in 1339 he had tried to make his council responsible for supplies granted by parliament. See the interesting correspondence printed by Baldwin, *op. cit.*, 476–9.

[4] Knighton (ed. Lumby) ii, 19.

[5] Baker, *Chronicon* (ed. Thompson), 72.

Now we have a circumstantial story in the French Chronicle of London which receives some corroboration from other sources. The chronicler evidently had the *libellus famosus* before him, and he describes how, during the summer of 1340, the king was in constant and fruitless correspondence with the *faus gardeins* in England who withheld from him the supplies which the commons had granted. One of these *faus treitres* ' *q'estoit jurée au roy* ' was better disposed towards him than any of the others. This man was well informed about all their secret business, which, together with the policy they had concerted, he set down in writing and transmitted to the king, to whom he suggested that further correspondence was idle. The only course that would serve him would be to come secretly to London, send for the mayor and serjeant at arms of the city, and try by their means to arrest and imprison certain persons, after which he would find treasure enough.[1]

According to this statement the plan was suggested to the king by a sworn member of the council. Now the composition of the council, as between the great men, the king's ' natural counsellors ', and the knights and clerks through whom, since Edward I's time at least, he had habitually done his work, was one of the standing political questions of the fourteenth century. The Lancastrian party, of which Stratford was one of the leaders, stood out for the council of magnates. Then another contemporary chronicler informs us that the king came back with ' his secretaries ', certain of whom, envying the archbishop, excited the king's wrath against him, and Stratford himself plainly denounced an intrigue against him in the council.[2] Further, we know who these secretaries that accompanied the king were, and two of them at least appear as leaders at each stage of the attack upon the archbishop.[3] From the moment when the first charge was made against Stratford in the Guild-hall down to the attempt to influence parliament by a demonstration of the Londoners, William Killesby and John Darcy are associated with every important step. Their official character and the party and policy they stood for are made apparent

---

[1] *French Chronicle of London* (Camden Soc., 1844), 82, 83.
[2] Avesbury (ed. Thompson), 323 ; Birchington, in *Angl. Sacr.* i, 36.
[3] *C.C.R.*, 1339–41, 653 ; *Foedera* II, ii, 1141.

enough in the attack which is alleged to have been delivered on them in parliament by Warenne, which will have to be considered later.[1] Stratford's biographer states this point in terms; he says that the *curiales* had conspired against the archbishop in Flanders, and adds : ' Verum non solum milites sed et clerici hoc fecerunt : et . . . duxerunt regem ad Angliam . . . et intrare fecerunt turrim Londoniensem.'[2] Behind the personal struggles and exchange of recriminations which are to follow, we have then the opposition of definite political principles and ideals.

On 30 November the king appeared at the Tower accompanied by Northampton, the constable, Killesby, keeper of the privy seal, Sir John Darcy, steward of the household, Sir Walter Manney, Giles de Beauchamp, and a number of other clerks and knights.[3] He sent for Andrew Aubrey, mayor of London, and caused the arrest and imprisonment of the chief justice of the common pleas, several of the judges—two were actually taken later, while holding the assize at Cambridge[4]— the chief clerks in chancery and the exchequer, and certain London merchants.[5] Later in the day the chancellor (the bishop of Chichester, Stratford's brother) and the treasurer were dismissed. It is important to notice the element of anti-clericalism in this; Hemingburgh writes, ' Non clericos immo seculares ad placitum suum substituit.'[6] The London chronicler gives the explanation in words that furnish the key to one phase at least of the whole dispute that followed. He says that after the dismissal, when two laymen, as we shall see, had been appointed to the vacant offices of chancellor and treasurer, the king swore that he would never again appoint clerics to any great office, but ' only such persons as, if convicted of treason he could cause to be drawn, hanged, and beheaded '.[7] Thus early in the dispute we may see that questions of *privilegium fori* and ministerial responsibility were raised.

The next step was the public accusation of the archbishop, and it is significant that this was accomplished by Killesby in the Guildhall as a preliminary to the more formal charges by royal letter.[8] Stratford, meanwhile, had withdrawn to Canter-

---

[1] *French Chronicle of London*, 90.   [2] Birchington i, 20.
[3] *Foedera* II, ii, 1141.   [4] *French Chronicle of London*, 85.
[5] *Ibid.*, 84–6.   [6] Hemingburgh ii, 363.
[7] *French Chronicle*, 86.   [8] Murimuth (ed. Thompson), 117–18.

bury. There he was found on 2 December by Nicholas de Cantilupe, a knight sent on the king's behalf, who reminded the archbishop that he was bound, as surety for the king's debts, to certain merchants of Louvain, and cited him to attend the king in London on the following Sunday, ready to cross to Flanders. Stratford asked for time, agreeing to send his answer later.[1] It can scarcely be supposed that the court party really hoped to get rid of the archbishop in this way, but at this stage their case was so weak that anything which would have the appearance of putting their opponents in the wrong was of value to them. Two deaths which followed closely on each other at this time, those of Thomas le Scrope and Burghersh, bishop of Lincoln, deprived the royalist party of experienced leaders and threw the king more and more into the hands of the younger men, among whom we should probably reckon Killesby and Darcy.[2] The archbishop's reply, which was sent, we learn, after a few days, does not appear to have been preserved. His biographer describes it as ' literas responsales et exhortatorias '.[3]

Meanwhile the king was forming his new ministry. The words used by the chronicler make it clear from what class and party they were drawn :

Fecit quendam militem cancellarium Angliae, videlicet dominum Robertum le Bourser, et alium thesaurarium, scilicet primo dominum Robertum de Sadyngtone et postea dominum Robertum de Pervenke.[4]

Bourchier had been a judge and a member of parliament and had seen service in Flanders.[5] Sadington was chief baron, and had been at the treasury as lately as June 1340.[6] Parning was chief justice of the king's bench, but this office passes to William Scot early in January 1341.[7] Though the appointments were not made formally until 14 and 15 December, these men were

[1] Birchington i, 21 ; *Foedera* ii, ii, 1152–3.

[2] Birchington, *loc. cit.* ; *D.N.B.* vii, 337 ; Murimuth, 118, ' et consilio iuvenum utebatur, spreto consilio seniorum.'

[3] Birchington, *loc. cit.*

[4] Murimuth, *loc. cit.*

[5] *D.N.B.* vi, 14 ; cf. Foss, *Judges* iii, 400 ff.

[6] *D.N.B.* l, 101 ; Foss iii, 485.

[7] *D.N.B.* xliii, 352 ; Foss iii, 492. It appears that this name is properly Parvynge ; it is so given by the editors of the Calendars and the London Letter Books. But I have thought it convenient to preserve the traditional spelling.

described by their official titles in an important commission on
10 December. This, as it marks the next step in the story we
are following, must now occupy our attention. It is a commission of oyer and terminer addressed to the chancellor, the
keeper of the privy seal, the treasurer, and William Scot—the
new ministry, in short—ordering them to inquire into the
conduct of ministers and justices towards the people and the
king since the beginning of the reign.[1] On the same day similar
commissions were issued to the same men to inquire into
' alleged oppression and extortions by justices and any other
ministers of the king '. Like commissions were issued for all
the counties of England.[2] It looks as though two sorts of
inquiry were here contemplated. The first would be largely
political in character, concerning itself ostensibly with the
conduct of all those who had held high offices under the king
since his accession; but as the king afterwards tried to make it
appear that Stratford had been responsible for the administration since Edward II's deposition, the attack was really
directed against him and his friends. The second seems to have
included the whole administrative system of the kingdom. It
may be that a thorough reform in good faith was contemplated.
Murimuth says that the king removed all sheriffs and other
administrative officers,[3] and for this we have the official order
dated 15 January 1341 and directed to all the counties of
England.[4] We know also that in the next spring a general
and searching investigation into the civil service of Ireland
was ordered.[5] But this was not the only purpose of the
inquiry.

The first of these two measures raised a grave constitutional
question, because it assumed that ministers were responsible to
the king alone and might be dismissed, their conduct in office
investigated, and their persons punished by him. Other views
were strongly held in the Lancastrian party, and we shall see
how the matter was fought out. The fact that Stratford and
his brother were bishops, and would be prepared to describe

---

[1] *C.P.R.*, 1340–43, 106. This was for Surrey, Middlesex, and London ;
similar commissions were issued for seven other counties to three groups of
four persons each.

[2] *C.P.R.*, 1340–43, 111–13.   [3] Murimuth, 118.

[4] *C.C.R.*, 1339–41, 607 ; cf. 663.   [5] *C.P.R.*, 1340–43, 207.

themselves as peers, raised questions of privilege.[1] The fact that on 13 January a new commission was specially appointed to try the judges and merchants who had been arrested on 1 December,[2] may perhaps be taken as an admission on the part of the government that the case of the ministers called for separate treatment. With regard to the several measures, it appears that the commissions under which the investigation was carried out were what are called commissions of trailbaston. Now it has been said that these commissions were unlawful :[3] they were certainly highly unpopular. It was one of the points raised in the Easter parliament that the king should revoke the ordinance of Northampton, which was perhaps confused with the statute.[4] Two observations are therefore to be made. It is plain that the first commission for the investigation of the conduct of the ministers might well be called into question as *ultra vires*, or at least as raising a constitutional point that required to be debated and defined. But the commissions of trailbaston to investigate the administration were clearly authorized by statute, and the parliament must have thought so or they would not have asked for the withdrawal of that authority. It is possible, however, that they may have thought that the words ' times past ' in the statute gave some ground for opposing the inquiry.

There may indeed have been another ground for complaint. There is evidence suggesting that these commissions were applied harshly and unjustly for the purpose of raising money by way of fines. The London chronicler, under the year 1301, has these significant words : ' In that year . . . to retrieve the great expenses of the past twenty years, he.[Edward I] caused justice to be done on malefactors, and it was called trailbaston and in that way the king gained great treasure.'[5] With regard to the present commission, the same writers says : ' In that

---

[1] The king had been dissuaded from arresting the bishops of Chichester and Coventry (Lichfield) on 1 December on this ground. But a number of the chancery and exchequer clerks were under the protection of the *privilegium fori*, so that the question was already raised.

[2] *C.P.R.*, 1340–43, 110–11.

[3] Ramsay i, 286–7 ; Vernon Harcourt, *op. cit.*, 338 ; Pike, *Year Books*, 14–15 *Edw. III*, xxxviii–xxxix.

[4] *Rot. Parl.* ii, 128, no. 13 ; cf. Pike, *op. cit.*, lvii–lix.

[5] *French Chron. of London*, 28–9.

time trailbaston lay throughout England . . . and great hardship was done to the people.'[1]   Murimuth agrees, but is more explicit ; the justices, he says,

tam rigide et voluntarie processerunt quod nullus impunitus evasit, sive bene gesserit regis negotia sive male, ita quod sine delectu omnes, etiam non indictati nec accusati, excessive se redemerunt, qui voluerunt carcerem evitare.[2]

Official records point unmistakably in the same direction. Late in January the commissioners were ordered to furnish the sheriff with lists of the fines and amercements made before them that he might levy and transmit them to the exchequer.[3] Soon after they were directed to take the fines of all those who wished to make them for such trespasses (i.e. those mentioned in the commission) up to 2,000 marks, and cause them to be levied agreeably to the king's earlier directions.[4] Later in the year issues of this sort from various counties were assigned for such purposes as the victualling of ships and security for money advanced.[5] The commissions of trailbaston then were opposed rather for the fact that they were used as instruments of extortion than because there was anything unlawful in their nature. Moreover an inquiry so searching and directed chiefly against those who held office could not fail—particularly since so little distinction was made between guilt and innocence— to involve some of the clergy and nobility, some, that is, who enjoyed or claimed to enjoy special immunity from the ordinary processes of law. As we have seen in the case of the clergy, the king had already anticipated this difficulty and infringed the principle in the matter of the arrest of the chancery and exchequer clerks.

It seems to have been intended to review the administration of London like that of the rest of the country, and possibly (but there is no direct evidence for this) a particularly rich harvest of fines was anticipated from that quarter. At all events, as early as 1 December people were asked to make their grievances known, officers and debtors were ordered to have their accounts ready against the New Year, and the sheriffs bidden to render

<hr>

[1] *French Chron. of London*, 89.   [2] Murimuth, 118.
[3] *C.C.R.*, 1341–43, 58.   [4] *Ibid.*
[5] *Ibid.*, pp. 58, 59 ; *C.P.R.*, 1340–43, 189.

every assistance to the new government.[1] On 21 December, in compliance with an order from ministers issued five days earlier, the sheriffs made proclamation summoning all who had grievances to appear at the Guildhall before the justices assigned. Twenty-four of the better men from each ward had already been cited to appear.[2] But the recorder, on behalf of the mayor, aldermen, and commonalty, challenged the commission of the justices as contrary to the city franchises, under which no justices were to sit within the liberty except at the Tower during an eyre. The case was argued and the matter postponed until 16 January, when, having consulted the king, the justices abandoned their commission, and the next day the king ordered writs to the sheriff for holding a general eyre at the Tower.[3] The king meanwhile had made his intention perfectly clear by holding a ' private council ' in London, at which it was determined to examine the private accounts of all the judges and administrative officers, who were therefore directed to produce their rolls at Westminster at an appointed time.[4] On 13 January a commission was issued to Parning, Sadington, and Scot, directing them to arraign, hear, and determine the cases of the judges and the clerks arrested on the king's return, who, ' by the common report and clamour of the people and divers petitions shown before him (i.e. the king) and the council ', appear to have borne themselves ' in divers manners unfaithfully in their offices '.[5]

Meanwhile arrangements for the eyre were proceeding. If the articles, as given in the London chronicle, are examined,[6] it will be found difficult to distinguish between the new commission, which provides for a searching inquiry into the conduct of a long list of named officials, and that of trailbaston, which had been withdrawn. No doubt the earlier commission was

---

[1] *Calendar of Letter Book F*, (ed. Sharpe, 1904), 58 ff. London was included in the trailbaston commission of 10 December, and the chancellor, treasurer, keeper of the privy seal, chief baron of the exchequer, and W. Scot assigned for ' city and suburb of London and counties of Surrey and Middlesex ' (*C.P.R.*, 1340–43, 111).

[2] *Calendar of Letter Book F*, 59–60.

[3] *Ibid.*, 59–60 ; Murimuth, 118–19 ; Baker, 73 ; *C.P.R.*, 1340–43, 79.

[4] *French Chron. of London*, 87. This is put on 3 January, but the dates afterward, as compared with the Letter Book (proclamation of the eyre) and Patent Rolls (trial of the judges), seem to be three days out.

[5] *C.P.R.*, 1340–43, 110–11.   [6] *French Chron.*, 88.

withdrawn because the statute of Northampton which authorized it contained a saving clause for the liberties of London, and
the newer one issued because the king had a grudge against the
city in the matter of the loan which they had practically refused
him the previous spring.[1] The articles, we are told, were drawn
up by Killesby and other members of the council, and the
proclamation which was made on 20 January directed that every
one, high or low, who owed fealty or service to the king,
should attend on the justices at the Tower on the first and
second Mondays in Lent.[2] The eyre was actually held on the
second of these dates (5 March), and the judges seem to have
sat for twelve days.[3] The session could not have come to much,
and there was certainly violence and even rioting on the part of
the Londoners, who seem to have understood (and quite rightly)
that their liberties were to be questioned and probably even
withdrawn.[4] At any rate, the eyre was adjourned under pretext
of the summons of parliament.[5]

The policy of the new government is now clearly before us.
In the execution of their scheme they had been obliged very
early to make a distinction between the great officers of state
and the rest of the administration, and the archbishop's case,
involving this principle as well as questions of privilege and
peerage, was, as we shall see, dealt with separately. For the
rest the policy was self-destructive, because the increase of
revenue could only be obtained by administering the reforms
harshly and unjustly. We must now return to the case of the
archbishop, whom we left at Canterbury, where, early in
December, he had issued his hortatory reply to the king's
summons in the matter of the Louvain merchants. The archbishop was now on his defence, and as the government proceeded energetically with the commission of inquiry, he no
doubt saw that he would be obliged to take a line. This line
was essentially an appeal to public opinion, but in form a repudiation of the king's charges, and a profession of readiness to

[1] Pike, *op. cit.*, xlii ff. ; Riley, *Memorials*, 209.
[2] *Calendar of Letter Book F*, 60 ; *French Chron. of London*, 88.
[3] *Cal. of Letter Book F*, 61 ; cf. Pike, *op. cit.*, xlvii–xlviii.
[4] Murimuth, 118–19.
[5] Early in the summer (3 June) the Londoners made their peace with the
king : *C.P.R.*, 1340–43, 223–4, 229 ; *Cal. of Letter Book F*, 61 ; Pike, *loc.
cit.*

answer them in particular in parliament. As soon as treason had been suggested (10 February), he stood on his privilege and repudiated the jurisdiction of any secular judge. The king appealed no less anxiously than the archbishop to public opinion, but he also attempted to vex and embarrass his opponent. This struggle which we now have to examine forms the second act of the drama, and extends from the first summons on 2 December 1340 until the archbishop's arrival in London to attend parliament on 23 April 1341.

On the feast day of St. Thomas the Martyr, 29 December, the archbishop preached at Canterbury, following his sermon with a kind of political speech in English, dealing mainly with the *privilegium fori* and the alleged infringements of the Great Charter by the king's special justices. This was followed again by a solemn general excommunication against persons offending in this way.[1] A general excommunication of this sort was no doubt part of the primate's right; but if it were to involve any of the king's officers in the discharge of their duty, it would equally no doubt be an infringement of the prerogative. The appeal to §§ 39–40 of the Charter[2] raised a delicate point, and we may well suppose that it was this that moved the king to deal with the arrested judges and clerks by special commission, as we have seen he did. His immediate answer, however, was to send Lord Stafford to Canterbury on 4 January to ask for the articles of the excommunication and summon Stratford to the king.[3] But the archbishop refused to make the excommunication specific or comply with the summons. He had meanwhile on 1 January addressed to the king a state-paper in the form of a vigorous letter in which he develops his views of the constitutional theory governing the situation.[4] These we shall have to

[1] Birchington, in *Angl. Sacr.* i, 21–2. The extracts from a sermon printed by Dr. Macray, *E.H.R.* viii, 85 ff., would suit well the first or formal part of Stratford's discourse. He treats of Becket's quarrel with Henry II over the Constitutions of Clarendon and justifies Becket on grounds, as it would seem, of natural law : in the course he took, either his reason justified him or it did not ; if it did not, he sinned, and was neither a martyr nor a saint, and whoever says that blasphemes. We should value the English part of the sermon more.

[2] The appeal was in fact to § 29 of the Charter of 1225, which replaced §§ 39–40 of the Charter of 1215, referred to above.

[3] Birchington i, 22.

[4] This important document is given in Avesbury, 324 ff. ; Hemingburgh ii, 363 ff. ; *Foedera* II, ii, 1143.

R

consider in their proper place. He further justified, upon the theory stated, his own share in the transactions of the summer and autumn and declared himself in all things ready to stand to the judgement of his peers, saving his estate. Meanwhile he protested that nothing should be believed against him before judgement had been given.

A new point was now raised which the archbishop turned to good account. The ninths granted in the previous March had, so far as the clergy represented in parliament were concerned, been understood to replace the clerical tenth granted in the preceding year. Nevertheless the collectors were taking both.[1] The archbishop regarded this as a breach of ecclesiastical liberties and forbade his suffragans to allow the collection of the ninth from those who were bound to pay the tenth.[2] This was some time before 26 January, when the king followed up his first summons by the issue of a safe-conduct and a formal summons delivered by Nicholas de Cantilupe.[3] On the same day Stratford was arrested, the sheriff of Kent was ordered to produce him before the king and council in London to answer for contempt, and this, as he said, prevented his making use of the safe-conduct. He seems to have let it be known in Canterbury that he did not consider it safe to go to the king except in full parliament as certain of the chief councillors had threatened him with death.[4]

On 28 January Stratford addressed letters to the chancellor and the king and council complaining of his arrest, by which the special privileges of the church and the rights of all secured by the great charter and the laws and customs of the land are infringed. Unless remedy is provided he will proceed to act under the bull of Innocent IV, which denounces excommunication for these offences.[5] On 30 January he took a still stronger measure for embarrassing the government by for-

---

[1] See Ramsay, *Genesis of Lancaster* i, 272 ; ii, 86.

[2] Birchington, *loc. cit.*

[3] *Foedera* II, ii, 1146 ; *C.P.R.*, 1340–43, 124. Stratford's letter to the king is in Birchington i, 27–36 ; on the present point see p. 32.

[4] This is reported by Dene, a contemporary Rochester writer, and distinctly asserted by Stratford in his reasoned reply to the *libellus famosus*. See the passages in *Anglia Sacra* i, 29, 374. He was no doubt serving political rather than precautionary ends in spreading this report.

[5] Hemingburgh ii, 368–70.

bidding the collection of all clerical aids throughout his province, unless the abuse in connexion with the ninths, to which we have already referred, were checked. The complaint is developed in a letter to the bishop of London, Stratford's nephew; and a form of excommunication against those who violate the privileges of the church or disturb the peace of the kingdom by their counsel to the king is addressed to all the suffragans of the province, with a formal covering letter.[1] The archbishop is careful to say that the abuse is unknown to the king; his councillors are of course responsible. The opinion of the country, we are plainly told, was at this time hostile to the archbishop,[2] whose claims of ecclesiastical privilege perhaps excited that anti-clerical feeling which was such a marked note of fourteenth-century England.

Down to this time the government had contented itself with action. It now made the mistake of resorting to rhetoric, and contrived to put its case in an unfortunate way. But first the archbishop and his suffragans were formally prohibited from publishing ecclesiastical censures against those appointed to levy the ninth.[3] This was on 10 February, and on the same day the *libellus famosus*, or infamous pamphlet as it was called, was issued.[4] This intemperate document, which takes the form of a letter addressed to the primate, is really an appeal to the country. The new government—it was well understood that the king did not write the letter himself—under cover of a review of the campaign during the past year, set forth its theory of ministerial responsibility, upon which the archbishop is held guilty of criminal negligence. The same point was developed by a further review of the events in England since the king's return. There was a good deal of ill-tempered personal abuse. Stratford was described as ' tumidus in prosperis, timidus in adversis ', and again, according to the proverb, ' mus in pera, serpens in gremio, ignis in sinu '; but the finest flight is a reference to the primate's ' fucatum zelum vulpinae calliditatis fuco

---

[1] Hemingburgh ii, 371–8, gives all these documents.

[2] *Ibid.*, 371 : ' De quo [i.e. Stratford] non pauca sinistra plebs indocta retulit, simplex et rudis, incertis ac rumoribus intenta, vanisque favor-abiliter aurem inclinans.'

[3] *C.C.R.*, 1341–43, 107 ; *Foedera* II, ii, 1147.

[4] The document has frequently been printed ; see *Foedera* II,ii, 1147–8 (from the Close Roll), and *Anglia Sacra* i, 23–27.

perizomate palliatum '. Towards the end of the document, the
ministers permitted themselves to make a formal charge of
treason. The archbishop, it was alleged, had taken bribes, had
dishonestly admitted to office improper persons, and had done
other things ' in status nostri detrimentum et dignitatis regiae
laesionem '. The most elaborate measures were taken for giving
publicity to this attack. Copies of the document were transmitted to the bishops of the province and to St. Augustine's,
Canterbury, with the strictest injunctions for publication.[1]
This was ' tuning the pulpits ' on a large scale, and from the
promptness with which the answering note sounded from
Canterbury itself we may judge of what went on in other
dioceses. The next week (18 February) the king's attack on the
archbishop was made public in Canterbury under conditions
calculated to arouse the liveliest and most widespread attention.
Killesby came to Canterbury and, having failed to force his way
into the archbishop's presence, read out the *libellus famosus* to a
crowd at the market cross. Subsequently the archbishop in the
course of a sermon recited the king's charges to the people and
denied them point by point.[2]

The king, on the other hand, did not neglect any means of
publicity. He announced through the sheriff of Kent that he
proposed to observe the statutes and not to take the ninth
irregularly.[3] On the same day, 6 March, he addressed to John
Grandison, bishop of Exeter, a reasoned remonstrance against
the latter's action in publishing ecclesiastical censures against
the special justices assigned under the new commissions in
Devon. This document states the government's case very
vigorously : after reviewing the campaign and its failure owing
to the alleged default of the ministers, the king declares that
his friends advised him that unless he dealt drastically with
the ministers there was danger of rebellion.[4] The bishop is
directed to see to it that the investigation is not further hindered

---

[1] *Foedera* II, ii, 1148.
[2] Spirited and detailed accounts of these proceedings are furnished by
Birchington i, 21–3, and by the prior of Canterbury in a letter to the earl of
Huntingdon, *Literae Cantuarienses* (R.S.) ii, 226–30, no. 696.
[3] *Foedera* II, ii, 1152.
[4] I do not think that the words ' se prorsus ab obsequiis nostris retrahere
proponebant ', bear any milder interpretation. This may be a clever
attempt to make capital out of the allusions to Rehoboam and Edward II

nor the king's people excited against him.[1] Finally, a week later
(14 March), the king brought his case before the pope. The
letter is a modified version of the *libellus famosus*, and, as in that
document, Stratford is accused of discrediting the king and his
government and exciting the people to sedition. His continuance in the kingdom would constitute a serious danger which
the pope is entreated to avert.[2]

Stratford now issued a long and reasoned reply to the *libellus
famosus*, which is quite the ablest document this whole controversy produced.[3] He begins by stating a theory of the
relations of the ecclesiastical to the civil power which reckons
the clergy as ' fathers and masters ' of kings, princes, and all
the faithful. He then proceeds to work out a constitutional
theory upon which ministers are only responsible to the king
collectively and when their policy framed in council and authorized by parliament has been carefully adhered to, which, as he
says, has not been done in the present case. He then deals with
the king's charges point by point, answering them all, as it
would seem, very satisfactorily. He expresses a desire publicly
to clear himself of these charges before the king, prelates,
magnates, and peers of the realm, although this is at present
impossible owing to hostile dispositions of the king's chief
councillors. He points out further that the king has charged
him with treason, ' quo casu rex nullus nec dominus temporalis
iudex noster competens esse potest ', and intimates that he will
wholly repudiate the jurisdiction of any secular judge. Finally,
he says, that if it were permitted to disclose the secrets of the
king's council, he could readily fasten the responsibility for all
that has gone wrong in the proper quarter.

The king had shot his bolt in the *libellus famosus* and
Stratford's reply was difficult to answer. Edward's ' excusatory
letters '[4] form a very feeble rejoinder, but he still sought
publicity. This was on 31 March and the inevitable parliament

---

in Stratford's letter of 1 January. Perhaps this or something like it was
really believed ; certainly it was said in Flanders that the Government
intended to depose the king (J. de Klerk, cited in Pauli, *Geschichte Englands* iv, 377, n. 2).

[1] *Foedera* II, ii, 1151–2.   [2] *Ibid.*, 1152–3.
[3] The letter is in Birchington i, 27–36. Only a brief summary is given
here, as its contents will have to come before us in some detail later.
[4] *Foedera* II, ii, 1154–5 ; *Angl. Sacr.* i, 36–8.

for which the archbishop had been asking was to meet in little more than a fortnight.[1]

II

It has been shown how the king's change of ministry in December 1340 and the subsequent measures which he took to fasten the responsibility for his failure in Flanders on the disgraced ministers had involved him in a serious dispute with the archbishop. The dispute turned on questions of class privilege and constitutional theory, and both parties to it had made vigorous attempts to arouse and form public opinion. The scene of these attempts now shifts from pulpit and market-cross to Westminster. From the outbreak of the controversy the archbishop had asked for a parliament and professed his willingness to stand trial by his peers and to clear himself in parliament. Down to March 1341 the king had contended that it was not ' convenient ' to summon a parliament at that time. Let us now see what occurred when the meeting took place.[2] Parliament assembled on Monday, 23 April, but no business was done until the following Thursday. On the Tuesday morning, however, when the archbishop appeared at West-minster he was directed by two of the king's council to go to the exchequer to answer certain charges.[3] This he did. Those who turned him away were Sir John Darcy, the chamberlain, and probably[4] the Darcy who was with the king on his return in November,[5] and Lord Stafford, the steward of the household, the same who had been sent to Canterbury by the king in the preceding January to summon the archbishop.[6] On Friday, 27 April, Stratford again attended at Westminster, where he was

[1] The writs were issued on 3 March, *Lords' Report* i, app. (vol. iv), 529 ff., and the parliament met on 17 April, *Rot. Parl.* ii, 126.

[2] See Birchington in *Angl. Sacr.* i, 37–8, and *Rot. Parl.* ii, 126 ff.

[3] I do not discuss here the question of the archbishop's business in the exchequer. Mr. Pike has done good service in dispelling the notion that he was, or could have been, tried there (*Const. Hist. of the House of Lords*, 186 ff.), and Mr. Vernon Harcourt has made it clear that the financial business on which he actually went was much more important than Mr. Pike had been willing to allow ; he names it a ' damaging incident ' for the archbishop, and ' useful material for cross-examination ' (*His Grace the Steward and the Trial of Peers*, 338 ff.).

[4] When Birchington mentions the father on the same page (p. 39) he adds ' senior '.

[5] Murimuth, 116 ; *Foedera* ii, ii, 1141.   [6] *Angl. Sacr.* i, 19 ff.

once more told to go to the exchequer, this time by Darcy, Giles de Beauchamp, who, like Darcy, had been with the king on his return, and Ralf de Neville. Stratford refused, and having made his way to the other bishops who were in the Painted Chamber, took his place among them. The king did not appear, but sent a message by Darcy and Adam of Orlton, bishop of Winchester.[1]

The next day the archbishop, continuing the rôle of Becket which he had assumed at Canterbury in December, took part in a scene which his opponents not unsuccessfully attempted to turn into ridicule. On presenting himself at Westminster he was told, civilly enough, by the sergeant at arms that the king was holding his parliament within and that they had orders not to admit him. He named his office, position, and writ, and was still refused admission, along with his brother and nephew, the bishops of Chichester and London. He declined to leave without the king's express command. Presently both the Darcys (father and son), Giles de Beauchamp, and Sir J. Medham appeared, and the elder Darcy angrily asked the archbishop what he was doing. Stratford reasserted his undeniable claim to enter and his intention to remain until it was satisfied. ' May you stay there for ever and never depart,' said Darcy. Stratford then assumed the rôle of Christian martyr, offering his body to torment and hoping to render his soul to his Maker, to which Darcy rudely replied, ' No such thing—you are not so worthy nor we so foolish '. When Stratford continued his high line, describing himself as having come humbly bearing his cross to his lord king, Darcy told him he was not worthy of the cross he bore and brought up the old charges of having misled the king in his youth. Beauchamp now intervened and with great violence accused Stratford of having wrecked the king's policy in France. Stratford repudiated the charges and launched a fine impersonal curse on all who might be responsible. Darcy and Beauchamp together expressed their expecta-

[1] Orlton was an old political rival of Stratford's, and so strongly suspected of having written the *libellus famosus* that he took this opportunity of assuring the archbishop that he had not done so. *Qui s'excuse s'accuse.* Avesbury says : ' Litera quam dominus Adam, Wyntoniensis episcopus, praefato domino archiepiscopo semper infestus, ad quorumdam ipsius archiepiscopi aemulorum instantiam, prout dicebatur a pluribus, fabricavit ' (p. 330).

tion of seeing the curse light on the archbishop's own head and
departed, thus ending a scene the indecency of which can
scarcely be excused on the ground of the sympathy which it
may be supposed to have attracted to the archbishop.

Having failed to turn the Stratfords away by coarse abuse,
the question must have risen as to how to deal with them. At
length the earls of Northampton—William de Bohun, another
of those who had been with the king on his return—and Salisbury appeared and, having agreed to take a message to the king,
led the whole party to the small hall, where they found the other
bishops. Birchington asserts that they then went to the Painted
Chamber, where, after some talk of a reconciliation, the king
withdrew and an angry debate ensued. Orlton, who is described
as the king's chief councillor, is alleged to have been convicted
by the peers of having made certain false charges against Stratford.
As the king did not return, the meeting broke up in anger. We
must not take the words ' per pares praedictos convictus ' too
literally, or indeed in a technical sense at all. What appears
to have happened is that Stratford received some support and
placed the government in a difficult position. It is not unlikely
indeed that the events of this day marked the beginning of
a defection of the peers from the government and their alliance
with the archbishop on the ground, as we shall explain presently,
of common interest in the matter of privileges and common
dislike of the councillors who were in control. Certainly this
would explain a scene described by the London chronicler,
which would seem to fit best at this point in the narrative. The
chronicler writes[1] that when parliament met, the archbishop,
his brother, and the bishop of London were excluded by the
contrivance of William de Killesby. At the end of the second
week—28 April, the date which we have reached suits this—the
earl of Warenne came to the king in parliament, where he found
Parning, Stafford, Killesby, Darcy, and others who ' ought not
properly to sit in parliament '.[2] This, of course, is the expres-

---

[1] *French Chron.*, 90. The text gives the bishop of Lichfield, but Stratford's nephew, the bishop of London, must certainly be meant.

[2] Stafford was summoned as a lord by the same writ as Warenne, and
Parning, as treasurer, had a special writ ; see *Lords' Report* iv, 530–1. No
doubt the others came as ordinary councillors without writs ; see Baldwin,
King's Council, 76, 312–13.

sion of a theory, not a constitutional rule, although it was as such, no doubt, that Warenne and his friends wished to treat it. The earl then turned to the king and took up his parable. ' How goes this parliament ? ' he asked. ' Those who ought to lead are excluded and others are here in parliament who ought never to be in such a council where only the peers of the land can support you, lord king, in your great need '. On this Darcy rose demurely and withdrew, and presently Killesby and the others followed him without a word. This was a blunt statement of the opposition programme, and it was so far relevant that there was no ground for excluding the archbishop once he had been summoned. The chronicle adds that Arundel then proposed to admit the archbishop and hear him, and if he were not able to clear himself, that they should deal with him.[1] This conjecture receives corroboration from the policy of the ministers on the succeeding days. On Sunday Darcy and Killesby tried to secure the support of London by bringing the mayor, aldermen, and *communitas* to Westminster and then laying before them certain articles against the archbishop ' ut sic contra eum dictam civitatem excitarent '.[2] On Monday they published certain articles addressed ' communitati Angliae ', ' ut sic ipse archiepiscopus totius communitatis Angliae perderet voluntatem; volentes ipsum archiepiscopum exulem fore a cordibus Anglicorum '. By the word ' communitas ' here we must understand the parliamentary representatives of the commons, for Birchington expressly states that nothing else was done in parliament on that day.

For the important events of the subsequent week, Birchington is evidently confused, but he has quite plainly used good authorities. Through his official Canterbury version of what happened we may discern with the aid of the rolls of parliament what appears to have been a neat piece of parliamentary manœuvring. Birchington says that on Tuesday, 1 May, the archbishop offered to clear himself in parliament of all the charges that had been brought against him and that a committee

---

[1] The chronicler adds that the king consented and that a list of articles was drawn up in writing, all of which the archbishop denied. But he seems to be confusing later events with what happened on this day.

[2] Such meetings of the Londoners at Westminster seem to have been usual enough ; cf. Riley, *Memorials*, 209.

of twelve peers, whom he names, was elected to advise the king in the matter. Now we know from the rolls that a committee, consisting of six peers, was appointed for that purpose on 12 May,[1] and also that on Thursday, 3 May, the committee named by Birchington actually was appointed for the purpose of considering, not the archbishop's case, but a petition of the lords for certain important legislation. If, then, we correct Birchington's chronology[2] and suppose that Stratford offered to clear himself on Thursday, 3 May, what follows in Birchington agrees perfectly with the evidence of the rolls and supplements it in some important particulars. On Friday, 4 May, then (Wednesday, in Birchington), the archbishop in the king's presence in parliament again asked leave to clear himself, but ' the aforesaid councillors of the king '—this must refer to Darcy and Killesby who have just been referred to as ' totius discordiae incentores '—refused to hear him, and when he persisted they shouted him down. Parliament was adjourned, and the next day a scene occurred which changed the whole complexion of affairs and must have placed the government in a very difficult position. An appeal on behalf of the archbishop was addressed to the king by a strong party of lay and spiritual peers, the mayor of London, the barons of the Cinque Ports, and the knights of the community of England; in reply Birchington says that the king received back the archbishop to his favour and held him excused of all the charges that had been made against him. But the statement, as we shall see, is a mistake. Still, from this moment Stratford's personal case falls more and more into the background, for he had succeeded in creating a parliamentary party[3] and his demonstration in force was precisely an announcement of that. An examination of the names given by Birchington reveals some interesting political changes. Stratford was supported by the bishops, three abbots, five earls, eight barons, and two lords, together with the commons, as it would seem, *en bloc*. But it is important to notice that he had succeeded in detaching a member of the govern-

---

[1] See below, pp. 254–5.
[2] For a re-examination of the chronological questions, more favourable to Birchington, see Wilkinson, *E.H.R.* xlvi, 183 *seq*.
[3] See, however, Wilkinson, *op. cit.*, 188–9.

ment, his old enemy Darcy the chamberlain, and the Londoners.[1]

On what basis, we must ask at once, was the new alliance made ? What inducement could Stratford hold out to bring together elements so divergent and some of them at least so recently hostile to himself ? If the king or his minister, Bourchier, the new lay chancellor, and Parning, the treasurer, asked themselves the question, they received an unmistakable answer when on the following Monday (7 May) the lords' committee reported. The terms of the reference had been relatively narrow—the magnates had asked for a declaration and extension of certain privileges of peerage in the matter of exemption from responsibility to the ordinary court. The committee reported favourably on the fullest measure of this privilege. They added in general terms a proposal for something like parliamentary control of ministers, and the observance of the privileges of the church, of the laws and charters and other franchises and liberties acquired and enjoyed by the city of London and the cities and boroughs, the Cinque Ports, and the *commune de la terre*. On this followed a series of petitions working out these points in detail and proceeding from the lords alone, the clergy, the lords and commons, and the commons alone. What was asked for was little short of revolutionary. On the same day the archbishop humbled himself before the king in full parliament and asked to be received back into his favour. The king consented and all the prelates and magnates thanked him. The archbishop then asked leave to clear himself in parliament before his peers ' that he might be openly held for such as he was ', that is, as a peer and entitled to at least some of the privileges of his rank. But this was to

[1] At first sight this would seem to be the point at which Warenne's protest should be introduced. But this would not leave time for the archbishop and the peers to have come to an understanding and concerted the action, which, as I try to show later, they actually did. Then, too, we must leave time for the opposition to approach and secure the Londoners and the commons. The ministers' action earlier in the week, and their apparent sense of security in shouting down Stratford on the Friday, would indicate that they supposed themselves secure of their support. If, however, after this scene Stratford could approach them with a programme powerfully supported by lay and spiritual peers, and some persons detached from the government, and a suggestion that this was the opportunity for securing the constitutional changes that were afterwards proposed and carried through, they may well have had reason to change their minds.

anticipate what Stratford's party was striving for, and the king therefore, while professing to agree, stipulated that the affairs of the kingdom and the common welfare, in other words, supply, must first be dealt with.

If now we consider the events that led up to this crisis and the demands that it produced, we shall see that practically every element in society whose existing privileges had been compromised by the king's actions since his return was combined not only to guarantee those privileges against further attack, but also to extend them as much as possible. These discordant elements had so much in common : they wished to be secured against the arbitrary administration of the king's officers, and they wished to increase their own privilege by limiting the prerogative. Yet even at the beginning of the week they seemed to have little perception of their common interest. The Londoners were being manipulated by Darcy and Killesby, animated perhaps by the anti-clericalism that had led five months earlier to the appointment of a lay chancellor. The magnates in their original petition were seeking the advantages of their own order. Who brought them together and made them perceive their common interest and the pressure which they could exert by common action ? We may ask another question, *Cui profuit* ? At the beginning of the week the archbishop was apparently isolated and discredited. The government attempted to embarrass and browbeat him, if possible to exclude him from parliament, and if not, to influence that body, through the Londoners, against him. But Stratford was in a very strong position and he seems to have known it. He met bluster and violence with melodrama, and stood out for a right—that of admission—which could not be denied him. Once in parliament, he was sure of his ground, and it is scarcely rash to conjecture that he gained some support among the peers during his altercation with Orlton on Saturday, the 28th, but did not see his real opportunity until the lords' petition was committed on the following Thursday, and that between that and the succeeding Saturday he was able to form a party, as has been suggested, on grounds of common interest.

We may now follow the parliamentary struggle to the end. The opposition had overreached themselves by asking too much; to have granted the demands of the peers would have been practically to constitute an irresponsible oligarchy, and it may have been with some apprehension of what was actually to take place that the peers asked for the inclusion of certain sages of the law in the committee. As has been pointed out, the first committee contained none such.[1] On Wednesday, 9 May, the king's replies to the petitions of the lords and commons were reported in full parliament, but they were not considered satisfactory, and the king was asked to amend them. We know from another quarter that the king and his government were resisting the demands of the opposition; Murimuth reports that for a long time the king refused the demands of the peers ' iuxta privatum consilium suum '.[2] The utmost that he would consent to at this time was the reference of the matter to a new committee which was to contain—and actually did contain— certain sages of the law. The changes in its composition are interesting but not altogether clear. Of the bishops London only remained; Durham, Ely, and Salisbury replacing Hereford, Bath and Exeter. Montacute of Ely and Wyvill of Salisbury seem to have been men of no political significance, and the same may be said of Charleton of Hereford and Ralph of Shrewsbury, bishop of Bath. But we know how Grandison of Exeter had aroused the wrath of the king, and Bury of Durham who took his place had been Edward's tutor,[3] and his appointment to the see of Durham was irregular, as another duly elected bishop had already received consecration.[4] Among the earls, Northampton, who, as we have seen, was with the king on his return in November, replaced Suffolk, who had spoken for the archbishop on the previous Saturday. The rest of the committee remained unchanged, except for certain important additions: the chancellor (Bourchier), the treasurer Parning (a judge), John de Offord, a civilian, William Scot, who had succeeded Parning as chief justice of the king's bench, and Robert de Sadington, who was chief baron of

---

[1] Vernon Harcourt, *His Grace the Steward*, 342–3 ; cf. Pike, *House of Lords*, 195, who seems to have been mistaken on this point.

[2] Murimuth, 119.

[3] Professor Tout sees reason to deny this ; *The Place of Edward II in English History*, 378 and *Chapters* iii, 25 ; but cf. Denholm-Young, N. *Collected Papers*, 4.

[4] Cf. Ramsay, *Genesis*, i, 239–40.

the exchequer.[1] Thus the king's party in the committee was strengthened, and the body further received a strong official and legal element.

After the appointment of the committee on 8 May the clergy submitted their petitions, to which the king's answers were reported on Friday, the 11th. These were debated in full parliament, were judged unsatisfactory (' pas si pleisantes come reson demanderoit '), were further debated and amended by the magnates, until at last an agreement was reached.[2] The next day (Saturday, 12 May) the king's answers to the lords and commons were delivered.[3] On the same day these replies were woven into a statute ' signed ' by the lords and commons and offered to the king as the price of a grant of thirty thousand sacks of wool.[4] Then the chancellor, the treasurer, and certain justices of either bench, when (along with certain officers of the king's household) they were sworn on the cross of Canterbury to maintain the statutes, ' made their protestation that they had not assented to the making or the forms of the said statutes, and that the statutes were contrary to the laws and usages of the kingdom which they were bound by oath to guard '.

Meanwhile the charges against the archbishop remained to be disposed of. They had, of course, ceased to have any practical importance for the actual political struggle, since all the principles involved in Stratford's personal case were covered by the provisions of the new statute,[5] and no doubt the best course was that actually taken, namely, to let the whole matter rest until such time as it could be decently extinguished. Accordingly, on 12 May, a committee consisting of two bishops and four earls was appointed to hear the archbishop's replies,

---

[1] Rot. Parl. ii, 129, no. 17. All these had had special writs to this parliament. Lords' Report iv, 531 ; Foss, Judges iii, 473, 485, 492.
[2] Rot. Parl. ii, 129–30, no. 26.   [3] Ibid., 130, nos. 34–41.
[4] Ibid., no. 42.
[5] He claimed, it would seem, the privilege of a peer in all cases except accusation of treason, when he fell back upon the privilegium fori. Of course, in view of the subsequent repeal of the statute, it was unfortunate for his party that his case was not actually brought before parliament. No doubt the government saw what an important concession they would make by doing so. On the other hand, the parliamentary record of the petitions and the statutes based upon them probably constituted an historical precedent at least as important as the legal one which the trial of the archbishop would have furnished. The whole question is instructively treated in Pike, op. cit., 186 ff., and Vernon Harcourt, op. cit., 338 ff.

and advise the king and his council as to the procedure which should be adopted. The whole record was to remain with Killesby, the keeper of the privy seal.[1] The committee informed Stratford that they could not then deal with the matter and so it remained in suspense.[2] In the parliament of 1343 the king directed that the ' record ' of the ' arraignment ' of the archbishop should be annulled as untrue and contrary to reason, and John de Offord (who was destined to succeed Stratford at Canterbury) was ordered to bring the documents into parliament and destroy them there.[3]

Having disposed of the troublesome case of the archbishop, it remained for the king and his ministers to get rid of the still more troublesome statutes. Edward has been so severely censured for his action in this matter, that it deserves to be examined with some care. On 1 October 1341 letters close[4] were issued to all the sheriffs of England directing them, under certain reservations, to proclaim the repeal and annulment of certain pretended statutes made in the last parliament. It is important to take account of these reservations. It is provided that whatever articles in the statute have been approved by other statutes of the king or his predecessors are still to be observed. The king justifies his action on constitutional grounds. Certain articles in the statute, he says, are expressly contrary to the laws and customs of the kingdom, and the royal rights and prerogatives. These the king is strictly bound by oath to maintain, and he wishes therefore to correct what has been imprudently done, and has consulted his earls, barons, and other councillors (*peritis aliis*). Protests, he adds, were entered against the statute when it was made and the king himself did not consent freely to it; there was great danger that the parliament would break up in discord with nothing done (that is, with no grant of supplies), and thus ruin the king's great undertaking; therefore he dissembled, as was proper, and allowed it to be passed. The council agreed that since the statute did not proceed from the king's free will it was null and ought not to have the force of a statute, and this doctrine was expressed

[1] *Rot. Parl.* ii, 131, no. 44 ; 132, no. 49.
[2] Murimuth, 120.
[3] *Rot. Parl.* ii, 139, no. 22.
[4] *Foedera* ii, ii, 1177 ; *Statutes of the Realm* i, 297.

in the rubric of the repeating ordinance, which runs ' de statuto revocando, quod a voluntate regis gratuita non processit '.[1]

Now this would seem to be a defensible position. There was a body of law and a prerogative, and the king was bound to defend both. He could no more diminish the rights of his subjects secured to them under the law than he could subtract from the right of his successors to enjoy the prerogative as fully as he himself had done.[2] Appeal might indeed be taken to the statute of York, which, by forbidding constitutional changes unless made in a prescribed fashion, did indeed admit the possibility of such changes; but to this it could be answered that the king's consent was essential to such changes.[3] Further, the changes contemplated by the statute of 1341, in so far as they were political, may well be thought to have been unworkable. We say, in so far as they were political, because the statute had this in common with the changes proposed in 1258 and 1311 that it combined constitutional innovation with much-needed administrative reform. What the king now proposed was to reject the one and accept the other, and if he had carried this through we could only have applauded his wisdom and discretion.[4] The ordinance repealing the statute had been made by the king and council, and although the theory was not yet perhaps clearly worked out, Edward would seem to have realized that in practice parliamentary confirmation was requisite. Hence the next parliament which met in the spring of 1343,[5] was the scene of the last act of the constitutional drama which we have been following. The details which we have now to relate appear to indicate that the lords and clergy, having been disappointed in their attempt to secure recognition of their special privilege by statute, had given up the still more difficult attempt at constitutional reform, although the commons stuck to it.

When parliament assembled the chancellor raised the whole question of the administration of justice, intimating that the king desired that ' the law should have equal course between poor and rich ' and should be properly observed, and charged

---

[1] *Foedera* II, ii, 1177.
[2] Cf. the discussion above, pp. 200 ff.
[3] Cf. above pp. 219 ff.
[4] Cf. above, p. 199.
[5] *Rot. Parl.* ii, 135–45.

the lords and commons to debate the subject separately and
report to the king.[1] The next day the commons reported,
advising that justices assigned should be elected and sworn in
parliament and that the articles of their commission should be
drawn up and approved by lords and commons.[2] On this the
king and the lords drew up a list of articles which they submitted to the commons for approval, but the suggestion of
the parliamentary control of the justices they appear to have
ignored.[3] The further discussion turned on the subject of
alien merchants, money and currency, and some technical
legal points. Then followed the quashing of the ' articles '
against the archbishop to which we have already referred, and
finally the formal record of the parliamentary repeal of the
statute, which contains a new and important point.[4] After the
words of repeal it is set forth that, since certain articles in the
statute ' were reasonable and according to law and reason, the
king and his council grant that such articles and others granted
in the present parliament should be made into a new statute by
the advice of the judges and other wise men and held for ever '.
Now this represents an advance over the words of the ordinance
of October 1341 in two points. In the first place, it is admitted
that certain innovations were reasonable and should therefore be
retained, and in the second a new statute is definitely promised.
But the great roll that contains the statutes of the seventeenth
and eighteenth years of Edward III shows that this promise
was not fulfilled.

A possible explanation of, though scarcely an excuse for,
this breach of faith, may be found in the parliamentary petitions
for 1343, which seem to reflect a great struggle. Those that are
relevant are as follows. The commons ask that the statutes be
maintained in their force, to which the king replies that they
should be examined and amended and the good ones observed.[5]
They then asked specifically for the observance and maintenance of the statutes of 1341, for which they had given the king
the ninth and 30,000 sacks of wool. To which the king replied
that he had repealed them as containing matter derogatory to

[1] *Rot. Parl.*, 136, no. 10. [2] *Ibid.*, no. 11.
[3] *Ibid.*, 137, no. 12. [4] *Ibid.*, 139, no. 23.
[5] *Ibid.*, no. 26.

S

the Crown and contrary to the law, but promised that whatever was honourable and profitable in them should be made into a new statute.[1] The commons then returned to the charge, petitioning against the repeal of statutes made by parliament, asking that the chancellor and treasurer should always be peers or other wise and sufficient persons, that no alien should be appointed, and that the chancellor and treasurer should not be justices.[2] In reply the commons were referred, as far as the statutes were concerned, to the answer already given. For the rest the royalist theory is bluntly expressed : ' The king may make such ministers as he pleases, as he and his ancestors have done in time past. It pleases him to make such ministers as be good and sufficient for him and for his people. As for their obedience, the king may charge his chancellor and treasurer to provide for the welfare [*faire le profit*] of him and his people, as may seem good to him and his council.'[3] Although this view of the constitution is not one that was destined to succeed, it is important to observe that in 1343 it had not yet failed.

Two reasons suggest themselves for the king's neglect to carry out his undertaking. In the first place, the fact that the commons were still pressing for the principle of ministerial responsibility to parliament, and were prepared to urge it even in the case of judges, might have made it very difficult to frame a statute containing the desired administrative reforms without in some way conceding the principle. In the second place—and this point, unfortunately for the king's credit, needs no labouring—the parliament of 1343 made no grants. It is not suggested that this is any excuse for Edward's conduct, but the view that he was acting in good faith until the temper of the commons alarmed and embarrassed him is not, I think, inadmissible. I believe that he was quite right to repeal the statute and that it was done in a regular way by an ordinance based on the judges' protest and confirmed by parliament; the wrong—and it is a comprehensible if not an excusable one—lay in not granting a new one.

[1] *Rot. Parl.*, ii, 139, no. 27.
[2] Parning became chancellor in October 1341.
[3] *Rot. Parl.*, ii, 140, no. 32.

III

It was said at the outset that the political controversy which we have just reviewed was essentially an attempt to settle certain constitutional questions. It would have been equally true to describe it as an attempt to convert certain political aims into constitutional principles. It will be profitable therefore to detach and examine some of these separately. We may begin, therefore, with what may be regarded as one of the few fixed points in the constitutional practice of the time. This was the idea that there was a certain body of privilege, custom, and law which should be regarded as inviolable either from customary sanction or because it could be referred to some definite transaction recorded in a charter or similar document. At every stage in the dispute both parties appealed freely to the Great Charter, the terms of which it was suggested were being infringed.[1] But the views taken of the authority of the Charter, its relation to the law of the land, the extent and fashion, in short, to which it could be invoked as a fundamental law restricting and sometimes, therefore, invalidating new legislation, varied considerably. Perhaps it is too much to say that the Charter or the laws connected with it were regarded as fundamental in the sense that they would limit the legislature and the Crown acting together. The older view, that they were concessions limiting the prerogative, purchased by the great classes of the kingdom and guarded by them as matters of privilege, seems rather to prevail. This is well put in the petition of the commons in the Easter parliament of 1341 :

The commons of the kingdom pray the king that the points of the Great Charter made by the king's ancestors and the magnates of the kingdom, wise and noble and then peers of the land, and other ordinances and statutes made for the profit of the common people containing the points of the Charter and others which are permanent should be observed without infringement, unless such be permitted by the peers of the land and that in full parliament. To this end the ninth was granted and the king renounced [March 1340] certain claims against his people. The king is asked to provide such remedy that every one shall be before the law according to his condition

[1] On this subject cf. Faith Thompson, *Magna Carta. Its Role in the Making of the English Constitution, 1300–1629* (1949), particularly pp. 80–84.

without in future being dealt with contrary to the law and the tenor of the Great Charter and all other ordinances and statutes.[1]

The view of the matter here taken seems to be that the sum of the customary law, the Charter and the statutes, forms that law which the king was bound by his coronation oath and paid by his subjects to observe. The notion seems to be that the king should act lawfully, rather than that he should be bound by any fundamental or organic law. There is a distinction here, because changes made by the king and parliament together would be understood as lawful action. Stratford had already warned the king that he was following a course ' contrary to the law of the land which he was bound by the oath taken at his coronation to guard and maintain ' ;[2] but he takes a different view of the Charter, as we shall see, emphasizing its ecclesiastical sanction. This conception of the law of the land comes out even more clearly in the terms of the statute :

The liberties of the church, the charters and other statutes made by the king and his progenitors the peers and commons of the land, for the common profit of the people are to be observed in all points. If any one of any condition infringes them let him be at the judgement of the peers in the next parliament. Whoever goes against any points of the Great Charter or other statutes or the laws of the land . . . shall answer in parliament . . . as well at the suit of the king as at the suit of party where neither punishment nor remedy was appointed before.[3]

This, no doubt, was what struck the chronicler as an attempt to enforce the observance of the Charter *ad unguem*,[4] but the liberties, charters and statutes referred to seem to be conceived much more as acquired privilege than any fundamental law.

Stratford's view of the matter holds it up in a somewhat different light. He distinguishes in his letter of 1 January between the law of the land to which the king is bound by his coronation oath and the Great Charter for the infringement of which he may incur excommunication. The distinction is quite clear, for he has already censured the king for arresting

---

[1] *Rot. Parl.* ii, 128, no. 9. Cf. p. 112, no. 6 (March 1340), where an aid is granted to obtain certain concessions, a committee is appointed, and to it are submitted ' les points et articles qe sont perpetuels '. I have given the substance of the petition in the text rather than a full translation.

[2] Avesbury, 325.

[3] *Rot. Parl.* ii, 132, no. 50. The translation is condensed.

[4] Avesbury, *loc. cit.*

people contrary to the law of the land and the Great Charter.[1] It was natural that Stratford should insist on the ecclesiastical sanction of the privileges secured by the Charter and think of enforcing their observance by excommunication, just as the commons had, by reminding the king that they had granted the ninth to secure a like concession, conveyed a threat of with-holding supplies. But even if one conceived of the Great Charter and laws and customs of the kingdom as a group of class privileges acquired and preserved in different ways, they operated, when they came to be enforced, as a fundamental law so far, at least, as the arbitrary exercise of the royal power was concerned. There is evidence for the theory that there was a mass of law, custom, and privilege, which, however sanctioned or acquired, ought not to be injured or altered. Even the king in his most angry moment admitted this by implication. The archbishop, he is made to say in the *libellus famosus*, has recently excommunicated violators of the liberties of the church and the Great Charter, ' to injure the king's reputation and defame his officers, excite the people to sedition, and withdraw the devotion of the magnates from him '.[2] The specification of the classes to be influenced is very instructive. The king admits, then, the existence of a body of law which he cannot afford even to appear to break ; but to this he can oppose another imperative principle, namely, the prerogative. This is brought out very clearly by the terms of the formal repeal of the statute which is described as contrary to the laws and usages of the kingdom and the rights and prerogatives of our lord the king,[3] and when the commons reminded the king that to obtain the statute they had made a special grant, they were told that ' the king lately perceiving that the said statute was contrary to his oath and in derogation of his crown and royalty and contrary to the law of the land in many points, caused it to be repealed'.[4] In other words, a fundamental law, if it existed, might work both ways ; the prerogative was no doubt as much part of the *lex terrae* as, say, exemption from arbitrary arrest. The commons in their petition, which we have already quoted, had suggested that certain things ought to be punishable as contrary to the law of

[1] Avesbury, *loc. cit.*
[2] *Angl. Sacr.* i, 26–7.
[3] *Rot. Parl.* ii, 139, no. 23.
[4] *Ibid.*, 139–40, no. 27.

the land, whether forbidden by statute or not, and this same principle was applied in a contrary sense by the king's great officers, the judges when they ' made their protestation '.[1]

Practice had, as so often before in England, outstripped theory, and an acute crisis had brought men to see that they were bound by two theories which might, and in this case had, come into collision. On the one hand was the permanent law of the land, consisting of various parts, produced and sanctioned in various ways and securing various privileges to various classes, but still capable of being conceived as an imperative whole. On the other hand was the royal authority undefined, except perhaps as consisting of all that had not definitely been taken away from it, and unlimited except by the *lex terrae* and the obligation imposed by the religious sanction of coronation and by the coronation oath to guard and observe the *lex terrae*.[2] Who, then, is the judge of what is contrary or conformable to the *lex terrae* ? The constitutional experience of six centuries has not produced a wholly satisfactory answer to that question, but it is important to note that the constitutional experience of less than two had sufficed to raise it in an acute form.

We may turn now to another aspect of the constitutional struggle, the attempt, namely, to deprive the king of the complete control of his ministers and to turn their responsibility, in some degree at least, to the parliament. It has been pointed out that the phrase ministerial responsibility is currently used to mean two quite separate things, the responsibility of ministers for the acts of the king, on the one hand, and their responsibility for their own acts either to the king or to parliament on the other.[3] These, of course, though different, are not unrelated, and both aspects of the matter were developed in the crisis of 1340–1, while the second occupies an extremely important place in it. There are two sides to the matter. On the one hand, there is the practical question of the way the king's government is administered, and I refer here particularly to local administration, having in view the sheriff and that group of officers and

---

[1] *Rot. Parl.*, ii, 126.

[2] Stratford could talk of ' iustitia . . . quae regibus dat regnare ' (Hemingburgh ii, 375), but I do not think that the conception of natural law was of much practical importance in medieval English politics.

[3] Dicey, *Law of the Constitution* (7th ed.), 321.

institutions throughout which his earlier plenary powers had been distributed. It has been well remarked that the Plantagenets from Edward I onward had the merit of perceiving that their interests and those of the community of the governed were identical and that the sheriff was the common enemy of both.[1] Some perception of this sort would account for the king's action in November—December 1340. Unfortunately the remedy was almost as bad as the disease. The measure raised constitutional questions of a very serious character. The king made his position quite clear from the beginning. The great officers of state are appointed and removable by him and by him alone. He says of the officers dismissed in 1340, ' a suis fecimus officiis prout nobis licuit amovere ' ; and, lest this should seem the exaggeration of anger—it is quoted from the *libellus famosus*— we may note that in answer to a petition of the commons in 1343 Edward replied, ' The king can make such persons as he pleases ministers, as he and his ancestors have done in times past, and he may charge his treasurer and chancellor with such duties as seem good to him and his council '.[2] The king's chief minister is the chancellor, to whom he has committed the administration of the whole state and the final conduct of affairs ; on his discretion and that of the other officials whom the king appoints to be of his council hangs the whole disposition of the kingdom.[3] The inferences which the king is made to draw from these principles, as that a minister who advises war is responsible for finding the resources to carry it on, we may dismiss as born of the heat of controversy, although it was a view that had its supporters.[4] The general principle here laid down, that ministers are appointed by the king and are responsible to him, and by implication, for him, is subject to one limitation. The king admits—indirectly, it is true, but it is none the less an admission—that he is in some sort bound to act by the advice of his council. He sets out in the *libellus famosus* that after repeated messages and letters sent without

[1] Riess, *Wahlrecht*, 3–6.
[2] *Angl. Sacr.* i, 25 ; *Rot. Parl.* ii, 140, no. 32 ; see above, p. 258.
[3] *Angl. Sacr., l.c.*
[4] Cf. Knighton ii, 19 : the king made the truce of 1341 because ' non esset ei ministratum de pecunia de communibus regni Angliae illi hactenus concessa pro defectu ministrorum suorum '. Compare the document printed in Baldwin, *The King's Council*, 351–2 ; cf. *ibid.*, 99.

result to the archbishop and his other councillors who followed him, he took the advice of his friends who had been abroad with him, who suggested in substance that it was no time for constitutional formalities.[1] Now the king here has the appearance of excusing himself for an irregularity which was justified by the urgency of the situation and the inefficiency of his official councillors. There is more than at once meets the eye here, because we know from other quarters that the king had an official council and a great seal in Flanders as well as in England;[2] and Stratford's sneer in his reply to the king, ' that those with whom he had taken counsel should proceed to find and punish the responsible person ',[3] indicates that the king had made the mistake of going outside the official circle.

The view that the king should govern by the advice and with the co-operation of the magnates, i.e. an official council drawn from the ruling class and not arbitrarily recruited by the king himself, was probably the most characteristic ' plank ' in the Lancastrian platform. It can be traced back to the ' paper constitution ' of 1244, and even then it would seem to have had a history in the desire of the great feudatories to be associated in the government of the kingdom and their suspicion and dislike of the *novi homines* with whom the king surrounded himself as early as the time of Henry I. This theory is developed at length in the very able state paper addressed by Stratford to the king on 1 January 1341.[4] ' The most sovereign thing,' he writes, ' that holdeth kings and princes in due and fitting estate is good and wise counsel, but now,' he proceeds, ' you are advised by people who are not as wise as they need be, and by others who desire their own profit rather than your honour and the welfare of the land, and you begin to follow unlawful and dangerous courses. Therefore take as counsellors the great and wise of the land as is customary, for without them you cannot govern well at home or succeed abroad.' If a council so constituted is to assume any responsibility, the king must stick to the policy which he and they have agreed upon; Stratford brings this out in his reply to the *libellus famosus*, where he is

---

[1] *Angl. Sacr.* i, 23.
[2] *Rot. Parl.* ii, 121 b, no. 28 ; *Foedera* ii, ii, 1141 ; cf. Baldwin, 396–7.
[3] *Angl. Sacr.* i, 30.
[4] Avesbury, 324 ff. ; Hemingburgh ii, 363 ff. ; *Foedera* ii, ii, 1143.

defending himself against the charge of having failed to furnish
supplies. Arrangements were made by the council in the
summer of 1340, based on contracts with certain merchants,
which seemed to the council satisfactory. The contracts were
violated and the money never came to their hands; he therefore
disclaimed responsibility : let them answer who broke the
agreements and spent the money badly.[1] He appears to admit,
on the other hand, that where the king and his ministers are
acting together, the ministers should assume responsibility.
In answering the charge of having attacked the king and his
government, he distinguishes : he never attacked the king, but
he has remarked certain administrative evils, things done ' by
the king's ministers without his knowledge ', and these he has
censured, not maliciously, ' but that remedy might be provided.'[2]

With regard to the responsibility of ministers for their
conduct of affairs, Stratford's position seems to be that they are
answerable to the council. He seems to understand this word
in its largest sense, defining it as ' great men, prelates and
peers ',[3] and it may be doubted whether he would distinguish
very sharply between this and parliament. The council, he
writes, should inquire into the whole question of the collection
and expenditure of supplies and punish such as are found
guilty according to law. In respect to his own conduct, the
archbishop undertakes in all things to stand by the judgement
of his peers (i.e. the council in the larger sense of the word)
raving his order and estate, for ' si gentz serront punis saunz
sespounse tout serra un juggement des bones et malveis '.[4]
This would seem to be a square statement of the traditional
Lancastrian principle that had already expressed itself in the
great attempts to set up oligarchy in England in 1258 and 1311.
The king should govern through the council; if he does not,
he must take the consequences alone. The council should
consist of the magnates, it should maintain solidarity, and to it
ministers should be responsible. To apply this strictly would
be, of course, to bring in oligarchy in an administrative way.
But two insurmountable obstacles stood in the way. The king
could dispose of the great seal and no effective grant of supplies

[1] *Angl. Sacr.* i, 30.   [2] *Ibid.*
[3] Avesbury, 325 ; cf. Baldwin, 101–2.   [4] Avesbury, 326, 327.

could be obtained without the co-operation of the commons. It was not until the reign of Richard II that the opposition attempted to cope with the first difficulty.[1] They tried now to meet the second by an alliance with the commons on the basis of extending the responsibility of ministers not to the council alone, even in its largest sense, but to the whole parliament, and of securing this by the appointment of officers in parliament and subject to its approval by requiring an oath of them. Further, the special claim of the commons in matters of finance was to be recognized by granting the audit of accounts. This comes out clearly enough in the content of the petitions in the Easter parliament of 1341 and the statute framed upon them.

These appear to be the conflicting views of what constitutional theory had been and was; it remains to show what the opposition thought it should be. As has already been indicated, a coalition seems to have been formed in the second week of the parliament for the purpose of weakening the prerogative in the interest of the peers and officials. An examination of their negotiations on this question of ministerial responsibility is very instructive. The question was first raised in connexion with the privilege of peerage. The magnates asked that the privilege should be extended to cover all official or ministerial acts, petitioning that ' peers of the land, officers, and others should not be held to answer for trespasses charged to them by the king except in parliament '. The king was advised that this was inconvenient and against his estate, and the matter was referred to a committee of twelve, consisting of four bishops, four earls, and four lords.[2] The committee reported favourably: ' peers who had held offices such as that of chancellor and treasurer should only be judged by other peers except that sheriffs and those who had money to account for should answer in the accustomed place ', namely, at the exchequer.[3]

The prelates and magnates then joined in a petition that all royal officers and justices should, on taking office, swear to

---

[1] Cf. Ramsay, *op. cit.* ii, 240.

[2] *Rot. Parl.* ii, 127, no. 7 ; p. 129, no. 17. Mr. Vernon Harcourt asserts against Mr. Pike that, in spite of the proposal to include ' sages of the law ', this was not done ; *His Grace the Steward*, 342. The second committee did, as we have seen, contain persons learned in the law, who afterwards protested against the statute.

[3] *Rot. Parl.* ii, 127, no. 7.

maintain and guard the laws of the land, the points of the Great
Charter, and the others ' made by the assent of the peers of the
land '. Further, they asked that any one procuring or advising
anything to be done to the contrary might be accused in parliament before the peers and awarded such judgement as they might
agree upon.[1] This was to be retroactive and permanent, and,
of course, implies the principle of direct ministerial responsibility to parliament. Then the magnates and commons united
to petition for an audit of all accounts whether foreign or
domestic.[2] The commons appear to have wished also to secure
some control over ordinary administration, for they petition
separately against ' general eyres commissioned without the
assent of parliament which have inquired into the acts of the
great officers, peers of the land ', and have occasioned certain
administrative abuses through the sheriffs. If the king feels
himself aggrieved by his ministers, they add, he should issue
lawful commissions with the assent of parliament.[3] The
magnates and commons also requested that ' because many
evils have arisen from bad councillors and ministers ', it
should be a law that the king should appoint his officers in
parliament and that they should take an oath there before the
peers to keep the law.[4] Since the magnates and prelates had
already asked for this, the petition may be regarded as having
the force of an expressed desire of the whole parliament, in
so far as the parliament at that time could be conceived of as a
whole.

The king's answers indicate an attempt to divide and rule,
and to grant, when he had to grant anything, to the council
rather than to the parliament. He began by presenting the
clergy with a dilemma. He remarks that the great seal is
a sufficient guarantee for the observance of the Great Charter
without an oath, and that ' the prelates who ought not themselves to take an oath without great and just cause should not
wish that people be charged with new oaths ', particularly as
there is already too much perjury in the kingdom.[5] This somewhat cynical appeal to professional interest, if it was intended

[1] *Rot. Parl.*, ii, 128, nos. 10–11.   [2] *Ibid.*, no. 12.
[3] *Ibid.*, 128, no. 14.   [4] *Ibid.*, no. 15.
[5] *Ibid.*, 130, no. 28. Stratford had forbidden people being put on oath
in Lent ; cf. *Foedera* ii, ii, 1151–2.

to detach the prelates from the lay lords, failed, and a day or two later the king gave a reply to the combined petition for the oath and ministerial responsibility. This answer in substance avoids the general constitutional principle which the petitioners had raised, and establishes the rule of law for the king's ministers. Anyone who in future shall do anything against the Great Charter or the law ' shall answer in parliament or else-where, where he ought to answer at the common law '. And this is to apply to things done at the king's command as well as of his own authority.[1] To the commons, however, the king grants the oath as it was asked for ; possibly his calculation was that if the clergy could be frightened from taking it, it would amount to very little. He granted them further the audit of accounts on condition that the treasurer and chief baron were among the auditors. With regard to the inquiry into the conduct of officers, the king undertakes that it shall be carried out by the council afforced ' by certain persons of the commons '. Finally, he agrees under reserve to the appoint-ment and trial of ministers in parliament. The words here are important :—

If any great officer of the king, named in the petition, should be deprived of his office by death or any other punishment, the king will take the advice of the lords who may happen to be near him along with the good council which he will have about him, and will put another suitable person in the office, and he is to be sworn according to the petition in the next parliament, and at every parlia-ment their offices are to be taken into the king's hand and they are to answer to all those who shall wish to make complaint against them. And if a complaint of misprision be made against a minister, and he be convicted of it in parliament, he is to be deprived of office and punished by judgement of the peers, and another suitable person put in.[2]

This was a considerable concession, although it was not all that had been asked for.

The statute framed on this answer was, as we have seen, protested against by the chancellor, the treasurer, and certain justices. This protest was no doubt directed against the un-warrantable extension of the privilege of peerage which the statute contained, and no doubt the protestants were right.[3]

[1] *Rot. Parl.* ii, 130, no. 37.　　　　[2] *Ibid.*, 130–1, nos. 37–41.
[3] *Ibid.*, 131, no. 42.

The statute itself contained some slight variations on the original demands.[1] All the barons of the exchequer were included, and all the judges, as well those of both benches as those assigned, and the council appointed for the duke of Cornwall,[2] but all the justices and the barons of the exchequer are exempted from the annual resumption of office although they are required to answer all complaints. The right of impeachment seems to be explicitly granted except that no corporate accusation is contemplated. Those who infringe any point of the Great Charter or other statute, or the laws of the land, whether they be royal officers or not, shall answer in parliament, and the plea that they have acted by the king's command or commission is not to avail them.[3] Parliament may therefore practically create new offences, by punishing official conduct which it determines to be contrary to the law and custom of the kingdom, that is, to the constitution. The principle of the responsibility of ministers to parliament could scarcely be more fully conceded. Even after the repeal of the statute, things were not quite where they had been before, because an important precedent had been registered. The commons had found themselves unable to act either corporately or independently ; they had therefore only secured what they might and should have demanded as a right, as a matter of special privilege, and in association with other privileges indefensible on any ground except that of class interest. The *privilegium fori* and the privilege of peerage as demanded by the lords spiritual and lay at this time were incompatible with any sound administrative system. On the other hand, it was but common justice that those who contributed for any given national purpose should ask that faith should be kept ; and a responsible administration—not necessarily responsible to parliament—is an elementary necessity of good government.

We may now consider what position the constitutional theory of the time would attribute to the parliament as a whole. It may be argued, of course, that except for purposes of supply no one thought of parliament as a whole, and some of the details

[1] *Ibid.*, 132, nos. 52, 53.
[2] He was keeper during the king's absence and a special council had been appointed for him ; *Foedera* II, ii, 1125.
[3] *Rot. Parl.* ii, 132, no. 52.

we have been examining would help to support that argument. Its predominance in matters of supply was admitted. There is also some evidence that the commons were coming to be associated with the magnates as guardians of the principle that the king should be under the law. From the point of view of the administration parliament was a body, or rather a collection of people, well fitted to assume responsibility and furnish moral support. Stratford in his defence availed himself liberally of this theory of parliamentary responsibility. The French crown, he says, was only claimed after a discussion in the parliament at Northampton,[1] and the continuance of the war and the alliance with the German princes followed on the discussion of the matter by parliament and its consent.[2] To the charge of having encouraged the king in making extravagant gifts, Stratford replied that he recalled no excessive gifts except those made to certain earls ' per vos nuper creatis denuo ex consensu parliamenti '.[3] The official records bear out Stratford's contentions in most points. In the archbishop's summons to the Lenten parliament of 1340 he is asked not to wonder at the king's change of style; it was done for many reasons which would be explained to the prelates, magnates, and commons in parliament;[4] not *to* parliament, it should be remarked, but to certain groups of persons *in* parliament. Again, the king announced that he was going abroad with the advice and consent of the prelates, magnates, and community of the kingdom,[5] and in 1341 it was roundly stated that the war was ' accorded and assented by the prelates, earls, barons, and community of the land in full parliament '.[6] With regard to the matter of the grants, the place of parliament is not so clear. In 1340 the king's brother-in-law, the margrave of Juliers, was created earl of Cambridge with a pension at the exchequer,[7] and this was afterwards confirmed by the magnates in what would appear to be a council minute.[8] On the other hand, an old councillor of the king's was pensioned ' per ipsum regem et concilium in parliamento '.[9]

---

[1] ' Quaestio . . . in parliamento . . . tractata et discussa ', *Angl. Sacr.* i, 29.

[2] *Ibid.*, 30.
[3] *Ibid.*, 35.
[4] *Foedera* II, ii, 1115.
[5] *Ibid.*, 1125.
[6] *Rot. Parl.* ii, 126–7, no. 5.
[7] *Foedera* II, ii, 1124.
[8] *Rot. Parl.* ii, 114, no. 35.
[9] *Foedera* II, ii, 1123.

One final point may be considered. Such a meeting, such a colloquy or debate as parliament was, carried on by estates and representatives, offered a quite exceptional opportunity for influencing public opinion.[1] The enormous importance attached to that ultimate political force is one of the most striking facts that emerges from the whole period of controversy and crisis. In the *libellus famosus* the king accuses Stratford of deliberately influencing public opinion to bring him and his government into discredit. He asserts that although he has always hated the abuse of power and wished to govern his subjects so that all should enjoy peace, the archbishop injures his good name (*innocentia*) and the faithfulness and diligence of his ministers by publicly preaching and writing open letters to the effect that nowadays people are unjustly oppressed by the royal power.[2] This anxious preoccupation with public opinion is reflected throughout the whole controversy. With the meeting of parliament, as has been pointed out, the scene changes, but the appeal, at least so far as it was made by the archbishop, does not alter substantially. The scene of melodrama at Westminster, already described, is evidence of this. Then it appears that the county members were anxious to get copies of the unlucky statutes to carry back with them, and they stipulated that these should be furnished gratuitously.[3] Finally, the importance attributed by the chroniclers to the whole episode indicates the extent to which the country at large was interested in, and, we may add, informed about it.

If we may speak of the English constitution as existing in the fourteenth century, it would be true to say that this controversy called its whole character into question. But it appears that precisely the most instructive lesson to be learnt from our study is that this judgement would be premature. The struggle must be considered in the light of fourteenth-century conditions when, if the English constitution existed at all, it was *im Werden*. If we applaud the tax-payer for trying to save his pocket, and the peer and the prelate their privilege, we must in common justice equally applaud the king for trying to save his prerogative. No doubt the structure of constitutional government

---

[1] On this see the interesting suggestions made by Dr. Riess, *ubi supra*.
[2] *Angl. Sacr*. i, 23–7.   [3] *Rot. Parl*. ii, 133, no. 61.

was in its main lines very nearly complete, but it is scarcely rash to say, in view of the welter of divergent and selfish interests we have been studying, that its real functions were not yet suspected. It may indeed be said that Edward III did not break the constitution, because there was no constitution to be broken, only precedents pointing in different directions.[1]

[1] I have adopted this phrase from Mr. Gooch's acute criticism of Hallam, in *History and Historians in the Nineteenth Century*, 293.

VII

THE PARLIAMENTARY TITLE OF HENRY IV[1]

I

IT is usually held that King Richard II was deposed by a parliament summoned, by writs issued in his name on 19 August, for 30 September, 1399. This body, having considered the king's abdication and a series of charges against him, and having set up a commission to depose him and heard its report, accepted Henry's claim to the throne, then observed to be vacant, and elected him king. This view of the transaction assumes that Henry and his friends sought the sanction of a parliamentary title for the new dynasty, and that their ' scrupulous attention for the forms of the constitution ' is evidence of this. 'Henry IV, coming to the throne as he did,' wrote Stubbs, ' made the validity of a parliamentary title indispensable to royalty.'[2] Now it may fairly be asked whether, under the constitution in 1399, parliament was competent to depose a reigning king and elect a successful rebel, to the exclusion of a legitimate heir whom it had already recognized as such. And if this question be answered in the affirmative, another and more embarrassing one arises. Do the facts as stated, or even as misrepresented, in the record really suggest that Henry wanted a parliamentary title ? The problem may be, and at this stage of the discussion should be, stated in less controversial fashion. What, on the evidence before us, is a fair inference as to Henry's aim and intention ? Now it is obvious that the parliament roll, if authentic, would be good evidence on that point and that the value of its testimony would be enhanced just in proportion as it had been tampered with in the Lancastrian interest.[3]

---

[1] Reprinted from *The English Historical Review* XLIV (1934), 423–449, 577–606.

[2] *Const. Hist.* ii (3rd edn.), 533.

[3] If the parliament roll were what it represents itself to be, we should have, of course, to accept the account which it gives as authentic, and reject such literary evidence as disagreed with it. There are good reasons for considering this unsatisfactory, but there appeared to be no way out of the difficulty until, a few years ago, the authority of the parliament roll was

T

We may therefore begin by summarizing the events as they appear in the official record, which may for convenience sake be designated the schedule.

On Monday, 6 October, a parliament met at Westminster in obedience to writs which had been issued in the new king's name on the previous Tuesday, 30 September.[1] As there was no time for an election, the commons were obviously the knights and burgesses who had been returned under the writs of 19 August summoning a parliament for 30 September.[2] This was reckoned the first parliament of Henry IV, and the new roll on which its proceedings were entered follows immediately upon that of the parliament of the twenty-first year of Richard II.[3] Thus the events at Westminster on 30 September are not entered as the proceedings of the parliament of 23 Richard II but under the title ' Record and Process of the Renunciation of King Richard the Second after the Conquest and the Acceptance of the same Renunciation together with the Deposition of the same King '. The document, therefore, contains the record of events occurring on the day previous to that for which parliament had been summoned as well as on the day itself, and is incorporated in the roll of the first parliament of Henry IV. The meeting of this body was opened by Archbishop Arundel not with the usual sermon (that came later) but with words which do, in effect, contrast the assemblies on 30 September and 6 October. On the earlier date, he reminded his hearers, King Richard had summoned his parliament to be held, ' which summons was of no force or effect ' by reason of the acceptance of the abdication of King Richard and of his deposition which were made on that day. Arundel then referred

challenged. Mr. Galbraith and Miss Clarke have raised a very strong presumption that it is not an impartial record, but a version of the transactions arranged in the Lancastrian interest. As evidence of fact, therefore, it has less, not greater, authority than contemporary literary evidence. See Lingard, *History of England* iii, 394 ; Webb, J., in his edition of Créton, *Archæologia* xx, 138 ; Williams, B., in his edition of the *Traïson*, Eng. Hist. Soc., 1846, 201, n. 2 ; Clarke and Galbraith, *B.J.R.L.* xiv (1930); Wallon, *Richard II* i, iv–v.

[1] *Rot. Parl.* iii, 415–24.

[2] A comparison of the returns and the writs *de expensis* confirms this ; see Hallam, *State of Europe during the Middle Ages* iii (11th ed.), 83.

[3] I cannot accept the argument that there may have been a separate roll for the parliament of 23 Richard II, subsequently lost or destroyed ; cf. below p. 362, n. 1.

to the events of 30 September which are set out in the schedule, and proceeded to deliver the traditional opening sermon on the text, ' Incumbit nobis ordinare pro regno '. He developed, as might be expected from such a text, the familiar doctrine of moderate Lancastrian constitutionalism. To this we shall have to return later. He then made an appeal to his hearers to be indulgent to what might seem to be irregular in the parliament and to keep it together, pending the king's coronation, partly for judicial purposes and partly to liquidate the business of the revolution. The day's session was brought to an end[1] by the appointment of receivers and triers of petitions, and the lists of their names on the roll are followed by the schedule of which we have already cited the full rubric. This official account of what is alleged to have taken place on 29 and 30 September may be summarized as follows.

On the morning of the 29th a committee of lords spiritual and temporal and other notable persons, chosen, it would seem, with a view to represent the ' estates ' of parliament and the sages of the law,[2] proceeded to the Tower to claim the king's fulfilment of the promise to abdicate which, as they were to remind him, he had freely made to Arundel and Northumberland when he was at Conway and before he was taken prisoner. We may ask whether this committee possessed an official character or authority, and the answer furnished by our text deserves close attention. It is that they were commissioned for

---

[1] Gower, *Cronica Tripertita* (in *Works*, ed. Macaulay, iv, 338) says of the meeting on 6 October, ' curia verbalis fuit et non judicialis ', meaning perhaps that no proper parliamentary business took place until after the coronation ; cf. Macaulay's note, p. 414.

[2] Adam of Usk, *Chronicon* (ed. Thompson), 31–2, says that the commissioners represented the greater prelates and lords and inferior prelates, the barons, the lesser clergy and the commons (' communitas regni '), and adds that the next day ' iidem domini ex parte tocius parliamenti, clerique et regni populi ', renounced allegiance to the king. The commission consisted of the archbishop of York and the bishop of Hereford, the earls of Northumberland and Westmorland, the lords Berkeley and Burnell, the prior of Canterbury and the abbot of Westminster, Sir William Thirning and John Markham, judges, Thomas Stowe and John Burbache, doctors of law, Sir Thomas de Erpingham and Sir Thomas Gray, William de Ferriby and Denys Lopham, notaries public. They are evidently representative in the sense mentioned by Adam, but he omits the judges and notaries and the fact that Stowe and Burbache were doctors of law. *Rot. Parl.* iii, 416. Northumberland was the spokesman. Lancaster, Archbishop Arundel, and a number of other lords attended in the afternoon, when the king read and signed the abdication.

this particular purpose—' ad actum subscriptum primitus deputati '—by the advice and consent of certain lords spiritual and temporal, justices, and other persons, proficient in the civil and canon laws as well as in the laws of the kingdom, assembled at Westminster ' in loco consueto consilii '. It can scarcely be supposed that the words were not intended to convey a suggestion—though necessarily a false one—and some at least of the chroniclers were quick to accept and develop it.[1]

The committee reminded the king of his promise and presented him with a form of abdication which had been previously drafted. This he asked time to consider and expressed a wish to see Lancaster and the archbishop. They came in the afternoon with certain other lords, and the king then read aloud and signed the document, adding that, if the matter depended on him, he would wish Lancaster to succeed him. He then appointed the archbishop of York and the bishop of Hereford as his proctors ' ad declarandam et intimandam cessionem et renunciationem hujusmodi omnibus statibus regni ut intentionem et voluntatem suam . . . populo nunciarent '. Finally, he gave Lancaster his signet, ' desiderans hoc ipsum, ut asseruit, omnibus regni statibus innotesci '. It will be noted that, although parliament had been summoned for the next day, it was to the ' estates ' that the formal announcement was to be made. The various senses in which the word ' status ' was used at this time need to be more accurately determined than has yet been done, but in this context it clearly means those persons who had been summoned by the king's writ to attend at Westminster and form, when duly convened and organized, a parliament. It should be remembered also that the committee which sought and obtained the abdication could have had no parliamentary sanction whatever, since the writ summoning the estates gave them no authority to convene as parliament until the next day, the 30th. This point is often lost sight of partly owing to Adam of Usk's account of the constitution of the committee—though Adam himself was quite clear that the estates could not and did not meet until the 30th—and

---

[1] See the account given in the *Traïson* of the scene in the Tower on 30 September, when Lancaster laid the whole responsibility for the king's restraint and isolation on the council, or the council and parliament. Below, p. 299.

partly because the authors of the *Lords' Report* have confused the date.[1]

We come now to the events of 30 September. The great hall at Westminster was prepared for the holding of a parliament. The vacant throne was ceremonially covered with cloth of gold, but there was no presiding officer of any sort. The attendance consisted of the lords spiritual and temporal and the people of the kingdom assembled in great numbers ' propter factum parliamenti '.[2] These words, again, are ambiguous and invite, if they do not admit, the interpretation that the assembly was in fact a parliament.[3] They should be compared with the otherwise irrelevant reference to ' the accustomed place of the council ' in the account of the events of the previous day, and it should be kept in mind that our text never gives the name parliament to the convention of the 30th. To this assembly, whatever its character may have been, the abdication was communicated by the archbishop of York. The estates and people, questioned severally and collectively, expressed their unanimous acceptance of the act. Those who were in charge of the proceedings appear to have felt that even this was inadequate to accomplish their purpose, for the record adds that, in order to remove all scruple or suspicion, it was considered expedient that the grounds of the abdication should be stated. To this end the form of the coronation oath and a selection from a formidable list of ' gravamina ' (which the record gives in full) were read aloud to the estates and people. This step puts the whole matter in a new light, for the body to which the charges were read takes on the aspect of tribunal. Its proceedings are beginning to look like an appeal ; they cannot constitute an

[1] The *Lords' Report* i, 349, states that parliament had been summoned for Michaelmas. A number of modern writers, beginning with Williams, *Traïson*, xiv, xv, have mistaken the dates in the same way, and even Mr. Galbraith and Miss Clarke refer to ' the second day of the deposition parliament '. *B.J.R.L.*, xiv, 146. Whatever the character of the body which deposed Richard may have been, its only session was on 30 September.

[2] These words can scarcely be restricted to the knights and burgesses, and as we shall see later more than one contemporary mentions the presence of a turbulent mob ; below, pp. 296, 301–3.

[3] Cf. Wallon, *op. cit*, ii, 301. He takes the words ' absque presidente quocumque ' to mean no more than that the throne was vacant. In that case they are redundant. But as we know that in the absence of the king he was normally represented, they serve to emphasize the abnormal fact that on this occasion it was not so.

impeachment, because the charges are not brought by the commons. They are not, however, an appeal, because the accused was not heard, and because the commons formed part of the tribunal that condemned Richard. Indeed, the fact that on 3 November the commons secured the agreement of the king and lords to a general statement in which they repudiated the obligation to act as judges in parliament[1] suggests that this last objection was clearly present in people's minds.

The confused document before us then records the next inconsequent step. The estates accepted the suggestion that the king, because he had broken his coronation oath and was therefore guilty of perjury on all the counts of the indictment, deserved to be deposed. They accordingly set up a commission to do so, not indeed as executing a judgement passed by themselves but on grounds of general expediency and ' ex habundanti . . . pro majori securitate et tranquillitate populi, ac regni comodo '. The tribunal has faded away, and we appear now to be dealing with a committee of public safety. Then the commission reports, not that it has executed judgement nor even that it has deposed the king, but that, if any royal honour or dignity remain in him, they declare him worthy to be deposed and ' ex habundanti et ad cautelam ' do so depose him. This may profitably be compared to catholic baptism administered ' sub conditione '. In order to know whether Richard had been deposed you must first be able to say whether his abdication had been effective. Having heard the report of the commission the estates, ' volentes ut nihil desit quod valeat aut debeat circa praemissa requiri ', appointed proctors to notify Richard of what had been done and to renounce their homage and allegiance to him. Then, ' since it was evident by reason of what had happened that the kingdom of England was vacant ', Henry of Lancaster claimed it in right of descent vindicated by conquest. Once more the lords spiritual and temporal and the estates were asked severally and collectively what they thought of the claim, whereupon ' iidem status cum toto populo ' agreed that the duke should reign over them. The new king (now first so styled) showed to the estates of the kingdom the signet that Richard had given him as a pledge of his will that he, Henry,

[1] *Rot. Parl.* iii, 427, no. 79.

should succeed and the archbishops thereupon enthroned him. There followed Arundel's sermon on the text, ' Vir domina-bitur populo ', which, unlike his constitutional discourse on 6 October, justified the rejection of Richard and the choice of Henry on grounds of expediency, contrasting the two as child and man.

What remained to be done was to offer some kind of apolo-getic explanation of the day's proceedings and to reorganize the administration and set it going under new authority. Henry, speaking in English, thanked the lords spiritual and temporal and all the estates of the land, and disclaimed any intention of pressing the consequence of his now admitted claim to rule by virtue of the reconquest of his inheritance, to the point of expropriation. All interests secured by law and custom were to be respected except in the case of persons that ' have been against the good purpose and common profit of the realm '. Then, since the authority of all justices, sheriffs, and other officers had lapsed during the vacancy of the throne following on the abdication and deposition, the king commissioned his chief officials and justices and received their oaths. An announcement, which amounted to an apology addressed to the estates of the kingdom, was then made on behalf of the new king. Writs had been ordered to be issued in his name sum-moning a parliament to meet on the following Monday, but the estates were assured that this ' abbreviatio assignationis diei parliamenti ' was not intended to prejudice them. The step was taken solely on grounds of expedience and convenience, in order to spare the labour and expense of the king's subjects and to facilitate the provision of remedy for their grievances. As new elections were impossible in the time allowed this was tantamount to inviting the commons to resume the authority they had lost by the cession of the crown without seeking a mandate in the constituencies and thereby creating an undesir-able precedent.[1]

This terminated the formal business of the day, which was concluded with a banquet. The next day, 1 October, the proctors appointed to notify Richard of what had been done proceeded to the Tower, where ' nomine omnium statuum et

[1] This, as we have seen, is what was in fact done ; above, p. 274. n. 2.

populi' they acquainted him with the acceptance of his abdication and the method, cause, and form of the sentence of deposition, and renounced, on behalf of their principals, all homage and allegiance. Thirning delivered a speech in English, and some of his cautious and carefully chosen words deserve particular attention. He began by reminding the late king that ' ther was a parlement somond of all the states of the reaume ' for 30 September, by reason of which summons all the states of the land were assembled, ' the whiche states hole made thes same persones that ben comen here to yowe nowe her procuratours . . . and so, Sire, thes wordes and the doyng that we sall say to yowe is not onlych our wordes but the wordes and the doynges of all the states of this londe and our charge in her name '. Thirning then informed Richard that the two bishops whom he had commissioned for that purpose had duly reported the abdication ' to all the states and all the people that were gadyrd ' at Westminster by reason of the summons to parliament, and that the renunciation was plainly and freely accepted and freely agreed to by all the states and people. These words leave us in little doubt as to what Thirning thought of the nature and character of the assembly that had met at Westminster on the previous day. It was a convention of the estates and people of the realm who were in London because some of them had been summoned to parliament.

Now how are we to interpret this document by itself ? Its credentials as an expression of the official Lancastrian view of the transaction are undeniable and are all the stronger if it turns out not to correspond with what actually occurred. Will it yield a self-consistent theory of what could and should have been done to give effect to the nation's will; for that appears to be the underlying idea ? The central problem appears to be that of determining when the cession occurred, because upon that must depend the character and constitutional authority of the body that assembled at Westminster on the morning of the 30th. The record states in terms that the cession occurred and the writs summoning, and therefore authorizing, the parliament were invalidated, by the acceptance of the abdication and the deposition. There are, however, reasons of two sorts which make it difficult to admit that this view, convenient as it was, could really have been held by those who caused the record to be drawn up. In the first place, it is contrary to the only precedent which was available. In the case of Edward II,[1] it is pretty clear that people thought that the throne had been effectively vacated when the king's abdication was accepted by the representative committee which parliament had sent to Kenilworth for that purpose. Edward III had been acclaimed king and his father deposed in London, but the official documents ran in Edward II's name until 21 January, when the abdication was accepted and the steward of his household broke his wand of office. Did Lancaster and his friends have this in mind when they suggested that the committee that waited on Richard on 29 September had been dispatched by the advice of lords and judges sitting in the wonted place of the council ? But the precedent was grounded in reason as well. If it is assumed that the relation between the king and his subjects had a contractual character arising out of the oaths of allegiance and of homage, then it might be thought to follow that an act of abdication would not take effect until it had been accepted by those who were bound by such oaths. But what if the relation between the king and his subjects (except those who had done homage) were not contractual ? If the coronation oath were no more than an unenforceable, moral obligation and fealty a responsibility incumbent on every man whether he had affirmed it by oath or not ? Surely in that case the king's act of abdication could alone suffice to vacate the throne ? No form of acceptance by the nation, whether in parliament or otherwise, would be necessary or even relevant.[2] No doubt both these views were held by some people in 1327. But public opinion (there can scarcely yet have been any public law on the matter) in 1399 would probably have been found to be less precise and less extreme. It could not have been forgotten either that Edward III like his father had come to the throne without any form of election by hereditary descent,[3] or that his coronation oath included a new clause introduced at his father's accession requiring him to maintain ' the laws and legal

---

[1] This will be examined in some detail in Part II of this article.

[2] This would seem to have been the view held by those who objected to the proposal that Richard should abdicate ; see below, p. 316.

[3] See the official proclamation of his peace in *Foedera* II, ii, 1.

customs which the community of the realm should choose '.[1]
Perhaps it was thought that, although there was no contract
enforceable against the king, his relation with ' the community
of the realm ' was bilateral. Upon any one of these views it
might have been argued that Richard ceased to be king when he
had signed and delivered his abdication to the committee
representative of the estates.

Now there are suggestions in our record which show that
these views were understood and taken into account. We have
seen that the meeting of 30 September was not entered on the
rolls either as the last parliament of Richard II or as the first
of Henry IV. It was not, indeed, recorded as a parliament at
all. Nor was it arranged or organized as a parliament. When
the estates were convened the throne was vacant, the king was
unrepresented, so that the meeting was without a presiding
officer, and no opening discourse constituting the parliament
and explaining the business in hand was delivered. The
commons did not retire nor did they choose a speaker; receivers
and triers of petitions were not appointed, so that the judicial
work of parliament remained unprovided for.[2] Again, emphasis
is laid upon the presence, seemingly encouraged or at least
welcomed, of a crowd of people who, since they are clearly
distinguished from the estates, cannot have been present in
response to any constitutional summons. Then, the record
consistently withholds the name of parliament from the assembly. The word, indeed, occurs at two points only, first in the
description of Westminster Hall prepared for the holding of a
parliament, and then, when Thirning at the beginning of his
speech in the Tower reminds Richard that the estates on whose
behalf he is speaking were actually gathered at Westminster
because there ' was a parlement somoned of all the states of the
reaume '. Finally, we should remember the grave doubt
expressed in the report of the commission set up to depose the
king : they acted only on what they appear to regard as an
unlikely possibility, namely, that any royal dignity or power
should still remain in him. They imply, that is, that the cession

[1] *Ibid.*, 36 ; cf. Ramsay, *Genesis of Lancaster* i, 11–12, 184 ; Wilkinson,
B., ' The Coronation Oath of Edward II ', *Historical Essays in Honour of
James Tait.*

[2] *Rot. Parl.* iii, 417 ff.

was complete either immediately after the abdication, or when it had been accepted by the estates. Now these arrangements imply that those who made them must have regarded very sceptically the doctrine formulated by Arundel in opening the new parliament on 6 October. The archbishop stated in terms that the writs were invalidated by the acceptance of the king's resignation and his subsequent deposition and this, of course, appears in the record. Obviously, any theory of a strictly parliamentary sanction for the new dynasty—any theory, that is, which would regard parliament as the authorized and constitutional organ for the expression of the national will in such a crisis—required that the writs should not be invalidated until after the deposition. If a parliamentary title was sought, one has to ask why the authors of our record gave away with one hand what they guarded, even to the point of self-stultification, with the other ?[1] What, in short, did parliament, as such, have to do with the events of 30 September as presented by the official Lancastrian view ? If we are obliged to answer ' Just nothing at all ', we shall not be without support from modern authority.[2]

The circumstances of the deposition, difficult as they are, constitute only one of the problems with which this record pre-

[1] The question of when the cession occurred is deliberately suspended here ; it will be discussed at some length, below pp. 321 ff.

[2] The *Lords' Report* (1820) states definitely that the body that deposed Richard was not a parliament but a convention of the states i, 348, 350. Hallam, writing two years earlier, saw the difficulty, but was apparently unwilling to face the consequences of it ; *op. cit.* iii, 82–3. Stubbs, when he came to reconsider the problem, showed some uneasiness, *Const. Hist.* iii (4th edn.), 6 ff. The *Returns of Members* i, 257, contains the note : ' the parliament summoned for 30 September 1399 was not held ', thus apparently accepting the view of the *Lords' Report*.

Apart from these notable exceptions, it is generally assumed that the change of dynasty was formally accomplished by parliament. Cf. Stubbs, *Const. Hist.* ii, 529. (The editors of the French translation of Stubbs present his account without comment, ii, 606 ; iii, 12–16). Gneist, *English Constitution* ii, 69–71 ; Wallon, *Richard II* ii, 293–313, 500 ; Wylie, *Henry IV* i, 8, 14 ; Ramsay, *Genesis of Lancaster* ii, 364 ; Hatschek, *Englische Verfassungsgeschichte*, 202 (a confused account based on Stubbs) ; Clarke and Galbraith, *op. cit.*, 146, 154 ; *Cambridge Medieval History* vii, 480. The *Interim Report of the Committee on House of Commons Personnel and Politics* (1932), App. I, p. 78, records a parliament of 23 Richard II, adding in a footnote, ' his deposition was a formal act of the parliament called in his name '. This appears to have the weighty authority of Mr. H. G. Richardson, cf. p. 59. In the writs *de expensis* issued to those who attended on 30 September, and afterwards at Henry IV's first parliament, both bodies are so described (Prynne, *Brief Register* iv, 450–6), but see below, p. 345.

sents us. There is another which requires provisional notice here. The terms in which Henry stated his claims to the throne are very difficult to reconcile with any theory which derives his title from parliamentary action. He asserted an hereditary right and claimed to have vindicated it by force of conquest. The claim was stated to, and admitted by, a body of people whom the Lancastrians chose to treat as somehow representing the nation for just this purpose. This body accepted the undeniable fact of conquest and the incredible story of hereditary right as antecedent to any part they had to play in the matter and thereby placed themselves, constitutionally speaking, very much in the position of the Witan which, lest a worse thing befall, entreated Duke William to accept the crown at Christmas 1066. They had, indeed, formally revived the very ancient practice of election, a practice which had fallen into disuse before we can properly speak of an English parliament. A right to elect asserted by an unorganized body that had admitted the facts of conquest and hereditary right does not afford much support for the doctrine of a parliament authorizing a change of dynasty in the interests of the nation and thereby modifying the power of the Crown.

Such is the official account of the matter and one may well ask why it was put in terms so faltering and inconsistent, and what impression it was intended to produce upon the minds of contemporaries and posterity ? Is it compatible with the current doctrine that Henry IV had a parliamentary title to the throne ? The solution of these problems requires something more than the study of the record itself.

The numerous contemporary or almost contemporary English chroniclers are in general well-informed. Their relations to one another are complicated and sometimes derivative, but as a rule each one makes some original contribution and might therefore be expected to form an independent judgement of the events which he recounts. On the other hand, we must not forget that the majority of them and certainly all the most important of them were strong partisans of, or at least favourably disposed to, the Lancastrian cause. Another and even more important fact tended to produce uniformity of judgement among them. The new government seems to have taken great pains to circulate copies of the official documents recording the steps by which it came into being,[1] and in consequence practically all writers had access to them either directly or indirectly.[2] Finally, with regard to the considerable body of French evidence we must keep two or three considerations in mind. In the first place, as to the events of 30 September, we cannot be sure that we are dealing with more than two independent authorities, namely the anonymous author of the *Traïson* and Froissart.[3] Then, the French writers are uniformly favourable to Richard and all of them are preoccupied with an aspect of the revolutionary movement that does not figure largely in the English accounts. In their view, it was expected from the moment of Richard's surrender that the dispute between him and Henry and later the charges of misgovernment and incompetence made against the king, would be submitted to the judgement of parliament. Moreover, their account of the proceedings of the convention, including the bishop of Carlisle's speech in defence of the king, gives them a contentious aspect wholly absent from the official record. Further, they appear to have confused the deposition on 30 September with the sentence of perpetual imprisonment passed on 27 October in what is generally accepted as a normal parliament, summoned by Henry's writs of 30 September.

With these general considerations in mind we may proceed to examine the account of the events of 30 September given by some of the more important English chroniclers. The *Historia Anglicana* was written early in Henry IV's reign and depends for the period 1399–1401 upon a source which is also used by the author of the *Annales Ricardi Secundi et Henrici Quarti*. The *Historia*, contrary to the opinion of its first editor, is now held to be entirely the work of Thomas of Walsingham, a St. Albans monk.[4] Thomas may also have been the author of the

[1] Kingsford, C. L., *English Historical Literature in the Fifteenth Century* (1913), 20.

[2] Andrew of Wyntoun, writing in Scotland about 1420, follows the account of *Rot. Parl.* pretty closely ; below p. 304.

[3] See A. Molinier, *Les Sources de l'Histoire de France* iv, nos. 3572, 3987, 3988, and C. Gross, *Sources and Literature of English History* (2nd edn.), nos. 1753, 1754, 1762, 1810.

[4] Thomas Walsingham, *Historia Anglicana*, ed. H. T. Riley, 2 vols. (R.S., 1863–64) ; Kingsford, *English Historical Literature*, cap. ii ; V. H. Galbraith, 'Thomas Walsingham and the St. Albans Chronicle,' *E.H.R.*, xlvii, 12 ff.

Annales, which in any case come from St. Albans.[1] Both writers, if indeed there are two, understood the nature of the parliament and the importance of the questions to be submitted to the meeting summoned for 30 September. Thus, Walsingham notices that the writs of 19 August were addressed ' ad personas regni qui de jure debeant interesse parliamento '.[2] In the *Annales* for ' personas ' we have ' omnes status regni ' with the addition ' ut ad parliamentum Londoniis celebrandum . . . occurrerent; eo studiosius, quo in dicto parliamento ardua regni negotia fuerant pertractanda '.[3] Walsingham's account then follows and condenses the official record with some trifling verbal differences and some addition and omission of names. The convention at Westminster, therefore, is never described as a parliament. We hear only of the estates of the kingdom there assembled, but it may be significant that there is no reference to the presence of ' the people ', who figure so largely in the official record. The author of the *Annales* follows the same plan, but when both writers reach 6 October they describe the body which assembled on that day as a parliament.[4]

The composite and anonymous work known as the *Continuatio Eulogii Historiarum* cannot have been finished before 1428; it depends for our period on the official documents and a brief Latin Chronicle written possibly at Canterbury not later than 1401.[5] The author gives a good deal of information not to be found elsewhere, to some of which we shall have to return later; for the moment it is important to notice that in his account of the change of dynasty he does not apply the word parliament to the convention of 30 September. Nor do we get, as in the schedule, the term ' estates ' ; the author prefers general words which suggest some kind of national authority behind the convention. He says that, when Henry had heard mass, he entered Westminster Hall and took his seat next to the bishop of Carlisle.[6] Then in the presence of all the bishops

---

[1] Ed. H. T. Riley in *J. de Trokelowe et Anon. Chronica* (R.S., 1866).

[2] Walsingham ii, 234.　　　　[3] *Annales*, 251–2.

[4] Walsingham, ii, 238 ; *Annales*, 288.

[5] *Eulogium Historiarum*, iii (ed. F. S. Haydon, R.S., 1858–63) xlix–lxxxii, 382 ff. ; Kingsford, *op. cit.* 28–30.

[6] *Eulogium* iii, 383 ; cf. Clarke and Galbraith, *op. cit.*, 154 n. 1, who point out that the miniature of the deposition scene, reproduced in Webb's edition of Créton (*Archaeologia* xx, plate xvi), shows that the spiritual and temporal peers sat on opposite sides.

and lords of the kingdom and ' populus multus ' the instrument of abdication and the charge against the king were read
out and he was deposed. After this the proctors ' vice omnium
de regno assignati ' renounced homage. When Henry had
made his claim, the lords assented severally ' et communitas
communiter '. It will be seen that, while this account departs
from the model of the schedule in a good many respects, it
agrees with it perfectly in the point under examination. His
account, or the common source from which both derive, is
reflected faithfully in a later work, a version of the English
Brut generally known by the editor's name as *Davies' Chronicle*,[1]
which, however, adds one point that deserves attention. After
describing Henry's coronation he proceeds : ' Thanne continued he the parlement that king Richarde hadde begonne ',[2]
suggesting that the distinction so carefully made in the contemporary record which he is ' writing out ' had by this time
been lost sight of. The point of view of the *Continuatio*,
however, is maintained in the English *Brut* itself, which avoids
the term parliament and emphasizes the share of ' the common
people ' in the events of 30 September.[3]

The Chronicle attributed to Thomas of Otterbourne derives
from the *Annales* and the schedule in its account of the revolution, and was probably composed about 1423.[4] For the events
of 29 and 30 September it follows the schedule closely with the
omission of such phrases, e.g. ' ut apparuit ', as would suggest
the evidence of an eye-witness. The abdication was read to and
accepted by ' status regni et vulgus '.[5] After Henry had
challenged the throne, the earl of Northumberland questioned
' the lords spiritual and temporal and the people ' as to the
admissibility of his claim. The lords gave their answers
severally and the ' vulgus et populus ' by acclamation.[6] After
the new king had expressed his thanks and the archbishop had
delivered a sermon and given his blessing, ' licentiata fuit
congregatio '.[7]

[1] *An English Chronicle* [1377–1461], ed. J. S. Davies (Camden Soc.,
1856) ; cf. Kingsford, *op. cit.*, 29, 127–8.
[2] *Ibid.*, 19.
[3] *The Brut* (ed. Brie, E.E.T.S.), ii, 359.
[4] Ed. Hearne (Oxford, 1732) ; cf. Kingsford, *op. cit.*, 21–3.
[5] *Op. cit.*, 213.   [6] *Ibid.*, 219.
[7] *Ibid.*, 221.

We turn now to a group of writers who take a different view of the nature of the convention of 30 September without showing themselves in any way less favourable to the Lancastrian cause. We may begin with the monk of Evesham, whose work ' grew by accumulation ' and was probably completed by 1402–4.[1] Although the work does not become of the first importance until January 1400, it influenced Adam of Usk, a writer who had a first-hand knowledge of the events. The monk understood perfectly the composition of parliament, and notes that by Henry's command writs were sent in Richard's name, to all the lords spiritual and temporal and to the commons ' qui de jure habent parliamento interesse '. It was to these persons constituted as a parliament that the abdication was read. The words on this point are precise : ' In quo quidem parliamento, primo, videlicet, die parliamenti . . . rege Ricardo absente . . . ceteris dominis spiritualibus et temporalibus totius regni ac plebeis presentibus ' etc. ; yet he must have seen some at least of the official documents for, although he dates the writs wrongly and gives a very different account of the election, he transcribes Henry's words of thanks to the lords and commons and estates and his safe-guarding of property rights, and Arundel's sermon on the text, ' Vir dominabitur populo '. But he returns to, and emphasizes the point by the phrase, ' Et statim eodem die istud parliamentum dissolutum est, et aliud novum . . . assignatum.'[2]

We turn now to Adam of Usk and it would seem at first sight, having regard to his profession and the part he played in September 1399, that his view of the matter should be decisive. He was a trained canonist, a D.C.L. of Oxford who had practised in the court of the archbishop of Canterbury 1390–97, and a member of the commission set up in September to determine the method of getting rid of Richard. He was sent to visit the king in the Tower and was probably present at Westminster on 30 September. In short, ' he witnessed the fall of Richard II in the train of Archbishop Arundel '.[3] On

---

[1] *Historia Vitae . . . Ricardi II* (ed. Hearne, Oxford, 1729) ; cf. Kingsford, *op. cit.*, 24.

[2] Monk of Evesham, 157–60.

[3] Adam of Usk, *Chron.* (ed. Maunde Thompson, Eng. Hist. Soc.), vii–xx ; Kingsford, *op. cit.*, 32–4.

the other hand, he did not write until after 1415, and his book has been appropriately compared (and his authority thereby implicitly disparaged) to ' a modern volume of reminiscences describing his impressions of things seen and done '.[1] It is clear, moreover, that he could not always trust his memory, because he borrowed from the monk of Evesham. Again, his account of the events of 30 September differs in so many points from the schedule that it seems highly unlikely that he had it before him when he wrote. It must be remembered also that after 1415 there were reasons for attributing the deposition to a regularly constituted parliament that did not exist in 1400. Finally, there was a reason personal to Adam which may have disposed him to describe the body which deposed Richard as a normal parliament. The commission of which he had been a member reported against abdication and advised that the king should be deposed by the authority of the clergy and people who had been summoned for that purpose, that is to say parliament.[2] Adam may well have been chagrined that the considered advice of himself and his colleagues had been disregarded.

We shall note first in Adam's account, that he describes the commission that visited Richard in the Tower on the 29th to obtain the abdication as consisting of groups representing the great lords, the inferior prelates, the barons, the lower clergy, and the commons, and then adds that the next day ' iidem domini ex parte totius parliamenti, clerique et regni populi ', renounced allegiance to the king.[3] The first statement may perhaps be taken as supplementing the words of the schedule to the effect that the commissioners were deputed by certain great lords together with justices and jurists, if we suppose that the doctors who had advised as to the deposition together with some of the leaders of the revolution selected the commissioners with a view to their representing the interests specified. The second, however, is a direct traverse of the schedule, which refuses the name of parliament to the convention of 30 September, and the words may be taken as explaining what the commissioners meant when they advised that Richard should be deposed ' cleri et populi auctoritate '.

---

[1] *Ibid.*, 32.   [2] Adam of Usk, 29–30 ; see below, p. 316.   [3] *Op. cit.*, 31–2.

U

They must have intended that the necessary authority should be obtained from parliament. To this point Adam sticks : he says that Scrope read the abdication ' in pleno parliamento ' and, with a view to its acceptance, asked the assent of all and singular of the parliament. When he comes to the deposition his words suggest a doubt. Although the king had already deposed himself, he says,[1] out of an abundance of caution the sentence of his deposition was publicly and solemnly read aloud by the consent and authority of the whole parliament, and thus, he proceeds, the kingdom being vacant, the duke of Lancaster was set up as king by the consent of the whole parliament. Now this account is not self-consistent. Adam knew well the ordinary forms by which a regular parliament was convened and organized. We have only to turn to the passage in which he describes the proceedings of the parliament of 1397–98, to be sure of that.[2] He was also aware that the writs were invalidated by the cession of the crown,[3] and upon his own showing that must have occurred at the latest when the ' sentence of deposition ' was read out to ' the whole parliament' by the bishop of St. Asaph.[4] The body, therefore, that raised

[1] *Op. cit.*, 32.

[2] *Ibid*, 9 ff. The narrative, it is true, is borrowed from the monk of Evesham, ' but this appropriation, it is fair to suggest, need not be regarded so much as a theft as a testimony to the accuracy of that history, Adam himself having been present during the proceedings '; Maunde Thompson, *ibid.*, xxxvi.

[3] ' Quia per deposicionem Ricardi olim regis parliamentum, ejus nomine congregatum, fuit extinctum ', p. 33.

[4] *Ibid.*, 32. It is not easy to determine the moment at which, according to Adam, the cession occurred. In his narrative of the proceedings on 30 September he does not mention the act of deposition recorded by the schedule. The whole account bears a striking resemblance to the events of 20 and 21 January 1327, when, as we shall see, the cession occurred on the acceptance, at Kenilworth, and by the parliamentary commission sent for that purpose, of Edward II's abdication. It is true that this was subsequently reported to, and admitted by parliament, but Edward had ceased to be king when the steward of his household broke his wand of office on 21 January (see below, p. 311). Adam uses words that strongly suggest that he had this precedent in mind. He makes the surrender of homage the first step in the proceedings on 30 September and attributes to the commissioners the words ' nec pro rege set pro privato domino Ricardo de Bordux, simplici milite, de cetero eundem habituri '. Edward II was described as ' persona privata ab omni regia dignitate ' as soon as the committee of estates had surrendered homage to him ; *Bridlington*, ii, 90. There is an even closer parallel in the passage from the Lichfield Chronicle printed by M. V. Clarke, *Medieval Representation and Consent*, 184, n. 3 : ' ordinatumque est quod extunc non rex sed Edwardus de Karnarvan pater regis a modo vocetur.'

Henry to the throne could not upon any constitutional theory have been a parliament as Adam nevertheless calls it. Finally, he is quite clear that the parliament of 1397–98 was the last parliament of Richard II, for he so describes it in terms at least three times.[1] What parliament, therefore, accomplished the deposition ? Not Richard's, for his last was in 1398, nor Henry's, for his first was convened by the writs issued on 30 September.

If Adam had left us a self-consistent account written shortly after the events which he had witnessed and uninfluenced (as in fact his narrative seems to be) by the official documents, it would have been difficult to resist the authority of a witness of his training and opportunities of observation. As it is, it does not seem necessary to press the words of an old man writing long after the event, who thought at the time that the change ought to have been accomplished by means of parliament, least of all since, as we know, he did not revise what he wrote.

The case of Gower is very different. The section of the *Cronica Tripertita* dealing with the revolution must have been written very soon after the events which it recounts, for the author died in 1408, after some years of blindness. He had rallied to the Lancastrian cause, after having enjoyed Richard's personal favour, but it is not clear that he was a mere vulgar turn-coat.[2] In any case he held, and developed in another poem, a view of the nature of Henry's title which reduced the part played by parliament in the revolution to something almost negligible. This we shall have to discuss later, but it is important to bear it in mind in estimating his account of the events of 30 September. The content of the poem makes it probable that Gower knew the official documents either at first or second hand, and his language leaves no doubt that he considered the convention on the 30th to be a parliament like any other. It suggests, on the other hand, that the abdication was in itself so effective that nothing more was needed but some form of election to make

---

[1] Adam of Usk, 36, 39.

[2] The *Cronica Tripertita* is in G. C. Macaulay's edition of the complete works, iv, 314 ff. For the ' charge of time-serving timidity ' brought in connexion with the alleged alteration in the dedication of the *Confessio Amantis* after the revolution, see K. Meyer, *Gowers Beziehungen zu Chaucer und Richard II*, 23, 46–7, and Macaulay's note, *Works* II, xxi–xxvi.

Henry king. This, of course, would rule out the possibility of a true parliament, because the writs would have been invalidated by the cession on the 29th, but Gower does not notice this nor does he scruple to record a parliamentary deposition. Let us consider his account of the event beginning with the marginal analysis in prose which runs as follows :

> Qualiter primo die parliamenti rex Ricardus personaliter non comparuit, set alibi existens, titulo corone sue sub forma magis auctentica penitus renunciavit ; super quo, nobilis Henricus, universo populo in ejus laudem conclamante, ut rex efficiatur, electus est.[1]

The text of the poem develops and obscures this straightforward account. Thus :

> Tunc prius incepta sunt parliamenta recepta
> De quibus abstractus Ricardi desinit actus.
> Ecce dies Martis, nec adest presentia partis,
> Non sedet in sede, quem culpa repellit ab ede
>
> .   .   .   .
>
> R. non comparet, alibi et dummodo staret,
> Causas assignat, quibus H. sua sceptra resignat :
> Substituit aliquos proceres tunc juris amicos
> Ad quos confessus proprio fuit ore repressus.

If Richard's official life (actus) had come to an end before parliament met, terminated by his own confession of guilt and his attribution of the sceptre to Henry, the body that met on Tuesday in the presence of the throne so effectively vacant could not upon the accepted contemporary theory have been a true parliament. This was seen by Arundel, but does not appear to have occurred to Gower.

He goes on, however, apparently with the schedule before him, to refer to the deposition and election :

> Hunc deponebant, plenum quem labe sciebant,
>
> .   .   .   .
>
> H. fuit electus regno, magis est quia rectus.
> Sola dies tentum tulit istud parliamentum.[2]

He seems to regard the meeting on 6 October as an extension of the parliament elected under Richard's writs and incapable, as the king was not yet crowned, of doing more than listen to a

---

[1] Gower, *Works* iv, 337.   [2] *Ibid.*, ll. 290–300.

recital of the proceedings on 30 September, which were thereby entered on the parliamentary roll.

> Sexta dies stabat Octobris, quando parabat
> Rex novus optata sua parliamenta novata :
> Curia verbalis fuit et non judicialis,
> Ad tempus restat nichil et de pondere prestat :
> Dicitur expletum quod nil valet esse quietum,
> Donec persona regis sit operta corona.[1]

Gower has thus missed or suppressed the question of the validity of the writs altogether and consequently fallen into self-contradiction. If the meeting on 30 September were a competent parliament, what was the use of an adjourned meeting of the same body taking place before the new king was crowned ? As Gower says that it was a ' curia verbalis ' only (overlooking the facts that it had been summoned by the new king's writs and that it had appointed receivers and triers of petitions to facilitate judicial business), the answer can only be the one we have already suggested, to get the record and process on the parliament roll, and this would have been unnecessary if there had really been a parliament on 30 September.[2] This is as much of Gower's work as concerns us at present and it is perhaps not unfair to say that it is neither profound nor quite self-consistent.[3] But as we shall see later, Gower was interested in, and took pains to develop, a very different notion of Henry's claim to the throne.

We come now to a view of the whole transaction which puts it in a very different light. This reaches us as a survival from the first serious reaction against the revolution, and is based largely, though not wholly, upon what may be called the Percy tradition. This part of the evidence comes to us from the most untrustworthy quarter possible, Hardyng's *Chronicle*, but it receives a certain support from Archbishop Scrope's Manifesto (1405)

---

[1] Ll. 308–313.

[2] Macaulay, p. 414, comments ' the demise of the crown made such writs necessary, but the same parliament met again six days later '. But this misses the whole point. Although it was composed of the same people, it was a new parliament under a new executive.

[3] It may be noted that the recently published chronicles of Dieulacres and Kirkstall both describe the convention as a parliament. The *Dieulacres Chronicle* gives the date as 29 September. Cf. Clarke and Galbraith, *op. cit.*, 173 ; Clarke and Denholm-Young, *B.J.R.L.* xv, 134.

and from the recently published *Dieulacres Chronicle*. We shall consider the texts first, and then try to appraise their value.

Hardyng's own chronicle depends for the years 1399–1402 on a Latin version of *Davies' Chronicle*, which, as we have seen, speaks with two voices as to the share of parliament in the deposition. Hardyng completed his work in 1451 and presented it to Henry VI. Six years later he offered a revised version adjusted to Yorkist sensibilities to Edward IV. The obvious purpose in writing, and the circumstances under which he composed, two different versions would be enough to discredit him.[1] Still he doubtless reflects contemporary public opinion in attributing the leading role in the change of dynasty to parliament. The rubric of cap. cxcvi reads:

How duke Henry of Lancaster was made kyng by resignacion,[2] renunciacion, and deposayle, and election of the parliamente.

This is developed in the text, which describes the abdication and then proceeds:

> The parliament then, for his misgovernaunce
> Deposed hym so then by great ordinaunce.
> Then went they to a free election.[3]

They considered and rejected the claims of Mortimer, admittedly the nearest heir, and then:

> Consydred also the might of duke Henry,
> They chose hym kyng, there durst none it [*al.* hym] deny.[4]

The point is driven home in the rubric of the succeeding chapter (cxcvii), which runs:

Henry the fourth . . . was elect by yᵉ hole parliament the morowe after Michaelmasse,

and again in the text:

> But kyng he was the morowe after Mighelmesse,
> His reygne begynnyng that day without distresse.[5]

So much for Hardyng's formal chronicle which may well have represented the received view of these events in the middle of the fifteenth century. But Hardyng had something more to

---

[1] Kingsford, *op. cit.*, 141. The chronicle was edited by H. Ellis, London, 1812; on its character and value see Kingsford *E.H.R.* xxvii, 462–82; Clarke and Galbraith, *op. cit.*, 136.

[2] Ed. Ellis, 350.   [3] *Ibid.*, 351.   [4] *Ibid.*   [5] *Ibid.*, 352.

tell which could not be welcome to Lancastrian ears and for that very reason found an appropriate place in the version of the *Chronicle* presented to Edward IV. Hardyng was in the service, and in the confidence of, the Percies at the time of the change of dynasty and indeed up to 1403, and preserved from these years an oral tradition and certain documents bearing on their quarrel with Henry IV which he inserted in the form of a prose note in the second version of his *Chronicle*.[1] The story which he heard from Northumberland chiefly concerns Henry's claim to the throne by descent from Edmund of Lancaster and will be considered later in that connexion. At present we are concerned with the document alleged to have been sent to the king ' in the field ' just before the battle of Shrewsbury. It contains a series of charges made by a group of disaffected lords acting under the advice of Archbishop Scrope. Hardyng alleges that they were committed by letters bearing their seals, which he had seen and had had in his keeping. Now as long ago as 1913 the late Mr. Kingsford wrote of this evidence : ' The passages in which he treats of the exploits of his patrons the Percies . . . were no doubt written from his own knowledge and contain material not to be found elsewhere '.[2] To this cautious recommendation must now be added the fact that a passage in the *Dieulacres Chronicle* supplies independent and more nearly contemporary evidence of attempted negotiation just before Shrewsbury and the dissatisfaction of the Percies, or at least of Hotspur, with the change of dynasty. On this the editors of the *Chronicle* pass an important judgment. ' Hardyng is one whose testimony,[3] other things being equal, one would more readily reject than believe, but so confirmed, the genuineness of this proclamation [i.e. the document referred to above], which has a real bearing on the question of Richard's deposition, must be accepted.'[4] The passage in the proclamation relevant to our purpose alleges that Henry had sworn at Doncaster that he had come only to claim his inheritance and to oblige Richard to rule by the good advice of his

[1] The text is in Ellis, 351 ff. ; see Kingsford, *E.H.R.* xxvii, 462, Clarke and Galbraith, *op. cit.*, 136, cf. Stubbs, *C.H.*, iii, 12n.

[2] Kingsford, *Historical Literature*, 147.

[3] To fact, of course, not to contemporary opinion for which we have cited him.   [4] Clarke and Galbraith, *op. cit.*, 136.

lords, and instead of this he has forced the king to abdicate and :

Colore quarum resignacionis et renunciacionis, tuorum fautorum consilio, ac publica vociferacione vulgaris populi apud Westmonasterium per te et tuos complices collecti, tu te coronasti in regem.[1]

This account of the events of 30 September is confirmed and somewhat amplified by the story which Hardyng had from Northumberland. The earl, having recounted the history of the commission which examined and rejected Henry's claim by descent, added that Henry had

made kynge Richard under dures of prison in the Toure of London in fere of his life to make a resignation of his right to hym. And upon that a renunciation of the seide right. And tho [these] two declared in the counsell and in the parlement at Westminster what of his myght and his wilfulness and what by certyne lords and strength of the comons, he was crouned ayenst his oth made at the White Ffriers at Doncaster [and against the will and counsel of the Percies].[2]

This passage recalls certain ambiguous phrases in the schedule—the appointment of the commissioners to take the abdication by the advice and consent of certain magnates and justices and jurists assembled at Westminster ' in loco consueto consilii', the Great Hall at Westminster ceremoniously prepared for the holding of the parliament, and the crowd of people gathered ' propter factum parliamenti '—words that suggest what they will not state. Northumberland uses the words council and parliament, but what he describes is something unusual and irregular. Besides this must be set the evidence of the *Dieulacres Chronicle*, which states that just before the battle of Shrewsbury in 1403 the king learned from Thomas Percy that he was being attacked by reason of his usurpation of the crown which by hereditary right should have gone to the son of the earl of March.[3] The chronicle proceeds :

Consiluit proinde rex discedere sine cede et convenire ad parliamentum nonobstante quod specialiter per eos et per proceres electus fuerat; sed probabile signum erat quod Henricus Percy ad hoc non consenciit quia in die coronacionis ad festum non incedit quia pro certo ipso invito coronacio facta fuit quia Henricus dux juravit aliis

[1] Ed. Ellis, 352.   [2] *Ibid.*, 353.
[3] Henry's treatment of March is the subject of one of the sections of the proclamation.

duobus Henricis super reliquias de Bridlynton quod coronam nunquam affectaret, et tunc dixit si aliquis dignior coronam inveniretur libenter cederet.[1]

Now the historical truth of the facts so alleged need not be discussed here. What is relevant to our purpose is that such views should have been held, or at least expressed, as early as 1403, and this seems to be pretty well established.

We have to consider in the light of these facts the charges made against Henry, in respect of his alleged usurpation, by Archbishop Scrope in 1405. They are contained in a manifesto issued in justification of his rising, which has been transmitted to us through various channels and in various forms.[2] Scrope's charge, which agrees in substance with the story told by Northumberland, or at any rate is not irreconcilable with it, alleges that Henry took and imprisoned King Richard in the Tower and proceeds :

Et eodem rege sic incarcerato et absente, parliamentum tenuit, in quo eundem dominum regem Ricardum resignare jus regni et coronae regiae per metum mortis compulit et artavit. Qua resignatione sic facta, quamvis nulla, nec de jure nec de facto, idem dominus Henricus coram parliamento surgens, superbe ac pompacite coram omnibus dicens regnum Angliae et coronam ejusdem et regaliam ejusdem immediate ad se, et ad nullum alium, tunc temporis, de jure pertinere; quod falsum fuit, est, et erit in aeternum . . . sed tandem per fas et nefas seipsum in regem promovit et exaltavit.[3]

This, of course, is propaganda. Scrope was intimately concerned with every step in the revolution, he was among those who went to the Tower on the 29th to receive the abdication, which, by Richard's commission, he and the bishop of Hereford were appointed to lay before the assembled estates, and when the time came he helped to enthrone Henry. He must have known, therefore, that the cession of the crown, whenever it occurred, would invalidate the writs by which the parliament was authorized. And yet the account he gives of

[1] Clarke and Galbraith, *op. cit.*, 179 ; cf. pp. 134–5.

[2] On the forms of the document and the places in which it may be found in print, see Stubbs, *C.H.* iii, 50–1. It is conveniently given in *Historians of the Church of York* (ed. Raine, R.S.) ii, 292–304 ; cf. also pp. xix–xx.

[3] *Op. cit.*, 297. It should be noticed that the *Annales*, 403–5, give a version which professes to be translated from an English original, and does not mention parliament. The version given in the *Continuatio Eulogii* 406, stresses the importance for reform of a freely elected parliament, containing lawyers and sitting at London.

the matter suggests that Richard's act vacated the throne (or would have done so had the act been voluntary), and that Henry immediately submitted to parliament (which could no longer be a parliament) a claim which, if admitted, would exclude it from any further part in the proceedings. But there is little room for constitutional consideration or argument in a document of this kind. Henry had reached the throne ' per fas et nefas ' and the archbishop was trying to bring him down.[1]

We may turn now to consider the impression produced by the events of the revolution upon the minds of foreign observers, and we must examine first the group of French chroniclers who have treated of the matter. The two writers whose works are devoted exclusively to Richard and his affairs may, to begin with, be pretty safely reduced to one. Créton on his own showing had left England shortly after the king's captivity, and received his information about subsequent events from a French clerk whom Henry had taken with him from Paris to England. This man might have been present at Westminster on 30 September and subsequently at Henry's first parliament, but he appears to have returned to France soon afterwards, there met Créton, and supplied him with information.[2] The anonymous *Traïson* appears to have been composed before 1412, and its editor, Williams, thought that the author was himself the very clerk who supplied Créton with his information.[3] He tells us that a deputation of Londoners had waited upon Henry at Coventry on his way from Bristol to London with Richard in his train, and begged him to behead his captive. Henry replied that he would in no circumstance do so, as he intended to bring the king to London and there refer to parliament the question of what was to be done with him.[4] Then

---

[1] On the Percy tradition in general see the long note of Webb in his edition of Créton, *Archaeologia* xx, 183–8. He thinks that the Percies really did not intend that Richard should be deposed, but when confronted with a *fait accompli* accepted office, in order that they might strike later, as they did at Shrewsbury. He says that, when charged with the deposition, Henry had no answer but force of arms ; but the *Dieulacres Chronicle* shows that he wished to negotiate and more than suggests that the Percies aimed at the crown themselves. Cf. Clarke and Galbraith, *op. cit.*, 134–5.

[2] Créton, ed. Webb, *Archaeologia* xx, 190.

[3] *Traïson* (ed. Williams, Eng. Hist. Soc.), 3 ; cf. Molinier, *op. cit*, iv, no. 3988.

[4] *Traïson*, 62.

there is a spirited account of an interview between Richard and York, Rutland, and Henry, who visited him in the Tower on 30 September. Henry met the king's protests against his confinement and isolation by disclaiming all responsibility; Richard was detained by order of the council of the realm pending the meeting of parliament. When the king furiously upbraided York and Rutland and challenged any four of his adversaries to meet him in personal combat, Henry fell on his knees and besought him ' to be quiet until the meeting of parliament and there every one would bring forward his reason '. To this the king replied by demanding that at least he might be brought to trial ' that I may answer to all they would say against me ', but Henry evaded the point by an answer evidently intended to be reassuring and non-committal : ' My lord, be not afraid, nothing unreasonable shall be done to you '.[1] On this follows an account of the deposition, introduced by the phrase ' after this began the parliament '. The confused and incoherent story can be made to take some sort of order by supposing it to be a conflation of the official records of the proceedings on 30 September and 6 October. It is not our business to investigate its sources or endeavour to determine what historical truth it may contain. What concerns us is to see the part assigned by the author to the council and parliament. The duke is described as attending in state. When he had taken his place, his steward introduced him with the cry, ' Long live Henry of Lancaster, king of England ',[2] on which all the lords, prelates and commons of England exclaim, ' Yes, yes, Henry of Lancaster shall be our king and none other '. Thereupon the duke took his place upon the throne and delivered a speech which appears to be some kind of an echo of the events of 30 September as recorded in the schedule. It contains in substance Henry's claim to the throne, and is followed by a series of charges against Richard, not corresponding to those in the schedule. Henry then submitted that Richard had forfeited his crown and asked the council of the country and the parliament to give judgement. They replied :

[1] *Ibid.*, 67-8.
[2] Obviously this is intended to announce a claim rather than to anticipate the formal election which was to follow. Edward III was acclaimed king in parliament a fortnight before his reign began.

' Tomorrow, my lord, we will give you our decision ', ' and such ', the writer adds, ' were the first day's proceedings of the duke of Lancaster and of his parliament '. Clearly ' the first day of the parliament ' is 6 October and the anonymous author has represented the king and not Arundel as addressing the assembly, and giving them directly, instead of with reference to a previous meeting, the case for his succession.

What follows is even more confused. The events of the ' morrow ' on which the new king was to have his answer are made to include the sentence of imprisonment passed on Richard and the bishop of Carlisle's speech in his defence, and all this before the coronation, which took place on 13 October. There is little to be made of it for our purposes, although the document published by Miss Clarke and Mr. Galbraith raises a strong presumption that there is a residuum of historical truth in the whole story. Meanwhile, it is difficult to suppose that the author understood very well the details of the matter he was describing. If, therefore, we find him laying particular emphasis on one point, it is fair to suppose that his informants or his sources had stressed it. Now precisely this is the case with the parliament. Our author recounts that on New Year's day 1400 certain lords asked the king to put Richard to death, and received the answer that he ' was sentenced and condemned in open parliament to perpetual imprisonment . . . and I will by no means act in opposition to open parliament '.[1] Shortly afterward he reports that when Henry was marching against the insurgents (January 1400) Warwick said to him : ' Dear Sire . . . if you had followed the counsel of the commons and the open parliament, there would have been no occasion for this day '. To which the king replied ' What reason had I to put such a lord to death ? '[2]

Créton reproduces much of this material, but it is significant that he lays emphasis of his own on the importance of the role of parliament. This is noticeable in two passages in which he seems to be using another source than the author of the *Traïson*, one that was common to him and the monk to Evesham. He recounts that, when Henry had lodged his prisoner in the Tower, he retired to the country and remained there until he

---

[1] *Traïson*, 78. [2] *Ibid.*, 82–3.

received word from the commons that the day for the meeting of parliament was fixed, whereupon he returned to London. At the meeting of parliament—like the monk he applies that term to the convention on 30 September—there were present, beside the lords and prelates, ' knights, squires, varlets and archers with many sorts of folk who were neither noble nor gentle . . . in such great heaps . . . that the officers could scarcely enter the hall '.[1] This is not the sort of detail that we should expect a foreigner ' writing out ' the substance of the *Traïson* to invent, and it corresponds remarkably with the words of the Percy manifesto accusing the king of having secured the crown ' publica vociferacione vulgaris populi apud Westmonasterium per te et tuos complices collecti '.[2] The resemblance of these two texts can scarcely be accidental.

Créton's account of Henry's election takes a form which he is not likely to have invented for himself. He says that various members of the royal family were proposed to, and rejected by ' the people ', who acclaimed Lancaster. The next day the two archbishops approached the duke, ' who was now elected king by the common people ', and said to him ' the sovereign princes here present and the prelates in goodly manner elect thee and call thee king : consider if thou thyself consent thereto '.[3] With this passage should be compared the words of the monk of Evesham. After the deposition and the consequent vacation of the throne, he says : ' cum tractaretur inter dominos de rege futuro, populus totus acclamavit dominum Henricum ducem Lancastriae, ipsumque in regem elegerunt '.[4] This tradition of a free election is preserved in Hardyng[5] and Chaucer.[6]

Froissart's account of the revolution appears to have been completed in or shortly after 1400. He had few written sources that can be identified,[7] and it would be hard to recover any definite historical fact from his reckless and confused story. We may note, however, his impression of the share and importance of parliament in the events which he was professing to record. He shifts the scene at Bristol to London, and makes Richard propose abdication in consequence of the execution of

[1] Créton, 191–2.   [2] Above, p. 296.
[3] Créton, 200–1.   [4] *Op. cit.*, 159.
[5] Ed. Ellis, 351.   [6] *Works* (ed. Skeat) i, 406.
[7] Pauli, *Geschichte Englands* iv, 732 ; Molinier, *Sources* iv, no. 3094.

his counsellors by the Londoners.[1] When Henry heard this he replied that it would be necessary to consult ' plusieurs des trois étas ' of England, and that he had summoned the prelates and nobles and the councils of the good towns, and in three days ' there will be enough to enable you to make your resignation in due form '.[2] Subsequently Richard, dressed as king, crowned and bearing the sceptre, was brought from the Tower ' au chastel ', where, in the presence of certain lords and prelates, he made a formal resignation, and ceremonially transferred the regalia to Henry.[3] This is worth noting, as it may be a distortion of a circumstance recorded in the *Dieulacres Chronicle*, which says that in parliament at London at Michaelmas[4] 1399 it was intimated to the king that, with a view to his deposition, the magnates and commons were about to make certain accusations against him : ' Unde ne parliamentum intraret humiliter, ut dictum est, rogavit ; et corona regni super humo posita Deo jus suum resignavit '.[5]

Froissart proceeds to say that, the abdication thus accomplished, Henry and his friends awaited the day of the council and parliament which were to be held at Westminster. On 30 September he ' held parliament ' there, at which were present ' all the prelates and most of the clergy of England and all the dukes, earls, nobles and the commons of every town '. There Henry challenged the kingdom and submitted his claim

[1] Froissart, *Chroniques* (ed. Kervyn de Lettenhove) xvi, 192 ff.
[2] *Ibid.*, 199.
[3] *Ibid.*, 202–3.
[4] The date is, of course, wrong : the writs state that parliament was summoned for the morrow of Michaelmas.
[5] Clarke and Galbraith, *op. cit.*, 173. The editors are inclined to accept this, and certainly the trait is characteristic. But what sort of a crown would have been available to Richard in the Tower ? The regalia which he had taken to Ireland had been captured by the Lancastrians in Wales (Palgrave, *Antient Kalendars* iii, 358), and since he began his journey to London he had been wearing a priest's hood (' en guise de preste ', *Traïson*, 59). Créton, 77, says that he disguised himself in the habit of a Minorite on landing in Wales, and the miniatures e.g. plates xiii, xiv, xv, appear to confirm this. Adam of Usk, *Chron.*, 28, says that Richard surrendered his two crowns to Arundel and Northumberland at Conway. If the words could bear a conditional construction and give the sense that Richard was ready formally to resign his crown to God in parliament, the difficulty would be overcome and our text would agree with the whole tradition of the French sources that Richard wished to be heard in parliament. See the version printed in the *Traïson*, 283, which perhaps points in this direction, although the manuscript from which it is printed is corrupt.

' a tout le peuple qui la fut, que de ce ils desissent leur bonne voulonté '. Whereupon the people replied with one voice that it was their will that he should be their king, and that they wished to have none other than he. Having put the question again and received a second acclamation, he took his place upon the throne and the people ' tendirent leurs mains contremont en luy prommettant foy et faisant grant'liesse. Et lors fut ce parlement conclu '.[1] The connexion between this account and those given in Créton and the Percy manifesto, is obvious. Although Froissart uses the term parliament, he emphasizes the manifestly irregular presence of a mob, to which Henry appealed. Its composition may well have been such as is described by Créton, and its decision, both in form and substance, is probably given accurately enough by the ' publica vociferacio vulgaris populi ' of the Percy manifesto.

If we ask what impression is left by the evidence of the chronicles a few generalizations may be formulated. In the first place, even the most orthodox of the Lancastrian writers, such as Walsingham and the author of the *Eulogium*, when closely examined, begin to lose that atmosphere of serenity, goodwill, and mutual accommodation so sedulously diffused through the official record and to suggest an underlying doubt, or at least an ambiguity in the presentation of the tale. Then, we must take account of what appears to have been a very general expectation from the moment of Richard's surrender, that the charges against him, including Henry's personal grievances, were to be submitted to the judgement of parliament. We may notice, too, that the convention of 30 September, whether by its composition, its warrant, or its acts, seemed to a good many observers to fall short of these expectations. Then there is the suggestion, just hinted at in one of the Lancastrian historians and openly formulated in hostile writers, that the proceedings on 30 September were conducted in a body irregular in character and composition, and turbulent and partisan in action, which refused the king the common justice of a hearing. There is, indeed, a strong suggestion of disappointment and disapproval that Richard should have been condemned unheard. When, if at all, Bishop Merks delivered

[1] Froissart, 204.

his speech of protest is a matter of dispute,[1] but the sense of injustice which it expresses animates the documents of the Percy tradition, is stated in Scrope's Manifesto and is clearly put in the words of a Scottish observer writing twenty years after the event.

Andrew of Wyntoun was well-informed as to the English revolution and evidently had the official documents before him, and knew more than he thought it discreet to say. He considers that Richard had been harshly treated and that the proceedings on 30 September were arbitrary and irresponsible. Richard, a crowned and experienced king, known to his people and no heretic,

> Al ꝑus undon amange his awyn
> As ane awld abbot swa put don
> For opyn dilapidacion
>
> . . . .
>
> Swylk abbotis ȝhit sulde ioys defens.[2]

It was bad enough, Wyntoun thought, that the accused should not be heard in his own defence, it was worse that the body that judged and condemned him had no authority to do so.

> Don, na in fayr competent
> Na be ony auctoryte.
> Or ꝑa ꝑat sulde his jugis be.[3]

Here we have put pretty plainly the doubt that haunts even the official account and the orthodox Lancastrian historians and is more openly expressed by hostile English writers and the French authorities, and the kernel of it, I think, lies in the analogy between a legitimate king and a Benedictine abbot who is a responsible ruler but not responsible to his chapter. It may be put briefly thus : parliament, even in its capacity as supreme tribunal, has no power to judge a legitimate king, but if it undertook to do so, it should in common justice at least hear him in his own defence. The first proposition agrees with Bracton, but as we shall see, English political theory had gone somewhat

---

[1] Miss Clarke and Mr. Galbraith, op. cit., 154, argue (as it seems to me, convincingly) that the speech was in fact delivered on 30 September when, as we know from the Eulogium iii, 383, the bishop was present in Westminster Hall.

[2] Andrew of Wyntoun, The Orygeynale Cronykil of Scotland (ed. Amours, Scottish Text Soc., vi), 384 ff.

[3] Op. cit., 388–9.

farther than this by 1399. As to the second, it is unanswerable if the action of parliament takes a judicial form, as it did at one stage of the proceedings on 30 September. But the essence of the doubt, of course, is whether the deposing body was in fact a parliament.

II

The Lancastrian doctrine of constitutional government was set forth both directly and by implication in the proceedings of the convention on 30 September and at the meeting of Henry IV's first parliament a week later. The text of Arundel's sermon on the latter occasion, ' Incumbit nobis ordinare pro regno ', was not chosen at random, and the discourse itself develops the duty of a constitutional king. He postulates three things which are indispensable to the government of every kingdom : justice, the observance of the laws of the kingdom, and the maintenance of every man in his estate and degree. The new king, therefore, will not be governed by his own will, arbitrary purpose, or personal opinion, but by the common advice, counsel, and assent of the wise and responsible men of his kingdom.[1] The week before, in his sermon after Henry's acceptance, he had charged the new king to look to it that he did the will of God and not his own, and to remember that, where arbitrary will rules and reason departs, there is no coherence in government and great danger is imminent.[2] This is Bracton's teaching almost *verbatim*. The king is under God and the law and as God's vicar can do nothing except what is conformable to the law.[3] The same theory is derived from the text of the coronation oath and the long series of gravamina by which the estates justified their rejection of Richard. The point which is developed most fully and emphasized most strongly is the relation to the king of the law, its supremacy, its integrity, and the guarantee which it provides for the protection of individual rights. The law, whether formulated in statutes and judgements or existing as the ' leges et consuetudines regni ', is supreme and the king is its agent, and therefore the theory of constructive sovereignty which is

---

[1] *Rot. Parl.* iii, 415.   [2] *Ibid.*, 423.
[3] Bracton, fo. 5*b*, fo. 107*b* ; ed. Woodbine ii, 33, 305.

X

attributed to Richard in these articles amounts to ' perjury ', that is to say, a breach of his coronation oath.[1] On the other hand, the law consists of, or at least includes, the sum of the subjective rights of all members of the community. This proposition is made with reference to the thirty-ninth chapter of the Great Charter, and illustrated by the citation of special cases in which the king is alleged to have deprived his subjects of rights so secured to them, whether by forcing them to defence by the duel in the military courts or by other and still more irregular methods.[2] Two of these deserve particular notice ; the king is charged with imposing a special oath on the sheriffs by the authority of the signet, requiring them to arrest persons on suspicion, and with employing the same authority to issue writs of prohibition which the chancellor had refused on the ground that the business involved was *mere spiritualia*.[3] Thus a subject could be arrested although no presumption against him had been legally established, and could also be deprived of the advantages of access to the ecclesiastical courts in a case which should have been dealt with by the canon law.

All this, of course, goes in principle very little beyond the Great Charter and Bracton, but the group of articles we have now to consider introduces a further motive. The king is charged with having alienated the property of the crown and with conveying away the crown jewels and regalia ' without the leave of the estates of the kingdom '.[4] The distinction between the king and the crown had been clearly drawn by the younger Despenser, but he was blamed for doing so, and the notion as he stated it does not seem to have had much influence on English political thought in the fourteenth century.[5] On the other hand, much the same idea, though formulated rather differently and reached probably by empirical methods, is contained in the charge that has just been quoted. The nation has interests in what nominally belongs to the crown and these

---

[1] The gravamina are in *Rot. Parl*. iii, 417–22, nos. 18 to 51, incl. The law is in the king's breast and mouth, he is not bound by statutes, and the lives and goods of his subjects are at his disposal, nos. 33, 34, 43.

[2] Nos. 21, 28, 29, 30, 44.   [3] Nos. 37, 46.   [4] No. 41.

[5] Tout, *Place of Edward II*, 144 ; Ehrlich, *Proceedings against the Crown*, 127 ff., 148 ff. ; Davies, *Baronial Opposition to Edward II*, 24–5 ; Ramsay, *Genesis of Lancaster* i, 14, 118 ; and see above, pp. 174 ff. The text is given in *Statutes of the Realm* i, 181–2.

interests may be compromised or destroyed by the personal action of the king. The king in such cases must seek the permission of the ' estates of the kingdom '. Now, of course, this identification of the king (or rather the crown) and the ' respublica ' is found in Bracton :

Rex sapiens judicabit populum suum. Si autem fuerit insipiens perdet illum, quia a capite corrupto descendit corruptio membrorum, et si sensus et vires non vigeant in capite, sequitur quod cetera membra suum non poterunt officium exercere.[1]

This passage must have been known to Gower, who reproduces the substance of it in the following lines :

Ordine quo regnant reges, sua nomina pregnant,
Quo caput infirmum, nichil est de corpore firmum,
Plebs neque firmatur, ubi virtus non dominatur.[2]

The same idea must have been familiar, or at least welcome, in circles ignorant of Latin, for it is in effect the subject of Langland's fragment, *Richard the Redeless*, which was written a few weeks before the deposition.[3] The poet blames Richard for upsetting the social order of counsellors, warriors, and labourers upon which the realm is based, and ' breaking his crown ' by making grooms and nobles equal and giving power to young and giddy favourites instead of choosing responsible counsellors from the class that was wont to furnish them. No doubt it was current talk at the time, for Arundel used much the same language in the tirade which he addressed to the king at Flint.[4]

A further step is taken when it is suggested in the gravamina that the interests of the nation which the king by arbitrary or personal action might infringe should be protected by parliament. He is charged with having corrupted the public records, with having secured the pope's confirmation of certain statutes ' contra coronam et dignitatem regiam ac contra statuta et libertates . . . regni '.[5] The committee which the king set up

---

[1] Bracton, fo 107*b* ; ed. Woodbine ii, 306.
[2] *Works* iv, 364 ; it is also given in *Political Songs* (ed. Wright, R. S.) i, 362.
[3] *Works*, ed. Skeat, 469 ; also in *Political Songs* i, 368 ff.
[4] *Cont. Eulog.*, 382.
[5] *Rot. Parl., loc. cit.*, nos. 27, 41 ; cf. *ibid.*, 359, no. 52. Had it been forgotten that the commission of doctors and jurists had advised the deposition of the king on grounds drawn from the canon law ? Cf. Adam of Usk, 30.

to complete the work of the parliament of Shrewsbury is condemned as an infringement of the ' potestas et status parliamenti ', and the king is himself accused of destroying the integrity of parliament by tampering with elections.[1] The nation, on this view, is entitled to the protection of an institution which works by its own recognized rules, and should be secured from arbitrary interference on the king's part.

But what if the king did none the less interfere ? Was it possible to restrain or coerce him ? Archbishop Arundel thought, or affected to think, that such power lay with the great lords of the kingdom, and at Flint he told Richard so bluntly. He reproached the king for disregarding the wise counsel of the great lords and his relatives and persecuting them, ' quia volebant tuam proterviam compescere, sicut per statuta regni potuerunt et in periculo regni debuerunt '.[2]

This is, of course, the crux of the whole constitutional problem. Who may judge the king ? Bracton's doctrine is unmistakable ; the king cannot be judged by any man, and if he persists in doing wrong, his punishment must be left to God.[3] But Bracton saw the practical and political difficulties of this doctrine, and was prepared to consider another opinion. Who is to be judge, for example, in an accusation of high treason ? Not the king, because he is a party to the action, nor the justiciar because he represents the person of the king. It would seem, subject to a better opinion, that the court and the lords (curia et pares) should judge.[4] But what of such a political situation as Arundel contemplated ? Must the nation still await the action of an avenging God ? Bracton seems to think so, although indeed he allows that it might be argued, in such a case, that the ' universitas regni et baronagium suum hoc facere debeat et possit in curia ipsius regis '.[5] This would appear to be as far as Bracton was prepared to go and he is by no means committed even to this view. There is, however, a

---

[1] Nos. 25, 36, 41. It would seem that the king had, in fact, tampered with the parliament roll in order to increase the power of the committee ; cf. Edwards, J. G., *E.H.R.* xl, 321 ff.

[2] *Cont. Eulog.*, 382 ; cf. *Davies' Chronicle*, 16.

[3] Fo. 5*b* ; ed. Woodbine II, 33.

[4] Fo. 119*b*, *ibid.* II, 337.

[5] Fo. 171*b* ; *ibid.* III, 43.

famous passage in his text,[1] now recognized as an accretion, which in rather excited language treats as settled law the opinion which Bracton thought might perhaps be discussed. The king is subordinate not only to God and the law but to his court and baronage as well, and they ought to check him if he departs from the law. Otherwise, they too will be lawless and unrestrained, and the subjects will appeal to Heaven to put bit and bridle upon their jaws, and God's answer will be to bring a distant and mighty people upon them who will root them up and cast them out because they refused to judge men justly.[2] This passed into the text of *Fleta*[3] and should, therefore, have been familiar to those who concerned themselves with such matters in the early years of the fourteenth century. But in the course of that century the king's court had become a national parliament, and it might be that people would attribute to it in its new capacity a power that some, at least, thought that it might, or ought to have had in its old. No one doubted, of course, that a tyrant might be forcibly put down. But that is not enough; there should be a way of enforcing the nation's will without the use of violence and perhaps parliament would be the right instrument. Certainly, from the beginning of the fourteenth century the political importance of parliament advanced rapidly and the precedents thus created might later be of service in constructing a constitutional doctrine.

The Ordinances had stipulated for annual parliaments at least, and the Statute of York which undid the work of the Ordainers laid down a rule which, however its aim may be interpreted,[4] contemplated for certain national purposes the joint action of the lords and commons in parliament assembled. The precedent of January 1327 as bearing directly on our problem must detain us for a little. The leaders of the rebellion

---

[1] Fo. 34*b* ; *Ibid.* II, 110. Professor Woodbine thinks that this is a very old *addicio* (probably a ' not very distant echo of the trouble between Henry III and his barons') ; but that the authority on which it rests is not sufficient to allow us to attribute it to Bracton ; *ibid.* i, 333. Ehrlich, *Proceedings against the Crown*, 203, takes a contrary view for reasons that do not appear to me convincing ; cf. above, p. 23, n. 2.

[2] The various scriptural quotations held in solution in this passage have been precipitated by Dr. Ehrlich, *op. cit.*, 205.

[3] See Holdsworth, *H.E.L.* ii, 255 ; cf. Davies, *Baronial Opposition,* 16–17.

[4] See above, pp. 153–228, and the works there cited.

which made Edward III king during his father's lifetime refused to throw any official responsibility upon parliament or to attribute to it any share in the transaction. The rolls of parliament contain no account of the proceedings between 7 and 25 January. When the new king's peace was proclaimed on the 24th it was announced that Edward, formerly king of England, had, of his own free will, and by the advice and assent of the prelates, nobles, and the whole community of the kingdom, retired from the government and intimated that it should pass to his eldest son and heir.[1] There is, therefore, no official precedent for a deposition, although the part played by parliament in the transaction was well known to the chroniclers. On the other hand, it is clearly held that abdication could not be accomplished by a unilateral act; it required the assent, if not the advice, of the estates of the kingdom using the term estates in no technical sense.[2]

Parliament, summoned by Edward II's writs, met in London on 7 January, and was almost immediately invaded and terrorized by a turbulent London mob. The intention of the leaders seems to have been to charge and judge the king, and then either persuade or compel him to abdicate in favour of his son, in parliament. Stratford and Orlton had been sent to Kenilworth to persuade him to appear, but were met with an indignant refusal. Meanwhile, parliament was being harangued by the bishops and bullied by the London mob. It heard a series of formal charges drawn up by Stratford and enumerating the points in which the king had offended against the orthodox constitutional doctrine. When the question was at length put, parliament acclaimed Edward III.[3] A commission representative of all the elements of parliament was then sent to the king at Kenilworth, where on 20 January he was tricked and bullied into abdicating in favour of his son. The next day, 21 January, Sir William Trussell, who spoke on behalf of the commission and was described by some chroniclers as *totius*

---

[1] *Foedera* II ii, 683. A notification to the sheriffs made five days later is a somewhat condensed Latin version of this.

[2] Cf. Hale, *Pleas of the Crown* (ed. 1736) i, 104 ff.

[3] Some but not all of the chronicles say that Edward II was deposed, e.g. *Lanercost*, 258 ; *Annales Paulini*, 323 : the point is only a verbal one, as all agree that Edward III was acclaimed and the commission deputed to surrender homage and fealty to his father.

parliamenti procurator,[1] renounced homage and allegiance, and the steward of the king's household broke his wand of office. The commission, that is to say, had accepted the abdication on the part of parliament, and the throne was vacant. This was not, however, taken as invalidating the writs by which the parliament had been summoned. It continued in being and, when the writs *de expensis* were issued, sixty-nine days of continuous service were reckoned. The last parliament of Edward II was also the first of Edward III.[2]

The part which parliament took in these transactions, if we look at it from a political point of view, is both important and obvious. If we ask, however, how those who thought in terms of law would have described it, an answer is not easy to find. We must keep two facts in mind. In the first place, the throne was not vacant until the commission had accepted the king's abdication on 21 January. Public documents still ran in Edward II's name on 20 January. When Trussell had accepted the abdication on behalf of the commission he is reported to have said : ' Te reputant et tenent amodo personam privatam ab omni regia dignitate '.[3] Thus the acclamation of Edward III and the deposition of his father in parliament and the determination to renounce homage and allegiance had not sufficed to produce the legal effect required. In the second place, there is the official version of the matter. No doubt, to represent the change as having been accomplished by the voluntary act of the last king was in the circumstances a wise precaution. But, even so, political discretion did not require the complete exclusion of parliament. The advice and assent of the elements that composed parliament are specified in the official announcement; why should not the acceptance of the abdication have been entered on the parliament roll ? It is hard to avoid the conclusion that people were still very uncertain about the legal position of parliament and were very reluctant, particularly in so grave a matter as this, to create a precedent. In consequence the precedent that actually did arise was probably, as

[1] See Clarke, M. V., *Medieval Representation and Consent*, 185 ; Richardson, and Sayles, *B.I.H.R.* xi, 151.
[2] See Prynne, *Brief Register* iv, 78 ff.
[3] *Bridlington*, 90.

Maitland thought, one for revolution rather than for legal action.[1]

The crisis of 1340–41 equipped parliament with the means of bargaining with the Crown, making it a valuable ally whose help the Lancastrians invoked to secure their traditional aim of controlling the selection, and the conduct in office, of the king's ministers. Their success, it is true, was premature, and the repeal of the statute of 1341 left the work to be done over again, but the precedent was on record, and the parliament was fortified by the Crown's practical acceptance of the doctrine of peerage and of the constitutional necessity of securing the consent of the commons to taxation.[2] The opposition returned to the attack in 1376, and the death of the old king and the subsequent formation of a new court party about Richard at length precipitated the inevitable crisis. The commission of 1386 secured in practice that degree of parliamentary control at which the opposition aimed, but it was the king's appeal to the judges in the following summer and the consequent statement of the royalist constitutional doctrine that resulted in the formulation of a theory of parliamentary supremacy in February 1388.

The point was raised on a technical matter, the form in

[1] *Annales Paulini* (ed. Stubbs, R.S.) i, 322–4 ; *Chron. de Lanercost* (ed. J. Stevenson), 257 ff. ; *Chron. Galfridi le Baker* (ed. E. M. Thompson), 26–8 ; Willelmi de Dene, *Historia Roffensis*, in *Anglia Sacra* i, 367 ; *Apologia Adae Orleton*, in Twysden, *Decem Scriptores*, 27, 63–8 ; *Gesta Edwardi . . . auctore canonico de Bridlington* (ed. Stubbs, R.S.) ii, 90–1 ; *Vita Edwardi II*, ed. Stubbs, *Chronicles of Ed. I and Ed. II* (R.S.) ii, 289–90 ; *French Chron. of London* (ed. Aungier, Camden Soc.), 57 ; Stubbs, *C.H.* ii, 377–86 ; Lingard, *History of England* iii, 70 ff. ; Ramsay, *Genesis of Lancaster* i, 160–6 ; Tout, *Chapters* iii, 1–5 ; Maitland, *C.H.*, 190–1 ; Clarke M. V., ' Committees of Estates and the Deposition of Edward II ', *Essays in Honour of James Tait*, also included in *Medieval Representation and Consent*, 173–193, a lucid and critical account partly based on a contemporary chronicle still unpublished. Miss Clarke thinks that the delegation sent by parliament to notify the king of his deposition and renounce homage and allegiance after accepting his abdication was not an unprecedented device. She treats it as a committee of estates modelled partly on revolutionary precedents since 1244 as modified by the recognition of the commons in the Statute of York, partly by the tenth chapter of the *Modus*. It was ' an extension not so much of power as of responsibility ', and ' renunciation of allegiance was transmuted from feudal defiance to the will of the commonalty and the king was rejected not by vassals but by subjects ' (pp. 42–3). It should be observed, however, that the king was not effectively rejected until he had abdicated.

[2] See above, pp. 231–272 ; cf. Tout, *Chapters* iii, 126 ff. ; Clarke, *Fourteenth Century Sudies*, 127 ff. ; Wilkinson, *E.H.R.* xlvi, 177 ff.

which the accusations had been drafted. After the appeal had been heard and the default of the appellees noted, the lords of parliament formally demanded the advice of the ' sages of the law ' (including of course the justices and serjeants) as to how they should proceed in the matter. The common law experts sought the help of the civilians and after deliberation informed the lords that the appeal was irregular in form, whether it were judged by the common or the civil law.[1] This produced a reply that disposed of the question of form by rejecting the suggestion that parliament was bound by the technical forms of any system of law. The lords observed that this was a matter of state which it was for parliament alone to settle, since it involved the person of the king and welfare of all the kingdom. They repudiated in terms the authority of the civil law and declared that in this matter parliament will be ruled by its own law and custom and by none other. The reason they give for this is, that the lower courts which are bound by rules and order of procedure are no more than the executors of the ancient laws and customs of the kingdom and of the ordinances and statutes of parliament.[2] The point is driven home in one of the articles of the impeachment of Burley and Beauchamp, where it is laid down that the law of the land is made in parliament by the king, the lords spiritual and temporal, and the whole community of the kingdom.[3] These texts amount to ' the declaration that parliament, as the law-maker, could over-ride the executive officers of the law ', and involve ' an assertion of the ultimate sovereignty of parliament '.[4] We must, of course, make full allowance for the political tension in which this declaration was made and for the provocation given by the royalist doctrine obtained from the judges in the previous summer.[5] The Lords Appellant in their attempt to secure their work against repeal by a future parliament did of course contradict the most import-

---

[1] It was originally intended that the appeal should be heard in the court of the constable and marshal where the civil law was used. The promise of a parliamentary inquiry was made by the king ; see Clarke, *op. cit.*, 134–5.

[2] *Rot. Parl.* iii, 236.

[3] Monk of Westm., in Higden, *Polychronicon* (R.S.) ix, 146, cited in Tout, *Chapters* iii, 432.

[4] Tout, *loc. cit.*

[5] *Rot. Parl.* iii, 233–4. The whole incident is carefully discussed in Miss Clarke's study, cited above pp. 29, 31, 312.

ant implication of their doctrine. But this did not, in fact, obscure it to those who came after them, and the meaning of the words they used is indeed plain enough. If the law is made by parliament and can be altered by it so that no one parliament can bind its successors,[1] then the doctrine of the sovereignty of the law taught by Bracton falls and the king will not be under God and the law but under God and the parliament that is superior to the law since it can make and unmake it. Now I believe there are reasons which should dispose us to think that those who managed what may be called the constitutional side of the change of dynasty in 1399 had this doctrine and many, if not all, of its implications in mind.

Two days after the coronation the commons asked that the parliament of the eleventh year of Richard II, having been of great honour and general benefit to the kingdom, should be recognized and confirmed in all its acts, with the proviso that, if any of them should appear to be unnecessary or undesirable, its repeal might be asked for in the course of the session. All this was granted by the king and lords.[2] Now Richard had obtained in 1398 the disavowal and reversal of the parliament of 1388 and all its works.[3] But the record, of course, remained, and there were passages in it which might prove extremely embarrassing to those who maintained the doctrine of parliamentary supremacy. The Appellants had caused parliament to define as treason any attempt to undo their work by securing judicially or otherwise the reversal or repeal of any of its statutes, ordinances, or judgements,[4] and as though this were not enough, they had at the end of the session ' betrayed the secret trouble of their hearts ' by imposing an oath to the same effect upon all the lords and commons.[5] This, of course, is incompatible with parliamentary supremacy, and the commons in October 1399 therefore petitioned for and obtained its repeal on the ground that the king's subjects should be free to make their complaint of any wrong done them in that parliament, as was just, reasonable, and customary.[6] But Richard in his hour of triumph

[1] See below, p. 315, n. 3.
[2] *Rot. Parl.* iii, 425, no. 67.　　[3] *Ibid.*, 357, no. 47.
[4] *Ibid.*, 250.
[5] *Ibid.* iii, 252, no. 48 ; cf. Ramsay, *Genesis of Lancaster* ii, 257.
[6] *Rot. Parl.* iii, 442, no. 143.

had been no less anxious than his adversaries to protect what he had secured against the action of future parliaments, and it had therefore been enacted at Shrewsbury that any attempt to repeal or overthrow the statutes or judgements of 1397–8 should be reckoned treason.[1] This had already been censured in the gravamina,[2] and it was repealed on the petition of the commons at the same time as the similar act of 1388.[3]

The effect of these measures was to extricate the doctrine of parliamentary supremacy from the stultifying and contradictory precautions with which it had been overlaid in 1388 and 1397. Now such a doctrine so liberated did not need to be pressed very far to warrant a national parliament in judging and dismissing a king who could be shown to have disregarded the obligations imposed by the coronation oath and broken the law in other respects. Deposition by some method had been within the range of practical politics ever since the parliament of 1386 had threatened Richard with the fate of Edward II, and it is not impossible that a *de facto* deposition of Richard himself may have taken place in the last days of 1387.[4] We should recall in this connexion the angry words which Arundel addressed to the king at Flint, reminding him that the great lords had by the law of the kingdom the right to restrain him and in time of danger were bound to do so. This must refer to the alleged statute under which Edward II was deposed, with which parliament threatened Richard, and amounts therefore to a scarcely veiled threat. Something of the sort appears in one of the gravamina laid before the convention on 30 September. It alleges that Arundel at the time of his banishment had

[1] *Ibid.*, 359, no. 51.   [2] *Ibid.*, 421, no. 48.

[3] *Ibid.*, 425, no. 66. Miss Clarke in her valuable study, ' Forfeitures and Treasons in 1388 ', *T.R.H.S.*, 4th ser. xiv (1931), 65–94 (reprinted in *Fourteenth Century Studies*, 115–145), argues that the leaders in 1388 ' neither believed in nor understood their own declaration of parliamentary supremacy, since they failed to recognize that what one supreme parliament could do another could as easily undo ' (p. 92). But in 1388 the return of the king to some degree at least of power was certain, while in 1399 the chances of such a return were almost negligible, and the way in which Henry's first parliament dealt with the acts of 1388 and 1397–8 does at least raise a strong presumption that the Lancastrians in the autumn of 1399 understood the doctrine of parliamentary supremacy and many of its implications.

[4] Cf. Clarke and Galbraith, *B.J.R.L.* xiv, 157–161. See in particular the discussion of the subject among the insurgent lords in November 1387 reported by the Monk of Westminster; Higden, *Polychronicon* ix, 109–10.

warned the king that his harshness would return upon his own head, to which he replied that he scarcely thought that it would happen that ' per ligeos suos a regno suo deberet expelli '.[1] Perhaps this was bravado, for the possibility of deposition was not absent from the king's mind in 1398 when ' compassing the deposition of the king ' was declared high treason by parliament.[2] Now we have what very nearly amounts to direct evidence that the Lancastrians in September 1399 intended to proceed by way of parliamentary deposition. They set up some weeks before the meeting of parliament a committee of learned men, doctors, jurists, and bishops, who were instructed to find a way by which under the forms of law Richard could be disposed of and Henry made king.[3] The commission considered the charges against Richard—perhaps they actually drafted the gravamina which are recorded in the schedule—[4] and, having in mind the proceedings against the Emperor Frederick at the Council of Lyons, agreed that there was good ground for deposition, and the report proceeds :

Et, licet cedere paratus fuerat, tamen ob causas praemissas ipsum fore deponendum cleri et populi autoritate, ob quam causam tunc vocabantur, pro majori securitate determinatum.[5]

It is hard to see how the commission expected the authority of the clergy and people to be obtained except through parliament, and this would appear to have been Adam of Usk's meaning when he says that they were summoned for that purpose. It is surely legitimate to assume that the commissioners who counselled that the king should be deposed rather than allowed to abdicate knew what powers had been claimed for parliament in 1388, and what use could be made of the doctrine then formulated in the present crisis. The measures taken on 15 October could scarcely have been impromptu. It is pretty clear, therefore, that they intended that the ' authority of the clergy and people ' should be furnished by the parliament, which had already been summoned. How else, indeed, could it be obtained ?

---

[1] *Rot. Parl.* iii, 422, no. 50.
[2] *Statutes of the Realm* ii, 98.
[3] Adam of Usk, *Chron.*, 29–30.
[4] Stubbs, *C.H.* ii, 528, states this as a fact, but cites no authority.
[5] Adam of Usk, 30. The reference is c. 2 in Sext., l. II, tit. xiv.

Now the question of getting rid of Richard was not the only one that had been referred to the commissioners. They had been asked as well to indicate a legal or at least a formal way to make Henry king. If they gave a direct answer to this it has not been transmitted to us, but we can scarcely doubt what their advice must have been. The question of the succession in the event of Richard's remaining childless had been raised earlier in the reign, and parliament had settled it by declaring Mortimer the heir.[1] What was to prevent its altering this decision by recognizing and electing Henry as soon as the throne was vacated by his cousin's deposition ? Henry and his friends would thus appear to have been confronted with what the French call a *situation nette*, imposing upon them a simple and straightforward course of action. If, in the light of this conclusion we look again at the confused and ambiguous account of the events of 29 and 30 September, we can only ask in bewilderment why a simple thing should have been done in a manner so obscure and elaborate. Two possibilities suggest themselves : the difficulty to be overcome was either formal or material, it derived either from the need of observing ' the forms of the constitution ' or from some objection arising out of the very nature of the proposed parliamentary action. For the moment we are concerned with the sequence of events rather than the exact chronology. Adam says that on his arrival in London Henry placed King Richard in the Tower for safe-keeping. Adam then speaks of the king's ill-treatment of the magnates, tells the story of Arthgallo, a British tyrant deposed by his barons, and refers to the scandalous rumours of Richard's illegitimacy. Immediately on this follows the account of the setting up of the commission and its report of which we have already taken account. Then follows Adam's narrative of his visit to King Richard in the Tower on St. Matthew's day, 21 September, whereupon he returns to the work of the commission with the words, ' one day in the deliberations of the aforesaid doctors, "in concilio per dictos doctores habito"', the question of the succession was raised by certain of them in connexion with the story of Edmund Crouchback's alleged seniority to his brother Edward. Adam had evidently interested

[1] *Cont. Eulog.*, 361, 369.

himself particularly in this, and he cites the passages from the chronicles the examination of which convinced him, and presumably his colleagues in the commission, that the story was groundless. He then passes immediately to the events of 29 September.[1]

Now the author of the *Annales* couples the issue of the parliamentary writs and the letters of privy seal directing the monasteries and principal churches to search out and transmit chronicles relevant to the problems before the commission as though they formed part of a single design, but dates them after Henry's arrival in London (3 September). We know that this is three weeks too late in the case of the writs, which were issued at Chester on 19 August, and it is likely, therefore, that the letters of privy seal were also issued earlier.[2] Among the chronicles which Adam cites in connexion with the fable of Edmund Crouchback's seniority there is one, at least, that is not very likely to have been available in London, namely, the chronicle of Gloucester.[3] If, therefore, we take the date of the letters of privy seal as 19 August, there would have been time to make a search and send a manuscript from Gloucester to London, by 21 September. This would scarcely be the case if the letters had not been issued until 3 September. It looks, therefore, as though the plan of summoning a parliament and submitting to it a considered scheme for the removal of Richard and the substitution of Henry had been settled as soon as the king was a prisoner. It is impossible to suppose that the commission did not consider very carefully the only available precedent. Indeed, it is directly referred to in connexion with the commission that was sent to Richard in the Tower which was to speak on behalf of the estates ' prout in consimilibus casibus de antiqua consuetudine dicti regni fuerat observatum'.[4] The adversaries of Richard II had had the deposition of his great-grandfather in mind at least since 1386. We need not pause now to consider whether any one really believed in the existence of the

[1] Adam of Usk, 29–31.
[2] *Lords' Report* iv, 465 ; *Annales*, 251–2. I am indebted to my friend Mr. A. B. Steel for this and a number of other suggestions and criticisms by which I have greatly profited.
[3] Adam of Usk, 31.
[4] *Rot. Parl.* iii, 422, no. 51.

statute that was invoked at that time ;[1] it is sufficient to recall that
the chronicles afforded abundant details of what took place.
These, indeed, were disregarded and even directly contradicted
by the official account, so that the precedent could be represented in two aspects. This fact must have been before the
commissioners, who must also have been aware that, whatever
view you took of the precedent, you could not invoke its
authority without employing the form of abdication. This
course, as we know, they deliberately rejected, and we are
entitled to assume, therefore, that they had with equal deliberation settled to disregard or at least to depart from, the precedent. Now Adam is quite clear that the terms of reference
were, as we have stated them, to substitute Henry for Richard,
and the question of the succession accordingly would not fail
to be discussed; it would remain only to determine upon what
ground Henry should be accepted. Since it had been settled
that Richard should be deposed by parliament, it would seem to
follow that Henry should be set up by the same authority.
Now Hardyng says that Northumberland told him that Henry
submitted the forged chronicle ' to the council ' on St.
Matthew's day and they rejected it. It can scarcely be a coincidence therefore that Adam uses the words ' in concilio ',
places the discussion of the story, and cites the evidence against
it, immediately after his account of his visit to the king in the
Tower on St. Matthew's day. If we allow three days, and that
would be barely sufficient, for Adam's search among the
chronicles and the council's discussion of the evidence which he
submitted to them, we shall have reached 25 September. The
situation would then be that within five days of the meeting of
parliament the official plan was to submit a case against the
king which would justify his deposition and, presumably, Henry's
election as his successor, his claim to succeed by independent
hereditary right having been examined and rejected. Yet within
four more days the necessity of an abdication had been admitted,
and the embarrassing consequences of the doctrine of the invalidation of the writs by the cession of the Crown recognized.

---

[1] Miss Clarke, relying on a passage in Knighton, thinks that an account
of the deposition of Edward II ' ex antiquo statuto ' may have been shown
to Richard in 1386 and afterward destroyed by his direction ; *Medieval
Representation and Consent*, 177 n.

This, it is submitted, is a reasonable interpretation of the only direct and more or less contemporary evidence we have on the subject, namely, that of Adam of Usk, the story that Hardyng had from Northumberland, the schedule, and the passage in the *Annales*. The difficulty then was not, as Stubbs supposed, a formal one recognized and provided for at the outset.[1] It arose rather from an emergency creating a new situation. It had been recognized all along that an abdication could be obtained, but the formal difficulty arising from the theory that it would automatically dissolve parliament appears to have occurred first at this time. It was brought forward, perhaps, as an objection; but it need not have been an insuperable obstacle to parliamentary action. What was to prevent the estates being convened, and parliament opened by commission and organized with all the accustomed forms, on the appointed day ? It could then have fixed the succession in Henry and his line. If it be objected that this was *ultra vires*, the answer is that parliament had already fixed the succession in the line of Mortimer and was to do so again in that of Lancaster. To the further objection that Richard was not a free agent and that his formal consent might be repudiated on that ground it may be answered that that was true of any course that might be adopted. If these measures had been taken, parliament could then have proceeded to depose Richard, thereby, of course, terminating its own existence. It would then have been open to Henry as king by succession to issue new writs and obtain an abdication from Richard *ex abundantia cautelae*. On the meeting of the new parliament he could have been recognized as king, as Edward III had been recognized, and the disposal of Richard's possible claims completed by the acceptance of his abdication by the parliament. No doubt this course, had it been taken, would have suggested a certain scepticism as to the authority of parliament, but abdication could not be had at any less price,

---

[1] *C.H.* ii, 528–9. Stubbs describes a plan proposed by Edmund of York (after it had been determined to proceed by way of abdication and deposition) ' which under these complicated contrivances should save the forms of the constitution '. He further attributes to Arundel the objection that the abdication would invalidate the writs. He cites no authority and I have been unable to discover any. His account cannot be reconciled with the evidence of Adam of Usk and the device by which he says Arundel's objection was met could not have had that effect.

and the face of parliament would have been saved to a far greater extent than was done by the procedure actually adopted.

If, therefore, we reject the orthodox account of the matter and accept the results yielded by the evidence at our disposal, we are left with a difficult but not, I think, an insoluble problem. We shall have to fit into the days that lie between the commission's rejection of Henry's claim to succeed by inheritance, say 25 September, and the king's abdication on the 29th, a series of well-attested events that may be taken as accounting for what was done on the 29th and 30th and the official report of these transactions set out in the schedule. These events may be enumerated without at present attempting to establish their sequence, as follows : Henry's proposal to rest his claim on conquest, Thirning's objection and the modified form in which it was allowed to appear, the eventual admission of Henry's claim by inheritance, and the proposal that an abdication should be obtained which prevailed in spite of the objection that it would invalidate the writs and render action through parliament impossible. Taken together these things constitute a surrender of the original, straightforward scheme for accomplishing the revolution by means of parliamentary action, and the change, I suggest, can best be accounted for on the assumption that Henry disliked that scheme and was determined to obtain the crown by other means. Three considerations suggest that Henry was dissatisfied with the arrangements that his friends had concerted for a parliamentary solution of the problem, and these may be examined in order.

In the first place, however we may judge the disorders and disaffection that culminated in the battle of Shrewsbury and the movement that cost Archbishop Scrope his life, one inference is almost impossible to resist. Many of those to whose help and support Henry owed the crown regretted the method if not the result of the revolution. We must not, of course, lose sight of the partisan character of the document sent to Henry on the eve of Shrewsbury and the manifesto that was issued in Scrope's name. Thus against the Percy allegation that Henry was bound by his oath at Doncaster not to take the crown we must set Adam of Usk's record that his commission was instructed to

Y

report on the best means of substituting Henry for Richard, particularly as, quite apart from intrigue and possible designs on the crown, one would not be disposed to trust the Percies. If on the other hand we accept the view that has been advanced here that up to 25 September the agreed policy of the revolutionary party was to proceed by parliamentary deposition and election, some of the points made by the Percies and Scrope become highly relevant. We shall recall the allegation of the Shrewsbury document that Henry had secured the crown by the acclamation of a packed and mob-ridden assembly; Northumberland's story that Henry had carried his point in council and parliament by his might and wilfulness and by the support of certain lords and the strength of the commons; and finally Scrope's charge that Henry, having coerced and terrified Richard, held a parliament without him, where arrogantly and insolently he had declared that the crown of England belonged immediately and by right to him and to none other.[1] Webb, as we have seen, took all this so seriously as to believe that from the first the Percies intended that March should succeed, and only acquiesced in what occurred and accepted office, in order to strike more effectively at Henry when the time came.[2] It is not necessary to go so far, however, to admit the inference that they and their friends offered Henry the crown upon terms which he was unwilling to accept, and that he was able at the last moment to obtain it upon his own.

We come now to two points which are perhaps best considered—as they eventually appeared—in relation to each other. These are Henry's proposals to claim the throne by right of conquest and/or as the legitimate heir. As to the first of these it should be remembered that it was an historical fact which, however embarrassing it might be to the constitutional issue, no one could deny; with regard to the second we may be equally

---

[1] References are given above pp. 295–8. Scrope's insistence on the importance for reform of a freely elected parliament, containing lawyers and held at London, should be remembered ; *Cont. Eulog.*, 406.

[2] *Archaeologia* xx, 183–8. It should not be forgotten that the *Dieulacres Chronicle*, 179, states definitely that Henry Percy had been so displeased with the turn of events that he refused to be present at the coronation banquet. It should also be recalled in this context that on the first day of parliamentary business after his coronation, Wednesday, 15 October, Henry secured from parliament the recognition of his son as heir-apparent ; *Rot. Parl.* iii, 426, no. 71.

clear that it was a preposterous story which no one could
believe. Further, it may be noticed that either of these claims,
or alternatively the ingenious combination of them to which
Henry finally resorted, would be fatal to the course proposed
by the commission. In connexion with the first we may notice
two texts. Adam of Usk describes Henry's arrival in London
with the captive king in his train, in these words : ' Et sic
dux, rege et regno per eum infra l. dies gloriose conquesto,
Londoniam transiit '.[1] A passage in the *Annales* makes it clear
that Henry proposed that his victory should yield him something more than glory :

> Proposuerat namque vendicasse regnum per conquestum; sed
> hoc omnino prohibuit Dominus Willelmus Thernyng, Justiciarius;
> quia tale occasione commovisset bilem totius populi contra eum; eo
> quod visum fuisset populo, si sic vendicasset regnum, quod potuisset
> quemlibet exhaeredasse pro votis, leges mutasse, condidisse novas,
> et veteres annullasse; et per consequens nullus securus fuisset de sua
> possessione.

The interpretation of these words depends in a great degree
on the question of when and in what circumstances the proposal
was advanced, and this we shall have to discuss later. What
concerns us for the moment is the combination of the two claims
which was eventually accepted and incorporated in the schedule.
The nature of the case becomes clear if we take the account of
Thirning's intervention in conjunction with the words Henry
used in thanking the estates for their acceptance of him.[2] The
new king disclaimed any theory of general expropriation which
might otherwise be expected to result from the admission of his
right by conquest. If he had not asserted such a right, the
explicit repudiation of one of its results would have been
meaningless and irrelevant, and the exception of those who
' had been against the good purpose and common profit of the
realm ' shows that, in their case at least, the result did follow.
But the point is scarcely worth labouring further in view of the
general agreement of the chronicles, royalist and Lancastrian
alike, that is tersely expressed in Chaucer's[3] well-known envoi.
To this may now be added the testimony of Froissart, who says

---

[1] *Chronicon*, 29.
[2] See above, p. 279.   [3] The lines are cited below, p. 328.

that Henry claimed to be king on three grounds (par trois
manières de cas), by conquest, because he claimed to be the
right heir, and because King Richard had freely and formally
resigned the kingdom into his hands,[1] and of Gower's marginal
summary of his own verse : ' Nota, qualiter jura corone
serenissimo jam regi nostro Henrico quarto tribus modis
accrescunt :   primo successione :   secundo eleccione :   tertio
conquestu sine sanguinis effusione.'[2]

But clearly Henry did not intend his claim by conquest to
be considered alone. He represents it as a conquest that was at
once justified and limited by his claim to an hereditary right to
the crown superior to that of Richard himself. If you admit
these two claims, as the estates are reported to have done, no
discretion is left to parliament. Henry has not merely removed
a tyrant who was oppressing England, he has disposed of an
usurper and put himself into actual possession of what had
always been his by right and law. To this last point we must
now address ourselves.

Henry's claim by inheritance is stressed by all the chroniclers, and this evidently corresponded with his own wish
expressed or implied. It is important, therefore, to be clear as
to what he really understood and meant to convey by his
assertion that he was descended in the right line from King
Henry III. The formula contained in the schedule is developed
and emphasized in the chronicles. He is the next heir by
hereditary right, in the right line descending from the noble
king, Henry III,[3] or he reads his speech from a manuscript
held in his hand and describes himself as the next heir male,[4] or
again he is represented as presenting the estates with an accomplished fact, a declaration ' quomodo, et sub qua fortuna, jus
et titulus regnorum, tunc vacantium, ad eum jure hereditario
spectabant, et ad ipsum fuerunt jure devoluta ',[5] and, as we
have seen, Scrope's manifesto describes Henry as arrogantly
and ostentatiously asserting that the kingdom and crown of

---

[1] *Chroniques* xvi, 355.
[2] *Works* iv, 338. In his text, however, the order is conquest, which
proved his right of succession, and election which confirmed it.
[3] Monk of Evesham, 160.
[4] *Cont. Eulog.*, 383.
[5] Otterbourne i, 219.

England belonged by right to him and to no other living man.[1]

Now we know that this question had been before the commission. Adam of Usk says[2] that it rested on the allegation that Edmund of Lancaster and not Edward was in fact the eldest son of Henry III, but had been postponed to his brothers and excluded from the succession ' propter fatuitatem '. The commissioners, as we have seen, took some pains to investigate the matter and reviewed a certain amount of historical evidence, more perhaps than the absurd story deserves. Hardyng alleges that he had heard the earl of Northumberland say that Henry had presented his story of the seniority of Edmund of Lancaster in the form of a chronicle which he submitted to the commission on 21 September, and on this the chronicles of Westminster and other houses ' were had in the council at Westminster ', and as the lords found in them no support for what Henry had submitted it was ' reproved and annulled '. The earl added that the chronicle in question had been forged and deposited in several monastic houses by the order of John of Gaunt when he had failed to persuade the commons to recognize him as heir-apparent on the ground that Richard was unlikely to have issue. John of Gaunt, he told Hardyng, wished to make a title for his son, and ' wolde have had the seide erle of Northumberland and sir Thomas Percy his brother, of counsaile thereof, for cause thei were descent of the said Edmunde be a suster; but they refused it '.[3]

Commenting on this Stubbs observes :[4]

Hardyng's story that John of Gaunt procured the insertion of the forged pedigree in several monastic chronicles is not borne out by any known evidence. If it is true, it must be referred to the year 1385 or 1394, when it is said that he tried to obtain Henry's recognition as heir, and when the earl of March was preferred[5] . . . But the

[1] *Historians of the Church of York* ii, 297.   [2] Adam of Usk, 30–1.
[3] Hardyng, *Chronicle*, 353–4.   [4] *Const. Hist.* iii, 12 n.
[5] *Cont. Eulogii*, 361, 369, where it is stated that John of Gaunt told the story of Edmund Crouchbacks' seniority in parliament and was given the lie by March. Cf. Armitage-Smith, *John of Gaunt*, 359–62. The late M. V. Clarke, in a letter of October 1934 to the writer, expressed the opinion that the story of the parliamentary recognition of March was ' a bogus tale, put about by the Yorkists under Henry VI, appearing only in a late authority and under the unconvincing date of 1385.' In any case, she pointed out, March's position would not have passed automatically to his heir on his death in 1398.

words of Henry's challenge do not necessarily imply that he meant to assert the forged pedigree; they need imply no more than that succession through females was regarded as strange to the customs of England. It is on the exclusion of females that Fortescue urges the claim of the king's brother as against the grandson of a daughter . . . if that were accepted, Henry might fairly call himself the male heir of Henry III. It was, moreover, on this principle probably that he tried to restrict the succession to male heirs in 1406.

The exact form of the alleged pedigree has not been preserved, but Henry was in fact descended from Edmund of Lancaster through his mother Blanche, great-granddaughter of Edmund Crouchback, and daughter and heiress of Henry, first duke of Lancaster, and Hardyng's story with its reference to the Percy descent suggests that this was the line taken. Stubbs appears to mean that succession through females was strange to the custom of England if any heir in the direct male line were available. Otherwise the succession of Stephen and Henry II would be proof to the contrary. Therefore the case contemplated by Stubbs now arose for the first time,[1] unless indeed we except Edward III's claim to the French crown which might be taken as indirectly admitting succession through females.[2] Without insisting on that, however, it may be pointed out that upon Stubbs's view Henry was the proper heir of Richard II as descended from Edward III in the eldest surviving direct male line, and that his claim by descent from Henry III was barred because it was transmitted through his mother. It is difficult to see how even a forged pedigree could have provided him with a Lancastrian descent in the direct male line from Henry III. So matters stood in 1399, and Fortescue's argument framed in conditions nearly half a century later is scarcely relevant. If, therefore, as Stubbs suggests, the point of Henry's argument had been to discredit Mortimer's claim as being transmitted by a woman, he would surely have emphasized his own position as the true heir of Edward III in the direct male line. It is

[1] Cf. Maitland, *C.H.*, 191.
[2] The arrangements made in the treaty of 1388 for securing to the descendants of the duke of York the contingent rights to the crown of Castile are perhaps worth noting in this connexion. They provide for succession in the direct male line, but failing that recognize the right transmitted by the Castilian princess whom the duke had married. Walsingham ii, 194 ; Armitage Smith, *John of Gaunt*, 330–3.

scarcely likely that he would have sacrificed the advantage of
the undeniable fact that he was the grandson of the last king
but one, to depend upon a claim deriving from Edward's
great-grandfather, which every one knew to be false. Henry's
formulation of his claim could not have been made at random
nor without some solid reason,[1] and we are entitled to assume
that succession through females (in Stubbs's sense) was contemplated in English practice (we can scarcely say more since
the case now arose for the first time), because Mortimer had
been recognized as Richard's heir and the principle had been
admitted in Edward III's claim to France.[2] This being so,
Henry's claim to descent from Henry III by an elder line would,
if it were true, automatically exclude Mortimer and entitle
Henry to the crown. If Edmund Crouchback's seniority were
admitted, no new pedigree would be needed : Henry's descent
through Blanche of Lancaster (to whom the whole inheritance
came) would enable him to meet and beat Mortimer on his
own ground. Here, therefore, was sufficient reason both for
discarding the pedigree and sticking to the fable of Edmund
Crouchback's seniority. Thus, having come into his inheritance
by an act of excusable self-help, he would be inviting an assembly of persons, representative, it is true, but unauthorized and
turbulent, to accept the *fait accompli* which he submitted. This
is obviously very far from what had been contemplated by the
great nobles and other persons of influence who surrounded
him. It must have needed all the ' might and wilfulness ' that
Northumberland attributed to him[3] in this business to overcome Thirning's opposition, to set aside the considered judgement of the commission, and to alter fundamentally the

---

[1] Macaulay's suggestion (in Gower, *Works* iv, 414) that it was because of
the identity of names, can scarcely be so described.

[2] In 1404 the succession to the crown was fixed in the prince of Wales
and the heirs of his body, which failing, to his brothers and their issue
successively and heritably according to the law of England ; *Rot. Parl.* iii,
525. In June 1406 this was altered and the succession limited to the prince
and his heirs male and then to his brothers and their heirs male in order of
seniority ; *ibid.*, 574–6. In the following December parliament asked that
the restriction be removed on the ground that it limited unduly the prospective rights of succession of the princes. In granting this the king
described it as *supplicatio juri consona* ; *ibid.*, 580–3. This does not look as
though succession through females in Stubbs's sense were repugnant to
English custom.

[3] Hardyng, 353.

plan which it had proposed. If now we ask his reasons for that dislike, we must look for our answer to what he accomplished, which was in fact to make the parliamentary title which had been proposed for him formally impossible and to substitute a title by legitimate descent, vindicated by conquest, and admitted by some form of popular acclamation. His purpose, therefore, would seem to have been to make himself what parliament could never make him nor revolution either, a legitimate king having no less a measure of power than, and no sanction inferior to, those that Richard had enjoyed. Now this is not merely inference from events, still less guesswork, there is direct evidence of the importance which Henry attached to his claim to legitimacy.

In the first year of his reign the new king was addressed by two poets each of whom, having something to gain, may be presumed to have informed himself of the terms which would be most pleasing to his prospective patron. Chaucer's begging letter consisted in an old set of verses, addressed to his purse, supplied with a new envoi,

> O conqueror of Brutes Albioun,
> Which that by lyne and free eleccioun
> Ben verray king, this song to you I sende;[1]

Gower's contribution was more substantial. He offered not only a new poem but, what is much more to our purpose, an interpretation of the facts of Henry's accession which must have been profoundly gratifying to the new king.

Gower's poem is without title, and his editor has conveniently if not very accurately named it *In Praise of Peace*.[2] It is in fact an argument in verse based on the terms of Henry's challenge and directed to show that the revolution was the act of God, who has blessed and sanctioned a measure of warfare which ridded England of a tyrant and brought the legitimate heir to the throne. The argument therefore starts from Henry's own words, ' that right [i.e. inheritance] that God of his grace hath sent me, with the help of my kin and my friends to

---

[1] *Works* (ed. Skeat) i, 401.

[2] *Works* (ed. Macaulay) iii, 481 ff. ; on grounds of internal evidence the poem is assigned to the first year of Henry IV's reign ; *ibid.*, pp. 550–1. This dating is accepted by R. B. Daniels, Studies in Philology xxxii (1935), 62–73.

recover '.[1] Before developing his argument the author makes its drift clear in a Latin quatrain, as follows :

> Electus Cristi, pie rex Henrice, fuisti,
> Qui bene venisti cum propria regna petisti;
> Tu mala vicisti qui bonis bona restituisti,
> Et populo tristi nova gaudia contribuisti.

From this we may turn to take account of some of the more significant passages in the poem itself :

> O worthi noble kyng, Henry the ferthe,
> In whom the glade fortune is befalle
> The poeple to governe uppon this erthe,
> God hath the chose in comfort of ous alle :
>
> .   .   .   .
>
> The highe God of his justice allone
> The right which longeth to thi regalie
> Declared hath to stonde in thi persone,
> And more than God may no man justefie.
> Thi title is knowe uppon thin ancestrie,
> The londes folk hath ek thy riht affermed;
> So stant thy regne of God and man confermed,
> There is no man mai seie in other wise,
> That God himself ne hath thi riht declared,
> Whereof the lond is boun to thi servise,
> Which for defalte of help hath longe cared;
> Bot now there is no mannes herte spared
> To love and serve and wirche thi plesance,
> And al is this thurgh Godes pourveiance.[2]

Gower then, by the examples of Solomon and Alexander, who asked respectively for wisdom and victory, raises the question whether a king can be justified in conquest :

> So mai a kynge of werre the viage
> Ordeigne and take, as he thereto is holde,
> To cleime and axe his rightful heritage
> In alle places wher it is witholde.[3]

In all other circumstances peace is to be preferred. This makes the two sides of Henry's claim depend on each other, and would have sufficed to meet Thirning's objection and make the new king's disclaimer unnecessary, for conquest so defined could give Henry no more than kingship under that law which

---

[1] *Rot. Parl.* iii, 423.   [2] Lines 1-21.   [3] Lines 57-60.

protected men's property by the same sanction as it secured the crown to him. Gower then argues that a king may properly make war to vindicate his right, since peace is the final end and aim of war, and illustrates his points with historical examples. The piece is followed by a Latin prayer, which serves to emphasize the conclusion that Henry is in fact a legitimate king brought to the throne by the intervention of God and ruling as his predecessors had done by divine sanction:

> Sancta sit illa dies qua tu tibi regna petisti,
> Sanctus et ille deus qui tibi regna dedit,
> Qui tibi prima tulit, confirmet regna futura,
> Quo poteris magno magnus honore frui.[1]

Clearly Gower was working from Henry's own words with perhaps a suggestion drawn from Arundel's sermon after the election. The archbishop there contrasts the new king with Richard who had acted as a capricious child, and says that Henry will on the contrary do the will of God, adding ' non veni facere voluntatem meam set ejus qui misit me scilicet Dei '.[2] But the poet's development of this material and the conclusion to which he brings his argument must also have been influenced by the elaborate ceremonial of the coronation. The ' premeditated pageant in Westminster Hall ' was only completed and its full intention disclosed in the coronation.[3] The underlying purpose of the elaborate symbolism with which that rite was accomplished originated with Henry and in spite of his advisers. The story of the phial of holy oil confided by the Virgin to St. Thomas of Canterbury with the prophecy that it would be used to inaugurate the reign of a king who should restore and extend the kingdom[4] is, of course, a clumsy forgery and may well, as Stubbs conjectured, derive from the same hand that framed the convenient legend of the Lancastrian descent. But Henry's unction produced the effect at which the

---

[1] P. 493, ll. 20–5.

[2] *Rot. Parl.* iii, 423. It seems to me possible that the antithesis between a child and a man on the throne, drawn by a forced interpretation of the text ' Vir dominabitur populo ', which forms the burden of the sermon, was aimed at the young Mortimer at least as much as at Richard.

[3] There is a minute account of the coronation ceremonies in Froissart xvi, 204–9 ; see also *Annales*, 291–300.

[4] *Annales*, 300 ; see also Bloch, *Les Rois Thaumaturges*, 241–3.

forger aimed, and the author of the *Annales*, having pointed out that Henry was the first of the kings anointed with the precious fluid sent, as it were, from Heaven, proceeds :

Quapropter pluribus credebatur, quod hic esset ille rex electus a Deo, cui talis unctio miraculose servabatur; cui et tanta gratia promittebatur quanta nulli alii que fuerat ante eum.[1]

From this point of view it was important, not only that the new king should assume the complete sanction of legitimacy, but also that his predecessor should be as completely divested of it. The instrument of abdication contains a very full enumeration of what may be called the content of the crown's sovereignty, with a comprehensive saving clause intended to secure for his successor all that Richard had had.[2] The author of the *Annales* relates that Richard took exception to the passage in Thirning's speech announcing his deposition to the effect that he had renounced all the honour and dignity belonging to a king. He objected ' quod noluit renunciare spirituali honori characteris sibi impressi, et inunctioni, quibus renunciare nec potuit, nec ab hiis cessare '.[3] To this Thirning answered, that his resignation was unconditional and could not be altered. Henry's claim to have all that his predecessor had enjoyed, and his willingness to exercise his power in conformity with the law which Richard was accused of neglecting, were officially recognized by his first parliament. The commons in a petition —which is in fact a memorandum—reminded the king that their predecessors had granted to King Richard at a parliament held at Winchester[4] that he should have as full a measure of wer (q'il serreit en auxi bon libertee) as his predecessors before him, and that he had interpreted this as authorizing him to act unlawfully in spite of his coronation oath. They proceed to say that, in this parliament, the commons have freely and voluntarily granted to the present king ' q'il soit en auxi graunde libertee roial come ses nobles progenitours furent devant luy '. This they did confiding in his high discretion and

---

[1] *Annales*, 300.   [2] *Rot. Parl.* iii, 417.

[3] *Annales*, 286 ; cf. Monk of Evesham, 159, who says that when he signed the form of abdication Richard protested ' quod noluit nec intendebat renunciare characteris animae suae impressis '.

[4] The only parliament held by Richard at Winchester was in his 16th year, 1393. There is no reference to the transaction in the printed parliament roll.

wise government. In return the king freely in open parliament made a reassuring statement. It was not, he said, his will or intention to distort laws, statutes, or good customs nor to take any other advantage of the grant the commons had made to him. On the contrary, it was his purpose to maintain the ancient laws and statutes ordained and observed in the time of his progenitors and to do right to all men in mercy and truth according to his oath.[1] The head of the house of Lancaster could give such an undertaking without a scruple or a regret, and it was, of course, perfectly compatible with his claim to legitimacy. He accepted no more from the commons than Richard had done, and imposed upon the prerogative no limitation that had not long been generally recognized and approved. What the commons may have meant to secure, beside the formal admission that the king is and should be below the law, is not very clear. If the words appear to suggest something more than a recognition of the king's legitimacy, they will scarcely bear the sense that the commons are the source of the prerogative.

Henry's course in this matter was no doubt the traditional policy of the usurper and could be matched among his own ancestors, Anglo-Norman and Capetian,[2] but Gower's argument, by representing Henry as the agent of divine justice,

---

[1] *Rot. Parl.* iii, 434, no. 108. The text appears to be a conflation of :

(a) The petitions of 14 and 15 Richard II, releasing the Crown from any restrictions imposed by the legislation of Richard's reign or those of his predecessors. In the later of these there is a clear reference to the statute by virtue of which Edward II was alleged to have been deposed. The two amount to ' a renunciation of political opposition [and] . . . must have been one condition of the promotion of the Arundels'. Stubbs, *C.H.* ii, 509–10.

(b) the undertaking given by the king *anno* 15, in return for a grant, to govern in conformity with the law. *Rot. Parl.* iii, 279, 285, 286.

[2] See Bloch's suggestion (*op. cit.*, caps. I and II) that the king's touch for scrofula was invented by Robert the Pious and imitated or adopted in England by Henry I, in whose time its origin was deliberately attributed to Edward the Confessor. On Henry's aspirations for legitimacy see Wallon, *op. cit.* ii, 312–13 : ' Porté au trône par une révolution, Henri aurait voulu élever sa dynastie au dessus de pareilles vicissitudes ; et sentant bien ce qui manquait à la légitimité de sa branche, il entreprit d'y suppléer par une autre sorte de droit divin'. I think that Wallon attaches too much importance to the perfectly normal religious forms observed before and during the proceedings on 30 September. But his phrase ' jamais on ne vit plus saint homme d'usurpateur ' deserves to be remembered. The point is well put in Cartellieri's phrase, ' Das heilige Öl ersetzte das fehlende Königsblut ' ; *Weltgeschichte als Machtgeschichte*, 152.

perhaps drew more from the material than the king was aware it would yield. In any case the poet represented it as a disinterested and patriotic act, in consequence of which the nation received peace and its legitimate king whom it had only to acclaim. This leaves little room for parliamentary election in any effective sense of the word and none at all for a deposition, and represents the whole transaction in a light that must have been unwelcome to many of the Lancastrian party. For it is reasonable to assume that the report of the commission represented their considered policy, and we have seen that the report was in effect disregarded. But the poet's business was to please the king and not his supporters, and we may fairly assume that he had rightly understood Henry's purpose and ambition. We can therefore construct a conjectural but not unreasonable explanation of what Henry did and the light in which he presented it, somewhat as follows. Between Richard's surrender and the last week in September the plans of the Lancastrian party had been framed. Public opinion was encouraged to assume that the matter would be referred to the parliament that had already been summoned. It was apparent that the country acquiesced in and even welcomed the accomplished revolution and the prospective change of dynasty. The Lancastrian leaders were free, therefore, to take any course that was within the range of their political experience and theory. Both of these pointed to the possibility of parliament deposing Richard and designating his successor, and this could have been accomplished even in view of the new doctrine that the cession of the crown invalidated the writs by which the parliament had been summoned and brought it to an end.

If now we attempt to arrange in order the events which produced the results we have to explain, we shall do well to begin by considering how much Henry had to gain by withholding his attack until the last possible moment. In the first place, by his birth, his wealth, and perhaps by his person and character he was in effect indispensable to the success of the revolution. This being so, if he was prepared with a policy that was destructive of the novel and radical plan which he had affected to accept and an alternative that was fundamentally conservative, though it afforded the radicals some opportunity to save their faces, his position would be almost impregnable. It was such a plan that was eventually adopted, but how was the way cleared for it ?

It is obvious that the weak point of the scheme proposed by the commission lay in the fact that it did not provide for the succession. They may have argued that the choice of the new king lay with the parliament that had deposed his predecessor, and this indeed would have resulted from their theory of parliamentary supremacy. A free choice among the possible candidates—and there were several even if you restricted the field to the blood royal—would have created a handsome parliamentary precedent, and Henry could probably be trusted to take care of himself. There are echoes in the chronicles that suggest that something of the sort was canvassed and perhaps even expected.[1] The practical objections to such a plan at such a time could not have escaped Henry, and he may well have pointed out to his friends the dangers involved. Mortimer was the recognized heir, but the election of a child of eight would require a regency throwing the direction of affairs into the hands of whichever of the lords was powerful enough to seize it, and the dissensions which would inevitably follow would open the way for Richard's return. Now we know that it is at least possible that in December 1387 considerations of the same sort, the rivalry of Gloucester and Derby, undid or prevented the deposition of Richard,[2] and, as we have seen, the Percies could not be counted on, either to desert Mortimer or to be themselves without designs upon the crown. It is at this point that I would place Henry's production of the chronicle in support of a claim which, as he might have argued, would cover the weak point in his friends' scheme without compromising its parliamentary character. This would be on 21 or 22 September and after the commission had made its recommendation in chief. It would overcome a practical difficulty, no doubt, for if Henry were the unquestioned heir the crown would pass to him by demise as soon as Richard was deposed. It was open, however, to two

---

[1] ' Et sic trono regio vacante, cum tractaretur inter dominos de rege futuro, populus totus acclamavit dominum Henricum ducem Lancastriae, ipsumque in regem elegerunt.' Monk of Evesham, 159 ; cf. Créton, 200–1, Shrewsbury Proclamation in Hardyng, *Chronicle*, 351.

[2] Clarke and Galbraith, *op. cit.*, 157–161.

fatal objections; it was impossible to accept it on historical grounds and it proved too much. The power of parliament to depose might seem to be vindicated, but the Lancastrians would have been left with a legitimate king on their hands. The step, however, served Henry's purpose, it emphasized an embarrassing difficulty, and it sensibly diminished the time before the meeting of parliament.

The rejection of his claim, say on 25 September, was the moment for Henry to unmask his batteries and develop his full attack by proposing to submit the brutal fact of conquest to parliament and base his claim to the crown upon conditions that nobody could deny. We may well suppose that Thirning's recorded objection gives us but a small measure of the scandal and dismay caused by Henry's suggestion. It was the atmosphere best suited for the form of compromise that was to constitute his next step. This I take to have been a proposal that in principle the precedent of 1327 should be followed. The part played by parliament in substituting Edward III for his father was in fact of first-rate importance, although it did not become a matter of record. Parliament acclaimed the heir as king and deposed his predecessor; it is open to you to do the same, Henry might have said, and, what is more, to cause the transaction to be entered on the parliament roll. You have only to obtain what is easily had, Richard's abdication,[1] and to declare what corresponds to fact though perhaps not to history, that I am his successor. This course will have given you the additional security of a voluntary abdication and will meet my views as well.[2] I will withdraw my unqualified claim to the crown by conquest, by limiting it to the vindication of my legal right and expressly securing all interests in property.

It we place ourselves in the position of such of the leaders of the rebellion as were still anxious to proceed with the agreed plan of deposition and election by parliament, it is not easy to see on what ground the proposal could be resisted. From a practical point of view, certainly, it had a great deal to commend it. It was conservative in so far as it complied with the ' forms

[1] The passage from the proclamation of 1403 quoted above p. 296, implies that the suggestion of abdication came from Henry.

[2] Because it would enable Henry to state both the claims which he had affected to abandon and save parliamentary forms.

of the constitution ' to the extent that such forms were available, and the abdication was calculated to supply additional security in case the revolution were put on its defence. Finally, it had the immense and immediate advantage of restoring harmony among the leaders. If an objection were sought, therefore, it must be in other quarters. It would have to be shown that in spite of its practical advantages the scheme was open to some fatal, theoretical objection. It is at this point therefore, between 25 and 29 September, that I would place the first formulation of the doctrine that the cession of the Crown invalidated the parliamentary writs that had been issued by its authority.

As far as I am aware this is the first appearance of a constitutional doctrine that was destined to hold its place, with some modification in 1688, until 1867.[1] As we have seen, it was unknown or unrecognized in 1327 and the last parliament of Edward II became the first of Edward III without challenge or question, to say nothing of the issue of new writs. As no parliament was in session or had been summoned when Edward III's death took place, the question cannot have arisen in practical form before September 1399. The surprising thing, however, is not the appearance of the doctrine at this time but the fact that it had not been formulated earlier, for it is founded on history and reason. If the king has his court in his council in his parliament, it is not likely that anyone considering the matter from a theoretical point of view would allow that these concentric institutions could subsist without the presence of the king either personally or by representation. And this is so because no one of them would, in such a case, have any reason for existence, their purpose being either to advise the king or to help him administer the *ordinaria* which he cannot delegate,[2] and from which he drew the remedies for new wrongs as they arose and the resolution of judicial doubts. The essence of parliament is the dispensation of justice by the king or some one who represents him;[3] a parliament without a king, therefore, could not exist.[4]

---

[1] Anson, *Law and Custom of the Constitution* i, 73 ff. ; cf. Blackstone, *Commentaries* i, 188, 249.

[2] Bracton, fo. 55b ; ed. Woodbine, ii, 167. Cf. above, p. 207 ff.

[3] Richardson and Sayles, ' Early Records of the English Parliaments ', *B.I.H.R.* v, 133.

[4] Two passages in the *Modus Tenendi Parliamentum* are worth considering in this connexion. The pamphlet has in itself no great evidential

Now, as we have seen, the difficulty was not felt in 1327, and this no doubt was because the crown passed by demise, i.e. there was a change of persons but no interruption of function, and officially, at least, parliament was not concerned in the change. In 1399 the situation was very different, unless men were prepared to accept March. Henry must be allowed to state and vindicate his claim to be the next heir, and there was a strong party that had determined that the whole transaction should be accomplished by parliament. It was natural, therefore, that the new doctrine should be brought forward either as an objection to the proposed plan or as showing the need of precautions. Stubbs states, though he cites no authority, that the doctrine was advanced by Arundel as an objection, and in a form in which it does not appear in the schedule, i.e. that parliament would be dissolved as soon as it met because of the abdication on the previous day. For two reasons this appears probable. In the first place, on our interpretation of the evidence an objection of a ' constitutional ' order was to be expected from the group that had advocated parliamentary action. In the second place, on the analogy of the precedent of 1327 the cession would naturally be held to have occurred at the moment when the abdication was accepted by those who had gone to the king to ask for it. This would be the case whether you follow the account given by the chronicles, which requires a deputation authorized by and reporting to parliament, or the statement of the official documents that the king had acted by the advice and consent of the magnates. For these reasons it appears probable that Arundel formulated and

value, but it was probably known to and valued by the Lancastrian party at this time, and if so they must have been aware that the presence of the king or his accredited representative was considered indispensable to parliament. Miss Clarke argues that the procedure in Edward II's deposition was influenced by cap. xvii of the *Modus*, cf. *Medieval Representation and Consent*, 189 ff. ' Rex est caput, principium, et finis parliamenti, et ita non habet parem in suo gradu, et ita ex rege solo est primus gradus '. ' Rex tenetur omni modo personaliter interesse parliamento [if, however, this is impossible] committere debet archiepiscopo loci, senescallo, et capitali justiciario suo, quod ipsi conjunctim et divisim inchoent et continuent parliamentum nomine suo ' *ibid.*, 378, 384. The fact that the king was neither present nor represented during the proceedings on 30 September was emphasized by a number of the chroniclers, although not by those who refuse the name of parliament to the convention, see above, pp. 288, 292, 297, 299, 302.

advanced the new doctrine as an objection to the course proposed by Henry on the ground that it would render all parliamentary action impossible. This brings us to our final problem: how was the objection met and Arundel and his friends induced to state the doctrine in the form (that can scarcely be reconciled either with reason or precedent) in which it appears in the schedule ?

In the absence of direct evidence we must take into account three considerations. In the first place, there is the extreme novelty of the doctrine itself formulated, as we have some reason to believe, almost as a debating point. It could scarcely have been reflected upon or its implications worked out, and this together with the real ambiguity of the precedent of 1327 (and this is the second consideration) would afford to Henry—whose taste for argument and even casuistry is attested[1]—a solid advantage. It is not difficult to construct a series of questions of a very embarrassing character. For example, if Arundel had urged (as appears to have been the case) that parliament would as a result of the abdication be dissolved as soon as it met, he could clearly be reduced to the position that the abdication took effect by the king's act alone and this was equally clearly contrary to the precedent. On the other hand, some body of persons having some sort of sanction (if only that of the leaders of the revolution) must visit the king and demand his resignation. Such a body, moreover, would necessarily comprise lay and spiritual magnates, for Richard was still king and you could scarcely send to him persons of no importance nor expect him to be influenced by them if you did. We know that in fact he was dissatisfied because Henry and Arundel were not among those who visited him on the morning of the 29th, and delayed his final answer until they came in the afternoon. In this case, if a deputation of magnates accepted the king's resignation before the day appointed for the meeting of parliament, would not that complete the cession on the analogy of the official version of the precedent of 1327 ? It is not difficult to see how such arrangements could be multiplied nor to estimate their embarrassing effect upon those who were using an unaccustomed weapon, a doctrine the full bearing and significance of

[1] See the striking passage from Capgrave cited in Stubbs, *C.H.* iii, 8.

which they had not yet completely understood or measured.
To this embarrassment must be added (our third consideration)
the urgency of the political situation. Time was very brief,
some decision must be taken, and Henry, who had shown himself so formidable and unruly, must be placated. What terms
could be got ? How much of the original plan of parliamentary
action could be saved ?

Henry had thus manoeuvred himself into a position which
enabled him to dictate his own terms with the appearance of
making substantial concessions. The point was to reconcile the
new doctrine (by guarding against its possible but not yet
wholly calculable consequences) with his earlier advice to
conform to the precedent, and in doing this it must be borne in
mind that, unlike the barons of 1327, the Lancastrians had no
parliament and no heir with an undisputed title. Further, in
the matter of the parliament it was at least doubtful when the
abdication would take effect and parliament be dissolved. On
the other hand, the precedent was ambiguous, and the doctrine
being new might be treated rather arbitrarily if due precautions
were taken against another interpretation prevailing in the end.
The precautions would consist in omitting to organize the
convention or to give it the name of parliament, while suggesting by other means that it was actually that. This suggestion
could be strengthened at the slight cost of a little further
ambiguity by definitely stating that the writs were not invalidated until the deposition had taken place. Here is something that can be represented as a concession. You have all the
elements of parliament judging and deposing the king and
thereby committing themselves, when under the new writs
they became parliament, to the revolution which they have
helped to accomplish politically if not quite constitutionally.
Further, you have the transaction incorporated in the official
record of parliament, where it may well lead people to believe
(as in fact it did) that it was itself the act of a parliament. On
the other hand, you can, if need be, fall back on a voluntary
abdication represented as cheerfully accomplished and duly
accepted by a body representative of the elements of parliament
and selected for that purpose ' in the accustomed place of the
council ', subsequently reporting to the estates and people

gathered in Westminster Hall ' propter factum parliamenti '. Finally, the arrangement must necessarily be agreeable to Henry, since it allowed him to state his claim to succeed by conquest of his inheritance, and provided for an effective if not exactly a parliamentary acceptance of that claim. If this last concession was accepted by Arundel as sufficient, we can then understand why Henry took care to make it vain, not by ' packing ' the parliament but by introducing the ' vulgus populus ', whose share in the transaction appears on the official record, but is best explained by the evidence of Créton, the Shrewsbury proclamation, the Percy tradition, and the Monk of Evesham. If he did so, he would be following the precedent of 1327 in form if not in substance. That, however, could not be foreseen, or at least could not have been guarded against, and in the anxious days before the meeting of parliament the proposed compromise offered many advantages. It conformed to tradition and precedent, it guaranteed the revolution, and saved the face of the parliamentarians by avoiding the question of when the cession occurred, or rather by giving an obscure and doubtful answer to it.

Perhaps we shall never know what really happened, but that is no reason for resting content with an account against which so much can be said as the one which is currently accepted. It will need, if the considerations advanced in the present study are admissible, a good deal of revision. To that end, I suggest that our evidence is best interpreted by supposing that Henry could have had a complete and technically correct parliamentary title, that his supporters intended that the revolution should be accomplished in that way, and that Henry by a *coup de main* at the last moment was able to obtain the crown on the grounds of conquest, inheritance, and some loose form of acceptance.[1]

---

[1] Did Stubbs have some possibility of this sort in mind when on reconsidering the evidence for his third volume he wrote : ' The deposition of Richard II and the accession of Henry IV were not the pure and legitimate result of a series of constitutional workings ' ? *Const. Hist.* iii, 6. A tone of doubt runs through the very significant pages that follow, which tends to modify substantially if cautiously the views expressed in the second volume.

It has been argued that the acts of 1404 and 1406 regulating the succession of Henry's sons did in fact create a parliamentary title. The argument is not valid. Parliament had admitted and recognised Henry's title in October 1399 ; it could not make itself the source of that title merely by determining how it should descend. See above p. 327, n. 2.

VIII

RICHARD II's 'LAST PARLIAMENT'[1]

The reconstruction upon which I have ventured in order to interpret the 'Record and Process' of the deposition of Richard II and its relation to the actual events of September 30th exposes me, I am well aware, to grave risks. I may be permitted therefore to say a word in defence of the hazardous course I have adopted. In the first place the character and quantity of the evidence is such as should protect me from the charge of resorting to mere guess-work. The attempt to solve the problems presented by the record and process by means of a suggestion drawn from a contemporary chronicler may give a wrong result, but it cannot fairly be called wanton. Again, every serious effort to make a body of evidence at once so rich and so recalcitrant yield a coherent and reasonable tale must render some service to future investigators. They will at any rate have something definite to criticize and if they show that some or even all of my conjectures are inadmissible certain paths will be clearly marked 'No Thoroughfare'. The work of Mr. Galbraith and the late Miss Clarke put Stubbs's account of the matter out of court and substantially increased the amount of evidence available. The challenge thus tacitly made I accepted in my earlier article and I could scarcely, therefore, refuse to go further and be more explicit when a more direct challenge from another quarter required it.

IN the preceding discussion of the parliamentary title of Henry IV it was argued that the assembly which on 30 September 1399 witnessed the change of dynasty was not, either in contemporary view or in fact, a true parliament. Mr. H. G. Richardson has questioned this view in the light of an official document that was culpably unknown to me when I wrote.[2] The text itself demands careful consideration, and I have too great a respect for Mr. Richardson's judgement and learning to differ from him lightly or willingly; I have therefore

---

[1] Reprinted from *The English Historical Review* liii (1938), 53–78.

[2] 'Richard II's Last Parliament', *E.H.R.* lii, 39–47. Mr. Richardson has been so friendly as to read the first draft of this article and to make a number of observations by which I have profited. He has further allowed me to cite and discuss the points he raised. I take this opportunity to acknowledge gratefully his courtesy and generosity.

studied attentively his new evidence and the arguments which
he uses. As they have not convinced me, I am bound to state
my reasons for remaining, though with diffidence and regret,
in disagreement with him.

The text to which Mr. Richardson draws attention consists
of the opening paragraphs of the coronation roll, which is an
official record of the proceedings of the court of claims set up
by Henry IV as his last act before rising from his throne at the
end of the session on 30 September, and of the services actually
performed at that coronation. Thus it appears to have the
credentials of a contemporary official document of an administrative kind and unlikely on that account to have been influenced
by any political considerations. This document records in
unequivocal terms that Richard's ' cession and resignation '
were announced and accepted and that he was deposed and
Henry succeeded him ' in parliamento . . . apud Westmonasterium convocato, ultimo die mensis Septembris '.[1] With this
' plain statement of what were presumably very plain facts '
Mr. Richardson contrasts unfavourably the more detailed
account of the same proceedings given in the document (also
official) known as the ' record and process ' of Richard's
deposition. This document, as stated above,[2] is inserted in the
roll of Henry IV's first parliament immediately after the report
of Arundel's opening speech and the formalities which occupied
the sitting on 6 October and terminated with an adjournment
until the day after the coronation. It takes its place there, in
Mr. Richardson's view, parenthetically, as it were, in consequence of Arundel's brief reference in his speech to the events
of 30 September.[3] He thinks that it was doubtless compiled and
copied in the chancery, and its character and attested diffusion
(it is reproduced in a number of important chronicles) show
that it was a deliberate piece of propaganda, a ' tendentious and
dishonest fabrication ', an *ex parte* revolutionary document; and
with this I quite agree. A copy of this document was in
chancery along with other available material when the parliament roll was made up by the enrolling clerk under the instruc-

---

[1] *Foedera* (1st edn.) viii, 90–1. Mr. Richardson prints the relevant
passage corrected from the original.
[2] Above, p. 274.
[3] *Rot. Parl.* iii, 416–24 ; Arundel's speech is on p. 415, nos. 1 and 2.

tion of the clerk of the parliament, and was included for the reasons given above. This, if I understand Mr. Richardson, is how it found a place in the parliament roll.

Now it is noticeable that whoever drafted this document was using words with the utmost caution so that ' its language is unusual ', and in no respect more so than the care with which the name ' parliament ' is withheld from the assembly in which the momentous events of 30 September took place. Mr. Richardson, if I have understood him, thinks that this is a formal rather than a material matter, and admits no difference in substance between the words of the coronation roll and those of Thirning's speech to Richard on 1 October, reported in the ' record and process '.[1] This speech like the rest of the document avoids a ' direct statement that certain proceedings took place in parliament—a parliament at some moment without a king '—because the speaker ' had no other word for the assembly '. Nor, indeed, Mr. Richardson adds, had Arundel, who in his speech on 6 October refers to 30 September as ' the day on which King Richard had summoned his parliament to be held '.[2] Still all through the ' record and process ' two words are used to refer to the body of persons that is hearing, acting or speaking : they are *populus* and *status*.[3] Mr. Richardson points out that these words may bear variable meanings in fourteenth-century usage and argues that the text, to be intelligible, requires them to be taken in different senses. With this combination of precision and ambiguity in a document primarily intended for circulation through the country, Mr. Richardson contrasts the clear language of the coronation

[1] The roll, however, states unconditionally that certain things took place in parliament, but Thirning says only that a parliament was summoned to meet on the 30th, not that it was held.

[2] Richardson, *op. cit.*, 40. He adds that, if Arundel ' referred to the assembly in any other terms they are lost to us '. But this is unlikely, for Arundel gives his reason for not referring to the assembly as parliament when he says, ' quele sommons ne feust du null force n'effect, a cause de l'acceptation de la renunciation fait par le dit Roy Richard, et de la deposition de mesme le Roy Richard qe feust fait le Maresdy suis dit '. It will be noted that, if Arundel has no single name for the assembly, he nevertheless describes its composition when he says that he had explained this point on the same Tuesday in the presence of King Henry, the lords spiritual and temporal, and the commons.

[3] The same words are used for the same purpose in Thirning's English speech on 1 October ; *Rot. Parl.* iii, 424, no. 59.

roll which had no purpose but record, and states unequivocally
that the transaction of 30 September took place in parliament.

Mr. Richardson then examines the assembly from another
angle, as who should say, ' if this was not a parliament what was
it ' ? He rejects the term used by the Lords' Committee ' convention of the states ' as a ' legalistic inversion of history ', and
refers to the events of January 1327 partly as a parallel (though
he will not admit that they were a precedent) and partly as a
warning to those who ' look for clear constitutional doctrines in
troubled times '. He holds that no coherent political or legal
theory can be devised to fit the facts of 1327 and that those of
1399 are in the same case, and he concludes that ' no consistent
doctrine will cover easily both the normal and the abnormal,
and no explanation we can offer will avoid the inherent difficulty
of reconciling violence and law '.[1]

Now if I have understood Mr. Richardson, he raises here a
new issue embracing indeed his earlier one but exceeding it both
in range and content. He sets out to discuss the question
whether the meeting on 30 September may properly be described as a parliament, and argues that the evidence of the
coronation roll contemporary, official and unbiassed, is conclusive in the affirmative sense. He then points out that the
whole transaction, like that of 1327, was an act of violence from
which, since *inter arma silent leges*, no valid constitutional
inferences can be drawn. This would be, I suppose, because
in such an act or series of acts form and matter are not *in pari
materia*. It would seem to follow then that the first question
has no reality, for so far as any constitutional significance goes
it would make no difference whether you called it a parliament
or not. These two issues I will discuss in order.

We return to the coronation roll, and observe that, while in
general a contemporary official document will have the highest
evidential value because it is likely to be disinterested and well
informed, this rule is subject to certain limitations. We must
consider, where we have the means, the draftsman's sources of
information, and we must allow for the possibility of his blundering through carelessness, inaccuracy, or stupidity, because
there is evidence that blundering of that kind occurred. These

[1] *Op. cit.,* 46, 47.

considerations are of the more importance in assessing the
value of the evidence of the coronation roll, because it is
directly traversed by another document drawn up in chancery
at much the same time as the coronation roll itself and possess-
ing therefore, in general, all the same credentials. This is the
form used for the writs of expenses for which the knights and
burgesses applied at the end of their service in Henry's first
parliament. In these writs the sheriffs were directed to allow
payment for attendance at the parliaments summoned by King
Richard and King Henry respectively, adding, with regard to
the first, ' licet parliamentum praedictum certis de causis
minime tentum fuerit '.[1] Mr. Richardson suggests that this
really means that the parliament was dissolved before any
normal business could be transacted. Now it should be
observed that the plain meaning of the words corresponds with
the language of the ' record and process ', which refused the
name of parliament to the session in which the king was
deposed. It is agreed that this document is mendacious, but it
is not denied that it represents the view of those in authority.
Now when the commons applied for their writs one of two
things must have happened. Either they were issued as a
matter of routine or the question obviously involved was
referred to those in authority.[2] In the first case we should
expect to find that the words of the writ agreed with those of
the coronation roll, and this is so because the clerk who prepared
the roll was concerned with politics only to the extent that the
business which he had to record had been consequential on
the political events of 30 September. He, like many other
people, expected that a parliament would be held, and therefore
notes clearly and precisely the events of the day ' in parliament '
including the accession of Henry of Lancaster. Mr. Richardson
finds it difficult to set this authority aside. ' These acts,' he
writes, ' according to an official document as nearly contemporary as we could hope for, took place in parliament ' (p. 45).
In the second case we should expect to find agreement with the
form of the ' record and process ', for the authorities who in

---

[1] The writ is cited above p. 283, but I did not realize its full evidential
value at that time ; it is printed *in extenso* in Prynne, *Brief Register* iv, 450.

[2] Alternatively they might have foreseen the difficulty and given
directions in advance, which would be materially the same thing.

that document had scrupulously withheld the name of parliament from the meeting of 30 September would scarcely have
stultified themselves by allowing it to be given officially in the
writ, least of all if they had been asked for an instruction on the
matter. The point may be put in another way. The question
did not concern the clerk who made up the coronation roll, but
on the answer to it depended the form which the writ was to
take. Payment was asked for services rendered; how were
those services to be described? The chief part of them was
parliamentary, but what of the attendance on the 30th? Should
there be two writs or one? In either case how should the
sitting of 30 September be described? Surely these were not
matters of routine, and since the writ like the ' record and
process ' withheld the name of parliament, it is a reasonable
inference that instructions were sought and given. The writ in
the ordinary course would possess the same credentials as the
coronation roll which it flatly contradicts. But if it were framed
after consultation with those who were responsible for the form
of the ' record and process ', it is, I submit, better evidence than
the roll of the official view of the nature of the meeting on the
30th. This reasoning Mr. Richardson does not think conclusive.
He finds it

very difficult to follow the suggestion that a presumably senior clerk
in chancery (the man responsible for the coronation roll) did not
know of the ' record and process ' or of its implications, whereas
those clerks who prepared the writs of expense and *a fortiori*, those
who prepared the parliament roll did. This seems to imply a lack
of cohesion and communication between senior chancery clerks
which is hard to reconcile with our general knowledge.

All this must be a matter of inference from that general knowledge of which Mr. Richardson has made himself a master; and
he has given a lead in another quarter to which I will refer in a
moment. Meanwhile, surely, what matters is not whether the
clerk knew the ' record and process ', but whether he had any
imperative reason for taking account of its rather ambiguous
form? Evidently the clerk who prepared the parliament roll
knew the document because he had to copy it, but its form and
substance had no effect on the rest of his task, which was to
produce, as he did, ' a sober and objective record '. It was

otherwise with the clerk who framed the writs, because he must
know whether the attendance on the 30th was to be paid for
and, if so, how the meeting was to be described. What I am
suggesting is that the professional civil servant, in the fourteenth century at any rate, could not necessarily be trusted to
use even the discretion of common sense in his work of drafting
or enrolment, and Mr. Richardson has himself established this
point. He reproved the late Professor Tout for inferring from
slips or contradictions in certain official documents that there
was confusion or disagreement among those who directed the
chancery. The evidence he cites suggests that the confusion
should be attributed to the mentality of men who, having been
trained to copy what was set before them or to follow precedent,
would sometimes distribute their material among the familiar
pigeon-holes without asking whether it made sense or not.[1]
Now, if we apply these general considerations to the particular
case, we shall recall first the actual situation, the crisis through
which the managers had passed, the obvious care which they
had bestowed on the drafting of the ' record and process ', and
the pressure they were under in connexion first with the coronation and then with the management of the political situation
and the business of the session. It would not be surprising if,
apart from the ' record and process ', they left the business of
the chancery to proceed on routine lines. If that were so, why
should the clerk who drew up the coronation roll concern
himself with the ' record and process ' even if he had read it ?
But if we suppose with Mr. Richardson that he had read it or
knew its implications, there would still remain a serious
objection to the conclusion that the acts which he records took
place in parliament. No contemporary with any knowledge of
the course of the revolution could have claimed that *all* the
events of the meeting of 30 September took place in parliament.
The new but unquestioned constitutional doctrine of the
invalidation of the writs by the cession made that impossible;
though it is hard to determine the exact moment at which the

[1] See *B.I.H.R.* viii, 71, 72 ; Tout, *Chapters* iii, 268, n. 4, 284, n. 3, 291,
n. 1 ; Pollard, *Evolution of Parliament* (2nd edn.), 388–91. In *B.I.H.R.*
xvi, 19, Pollard argues that the clerk who drew up the roll of Richard's
first parliament (1377) and gave a demonstrably wrong date for the last
day of the session, had not seen the writs *de expensis*.

cession was held to have taken place. The *terminus ante quem* is the scene in the Tower on the afternoon of the 29th, and the covered throne and absence of a royal commissioner to open the meeting next day suggest that that was the moment. The *terminus post quem* is the deposition, and there are words in the record to suggest that this was the moment. In any case after the deposition there was no king and the parliament, to use Adam of Usk's word, was extinct.[1] Therefore the coronation roll is certainly wrong in saying that Henry succeeded in parliament, and may not be right in saying that any of these events took place in parliament. There is probably a simple explanation for the words of the roll. The draftsman knew that a parliament had been summoned, that a meeting of those summoned had taken place on the appointed day, and that the events which then occurred made his roll necessary, and it was not his business to know more or inquire further. This is what we might expect having regard to the mentality of certain civil servants; the job could be done by routine, and why, unless one got orders to the contrary, should one concern oneself with political or constitutional questions ? On the other hand, as we have seen, the constitutional question must have intruded itself on the attention of the clerk who drafted the writ in the guise of a perfectly practical matter.

These are considerations which make it extremely difficult to treat the evidence of the coronation roll as conclusive, or to place it on the same footing as that of the writ of expenses. As far as this new evidence of Mr. Richardson's is concerned, then, we are, I venture to think, pretty much where we were before. We must return accordingly to the ' record and process ' and see whether it will yield a self-consistent account of how the managers of the revolution wished to represent the events of 29 and 30 September. If this is to be done, we must

---

[1] *Chronicon* (ed. Thompson) 33. Mr. Richardson writes of ' a parliament at some moment without a king '. Is such a thing conceivable before an omnicompetent parliament had made it possible by statute ? Would the notion have been admissible in October 1399 ?

It may be noted further that if Adam wrote or caused to be written the marginal note on p. 9, which describes the parliament of 1397 as *ultimum parliamentum regis Ricardi*, he is contradicting himself on p. 33. Unfortunately it does not seem possible to establish his responsibility for the marginalia ; cf. Thompson, *ibid.*, viii.

meet the objection raised by Mr. Richardson to which we have already alluded. The argument turns on the sense in which the words *populus* and *status* are used in the ' record and process ', and what is involved is Mr. Richardson's contention that as to the name and nature of the assembly on 30 September the evidence of our text is quite inconclusive. He argues that we should prefer the ' clear and precise language of the coronation roll ' to the ambiguities of the ' record and process ' on the ground that it is difficult if not impossible to determine exactly what the writer of that document intended his readers to understand. This arises from his use of the words *populus* and *status* in such a way that certain passages can only be interpreted by giving the words now one and now another of the senses in which they are used in the course of the fourteenth century. The difficulty is undeniable, but I feel that, before rejecting the testimony of a text that has such credentials to speak for the intention of the managers of the revolution, an attempt should be made to interpret it as a whole by such evidence as it furnishes itself or as can be derived from other texts closely related to it in time and provenance. A closer examination of Mr. Richardson's argument will make this clear. He begins by observing that the word *populus* in fourteenth-century usage may mean bystanders who were casually present at the meeting of parliament, or the *communitas*, the general body of suitors summoned to parliament, or the people of England at large, or even the magnates alone, or a group of unrepresentative petitioners. It seems to me that a more promising way of approaching the text would be to assume that its author knew what he intended to say and attached a definite meaning to the two words in question, and try to interpret it in a way that is self-consistent, reasonable, and conformable to what we know from other sources of the facts of the case. If these facts suggest that the words are being used in one of the senses which Mr. Richardson's evidence has shown to be possible, and we find no case in which that sense must be definitely ruled out because it would make the passage unintelligible, our assumption would seem to be warranted. It will be observed that the text uses the words *status* and *populus* to refer to two groups of people who were present and active at Westminster on 30 September, and that though these groups are clearly distinguished they are never dissociated. The word *populus*, therefore, cannot here mean either ' the people of England at large ' nor ' a group of unrepresentative petitioners ', because there is no question of petition in the course of the proceedings. It if can be shown that the word *status* is used to denote the lords spiritual and temporal and the elected commons (and this will shortly fall to be discussed), it will be, to say the least, improbable that *populus* can have the sense of the suitors summoned to parliament or the magnates alone. There remains of Mr. Richardson's alternatives only the sense of casual bystanders, and this he rules out on the antecedent improbability that they should have had any voice in choosing the proctors who visited the king on 1 October. Mr. Richardson writes :

the mob of followers was the ordinary accompaniment of fourteenth century parliaments, and in time of excitement these followers were apt to get out of hand. It seems worth emphasizing that 1399 was not singular in this respect. I still find it hard to take the word *populus* as meaning this mob in all the passages I quote on pp. 42 and 43.[1]

As to the mob as an ' ordinary accompaniment ' of parliament, I venture to think that the generalization is rather beside the point. The really relevant matter is not the presence of the mob but the extent, if any, to which it influenced or took part in the proceedings of those who had been formally summoned. Certainly it did so in 1327; there is some evidence that this was the case in 1399, and it would be agreed that both years were exceptional. No doubt there were other exceptional years as well, and 1399 was therefore not singular in being an exception. It must be remembered that the ' record and process ' has represented the action of a disorderly mob as the traditional share of the people in the formalities of the accession. As to Mr. Richardson's second point that the sense ' mob ' will not suit in the passages he quotes, we must take a distinction between the quotations from the ' record and process ' with which alone my argument is concerned and those from other texts where the sense is obviously inadmissible. Now, if the 'record and process ' were a credible account of what actually took place,

[1] Cf. *E.H.R.* lii, 42–3.

Mr. Richardson's objection would be hard to meet. But it is common ground between us that it is a tendentious and falsified document. If it can be shown that a turbulent mob influenced the proceedings, we need not be surprised to find their action presented in the ' record and process ' as an orderly share in extremely extraordinary proceedings. There is some very nearly contemporary evidence pointing in that direction. The Percy traditions preserved by Hardyng and Archbishop Scrope's manifesto are, of course, *ex parte* statements, but they contain accounts of what took place at Westminster on 30 September which cannot be neglected since the discovery of the *Dieulacres Chronicle*, a contemporary and trustworthy source, which in some respects confirms them. The same discovery has also tended to rehabilitate the authority of Créton. Now these sources agree in reporting that the proceedings on 30 September were contentious and that opposition had to be overcome. Créton and the proclamation issued by the Percies before the battle of Shrewsbury are precise in speaking of the presence of what might fairly be called a turbulent mob of Henry's supporters who enabled him to carry his point. The *Dieulacres Chronicle* reports that Henry Percy was so much displeased by what had taken place that he withdrew before the banquet on the day of the coronation.[1] This evidence need not now be

---

[1] The presence of the mob and its official recognition in the ' record and process ' present an important problem, but it cannot be discussed here. The evidence is cited and the whole matter discussed above, pp. 293–303. Three passages are worth reproducing here. The Lancastrian monk of Evesham says that, while the magnates were discussing the choice of the future king, ' populus totus acclamavit Henricum . . . ipsumque in regem elegerunt ' (ed. Hearne, 159). Créton, who may have been working from the same source as the monk, shows the facts in a different light. He says that there were present, beside the lords and prelates, ' knights squires varlets and archers, with many sorts of folk who were neither noble nor gentle . . . in such great heaps . . . that the officers could scarcely enter the hall ' (*Archaeologica* xx, 192). Then in the proclamation which the Percies sent to Henry before Shrewsbury they accused him of having obtained the crown ' publica vociferacione vulgaris populi apud Westmonasterium per te et tuos complices collecti ' (Hardyng's *Chronicle*, 352). To this may now be added a fact to which my attention has been drawn by Dr. Chrimes. In the summer of 1403 a certain Philip fitz Eustace, who was involved in the rising of the Percies, was reported to have spoken in derision of Henry ' as not elected by the magnates and the community of England, but by the London rabble '. See *Misc. K. R. Exchequer* E. 163/6/28 (' dixit quod predictus rex nunquam electus fuit neque factus per magnates et communitatem Anglie sed omnino per villanos civitatis Londonie ') ; cf. Wylie, *Henry IV*, i, 420–1.

pressed farther than to suggest that *populus* should here be
taken in the sense of a group of persons not summoned to
parliament but having a lively interest in the proceeding.

Now the most striking characteristic of the ' record and
process ' is to exhibit the events which it describes in the light
of an orderly proceeding following on the king's free acknow-
ledgement of his own incompetence and his desire that his
cousin should succeed him. It was, no doubt, part of this
plan to give to every step taken the appearance of what we may
for convenience' sake call constitutionality. We know that in
the case of Richard's betrayal and capture in Wales and his
behaviour in the Tower on 29 September the authors of our
text were not hampered by any regard for truth, and it is not
likely that they would have allowed themselves to be so hampered in any other part of the document. If, as we have seen
some reason to believe, they had to fit the action of an unruly
mob into their picture of the proceedings they must have cast
about for some constitutional form to which they could
assimilate it. It would be within the knowledge of many of
them that in the coronation office used in 1377 (to go no
farther back) the ' people ' had a formal part to play, and I
do not think it fantastic to suggest that the acclamation of the
people as described in the *Liber Regalis*[1] gave the suggestion
with which the authors of the ' record and process ' worked.
What was wanted was some authentic and recognized form
made use of in the normal passage of the crown which could be
extended to cover the irregular and disorderly acts they were
trying to disguise. Was there any other than, or at any rate any
other so well suited to the purpose as, the *collaudatio* of the
coronation office ? If the *populus* in the sense of bystanders
were present at Westminster on 30 September and at least
assented to the election of Henry and acclaimed him, why
should it be impossible to believe (as Mr. Richardson finds it)

[1] The text is given in Wickham Legge, *English Coronation Records*, 85 ;
cf. P. E. Schramm, *History of the English Coronation*, Oxford, 1937, Pt. II,
cap. vi, and particularly pp. 170–3 (I cite this with reserves as to Dr.
Schramm's inferences) ; Richardson and Sayles, ' Early Coronation
Records ', *B.I.H.R.* xiii, 129 ff., particularly p. 139.—This point, of popular
acclamation of the new king, is further developed by B. Wilkinson, ' The
Deposition of Richard II and the Accession of Henry IV ', *E.H.R.* liv,
215–239.

that ' they had anything to do with the choosing of the proctors'?
I should agree with Mr. Richardson's scepticism if we were
dealing with normal conditions or an ordinary historical
record, but the case fulfils neither of these conditions. The
question to be put and answered, therefore, is did the authors
of the ' record and process ' for reasons of their own represent
the *populus* in the sense of bystanders as having been associated
with the *status* in the proceedings, and I submit that there is
ground for answering the question in the affirmative.

If we turn now to the word *status* as used in the ' record and
process ', we find that Mr. Richardson supports his contention
by pointing out first that it is a ' word of vague meaning and
rarely used with precision ', and second by arguing that in one
passage in the document ' it clearly seems to be used ' in
opposition to ' commons ', in which case it could not consistently be taken to mean those who were summoned by writ
to attend. We may consider the specific objection first. It is
contained in the passage in the ' record and process ' ' where
there is told the story of the impeachment of Archbishop
Arundel by the Speaker of the commons [1397] " coram rege et
omnibus statibus regni " ' (p. 44), and Mr. Richardson seems
to imply that from the nature of the process of impeachment
the commons could not be included in the word ' statibus '.
I cannot feel as confident as Mr. Richardson that the word
status is here intended to exclude the commons. The context
does not say that the archbishop was impeached by the
commons but by the Speaker (unus de militibus comitatuum
. . . vocem habens eorum in parliamento[1]), and although the
official record[2] seems to distinguish between requests made by
the commons and by the Speaker on their behalf, and in this
particular case Adam of Usk, who was present, states that
Bushey alone was speaking,[3] it is pretty clear that the commons
were present throughout the proceedings, as we are told of the
special place that was assigned to them in the temporary
building that was constructed for the meeting of parliament.[4]
But even if they had been themselves absent (and we know

---

[1] *Rot. Parl.* iii, 421, no. 50.
[2] *Ibid.*, 348, no. 9, 349, no. 11, 351, nos. 14, 15.   [3] Usk, *op. cit.*, 12.
[4] *Annales Ricardi Secundi*, 209.

A a

that they did withdraw for consultation),[1] the Speaker represented them as an estate just as on this occasion Thomas Percy, as proctor of the spiritual lords, who were forbidden by the canon law to participate in a judgement involving bloodshed, represented their estate.[2] The act therefore took place in the presence of the commons unless the word *coram* is used here to distinguish between the accuser and the tribunal. This view might seem to derive support from a text just cited. The *Annales* state that the king provided in the temporary building *pro cunctis regni statibus locus largus*, adding that the appellants were accommodated on one side and the accused on the other and a place provided *seorsum vero pro militibus parliamenti*. Before taking this as conclusive evidence that the commons were not reckoned an estate of parliament we must consider the more authoritative testimony of the rolls. The bishop of Exeter in his opening speech (17 September 1397) stated that the king had caused the assembly of the estates of parliament in order to be informed on a number of points which the bishop proceeds to enumerate. On these matters, he added, the king wishes to be counselled by all the estates of parliament.[3] It is obvious that the quarter from which most of the information and at least some of the advice came was the commons. It seems difficult, therefore, to deny that in the text cited by Mr. Richardson, which refers, of course, to the proceedings of this parliament of 1397, the commons were regarded as an estate of parliament. Mr. Richardson comments on these observations as follows :

The difficulty of seeking some other meaning for ' coram rege et omnibus statibus regni ' than that which I have suggested seems to me to be that any alternative implies that the commons were judges. This would raise a very serious issue. The presence of some of the commons at such trials is well attested : but this does not seem to me to be to the point. I did not intend to imply that the ' commons ' *could* not be among the ' estates ', but that in certain contexts they may not be included.

Since Mr. Richardson did not intend his citation necessarily to rule out the inclusion of the commons in the word *status* in

[1] Usk, *op. cit.*, 10.   [2] *Rot. Parl.* iii, 348, no. 9.
[3] *Ibid.*, iii, 347.

this context, and since there is other evidence for such inclusion, the matter might be left there, but for the other point which he raises, the suggestion, namely, that the commons were judges. This has an important bearing on the main point of this discussion, for I think it can be shown that the commons were in fact judges on 30 September, and that they afterwards took a step which at any rate implies that the assembly which deposed Richard was not a parliament. As to the first of these points there are words in the ' record and process ' which appear to be decisive. They occur in connexion with the deposition which was accomplished by a commission authorized to act ' vice, nomine et auctoritate omnium statuum . . . prout in consimilibus casibus de antiqua consuetudine . . . regni fuerat observatum '. It consisted of a bishop, an abbot, a duke, a lord, two commoners (one of them a knight of the shire), and a judge, and they described themselves in their report as ' per pares et proceres regni Anglie spirituales et temporales, et ejusdem regni communitates omnes status ejusdem regni representantes, commissarii . . . specialiter deputati, pro tribunali sedentes '.[1] Therefore the ' estates ' which judged that Richard should be deposed, and set up a commission to do so, included the commons, and they were represented on the commission. On the second day of Henry IV's first parliament, when the king's son was made prince of Wales, his father's accession was recalled in these terms :

coment toutz les estatz du roialme entierment et benignement et d'un accord et assent, luy ont acceptez en leur droiturel roy.[2]

Later in the session (Monday, 3 November) the commons petitioned the king as follows :

come les juggementz du parlement appertiegnent soulement au roy et as seigniours, et nient as communes sinoun en cas qe s'il plest au roy de sa grace especiale lour monstrer les ditz juggementz, pur ease de eux, qe nul record soit fait en parlement encontre les ditz communes q'ils sont ou serront parties as ascunes juggementz donez ou a doners en apres en parlement.

The king in his reply confirmed and expounded the constitutional rule formulated by the commons : judgement belongs to the king and lords, the commons are petitioners and

---

[1] *Ibid.* iii, 422, nos. 51, 52.   [2] *Ibid.* iii, 426, no. 71.

demanders except in legislation, the grant of supply, or similar matters of general welfare when the king may require their advice and consent.[1]

It is to be noted that this matter was raised independently of the formal protestation of the commons at the beginning of parliament, made on their behalf by their Speaker. This fact and the terms of the petition suggest a reference to a judgement given in the current session, because the commons ask that no record prejudicial to them shall be made in parliament. The reference can scarcely be to the judgement of imprisonment passed on the late king on 27 October, because the king and the lords were alone concerned in this.[2] But in the case of Richard's ' appellants ', against whom judgement was delivered by Thirning on 3 November (the day on which the commons submitted their petition), the commons were to a certain extent concerned. The proceedings had been initiated at their instance, and the lords were severally examined ' before the king and all the states in this present parliament '.[3] On the other hand, judgement was passed in the name of the king and lords alone. Now it must be remembered that the knights and burgesses who were so scrupulous in guarding themselves against even the appearance of taking part in a judgement in Henry IV's first parliament were the same men who had been summoned by Richard II's writ and had not hesitated to judge and depose him on 30 September.

If the meeting in which that momentous act was accomplished had been in fact a parliament, the commons would have created a precedent most damaging to the accepted view of their position and responsibility in parliament. If a few weeks later the same men took pains to guard themselves against establishing even the appearance of a precedent, *a fortiori* they would have sought the protection that parliament could give them against the consequences of their act on the 30th.[4]

---

[1] *Ibid.* iii, 427, no. 79.

[2] *Lords' Report* i, 353 ; cf. Ramsay, *Lancaster and York* i, 10, arguing that all three estates were parties to the transaction on the strength of a passage in the *Annales*, 313, but *Rot. Parl.* iii, 426–7, nos. 73, 74, is quite definite in the contrary sense.　　　　[3] *Ibid.*, 449, 451–2.

[4] Was this a factor in determining the form in which the proceedings on the 30th should be recorded ? If there were no parliament roll there would be no embarrassing precedent. Cf. below, p. 362, n. 1.

It appears, therefore, that there is no reason against the assumption that the word *status* is used in the ' record and process' to mean the lords spiritual and temporal and the commons, those, that is to say, who had been summoned by writ to attend parliament, although the alternative assumption that it means the social orders of the kingdom cannot be ruled out. The distinction, however, would be a formal one if the persons present and acting on the 30th were (as they said they were) representing all the estates of the kingdom.

Next we have to note two passages at the beginning and the end of the text respectively which may be thought to raise a strong presumption that its authors attached a definite meaning to the word *status*, and intended to be using it consistently throughout, whenever reference is made to the assembly of *status* and *populus* on the 30th and what it did and authorized to be done. First, we have the words attributed to Richard when he read his abdication to the commissioners in the Tower. He charged two prelates to announce and declare this his cession and renunciation ' omnibus statibus dicti regni '.[1] With this must be read the opening words of Thirning's speech on 1 October. He reminds the king that ' ther was a parlement somond of all the states of the reaume ... by cause of the whiche sommons all the states of this londe were ther gadyrd '.[2] He then proceeds to name the proctors whom the estates had commissioned to wait upon the king and the groups which they respectively represented. These were : 1, the archbishops and bishops, 2, the abbots, priors, and other clergy, 3, the dukes and earls, 4, the barons and bannerets, 5, the bachelors and commons of the north and south respectively, 6, two judges. It will be observed that these groups were all summoned to parliament, individually or in general, by writ, and this was true of all the proctors with the exception of Erpingham who represented the bachelors and commons of the south.[3] It will

---

[1] *Rot. Parl.* iii, 417, no. 14. In this and what immediately follows I have profited greatly by Dr. Chrimes' discussion of the whole question in *English Constitutional Ideas in the Fifteenth Century*, 81 *seqq.*

[2] *Rot. Parl.* iii, 424, no. 59.

[3] He is described (*loc. cit.*) as ' Sir Thomas Irpyngham, Chamberleyne '. He was one of three deputed to wait on the king in the Tower on the 29th, *ibid.* iii, 416, no. 10*b* (where the name is spelt ' Erpyngham '). He was one of ' the faithful followers ' included in ' the little retinue that surrounded

be observed further that we have here ' the estates on whose behalf and in whose name Richard was deposed set out not merely as particular persons, but as orders or ranks in the nation at large '.[1] A comparison with the unofficial accounts (which are all that we have) of the committee of estates that accepted the abdication extorted from Edward II at Kenilworth in 1327 is very instructive. The Lanercost and Pipewell[2] chronicles appear to be the best informed. They differ somewhat in detail, but as to the estates represented they agree : these (inferred from the members of the committee) are as follows, bishops and abbots (Lanercost adds priors and friars), earls, barons, knights of the shire (Lanercost records the distinction between the north and south),[3] the towns, and two judges (given only in Pipewell).[4] If allowance be made for the social and constitutional development of seventy-two years particularly in the notions of peerage, the resemblance makes it very hard to rule out the conscious use of the precedent.[5] In the case before us, therefore, it appears to me that two inferences may reasonably be made from the evidence. The first is that the authors of the ' record and process ' used the word *status* to mean the estates or social orders of the realm whenever they were referring to those who took part in the transactions of the 30th. The second is that they considered

Henry of Lancaster in exile ', and was appointed chamberlain on 30 September. See Tout, *Chapters* iv, 56 ; Wylie, *Henry IV* i, 28 ; and *D.N.B.* Suppl. ii, 189 ff. It will be recalled that William Trussel, a member of the king's household and not a member of parliament, spoke for the commons in 1343, and for the whole deputation that waited on Edward II at Kenilworth in 1327 ; see *Rot. Parl.* ii, 136, no. 9, and above, pp. 310–11.

Sir Thomas Gray was one of the knights of the shire for Northumberland in Henry's first parliament and had presumably, therefore, been returned first under Richard's writ of 19 August ; *Returns* i, 259.

[1] Chrimes, *op. cit.*, 114. This otherwise valuable discussion of the problem suffers from the fact that Dr. Chrimes has not attempted to account for the part attributed to the *populus* by the ' record and process '.

[2] The relevant portion is printed in M. V. Clarke, *Medieval Representation and Consent*, 193–5, where its origin is tentatively attributed to Pipewell Abbey, but see *B.I.H.R.* xiv, 146, and *History* xxii, 69.

[3] It may be noted that the Anonimalle Chronicle describes the speaker in the Good Parliament of 1376 as a knight from the south ; *Anon. Chron.* (ed. Galbraith), 81.

[4] See M. V. Clarke, *op. cit.*, cap. ix, where references are given and the matter worked out in detail.

[5] In the matter of the deposition the ' record and process ' states that the act was in accordance with the ancient custom of the kingdom in like cases, *Rot. Parl.* iii, 422, no. 51. The words are quoted above, p. 355.

that those estates were duly and adequately represented by the persons who were gathered at Westminster by reason of the summons to parliament. This implies a certain confusion of thinking, but not any ignorance or disregard of established custom. The judges were summoned to parliament and the king's officers had a place there, but neither represented the estates of the realm, yet it is clear that those whom the summons of King Richard had brought to Westminster were in fact ' omnes status regni qui parliamento interesse debebant ',[1] either senatorially or as charged with *plena potestas.* For practical purposes they were the obvious people to choose for the business in hand, and since if they had been organized into a parliament they would have spoken and acted with authority derived from the classes and communities they represented, the term estates of the realm was the obvious one to choose.

It will be noticed that, when the ' record and process ' has to describe those who took part in the proceedings of September 30th, it regularly couples the terms *status* and *populus.* This, indeed, is what we should expect if the word *populus* is used in the sense and for the reasons which we have suggested above. Mr. Richardson, however, appears to regard the association of the two words as adding to the confusion and ambiguity of the text. He observes that Thirning, in his speech to the king, after referring to the gathering of the ' states ' at Westminster, ' slips into references to " all the states and all the people that was ther gadyrd by cause of the summons forsayd ", and he finally refers to the proctors ' as elected by them (p. 43). I am not sure whether Mr. Richardson means to suggest that Thirning was speaking loosely or inadvertently. If so, it seems to me contrary to all antecedent probability that on such an occasion he should have done so or, if he did, that his words should have passed the scrutiny of those who drafted the text with such obvious care and caution. If we assume, on the other hand, that the words were consistent with the purpose the draftsmen had in mind, we shall find support in another and equally important part of the text. This is a passage to which we have already referred, and it may be cited here more fully :

Eboracensem archiepiscopum et episcopum Herefordensem, quos protunc suos constituit procuratores ad declarandum et intimandum

[1] *Annales,* 251 ; cf. above, p. 286.

cessionem et renunciationem hujusmodi omnibus statibus dicti regni, rogavit, ut intentionem et voluntatem suam in ea parte populo nunciarent.[1]

As the same section of the text records the presence of the *populus* at Westminster the next day and the question which, when the announcement had been made, the commission addressed to the ' estates and people ', we can scarcely take the king's words as meaning that his intention should be declared to the *populus* in the sense of the country at large. The king's words distinguish clearly between the estates and the people, but contemplate that both have a part to play. The course of the proceedings illustrates those points : the states act and the people concur. Thirning accordingly first describes himself and those who accompanied him as the proctor of the estates. He then reminds the king of his words on the Monday (which we have just quoted) and refers to the acceptance of the abdication by the estates and people, and the subsequent steps, and finally describes himself and his fellows as ' procuratours to all thes states and poeple ' charged and given authority by them to withdraw all homage, fealty, and allegiance to the king; ' and that non of all thes states and poeple fro this tyme forward ne bere yowe feyth, ne do yowe obeisance os to thar kyng '.[2]

Surely there is no inadvertence here but rather a perfect correspondence with what is represented as the intention of the managers for the course of the meeting on the 30th. The estates acted, and the people consented, and the language held by Thirning in his discourse reflects correctly the major and minor parts played by those for whom he and his fellows spoke.

The foregoing considerations suggest that the authors of the ' record and process ' used the words *status* and *populus* when referring to the meeting on 30 September to mean those who had been summoned by writ to parliament and those who were present at Westminster and were expected to take and did take a minor part in the proceedings there. We have some reason to

---

[1] *Rot. Parl.* iii, 417, no. 14.
[2] *Ibid.* iii, 424, no. 59*b*. On the constitutional theory of the ' record and process ' the ' people ' would properly take part in the election of proctors, one of whose tasks was to withdraw from the king the faith and obedience of all his subjects.

believe that the account is not without a basis of fact as far as
the composition of the meeting was concerned, and that it was
intended to represent its proceedings as orderly and in some
sense legal. The nature of the crisis in which the managers of
the revolution were involved and the character of the document
in which they affect to record what took place both suggest that
they were guided by some leading idea and wished to produce a
calculated effect. If we seek to determine what that idea and
effect were, three hypotheses present themselves. The first is
that implied by Mr. Richardson, which seems to be that the
meeting was in fact a parliament but an irregular one in the
sense that it was not organized and that the king was absent.
Moreover, the proceedings being revolutionary could not be
adjusted to any constitutional or legal form. In these circumstances the confused and self-contradictory narrative of the
' record and process ' will not yield any intelligible result and
must give way to the authoritative coronation roll which settles
the matter, in the sense that if the meeting was anything at all
it was a parliament. I have given some reasons why I cannot
admit the grounds upon which, in his article, Mr. Richardson
bases his scepticism as to the ' record and process '. If these
should prove acceptable we are left with the text as good evidence of what those who had in advance arranged the setting,
and tried to determine the course, of the proceedings on the
30th, wished us to think about it. I submit, therefore, that on
those who maintain in the face of this evidence that the assembly
was in fact a parliament there is the onus of meeting the following points : 1. Why is the word parliament never applied to it
in the ' record and process ' ? 2. Why was the throne covered
and the king unrepresented ? 3. On what we know of fourteenth-
century theory and practice can there be a parliament in the
absence, without representation, of a living king ? 4. If it
had been wished to give the assembly the form of a parliament
and the managers had really believed that the writs were not
invalidated until after the deposition,[1] why was not Richard
represented as sending his message of the 29th to parliament
and not to the estates ? 5. Why was not the meeting properly

---

[1] Arundel's words on the opening of Henry's first parliament appear to
have this meaning ; see below, p. 367.

organized the next morning and carried on until the deposition was accomplished ? 6. Why was not the record of the proceedings made up into the form of a roll ?[1] It seems to me that the evidence of the ' record and process ' as to the purpose of the managers is too good to be dismissed, as I understand Mr. Richardson would do, as a confused and ambiguous account of a very irregular meeting of parliament. There are, of course, two questions involved : one what actually took place and the other what the managers represented as having taken place, and I suggest that there is evidence enough as to both to charge the historian with the duty of framing a constructive hypothesis. If Mr. Richardson maintains on the authority of the coronation roll that the meeting was a parliament, then the objections I have just formulated ought to be met. For if, as he suggests, Henry ' felt able to use, and could conceive, only the normal constitutional forms even for an abnormal purpose ', it would follow that those who were giving a false account of what happened would be scrupulous to observe the normal forms, which is exactly what they did not do. For the sake of clearness this may be put in another way. If the meeting on the 30th were in any constitutional sense a parliament, then, on Mr. Richardson's view, the ' record and process ' should have emphasized instead of discredited its parliamentary character. Mr. Richardson adds ' no consistent doctrine will cover easily both the normal and the abnormal ', and these words appear to me to confuse the two questions to which I have referred. What took place was no doubt abnormal, but the arrangement of the meeting beforehand and the account given of it afterwards (both

[1] Mr. Richardson writes : ' It would be dangerous to argue that, because there is now no separate roll recording the meeting of 30 September, the inference must be that none was ever made. There is now no roll for many parliaments—e.g. that at Cambridge in 1388 '. I accept the general principle, but I cannot admit the application of it to the particular case for the following reasons. The ' record and process ' presents an account of the meeting in the form acceptable to the managers. We have reason to believe that it has suppressed some facts and misrepresented others, but it presents itself as a record of the material proceedings of the day. Is it likely that the managers would have allowed any other account to be drawn up ? Mr. Richardson argues that the parliament was dissolved before it could transact any formal business, and this would scarcely be denied. What then was there left to be put into a parliament roll, if there had been no formal business and all that was material was comprised in another official document ? I have suggested above, p. 356, n. 4., another possible reason for avoiding the form of a parliament roll.

of which were in the managers' hands) could, it seems, have been made to conform to normal practice if not completely, at any rate to a far greater degree than appears to have been done.

We must now consider the second and more constructive hypothesis. This is not new, but it has been recently revived and examined by Dr. Chrimes, who observes that the sanction of the estates was the only one invoked throughout the entire proceedings, and adds that it is possible that ' Henry was, in lieu of the parliamentary sanction, craftily using the idea of the estates for his own purposes '. He thinks, however, that this is improbable.[1] In this I agree with him, but I think that there is more to be said for the theory than he admits and I reject it for different reasons. The suggestion was first made by the authors of the *Reports on the Dignity of a Peer* who observed that ' the title of Henry the Fourth ... depended wholly on the authority of the lords and commons, summoned in the name of Richard to attend his parliament, assuming the character of representatives of the three estates of the realm ', etc.[2] This view Mr. Richardson qualifies as ' a mere legalistic inversion of history which views the past in the light of modern doctrine,' and adds, ' the men of 1399 would have been as puzzled to know what to make of a convention of estates as they would of a bill of rights '. In support of this he argues that ' no one is likely to have had any detailed knowledge of the Epiphany-Candlemas parliament of 1327, and [people] cannot be supposed to have been following precedents distant by seventy years '. In view of the evidence adduced by the late Miss Clarke[3] I do not think that the idea of the estates of the realm acting politically through representatives can be rejected in quite so summary a fashion. If so, the passage just quoted (apart from the word ' convention ' which is admittedly a modern convenience and not an indispensable one) perhaps deserves a little more attention. If we could be sure that the managers intended, in view of the abnormality of the situation and the recognized doubt of the possibility of

---

[1] Chrimes, *op. cit.*, 114.

[2] *Report* i, 348 ; on p. 350 the phrase ' convention of the states ' is used. Cf. above p. 283, n. 2, and for further discussion of uses of the expression ' estates ', see the correspondence in the *Times Lit. Sup.*, July 3rd, 10th, 17th, 1924.

[3] See above, p. 358, n. 2.

obtaining a valid parliament, to appeal to the authority of the influential classes of the nation who were present in person or by representation, and if they were aware that a committee of estates had been made use of in similar circumstances in 1327, many of the difficulties in interpreting the ' record and process ' would vanish. Richard's direction to the bishops to announce his abdication to the estates, the covered throne, the absence of a presiding officer and of the formalities of organization, the avoidance of the word parliament and the remarkable correspondence in point of composition, even to the distinct representation of the knights from the north and the south,[1] between the deputation which waited on Richard in the Tower and that which had been sent to his great-grandfather at Kenilworth would fall into place. We should have an intelligible and self-consistent document representing an attempt to give an appearance of legal form or at any rate of political authority to abnormal proceedings by the extension of a theory attested by precedent. There are, however, two considerations which, taken together, seem to me to be fatal to this view. The first is that it cannot account for the use of the word *populus* and all that it may connote in the text. An appeal to the social orders of the kingdom through their representatives who had been actually summoned to parliament might be suggested by precedent, but on what ground could you include the people in what was in effect a convention of estates in the sense in which the term is now used ? The second objection lies in what we know or may reasonably conjecture of the events of the ten days immediately preceding the deposition. I have discussed the evidence in my former article and suggested certain inferences which I will state presently. Could we expect, at a moment when Henry had thrown all arrangements into confusion, an agreement upon a plan which, whatever its advantages, abandoned any appearance of parliamentary action and allowed him to succeed by birth, conquest, and the acceptance of the estates ? Surely those who only ten days earlier had intended to proceed by parliamentary deposition alone would not have agreed to an alternative which contained

[1] Above pp. 357–8. Note also the parallel between ' Richard of Bordeaux, and ' Edward of Carnarvon ', above p. 290, n. 4.

no element of compromise ? Nor, it may be thought, is it likely that Henry would have tried to impose his will on them without even the appearance of a concession. Again, the plan of a convention of estates consciously used as a substitute for parliament, although it might have been based on the habit of thinking and acting in terms of ' estates ' and ' committees of estates ', would still be a new constitutional device. As such it might be expected to have resulted, if at all, from reflection and a common effort to find a way out of a difficulty not made by party conflict, conditions that were not present at the end of September 1399. Finally, it seems to me incongruous with the institutional and theoretical development of parliament in the fourteenth century. For these reasons I agree with Mr. Richardson and Dr. Chrimes in rejecting the hypothesis of a deliberately planned convention of estates.

The third hypothesis is substantially that which I put forward in my earlier article and for convenience' sake I will summarize the argument. Parliamentary action by way of deposition and election, as recommended by the commission, was unacceptable to Henry. Personally and politically he was indispensable to the Lancastrians, particularly as the succession was not determined in law. Henry, having in fact settled it by conquest, had proposed to assert the seniority of his line to that of Mortimer on patently spurious historical evidence which the commission very properly rejected. He then, within a week of the meeting of parliament, announced his intention of basing his claim on conquest alone; as a compromise he proposed the scheme of a combined abdication and deposition which would have the warrant of precedent, secure parliamentary forms and at the same time allow him to allege his claims by inheritance and (under reasonable safeguards) by conquest. This was accepted but not without opposition, in the course of which the doctrine that the cession of the crown would invalidate the writs of summons was formulated. This could not be denied nor upon the scheme proposed could anyone be certain when the cession would occur. Henry's adversaries had thus been outwitted by an astute and very likely unscrupulous leader who had most of the trumps in his hand. They had conceded the abdication to save parliamentary deposition, and had been

manoeuvred into the position of finding themselves on the very
eve of the meeting of parliament without the possibility of
holding a parliament at all unless they were willing to allow
Henry to announce his succession by birth and conquest before
issuing the new writs. What compromise could Henry offer
them ? I suggest that it was in substance this : ' gather those
who have been summoned to parliament, let them be notified
of the abdication and go through the forms of accepting it,
judging and deposing Richard, hearing and admitting Henry's
claims; let them meet again under the writs which on the 30th
shall be in readiness, and when they are organized as an unquestioned and regular parliament their tacit acceptance
of the accomplished fact will give something that can be represented as parliamentary warrant for it.'[1] The concession was
not great, but it was at any rate better than the alternative.

The procedure to be followed on the 29th and 30th we may
suppose to have been hastily arranged on two assumptions, the
one that the meeting could not in fact be a parliament and the
other that the use of committees or bodies of commissioners
drawn from and representing the various orders of society (a
practice sanctioned by tradition and parliamentary usage)
would give some appearance of regularity and legal form to the
proceedings. The practical advantage to be expected was that
the personnel of the new parliament would be committed
beforehand to the revolution. In the course of the meeting,
however, opposition developed, and was overcome or at any
rate silenced by Henry's ' might and wilfulness ' and the ' publica vociferacione vulgaris populi '.

When the revolution was accomplished and those who had
sought a parliamentary solution came to take stock of their

---

[1] Something of the sort may have been in Stubbs' mind when he wrote
a page that has puzzled many who have worked at this subject, see *C.H.* ii,
528 and my comment, above, p. 320, n. 1. The passage is too long for
quotation and it is entirely unsupported by relevant evidence. The
substance of it is that the combination of abdication and deposition was
settled before the commission reported ; that the duke of York arranged
the order of proceedings and met Arundel's objection that the king's
resignation would cause the parliament to be dissolved as soon as it met
by the preparation of new writs to be issued on the day of the resignation.
Obviously this device could not ' save the forms of the constitution ' in
the sense which Stubbs evidently attached to the words. It could, however,
have the practical (though not ' constitutional ') effect which I have
indicated in the text.

situation, they would have to reckon with two considerations. They had to all appearances surrendered the principle of parliamentary action, and events had occurred which were known to too many people to be passed over in silence. With these things in mind and time for reflection they may be supposed to have approached the task of putting the best face they could on a bad business. If we look at the ' record and process ' from this point of view, it will appear consistent and intelligible. Clearly the best way of treating the facts in so far as they could be admitted at all would be to misrepresent them. The turbulent mob will become the acclaiming people, Richard the gentle and contrite prince owning his failure and recognizing his cousin as the man best qualified to succeed him. The momentous events of the day will be accomplished in an atmosphere of grave and orderly unanimity with a suggestion of conformity with ancient custom and forms of law. But when the utmost had been done in this direction the awkward fact would still remain that they had not dared to say or to show that the meeting was a parliament. What means could be used to cover this admission ? The answer I think will be found in the words used by Arundel in opening the first parliament of Henry IV. He refers to the meeting on the 30th :

a quel jour le roy Richard . . . avoit somonez son parlement d'y estre tenuz; quele sommons ne feust du null force n'effect, a cause de l'acceptation de la renunciation fait par le dit roy Richard, et de la deposition de mesme le Roy Richard qe feust fait le Maresdy suis dit, come par le record et proces ent faitz et enrollez en cest rolle du parlement piert pluis au plein.[1]

Now on this theory the writs were not invalidated until near the close of the proceedings, and the meeting could therefore have been organized and acted as a parliament up to that moment. The constitutionalists would thus have had their way or very nearly had it, and the abnormal arrangements for the meeting would have been unnecessary and inappropriate. Why, then, were they made, and (what is more important) why do they figure in the ' record and process ' ? A satisfactory answer to both questions will be forthcoming if we assume that this doctrine was the fruit of reflection, an afterthought and

[1] *Rot. Parl.* iii, 415.

perhaps a desperate one in the sense that it was not held with conviction. On that assumption the abnormal arrangements of the meeting would represent the earlier theory that the cession must occur at latest when the abdication was announced, for why should they have been made if Arundel's argument of 6 October had been available a week earlier ? They would be known, however, to too many people to be denied, and would constitute an admission that would make it impossible to describe the meeting as a parliament. Better, therefore, avoid the word, describe the arrangements in such terms as to suggest a parliament and fortify this *suggestio falsi* by the formulation of the new doctrine. This suggestion of deliberate ambiguity is contained in my earlier article, where I have treated it at greater length than there is room for here, although I did not then see how much my point could be strengthened by regarding Arundel's words as an afterthought.

Mr. Richardson suggests the difficulty

that the language of the record and process was such that, if its authors had intended the inference to be drawn that the assembly was not a parliament, a fairly representative selection of its readers, including a chancery clerk, failed to draw that inference. May that not lead to the dilemma either that the language was so obscure that even contemporaries did not understand what (on this point) they were driving at or, alternatively, that they did not intend that inference to be drawn ? Why should not such common words as ' tractatus ' or ' consilium ' have been used if it was desired to avoid parliament ?

My point is that the authors of the ' record and process ' dared not say that the meeting was a parliament, but so arranged their narrative that the contrary inference might be drawn. Readers who, like a chancery clerk, expected a parliament or, like some of the chroniclers who hoped for as well as expected one, might be misled. Any contemporary examining the text with a view to finding out what the meeting really was could not, I think, have failed to see the difficulties which are evident to us as indeed they appear to have been to the chancery clerk who wrote the writs of expenses. If the document was drafted in bad faith with the desire to mislead, then, I submit, Mr. Richardson's dilemma does not arise. As to his last point I would ask whether a ' tractatus ' or ' consilium ' to consider national affairs could have been assembled without a royal writ ? If not, the words were open to the same objection as the word parliament.

Now it is evident that this reconstruction depends, though in differing degrees, on two propositions. The first is that the effect of the demise of the crown upon the writs issued under its authority was new and imperfectly understood doctrine in 1399 and the second that the procedure eventually adopted for formally effecting the change of dynasty was influenced by the precedent of 1327. These points I have treated in some detail in my former article. Mr. Richardson, however, dissents from both propositions. As to the first he writes :

In 1327 the ordinary processes of the courts, in theory at least, seem to have been interrupted : the same is true in 1399. By a parity of reasoning (there were no effective precedents) it would seem that some formal steps should have been taken in 1327 to restore the parliamentary machine, but so far as we know the necessity for such steps was ignored. I am not sure, however, that it was really ' new doctrine ' in 1399 that the demise of the crown affected the summons or proceedings of parliament. In any case I must not be understood to assent to the view implied by the words new doctrine.

If I have followed Mr. Richardson, he means that the appointment or reappointment of the judges on Edward III's accession implied that the effect of the demise of the crown on their patents was well understood in 1327, and that its consequences in respect to the writs under which parliament was sitting and continued to sit should have been equally understood. The point is interesting, because the extension of the doctrine from judges' patents to parliamentary writs is a logical one which might indeed have been expected in the circumstances of 1327.[1] It seems to me, however, that the writs of expenses which, as is well known, treated the whole life of the parliament as continuous,[2] are formal and conclusive evidence that the

[1] For a brief statement of the facts as to the discontinuance of legal actions on the demise of the crown from 1199 onwards, see Sayles, *Select Cases in the King's Bench* i, xlii–xliii. This might be related to (1) the cessation of the king's peace ; (2) the invalidation of the justices' commissions ; (3) the invalidation of the writs of summons and attachments. Mr. Richardson would seem to uphold theory no. (1) ; either (2) or (3) would offer a closer analogy to the parliamentary writs of summons.

[2] The writs of course ran in the name of Edward III, and the whole service was described as ' ad parliamentum nostrum ', Prynne, *Brief Register* iv, 78. If men had understood the doctrine as applying to writs of summons they would scarcely have failed to see the need of issuing new ones in Edward III's name. The need of new elections might have been passed over as it was in 1399.

B b

doctrine was not understood, and explain satisfactorily why no
formal steps to restart the parliamentary machine were considered necessary. As a like situation did not recur until 1399
we should scarcely expect to hear of the matter in the interval.
In 1399 both parts of the doctrine were known but were kept
separate. Henry's first act after his declaration made to the
estates, was to appoint or reappoint the justices, sheriffs, and
other royal officers throughout the kingdom whom the vacancy
of the throne had deprived of all power.[1] It is in another
context and on a later date that we have the first official reference to the invalidation of the writs of summons. If the point
had not been understood in 1327 and there had been no
practical reason to consider it again until 1399, it may fairly be
called new doctrine in that year.

I come now to the second proposition which concerns the
influence of the precedent of 1327. I find it difficult to follow
Mr. Richardson when, after observing that Edward II was
remembered at the crisis of Richard II's reign, he proceeds, ' no
one is likely to have had any detailed knowledge of the Epiphany-Candlemas parliament of 1327, and [people] cannot be
supposed to have been following precedents distant by seventy
years and more ' (p. 45). Surely no detailed knowledge was
required to grasp the relevance and the importance of the well-
known facts that a parliament which had affected to depose
Edward II had subsequently sent to him a representative
committee instructed to accept his abdication and renounce
homage and allegiance on their behalf ? These facts (refracted
no doubt through a tendentious mind) are referred to in the
Leicester chronicle and plainly stated by Higden.[2] Adam of
Usk owned a copy of Higden's work, and referred to it in connexion with Henry's attempt to establish the seniority of his
line.[3] Again, the resemblances in point of composition between
the committee sent to Kenilworth in 1327, and the deputation
that waited on Richard in the Tower as described by Adam of
Usk,[4] in themselves suggest a deliberate use of the precedent.[5]

---

[1] *Rot. Parl.* iii, 423, no. 57.
[2] *Knighton* (R.S.) ii, 219 ; *Polychronicon* (R.S.) viii, 322.
[3] Adam of Usk, *Chron.*, vi, 31.   [4] *Op. cit.*, 31–2; cf. above pp. 275, 318.
[5] Cf. M. V. Clarke, *op. cit.*, 177, and Richardson and Sayles, *B.I.H.R.*
xiv, 146.

To this Mr. Richardson objects :

One of the salient points of difference between medieval and modern procedure is the use of precedent, and my contention was that in this case any precedents followed were general and not particular. So far as we know, no attempt was made to consult the public records which might be supposed to afford detailed precedents.

I think that we are perhaps at cross-purposes here. The precedents to which I referred in my original article and in the words above were the alleged deposition and formal abdication of Edward II which are recounted in the chronicles.[1] I never meant to suggest that the effect of the demise of the crown upon the existence of parliament could have been discovered from the precedent of 1327, for it was and is part of my case that it was unknown at that time. If I understand Mr. Richardson, then, we are agreed on this point.

We come now to the second of the two points raised by Mr. Richardson. Speaking of the events of January 1327, he says, ' no coherent political or legal theory can be devised to fit these facts ', and he extends this principle to the revolution of 1399, adding ' no explanation we can offer will avoid the inherent difficulty of reconciling violence and law '. Since the writs were issued as early as 19 August, he suggests that Henry's plans were already shaped, i.e. that he intended to proceed by parliamentary action, and could not be supposed to have had any other view, because ' he felt able to use and could conceive only the normal constitutional forms even for an abnormal purpose'.[2] Mr. Richardson appears to suggest that the discussion of the term is a vain one, because the action involved was the use of force and the whole situation abnormal. In these circumstances, he concludes, our best course is to follow the authority of the coronation roll and call the assembly parliament. I agree that it was intended from 19 August to refer the whole matter to

[1] See above pp. 318 ff. A passage in the ' record and process ' is relevant at this point ; having described the commission set up to depose the king in the name and by the authority of the estates, it adds ' prout in consimilibus casibus de antiqua consuetudine . . . regni fuerat observatum '. *Rot. Parl.* iii, 422, no. 51.

[2] Mr. Richardson has raised here an issue the discussion of which would require an article by itself. To use the words ' constitutional ' and ' normal' without a definite statement of what you mean by them can in such a discussion lead only to confusion and cross-purposes. I have tried therefore to avoid the general issue and confine myself to the particular case.

parliament and that at the date (probably 20 September) of the publication of the commission's report[1] the course contemplated was deposition. Thereafter there was a change of plan, it was decided to obtain an abdication before proceeding to the deposition, and it was then discovered that that might extinguish parliament. So far there is no departure here from what Mr. Richardson calls 'the normal constitutional forms' which alone Henry could conceive of using even for an abnormal purpose, but there is a very notable discovery made about one of them.[2] The question of the abnormal purpose need not have entered into the discussion at all; it was not necessary to ask whether parliament could lawfully depose the king; it was enough to point out that the existence of parliament depended on the official existence of the king who had summoned it. A new situation was thereby created, and it was a normal one because it arose out of an enlarged knowledge of the nature of an integral part of the government and the laws of its existence. There could be nothing in it, therefore, inconceivable to Henry or any others who had determined to give a constitutional veneer to their violence. To them, accordingly, as to us, the question of whether the assembly gathered on 30 September was a parliament would be an intelligible one and a matter of substance as well as form. So much for what appears to be the main point at issue between Mr. Richardson and myself. If space permitted a discussion of the larger question which he opens at the end of his paper, I would enter upon it. As it is I must content myself with one observation. In a society in which the forms of law have been prized as highly as they have in England revolutions may assume an important constitutional significance, not because of the material alterations they make but on account of the discoveries about the law[3] and its forms

[1] It will be remembered that the commission had rejected Henry's preposterous claim to be the legitimate heir. Mr. Richardson asks (p. 47), ' was there any other device [except reference to parliament] ready to a usurper's hand ? ' Answers are provided by this claim and the subsequent threat to challenge the crown by right of conquest alone.

[2] There is a sense in which abdication is abnormal because it is rare, but it is not a constitutional sense. As to whether parliament had power and authority to depose a king, perhaps the most that can be said here is that the Lancastrians had the power and professed that parliament had the authority.

[3] For reasons given above (p. 371, n. 2), I have used the word law instead of ' constitution ' not in a technical sense but having in mind Dr.

to which they lead. In the sense of the self-consistent development of constitutional principles it may be said of the crises of
1399 and of 1688 that 'out of the eater came forth meat'.

Pickthorn's generalization, ' the medieval idea of the supremacy of the
law . . . before the sixteenth century . . . was all there was in England in the
way of a constitution ', *Early Tudor Government* i, 55. Taken from their
context the words commit Dr. Pickthorn to more than he has said, and I
apologize to him for a condensation which serves to emphasize the main
point.

IX

THE PROBLEM OF THE NORTH [1]

THE task of bringing the border counties of England into line with the rest of the kingdom was not the least troublesome of the problems of internal policy that confronted Henry VIII and his ministers. Wolsey handled the difficulty with very indifferent success; it remained for Cromwell (or for the king acting through Cromwell) to deal with the Pilgrimage of Grace and to undertake, after that movement had been suppressed, the reconstruction of the North. For this purpose the northern counties were placed under the direct control of the king and his council, and consequently to a great extent beyond the reach of parliament and the common law. An offshoot of the privy council, called into being by royal commission under the official style of the President and Council of the North and vested with practically absolute administrative and judicial powers, was in 1537 placed at York.

This review of familiar facts raises the question of the origin of the problem which Henry VIII solved in this arbitrary fashion. The answer to that question will affect any estimate of the character and motives of Henry VIII. For if the disaffection of the northern counties and their subsequent rebellion was due to the king's determination to render himself absolute, even at the cost of a change of religion, then the harsh treatment they received must be condemned as mere tyranny. But if the causes of the trouble in the North lay deeper than this, if the northern counties had from early times been kept on a footing somewhat different from the other English counties, so as never to have been quite assimilated to the rest of the kingdom, then Henry VIII's measures will appear in an altered light. In the king's dealing with the North will be seen an effort to complete the consolidation of England which will go far to account for, if not to mitigate, the harshness and brutality which were undoubtedly practised. It is hoped that the present study will show this to be the just view of the case.

[1] Reprinted with permission from the *American Historical Review*, v (1900), pp. 440–466. Some of the matter contained in the following paper has also been discussed by R. R. Reid, 'The Office of Warden of the Marches,' *E.H.R.* xxxii (1917), 479–496, and *The King's Council in the North* (1921).

The circumstances which differentiated the northern counties from the rest of England were, first, the fact that they did not actually form part of the kingdom until late in the reign of Henry II; second, the development, in the thirteenth century, of a special jurisdiction of the marches which in military and (although in a less degree) judicial affairs extended over Northumberland, Cumberland and Westmorland, and influenced Lancaster, Durham and York; third, the war with Scotland during the fourteenth and fifteenth centuries, which tended to throw the administration of the border counties directly into the hands of the king and his council and to retard civilization by frequent devastations of the North; last, the circumstances of the Wars of the Roses, during which the extensive influence exerted in behalf of a revived feudalism by the families of Nevill and Percy created a feeling of local independence and segregation from the rest of the kingdom. These, in the main, were the factors that went to make up the problem which presented itself in the beginning of the sixteenth century. Some consideration of the points here suggested is necessary before passing to the efforts to solve the problem which culminated in the erection of the Council of the North.

The counties of Westmorland, Cumberland and Lancaster, and Northumberland, Durham and York, formed parts respectively of the ancient kingdoms of Cumbria and Northumbria. The kingdom of Northumbria extended northward to the Forth and southward to the Humber, and the district between Forth and Tweed known as Lothian was not obtained by the Scots king until the year 1018.[1] Northumbria was conquered by Wessex and divided, and eventually the ancient kingdom split up into the two earldoms of Northumberland and York. It has been convincingly argued that the independence of the Northumbrians survived their conquest by the West Saxons, expressing itself at first in the influence exerted by the local witan in the choice of rulers, and later in the persons of the earls of Northumberland and the lords of the great northern franchises such as Durham, Richmond, Lancaster, Hexham and Tynemouth.[2]

---

[1] Hume Brown, *History of Scotland* I, 43.
[2] W. Page, 'Northumbrian Palatinates,' *Archaeologia*, LI, 143 ff.

The north-western part of England had been, since the year 945, held by the Scots kings, of the English crown. But the suzerainty thus exercised was very vague and ill-defined.[1]

The counties of Northumberland, Cumberland, Westmorland and Durham were not included in the Domesday Survey, and the accounts of Cheshire and Yorkshire show that the King had but a limited interest in those districts.[2] The absence of the northern counties from a survey which was intended to embrace the whole territory of England has never been satisfactorily explained, although it is generally accounted for on the ground that the North had not yet sufficiently recovered from the Conqueror's devastations to make it worth while to send commissioners there.[3] Now the county of Durham is understood to have been more effectively ravaged than any other part of the North.[4] But if the theory be accepted that in six years this county had not sufficiently recuperated to make it worth the king's while to send his commissioners there, how is this to be reconciled with the fact that in another six years[5] the Bishop of Durham was able to build the greater part of what to-day remains the most splendid ecclesiastical fabric in England ? It has been more plausibly suggested that the omitted counties were either in the hands of the Scots, ' or else in such condition as no Commissioners dare adventure into them, to take the Returns of Juries, and make the Survey '.[6] At this time, probably, there was no very clear distinction between Lothians and Northumbrians as Scots and Englishmen, and the undescribed district included the earldoms of Cumberland and Northumberland, both of which possessed a high degree of local independence.[7] Domesday Book was primarily a geld-book,

---

[1] *Anglo-Saxon Chronicle*, A.D. 945 (Rolls Series), I, 212–213 ; Stubbs, *C.H.* I, 595.

[2] *Domesday Book* I, 262–270, 298–333.

[3] Kelham, *Domesday Book Illustrated*, 15 ; Ellis, *Introduction to Domesday* I, 35–40.

[4] William of Malmesbury, *Gesta Pontificum* (R.S.), 271 ; *Domesday Studies* II, 494.

[5] This is the extreme limit. William de St. Carilef, Bishop of Durham, was banished in 1088 and did not return to England until 1093, when he immediately began the construction of Durham cathedral. But there is nothing to prove that he might not have undertaken the work in 1088.

[6] Brady, *Introduction to the Old English History*, App., p. 17.

[7] *Pipe Rolls for the Northern Counties* (Society of Antiquaries of Newcastle-upon-Tyne), iv.

and the chief purpose of the survey was to increase the king's revenue.[1] Therefore the king would not send his commissioners into districts where he could not expect to take revenue. But it has been seen that the earldoms of Cumberland and Northumberland were independent of the crown in local affairs, and Durham and Chester, although not yet palatinates, already enjoyed high immunities.[2] Again, the king had as yet no castle north of Tees. Bamborough belonged to the earls of Northumberland, Norham and Newcastle were still to be, and Durham, although founded by the Conqueror, belonged to the bishop.[3] In the eleventh century, then, the northern counties did not, for administrative purposes, form an integral part of the English kingdom.

During the first half of the twelfth century the Scots kings made an attempt to attach the north of England to their kingdom. This effort was much favoured by the feudalization of the Scottish lowlands at the hands of Norman adventurers whose rapid success went far towards obliterating any distinction that might earlier have existed between the north-country Englishman and the lowland Scot. The Normans were welcomed by the Scots kings, from whom they obtained grants of land. They built castles and founded great families which, extending across the border in either direction, did homage to both kings.[4] The families of Bruce and Balliol were English before they were Scottish, and David I. was an English earl, as well as the Scots king.[5] In the law, as well, distinctions

---

[1] Maitland, *Domesday Book and Beyond*, 3.

[2] Page, *op. cit.* 143 ff. ; Sitwell, *The Barons of Pulford*, ix ff.

[3] Symeon of Durham (R.S.), II, 199–200, 260 ; Brand, *History of New-castle-upon-Tyne*, II, 127 ff. ; *History of Northumberland* (Northumberland County History Committee), I, 22.

[4] Stubbs, *C.H.* I, 596–597 ; Burton, *History of Scotland*, II, chs. xiii–xiv ; Neilson, ' The Motes in Norman Scotland ', *Scottish Review*, 1898. The latter writer shows that no less than fifty-one Norman castles, constructed at this period, are still to be identified in the Scottish border counties.

[5] A less prominent but equally striking example of this feudal interpenetration of the two kingdoms is furnished by the family of Umfraville. In the thirteenth century Gilbert de Umfraville was earl of Angus in Scotland and also an English baron with wide estates in Durham and Northumberland. In 1297 his summons to the English parliament as earl of Angus created much perplexity. Again, in the early twelfth century the Scottish lordship of Liddesdale was held by Randolph de Soulis, a baron of Northamptonshire who had estates in Northumberland as well (*Placita de Quo*

vanished and in the next century a version of Glanvill's book became popular in Scotland.[1]

So the similarity of language, institutions and religion, on either side of the border, conspired to make the adhesion of the northern counties of England to one or the other crown a matter of political convenience. The territory was equally fit to be worked into either kingdom in the then state of the royal power. Still, the English kings would no doubt have the more difficult task in proportion as they were able, in the rest of their kingdom, to apply strict principles of royal as opposed to feudal government. The body of the English kingdom could be controlled or coerced by a strong king, but in the North the feudal lords emulated the independence of their fellows across the border where the feudal system had reached a high development. This difficulty was complicated by that feudal interpenetration which has already been noticed and which proceeded to such an extent that many great barons could hardly have known to which nation they belonged.[2]

The history of the attempt of the Scots kings to acquire the northern counties of England, and the ultimate failure of that attempt, need not be reviewed here.[3] But one often unnoticed phase of the struggle is worthy of attention as showing the undecided—it is too early to call it disloyal—state of the North. Both David I and William the Lion intrigued to bring the bishopric of Durham under their control, and nearly succeeded. The bishops of Durham were already great among the greatest of English immunists, and were practically independent local rulers. Upon the death of Bishop Geoffrey, in 1140, William Cumin, a creature of David's, attempted to force himself into the vacant see. Cumin secured the adhesion of the majority of the barons of the bishopric and got *de facto* possession of the temporalities, which he held for three years. But he could not obtain either election or consecration, and in 1143 he was obliged to give way before a canonically elected bishop sup-

Warranto, Rec. Com., 604 ; Banks, *Baronia Anglica Concentrata* i, 103–105; Armstrong, *History of Liddesdale,* 123–125).

[1] Pollock and Maitland, *H.E.L.* i, 145, 200–201.
[2] Stubbs, *C.H.* i, 597 ; Pollock and Maitland, *H.E.L.* i, 202.
[3] See Burton, *History of Scotland* ii, chs. xiii–xiv ; Stubbs, *C.H.* i, 596–597.

ported by a few of the barons of the province.[1] Again, in the rebellion of 1173 Bishop Pudsey intrigued with William the Lion, agreeing to allow the Scots to pass through the bishopric and to permit the landing of French and Flemish troops at his seaports.[2]

Even after the treaty of Falaise (1174), when the captive William was glad to accept what terms he could obtain, the Scots kings did not abandon hope of pushing their frontier southward, and it was not until 1238 that anything like a definite boundary between the two kingdoms was determined.[3] Meanwhile Henry II's reorganization of the central government had accomplished the formal attachment of the northern counties to the English crown. But although the danger of these counties ever becoming Scottish was thus averted, a difference between them and the rest of England was frankly acknowledged in the institution and government of the marches against Scotland. Accordingly the nature of the march government and its reaction on the adjacent counties must be considered.

Such natural boundaries as the river Tweed and the Cheviot Hills could be, and were, defined and defended by castles of which Berwick, Norham and Roxburgh are types. But even these natural and artificial defences did not prevent constant raids and petty warfare which kept the whole country north and south of the border in a state of perpetual demoralization. Further westward, where the natural boundary failed, this dislocated condition was aggravated by the presence of a strip of debatable land. The most definite part of the border was open to dispute, and was much questioned even during the peaceful time in the thirteenth century.[4] But the marches do not clearly come into view until 1249, when, by a treaty

[1] Symeon of Durham (R.S.) i, 143–167. The story is told at length, and in very indifferent verse, in the *Dialogues* of Laurence, prior of Durham, edited for the Surtees Society by the late Canon Raine, who discussed the whole question in an interesting preface. Laurence's account is contemporary.

[2] Geoffrey de Coldingham, *Historia*, cap. vi, in *Historiae Dunelmensis Scriptores Tres* (Surtees Society), 10 ; Jordan Fantosme, *Chronicle* (Surtees Society), 26, 72 ; Jerningham, *Norham Castle*, 100.

[3] Burton, *History of Scotland* ii, 77–82.

[4] *Royal Letters of the Reign of Henry III* (R.S.) i, 186–188 ; *Foedera* (Rec. Com.), i, ii, 544–565.

concluded in that year between Henry III and Alexander III, the vague body of rules that had hitherto formed the *modus vivendi* on the borders was arranged and amplified.[1] The east, middle and west marches of England against Scotland comprised parts of the counties of Northumberland and Cumberland and contained the fortified cities of Berwick-on-Tweed and Carlisle. This district was placed in charge of wardens of the marches, who administered march law, and had general civil and military powers. Under certain conditions their authority extended over the adjacent counties. The courts of the marches, or warden courts, concerned themselves chiefly with criminal matters such as march treason, which consisted of illicit communication with the Scots and was punishable with death. But they also entertained some contentious litigation.[2] At the commencement of the fourteenth century the military authority of the march officials began to be extended over the adjacent counties. Their powers were much increased, and they were sometimes styled wardens of Cumberland, or Westmorland, or Northumberland and the adjacent marches.[3] The bishopric of Durham was at this time a county palatine into which the king's officers could not enter in the discharge of their duties. Chester, on the west, was in the same position, and north of Chester lay the great honour of Lancaster, soon to be raised to the palatine dignity.[4] Thus at the beginning of the fourteenth century the whole of the north of England was under special or extraordinary administrative conditions.

In 1333 the judicial functions of the wardens of the marches were extended so as to include a kind of high police jurisdiction, with powers of arrest and imprisonment. Those who were imprisoned by this authority could not be brought to trial before the justices of gaol-delivery, but had to wait the king's special command. As this authority extended beyond the marches to the adjacent counties, these counties were thus to a certain

---

[1] Nicolson, *Leges Marchiarum*, 1–9.

[2] Nicolson, *op. cit.*, 3 ; Redpath, *Border History*, 17–96 ; Armstrong, *History of Liddesdale*, 1–13.

[3] *Rotuli Scotiae* (Rec. Com.) I, 135, 140, 141, 149, 166, 189, 194, 203 ; *Foedera* III, 495.

[4] Surtees, *History of Durham* I, xv–lv : Ormerod, *History of Chester* I, 9–55 ; Baines, *History of Lancaster* I, 199–240.

extent withdrawn from the jurisdiction of the common law.[1]

In 1370 the wardens of the marches were commissioned to visit all liberties, castles, and privileged districts in the northern counties, for the purpose of arresting offenders against their authority and, in general, of correcting abuses. They had also the duty of maintaining the truce recently concluded with Scotland, which involved a civil and criminal jurisdiction over causes and offenses arising under the terms of that truce.[2] Similar commissions issued in 1377.[3] It may be inferred that the policy indicated in this extension of the wardens' authority was made necessary by the demoralized state of the northern counties after nearly a century of war with Scotland.[4]

Again, under pressure of the disorganizing effects of the war in the fourteenth century the plan of bringing the northern counties immediately under the control of the king and his council began to take shape. Already in 1297 the sheriffs of Lancaster, Westmorland and Cumberland had a special responsibility to notify the king of invasions.[5] In 1314 a special commission, including several of the king's ministers, was sent down to confer with the wardens and local magnates with regard to the safe-keeping of the marches and northern counties.[6] In 1345 the northern prelates were commissioned to collect a similar assembly in the king's name, the decisions of which should be binding on the marches and neighbouring counties.[7] In the meantime the king was strengthening his personal hold on the North. In 1362 the duchy of Lancaster was erected into a palatinate for John of Gaunt, and in 1378 that prince was created king's lieutenant in the North and warden-general of the marches.[8]

The palatine earldom of Chester was attached to the crown

---

[1] *Rotuli Scotiae* I, 257, 276, 282, 398, 436.

[2] *Foedera* III, ii, 895–896.   [3] *Rotuli Scotiae* II, 2.

[4] In the course of the fourteenth century there was a deliberate, but not very successful, effort to draw the northern counties closer to the English system by planting English colonists on, and even across, the borders. We hear a good deal of *Scotii Anglicati*, and even of *Scotia Anglicata*. But this effort, in spite of much encouragement at the hands of the English government, produced little effect. *Rotuli Scotiae* I, 658, 752–753, 794, 856, 887, II, 207 ; Armstrong, *History of Liddesdale*, 131–134.

[5] Nicolson, *Leges Marchiarum*, 368–370.   [6] *Rotuli Scotiae* I, 113, 139.

[7] *Ibid.* I, 663   [8] *Rotuli Scotiae* II, 14, 27, 36.

in the person of Edward I, and in 1389 it was permanently connected with the principality of Wales. Finally, towards the close of the century the privy council begins to concern itself with the administration of the marches, auditing the accounts of the wardens and authorizing their appointment.[1]

Thus during the fourteenth century the northern counties were kept on a different footing from the rest of England. Durham, Chester, and Lancaster were palatinates, and the two former sent no representatives to Parliament.[2] Large parts of Northumberland and Cumberland were included in the marches, and the increased powers of the wardens, extending for certain purposes over all the northern counties, together with occasional special commissions, brought these counties more and more under the direct control of the king and his council, withdrawing them proportionately from the ordinary administration of the kingdom.

During the fifteenth century this tendency advanced more rapidly. In 1400 the council urged the king to go in person to the North to establish order, which was the more necessary as Richard had been very popular in that region.[3] Later in the same year the council, sitting at Durham, adopted several measures for the defence and control of the marches. Two general superintendents were appointed, who, in association with the ordinary march authorities, formed a kind of conference or council. The loyalty of the North was doubted, for the superintendents were directed to see that the border garrisons be not composed of local troops.[4] In 1402 and 1405 the council was again busy with the affairs of the North.[5]

As in the preceding century, the council authorized the appointment of march officers, paid their salaries, and, in general, made provision for all expenses of defence and government in the North.[6] Through the officers of the marches the

---

[1] *Proceedings of the Privy Council* (Rec. Com.) I, 9, 11, 12; *Rot. Scot.* II, 96.
[2] This exemption was regarded by the other northern counties in the light of an enviable privilege. Stubbs, *C.H.* III, 463.
[3] *Proceedings of the Privy Council* I, 119.
[4] *Ibid.* I, 124–126.   [5] *Ibid.* I, 176–178, 255.
[6] *Ibid.* I, 333, 337 II, 8, 15, 17, 96, 108, 178, 213, III, 7, 8, v, 92, 100; *Rot. Scot.* II, 219–220; *C.S.P.* (Henry VIII), II, pt. i, No. 1365. Money for the expenses of the North was obtained by the council either as prestmoney, or by the assignment of the whole or part of some tax for this purpose.

council exercised a certain judicial authority in the North. This consisted chiefly in the application of measures for suppressing disturbances and as far as possible preserving order. But in this direction the wardens and other officers had less discretion than was allowed them in the last century. Their commissions, it is true, conferred on them more general powers of inquiry, arrest and imprisonment, but their instructions were more minute, and in most cases accused persons were to be referred to the king and his council for punishment.[1]

The increased occupation of the privy council with northern affairs also appears in the practice of sending, from time to time, a committee or deputation of that body to sit on the borders for some special purpose. This was generally to negotiate a truce with the Scots, or to adjust difficulties arising out of one already in force.[2] By a treaty in 1449 it was provided that in the event of either king's complaining of the state of the borders, or of infractions of an existing truce, the other should send down two or three members of his council as well to right the matter of immediate complaint as to take general cognizance of border affairs.[3] These commissions, although primarily of a diplomatic and international character, included considerable powers of supervision and administration of local affairs.[4] Also the influence of the king and his council in this direction expressed itself in the occasional organization of the march officers and local magnates into a kind of informal conference or council under the presidency of a royal lieutenant, foreshadowing the devices of the early sixteenth century which eventually crystallized into the Council of the North. This matter is of sufficient importance, as illustrating the conditions and requirements of the North in the late fourteenth and fifteenth centuries and their similarity to those of the sixteenth century, to require special attention.

---

[1] *Rot. Scot.* II, 287 ; *ibid.*, II, 470–471. The Commission to the Earl of Northumberland (A.D. 1480), referred to in the later citation, is of an unusually general character, which may be partly explained by the earl's great unpopularity in the North. He was afterward murdered in a popular rising. Holinshed, *Chronicles* III, 769–770.
[2] *Royal Letters of the Reign of Henry IV* (R.S.) I, 52–56.
[3] Nicolson, *Leges Marchiarum*, 131.
[4] *Cf.* Coke, *Fourth Institute*, ch. xxvi.

The lieutenant of the marches or of the North was, as his title implies, the *locum tenens regis* in those parts, representing the king and drawing his authority from the crown and council and not from parliament. The region placed under his control was therefore necessarily withdrawn from the ordinary administration of the kingdom.[1] The lieutenant of the North first appears, under that title, in 1378, but when Sir Andrew Harclay was created earl of Carlisle in 1322 he was given a general custody of the northern counties that amounted to a lieutenancy.[2] In 1334 and 1350 a *solus superior custos* and a *capitaneus* of the North occur.[3] In 1378 John of Gaunt was created king's lieutenant in the North, with wide civil and military powers and general authority over all the wardens of the marches and northern magnates.[4] He administered the North for four years and in 1380 received additional powers which rendered him virtually absolute there.[5] In 1384 he was replaced by the Earl of Northumberland, who was styled commissary general and had royal authority to grant pardons and to receive outlaws into the king's peace.[6] Similar appointments were made in 1387, 1391 and 1434;[7] but they do not occur during the Wars of the Roses. In 1484 the Earl of Northumberland was created *custos regis generalis* in the North,[8] and after the accession of Henry VII, he was reappointed with the specific purpose of pacifying that region.[9] In virtue of this office he was described as the ' Chiefe ruler of the North parts '.[10] After Northumberland's death Thomas Howard, earl of Surrey, was made lieutenant-general of the North and held office until 1497.[11] It should be observed that all of these appointments are of a temporary or provisional nature. Men are sent down to accomplish a specific purpose and return. The notion of a lieutenant in permanent residence, representing the continual presence of the king, does not appear until the sixteenth century.

[1] Cf. Armstrong, *History of Liddesdale*, 7–10.
[2] *Foedera* III, 495 ; Stubbs, *C.H.* II, 371.
[3] *Rot. Scot.* I, 277, 737.　　　　　[4] *Ibid.* II, 14.
[5] *Ibid.* II, 27, 36 ; *Foedera* IV, 99.　　[6] *Rot. Scot.* II, 65–66.
[7] *Ibid.* II, 89–90, 110, 287 ; *Proceedings of the Privy Council* IV, 269–277, 295–297.　　　　　[8] *Rot. Scot* II, 463.
[9] *Ibid.* II, 470–471, 484.　　[10] Holinshed, *Chronicles* III, 769–770.
[11] *Ibid.* III, 769–770, 782–783 ; *D.N.B.* XXVIII, 62 ff.
C C

Passing now to the conference or council organized by these royal representatives, it is clear that such a body would be a natural outgrowth of the conditions of the North. It cannot be supposed that a number of wardens, deputies, and other officers of the marches, all owing obedience to one superior officer and all charged with the same duty of quelling disturbances and protecting the country, should not have met together to determine upon common measures for the maintenance of order, defence, or aggression. This kind of conference or association of the march officers occurs as early as 1314,[1] and in the next year there is evidence that some sort of consultation regularly preceded all arrangements for truce or armistice with the Scots.[2] Instances of this sort of assembly, sometimes including the local magnates and sometimes only the march officers, recur in 1345, 1352 and 1370.[3] Finally, in 1383, John of Gaunt, as king's lieutenant in the North, presides over such a meeting.[4] In the beginning of the fifteenth century John of Lancaster, second son of Henry IV, represented his father in the North, administering that region in association with a kind of council of march officials.[5] The plan of combining the local authorities into a sort of council for the defence and administration of the North is apparent in the arrangements made by the privy council preparatory to the king's departure for France in 1415.[6] The idea is continued during the fifteenth century by the frequent commissions which issued for the negotiation of truces and for their subsequent application and maintenance. These commissions generally included the officers of the marches and several of the northern barons and prelates, and were presided over by the royal lieutenant, if such an officer happened to be present. They were authorized to hear and determine litigation arising out of the terms of the truce and to take and imprison those who neglected them.[7] Finally,

[1] *Rot. Scot.* I, 113, 139.
[2] *Rot. Scot.* I, 151 ; *Foedera* III, 540, 541.
[3] *Rot. Scot.* I, 663, 670, 752, 940.
[4] *Foedera* (original edition) VII, 425.
[5] *Proceedings of the Privy Council* I, 315, 333, 350, II, 91–96, 136–139 ; Stubbs, *C.H.* III, 60–61 ; Scott, *History of Berwick-on-Tweed*, 85 ff.
[6] *Proceedings of the Privy Council* VI, 165.
[7] *Rot. Scot* II, 237, 256, 266, 267, 268, 272, 286, 287, 292, 294, 345, 387, 390, 413, 434.

when the young Duke of York became lieutenant of the North in 1498, a council of local notables was appointed to assist him.[1]

Another and a powerful force was tending, during this century, to separate the North from the rest of England. This was the increasing local influence of the baronage expressing itself in a kind of feudal reaction. Nowhere was this tendency more apparent than in the great northern families of Nevill and Percy. The barons were the shepherds of the people, and the people recognized them as their leaders.[2] The new and vicious feudalism of the fifteenth century, with its livery and mainten-ance, superseding the national military system and defeating justice, tended to loosen the bonds that drew the whole kingdom together and to foster a sense of remoteness and self-sufficiency in the North.[3] Symptoms of this appear as early as 1404.[4]

The northern baronage also contrived to keep the adminis-tration of the marches almost continuously in their own hands. Throughout the century Nevills and Percies are appointed and reappointed to the wardenships.[5] Dacres, Scropes, Mowbrays, Cliffords and De Roos, as well as the palatine bishops of Durham, also appear frequently in this capacity, and these names fill out the list of northern barons who exerted local influence.[6] Thus the ordinary local influence of the baronage was intensified by their extraordinary powers as lords marcher, and this second power was so constantly exercised by the two greatest northern families that men could not discriminate between the ordinary and extraordinary authority of the Percies and Nevills. Finally, the disruptive clan system obtained on the English side of the border to a much greater extent than is commonly supposed.[7]

These, then, were the conditions and forces tending to differentiate the North from the rest of England up to the

---

[1] *Ibid.* II, 517.   [2] Stubbs, *C.H.* III, 561.
[3] *Ibid.* III, 548–555.
[4] *Royal Letters of the Reign of Henry IV* (R.S.) I, 206, 207.
[5] *Proceedings of the Privy Council* I, 337, II, 213, IV, 269–277, VI, 65–66 ; *Rot. Scot.* II, 287, 313, 321, 355, 372, 377, 402, 407, 422, 442, 463, 484.
[6] *Ibid.* I, 940, 962, II, 53, 266, 399, 472, 486, 498, 501, 517, 522 ; *Pro-ceedings of the Privy Council* VI, 65–66 ; *Foedera* (original edition) XII, 399, 617 ; Stubbs, *C. H.* III, 517.
[7] *Tract illustrative of the Border Topography of Scotland* (ed. H. Ellis), *Archaeologia* XXII, 161–171.

beginning of the sixteenth century. The demoralizing effect
of border warfare is readily enough understood, but the
statement that the disorganization extended beyond the marches
to the five northern counties needs some illustration. In 1384
it was complained in parliament that people from Durham and
Chester were in the habit of making raids, for cattle-lifting
and the like, into the adjoining counties and then returning
to their privileged districts beyond the reach of punishment.[1]
In the fifteenth century an effort was made to correct these
disorders by legislation, and the statute prepared for this
purpose also sought to check the abuse of livery and maintenance. But the futility of the act is apparent in the means taken
to enforce it. The lords in parliament and all lords of franchises
were asked to take a personal oath to support the statute, which
was also communicated to the bishop of Durham and the
chamberlain of Wales with directions that they should exact a
similar oath from the people of the two palatinates.[2] In 1488 the
people of the North declined to pay their share of a tax on
movables which had been granted to the King for the war in
Brittany. The Earl of Northumberland, then lieutenant in the
North, brought the matter before the king who, fearing to
establish a precedent, refused to remit any part of the tax.
The earl was unpopular in the north, where Richard III had
been in great favour, and when he reported the king's answer,
' the rude and beastlie people . . . furiouslie and cruellie mur-
thered both him and diverse of his household servants '.[3]
This outbreak originated in York and Durham.[4]

Thus, by way of recapitulation, it appears that up to the
accession of the Tudors, the North had never been governed
like the rest of England. Not definitely English until the close
of Henry II's reign, these counties might still have been assimilated to the general system of administration had not the failure
of the royal line in Scotland plunged the two countries into a
war which was destined to last into modern times. In the mean-

[1] *Rot. Parl.* III, 201.
[2] *Ibid.* IV, 421–422 ; Bishop Langley's Chancery Roll, C., ann. 30, m.
10, *Durham,* Cursitor, 36 (Record Office) ; Calendar of Welsh Records,
Deputy Keeper's Report XXXVI, App. ii, 135.
[3] Holinshed, *Chronicles* III, 769–770 ; *Materials for a History of the
Reign of Henry VII* (R.S.), II, 480.
[4] Holinshed, *Chronicles* III, 769–770.

while, the necessity for keeping the marches in order quite withdrew portions of Cumberland and Northumberland from the regular administrative system and strongly affected the government of the neighbouring counties. Repeated invasions and expeditions against Scotland, bringing large armies through the North, impoverished and demoralized the country, occasioning disorders which demanded some special form of government. The administration of justice and the maintenance of the peace were seriously crippled by the large number of privileged districts and the undue local influence of the baronage. The effort to meet these difficulties by placing the North under the immediate control of the king and his council did not prove effectual, and probably contributed to increase the existing disorganization. In this way it came to pass that the problem of incorporating the northern counties with the rest of England was yet unsolved at the accession of the house of Tudor. It cannot be said that Henry VIII reached a final solution of the problem. He crushed, however, a dangerous rebellion in his own time and submitted the northern counties to such a discipline, that they were able a century later to take their natural place in the kingdom.

Some notion of the conditions and requirements of the North at the beginning of the sixteenth century has now been obtained; it remains to examine the attempts made to meet these requirements up to 1537, when a policy was adopted that for a century served its purpose well. After Surrey had suppressed the rebellion of 1488, Thomas, Lord Dacre of Gilsland, a nobleman of much local influence in Cumberland, became warden of the marches and held that office with few interruptions until his death in 1525.[1] Up to 1522 Dacre, in association with Sir Anthony Ughtred, captain of Berwick, and Dr. Magnus, archdeacon of the east riding of Yorkshire, administered the North under the direction of Wolsey.[2] In this arrangement there is latent the notion of a lieutenant and council acting as the representatives of the central government, a notion which in its inception and rudimentary development has been traced through the fourteenth and fifteenth centuries. The warden

[1] *C.S.P.* (Henry VIII) iii, ii, no. 3096 ; iv, i, no. 1727.
[2] *Ibid.* i, no. 1850 ; ii, i. no. 1598 ; ii, ii, no. 3365.

corresponds to the lieutenant; he was in constant communication with the king and privy council, submitting to them detailed reports of his actions and receiving in return equally detailed instructions.[1] In 1516 and again in 1518 the warden's influence over the civil administration of the northern counties was increased.[2] Dacre's frequent consultations with Ughtred and Magnus, and their common reports to Wolsey, represent the local council.

After the victory of Flodden Field, in 1513, the chief duty of Dacre and his colleagues was to fortify the North and establish order. Their efforts to accomplish this end were continued with very indifferent success for eight years. But in 1521 it was made apparent to Wolsey that the existing arrangements were no longer adequate.[3] At the same time the king's intimate relation with the Queen Dowager and the infant King of Scots and the attitude of the Duke of Albany, who represented the French influence in Scotland, made it imperative that the English government should have such complete control of the borders as to prevent the unforeseen outbreak of hostilities.[4] New measures for administering the North were therefore devised, and this marks the close of the first stage in the development of the Council of the North.

Wolsey's device to meet the new requirements consisted in the mission of a royal lieutenant to put the North in order, and the organization of a secret, permanent council to aid the lieutenant and to carry on the policy he had inaugurated. It will be seen at once that this scheme contains no novelty beyond the definite and permanent organization of the council. All the elements were tried and familiar. In February, 1522, John Kite, the newly elected bishop of Carlisle, was sent northward with full instructions for organizing the secret council. The king,

[1] *Ibid.* I, nos. 380, 3577, 4105, 4870, 5090 ; II, i, no. 2620 ; II, ii, nos. 3386, 4547 ; III, i, no. 1169. Several of Dacre's reports are printed *in extenso* in Raine, *North Durham* vi, ff.

[2] *C.S.P.* (Henry VIII), II, i, no. 2481 ; II, ii, no. 4547.

[3] 'A bill of information made unto my lord Cardinal's grace for the repressing of maintainers of murder within the county of Northumberland.' *C.S.P.* III, ii, nos. 1920–1921. This document may have been the work of Dacre and his associates, but its origin is not clear. The original marginalia show that nearly all prisoners were sent up to London to be dealt with by the privy council.

[4] *Ibid.* III, ii, no. 2075.

it was explained, intended shortly to appoint some proper nobleman as his lieutenant north of the Trent, ' to set that country in readiness '. In the meantime Kite was to join Dacre at Carlisle and there to assemble certain northern gentlemen, designated as councillors.[1] The council was presided over by Lord Dacre, and Kite acted as treasurer. Troops and funds were placed at its disposal and it was entrusted with the general administration of the North.[2]

The appointment of a lieutenant was put off until the summer, but in the meantime the council met at the summons of Dacre.[3] It was not, however, as successful as had been hoped. In May, Kite reported to Wolsey complaining of want of money, charging various members of the council with inefficiency, avarice and dishonesty, and recommending that ' some good captains should be sent down '.[4] Wolsey at once remanded Kite to his diocese and deprived him of his office of treasurer to the council, which he conferred on Dacre.[5] It is clear that from the beginning Wolsey intended that the council should be no more than a convenient mechanism for carrying out his will in the North.[6]

The time had now come for the mission of a royal lieutenant and the choice fell upon George Talbot, earl of Shrewsbury. Shrewsbury, under the title of lieutenant-general of the North, was given wide powers and minute instructions. He was to go to York and there to take over the general command of the king's troops and garrisons in the North, to suppress disturbances and to administer impartial justice in all causes. In the matter of residence he was allowed to choose among the royal houses of Pontefract, Sheriff Hutton and Barnard Castle, the first two in Yorkshire and the latter in Durham. This point is of importance as defining the territorial extent of the lieutenant's jurisdiction, which was to extend southward over Yorkshire

---

[1] These were Sir William, Sir Robert and Sir Marmaduke Constable, Sir William Bulmer, Sir Christopher Dacre (one of the wardens of the marches), and Sir Anthony Ughtred, captain of Berwick. *C.S.P.*, iii, ii, no. 2075.

[2] *Ibid*. iii, ii, no. 2075. [3] *Ibid*. iii, ii, no. 2186.

[4] *Ibid*. iii, ii, no. 2271.

[5] *Ibid*. iii, ii, nos. 2294–2295, 2613. A letter from Kite to Wolsey announcing that he had transferred to Dacre the funds in his possession as treasurer of the council, seems to belong here rather than in the following year where it has been placed by Mr. Brewer. *C.S.P.* iv, i, no. 448.

[6] *Ibid*. iii, ii, no. 2318.

and to include the county palatine of Durham. Finally, he was
to accept the aid and advice of the secret council, to which he
was to add certain gentlemen designated in his instructions.[1]
It was not part of Wolsey's plan to keep a lieutenant permanently resident in the North. He seems to have thought that
for the purposes of ordinary administration, Dacre's long
experience aided by the collective wisdom and local influence
of the council, and occasionally reinforced by the presence of a
royal lieutenant, would suffice to keep the North in good order.
But this calculation proved to be incorrect.

Shrewsbury's mission was uneventful and not very successful.[2] Accordingly in the next summer (1523) the king sent
down Thomas Howard, earl of Surrey. Surrey joined the
council and lost no time in taking an active part in the civil,
military and judicial administration of the northern counties.[3]
He sat with the judges in their circuits, attempted to harmonize
local factions, and in general informed himself of the condition
and needs of the district under his control. In August he wrote
to Wolsey that the administration of justice was slack and the
abuse of livery and maintenance very prevalent, that the
intention of the government to put the North in order was not
taken seriously, and that Wolsey's method was ineffectual. In
conclusion he suggested that some great nobleman be appointed
to be continually resident, assisted by such a council as already
existed in the marches of Wales.[4] From this it appears that
the northern counties were still in the chaotic and disordered
state in which they had been in the preceding centuries. The
suggestion of a council cannot be taken to imply that the body

[1] These were the Lords Darcy, Latimer, Percy and Conyers, all north-
country names. The councillors were to take oath according to a form
subjoined to Shrewsbury's instructions. *C.S.P.* III, ii, no. 2412.

[2] *Ibid.* III, ii, no. 2544.

[3] *Ibid.* III, ii, no. 3200.

[4] The whole of this letter is important and interesting. Surrey complained that at Durham, where he sat with the judges, ' only one man, an
Irishman, was hanged '. At Newcastle twelve indicted persons had
escaped, and although eleven others were produced, it was impossible to
get evidence against them because ' so few of the gentlemen of Northumberland . . . have not thieves belonging to them.' The whole system is
weak, ' the whole country thinks the talk of administering justice here is
only intended to frighten them, as no man is appointed to continue among
them to see justice administered.' In conclusion he says that ' the judges
think it is ten times more necessary to have a council here than in the
marches of Wales.' *C.S.P.* III, ii, no. 3240.

organized the year before had been disbanded, for its report to Wolsey, in August, 1523, is evidence of its continued existence.[1] This document was clearly inspired by Surrey. It recommends that the privy council take active measures for the suppression of livery and maintenance in the North, that the local council hold four sessions annually for judicial purposes, and that ' some great and discreet nobleman ' should be made warden of the marches and required to remain permanently in the North to see that justice was effectually administered there.[2] Surrey saw what Wolsey could not or would not see, and if the lieutenant's policy had been immediately adopted it is by no means impossible that the central government might have obtained so firm a hold upon the North that it would have been able to withstand the great strain of the change of religion and its attendant circumstances that led to the rebellion of 1536. But Wolsey must have found it hard to accept the suggestion of his rival, particularly when that suggestion involved his resigning the personal direction of a part of the administration.

The plan was therefore received in a half-hearted way, and in October Surrey was made warden of the marches.[3] He had no wish, however, to remain long away from the court, and in December he left the North and was immediately succeeded in his office of warden by Dacre.[4] Early in the new year (1524) the secret council assembled to take action on instructions newly sent down by Wolsey.[5]

The change in the king's relations with Scotland which declared itself in the summer of 1524 made it imperative that the borders should be controlled and kept quiet. Elaborate preparations were made for the meeting between the chancellor of Scotland and Surrey (now duke of Norfolk), who was sent north to carry out the king's intention of ' erecting the young king of Scotland '.[6] The negotiation failed, the border relapsed into a disordered state and the council applied its energies to arranging raids—warden-rodes they were called—

[1] *Ibid.* III, ii, no. 3286.
[2] *Ibid.* III, ii, no. 3286.   [3] *Ibid.* III, ii, no. 3438.
[4] *Ibid.* III, ii, no. 3626.
[5] *Ibid.* IV, i, no. 219.
[6] *Ibid.* IV, i, nos. 474, 498, 506, 516, 525, 530, 535, 549, 571.

into Scotland.[1] It was now apparent that the secret council, even with the aid of a lieutenant, did not meet the require-ments of the case. The scheme had failed, and something new had to be devised. Here, then, closes the second stage in the development of the Council of the North.

In the summer of 1525, Henry Fitz Roy, a natural son of Henry VIII, was sent to the North as a permanent representative of the king's authority in that region. Henry, at this time six years of age, was created duke of Richmond, and appointed lieutenant-general north of Trent, keeper of Carlisle and warden-general of the marches.[2] To enable him to discharge the duties connected with these offices and to administer the North the young duke was surrounded with a council having very much the same membership as the earlier secret council. It contained also Dr. Magnus and William Frankleyne, arch-deacon and temporal chancellor of the bishopric of Durham, a man of the same stripe as Magnus and, like him, an agent of Wolsey. Richmond remained in the North, chiefly at Pontefract and Sheriff Hutton in Yorkshire, until 1532. During this period his council, under the close supervision of Wolsey as long as he remained in power, and afterwards with greater independence, conducted diplomatic relations with Scotland and adminis-tered the northern counties in the name of the Duke of Rich-mond. This is only a slight variation of the plan of a lieutenant and council, but it introduces the element of permanence and constant residence on the part of the royal representative. These arrangements form Wolsey's final contribution to the solution of the problem. If subsequent events proved it futile, it did at least last his time and was by him considered adequate.[3]

But Wolsey was mistaken. The acts of the duke's council and its relation to the central government show that it was ineffectual. A vigorous policy and sufficient independence to permit of immediate action in the face of difficulties, were demanded by the situation. Norfolk had seen this at once and

[1] *Ibid.* IV, i, no. 762 ; see Armstrong, *History of Liddesdale*, 217–220.
[2] *Ibid.* IV, i, nos. 1431, 1510 ; *D.N.B.* XIX, 204, 205.
[3] In 1526 the Scots king submitted to Henry VIII a list of gravamina entitled, ' Misrule of the Borders '. Wolsey endorsed this document thus, ' Provision is made already to this effect by the duke of Richmond's council ; ' showing that he considered the duke's council the solution of the whole northern difficulty. *C.S.P.* IV, i, no. 2292.

the failure of the secret council had corroborated him. But Wolsey shut his eyes to all this and kept the new council, as he had kept the old one, in close leading-strings. In the autumn of 1525 the duke's council wrote to Wolsey asking for money and for leave to appoint wardens and to fill a vacancy in its own body.[1] The North was now in a very disturbed condition and great efforts were made to establish order to promote the king's negotiations with Scotland. Magnus, now English resident at the court of James, went to the borders, and Norfolk was again sent down as lieutenant. But all to no purpose. In December the Earl of Westmorland, as a last resort, summoned an assembly of the gentlemen of the borders and the lieutenants of the marches and begged them to observe a kind of *modus vivendi* arranged by himself and the Earl of Angus.[2] In the meantime Wolsey sent for several members of the Duke of Richmond's council to confer with him at London.[3] By the spring some improvement had been effected,[4] and in the course of the summer the council bestirred itself and began to attend to the civil administration of the North.[5] In August it was sitting with the judges of assize at York and Newcastle in order to secure evidence and indictments, and was trying to keep the unruly clans or ' surnames ' quiet by paying them.[6] In December the council was alarmed at the consequences of its own activity. There had been serious disturbances in the North and a number of raids and robberies on the borders. The council had begun to repress these vigorously but soon found itself in conflict with the Earl of Northumberland. Terrified by the great local influence of the Percies it at once gave over the whole affair, referring it to Wolsey and the privy council.[7]

Thus ends the first year of the council's administration, a record of timorous ineptitude. But this was probably as much the fault of Wolsey as of the council. He allowed it little independence and, occupied as he was with questions of international policy, neglected the North. A new pope had recently

[1] *Ibid.* iv, i, nos. 1727, 1779.
[2] *C.S.P.* iv, i, nos. 1808, 1809, 1821, 1862 (ii).
[3] *Ibid.* iv, i, no. 1910.   [4] *Ibid.* iv, i, nos. 1980, 2004, 2031.
[5] *Ibid.* iv, ii, no. 2402.   [6] *Ibid.* iv, ii, no. 2402.
[7] *Ibid.* iv, ii, nos. 2729, 2993 ; also *ibid.*, no. 2608.

been elected and already the question of the divorce was beginning to overshadow all other problems; so Wolsey let affairs on the border take their course. The council, however, quite recognized its own inefficiency, and pointed out to Wolsey, in terms much the same as Norfolk had used four years earlier, the measures that ought to be taken to establish order in the northern counties. During the summer of 1527 it had continued its usual activities, corresponding with the Scots king about the affairs of the border and busying itself with the civil and judicial administration of the district under its control. It sat with the judges at York and Newcastle, and appointed members of its own body to the shrievalties of Northumberland and Cumberland.[1] But its authority was disregarded and, doubting its own legality, it implored the king to maintain its credit.[2] Uncertain and hesitating in ordinary affairs, the council found itself absolutely incapable of coping with a difficulty connected with the escape from prison of two members of the Lisle family, which in the course of the summer threatened to develop into a popular rising.[3] In November the council wrote to Wolsey confessing its entire inability to deal with the problems confronting it, and asking that some great nobleman be sent down, ' to lie continually in Northumberland '.[4]

The communication demanded and received instant attention. On December 2, 1527, the Earl of Northumberland was appointed warden-general of the marches with directions to govern the North with the aid and advice of the council which, for the rest, had undergone some reorganization.[5] The new warden went north at once, and after visiting the Duke of Richmond at Pontefract, joined the council at Newcastle.[6] He immediately proceeded to inaugurate a policy of greatly increased severity by proclaiming serious temporal and spiritual penalties against all who did not submit to the king's

---

[1] *Ibid.* IV, ii, nos. 3344, 3404, 3477, 3501, 3610.

[2] *Ibid.* IV, ii, no. 3383. This was in August, 1527 ; the letter is signed by Magnus, Parre, Bulmer, Foljambe, Tempest, Taite and Bowes, and countersigned by Uvedale, secretary of the council. See also *C.S.P.* IV, ii, no. 3552.

[3] *Ibid.* IV, ii, nos. 3383, 3501, 3552.

[4] *Ibid.* IV, ii, no. 3552.

[5] *Ibid.* IV, ii, nos. 3628, 3629.   [6] *Ibid.* IV, ii, no. 3689.

mercy.[1] On January 12 he held a march court at Alnwick, where nine persons were beheaded for march treason and five hanged for felony.[2] All through the year (1528) he and the council submitted to Wolsey constant and detailed reports of their doings.[3] Still the council was kept in leading strings, and when in March it undertook to appoint a *locum tenens* to supply the place of its secretary it was sharply snubbed by Wolsey.[4] In October the council professed itself unable to settle a dispute between the Earl of Cumberland and Lord Dacre and submitted the case along with a number of other similar matters to Wolsey.[5] But the chancellor continued to affirm the legality of the council's jurisdiction by occasionally referring to it cases of which it might appropriately take cognizance.[6]

For three years after the fall of Wolsey the history of the North of England is involved in great obscurity, owing to the extreme scarcity of documentary evidence. Towards the close of the year 1531 the Earl of Northumberland, still warden of the marches, submits to the king a long report on Scottish affairs and the condition of the North.[7] The council is not mentioned, but its continued existence may be inferred from its subsequent reappearance and from the fact that the Duke of Richmond remained in Yorkshire until the spring of 1532.[8] Richmond's departure marks the formal close of the third stage in the development of the Council of the North. But the next period, from 1532 to the outbreak of the rebellion in 1536, presents no new elements and is characterized by retrogression rather than development. After Richmond had gone there was some question of sending Norfolk again as lieutenant. But this was dropped and Northumberland retained the civil and military administration of the North.[9]

The council reappears in January 1533. Cromwell was now well established in power and through his agent Sir George Lawson, treasurer of Berwick, began to deal with the problem

[1] *Ibid.* IV, ii, nos. 3795, 3816.   [2] *Ibid.* IV, ii, no. 3795.
[3] *Ibid.* IV, ii, nos. 3849, 3850, 4132–4134, 4925.
[4] *Ibid.* IV, ii, no. 4042.   [5] *Ibid.* IV, ii, no. 4855.
[6] *Ibid.* IV, iii, no. 5430.
[7] *State Papers* (Rec. Com.) IV, nos. ccxv, ccxxii.
[8] *D.N.B.* XIX, 204–205.
[9] *State Papers* (Rec. Com.) IV, nos. ccxxv, ccxxix, ccxxxi, ccxxxv.

of the North. After Richmond's departure his council had joined Northumberland and they acted in common, under the style of the Lord Warden and Council of the Marches. Cromwell accepted the existence of this apparatus and controlled it through Lawson, who had charge of all the king's money which was applied to the defence of the borders. In January, 1533, Lawson wrote to Cromwell advising that the king should ' send a strait letter to my Lord Warden and the Council here ', with regard to the mustering of troops.[1] The council now consisted chiefly of the local gentry, each of whom was bound to produce a certain retinue or following when a ' rode ' was to be undertaken. They sat with the warden at Alnwick and were chiefly concerned with the defence of the borders and the arrangement of invasions or ' rodes ' into Scotland.[2] They were under the close supervision of the central government, reporting constantly to Cromwell or to the king (sometimes by letter and sometimes in the person of one of their members sent to London for the purpose), and receiving detailed instructions from them.[3] Besides this, Lawson, from time to time, communicated his opinion of the warden and council to Cromwell.[4]

Early in 1533 Lawson suggested that, instead of relying upon private retinues, the warden and council should resort to a general levy in the northern counties. This was partly owing to his distrust of the local nobility and gentry.[5] In February Lawson repeated his suggestion, with the significant recommendation that the troops raised in this fashion should be commanded by captains from some other part of England.[6] He continued to urge his plan, but Northumberland, who was looking back to the feudal glories of the Percies in the fifteenth century, successfully opposed it.[7] Had it been adopted it is possible that the rebellion might have been immediately crushed or even averted; but the king, like Wolsey when warned by Norfolk, would not or could not see.

The council at this time was composed of five or six persons

---

[1] *C.S.P.* VI, no. 16.   [2] *Ibid.* VI, nos. 51, 124, 155, 217, 260, 322.
[3] *Ibid.* VI, nos. 17, 107, 113, 322, 375, 606, 909, 1048, 1187.
[4] *Ibid.* VI, nos. 51, 217.
[5] *Ibid.* VI, no. 16.   [6] *Ibid.* VI, nos. 124, 145.
[7] *Ibid.* VI, nos. 145, 217, 269, 1589 ; *State Papers* (Rec. Com.), IV, nos. ccxxxv, ccxl.

several of whom had belonged to the Duke of Richmond's council.[1] It was occupied with fortifying the borders, treating with the Scottish commissioners and, in a small way, with the general administration of the North.[2] It was officially known as the Council of the Marches.[3]

This method of administration was continued up to the very eve of the rebellion.[4] Lawson's prudent suggestion of a general levy was not accepted,[5] but some slight ceremonial changes, emphasizing the character of the warden as immediate representative of the king, were introduced.[6] Under pressure of larger interests of state the king and Cromwell were neglecting the northern counties, or only dealing with the disorders there in an abrupt and intermittent fashion that produced exasperation without relief and was worse than total neglect.[7] Cromwell was conscious of this, for in June 1535 there appears in his memoranda a note regarding the suppression of riots in the North by means of establishing there such a council as already existed in the marches of Wales.[8] But the matter was allowed to stand over. In the meantime events were hurrying to a climax and no measures had been taken for controlling the North. Cromwell's agent, Barlow, wrote to him from Berwick early in 1536 describing the disordered condition of the North. 'Authority,' he says, ' must be given to execute justice without fear of partiality, otherwise admonitions only make things worse .'[9] Still Cromwell was not to be roused. In the course of the summer things rapidly grew worse, grew, in effect, as bad as possible, and in October the rebellion broke out. The story of the Pilgrimage of Grace has been told elsewhere;[10] for present purposes its consequences alone are important. The effort to restore order in the North after the close of the

---

[1] The members were : Magnus, Sir Thomas Clifford, Sir Thomas Wharton (who wore the Earl of Northumberland's livery but had been appointed at Cromwell's direction), and Sir Ralf Ellerkar. Both Magnus and Ellerkar had served on Richmond's council, *C.S.P.* vi, nos. 17, 51, 143, 150.

[2] *State Papers* (Rec. Com.), iv, nos. ccxliv, ccxlvi–cclii.

[3] *C.S.P.* vi, no. 150.   [4] *Ibid.* viii, nos. 696, 945, 992–994.

[5] *Iibd.* ix, no. 1078.   [6] *Ibid.* viii, no. 100.

[7] Froude, *History of England* iii, 96.

[8] *C.S.P.* viii, no. 892.

[9] *Ibid.* x, no. 286.

[10] Best of all by M. and R. Dodds, *The Pilgimage of Grace* (1915). Gairdner's account will be found in the introduction to the *C.S.P.*, Vol. xi, Froude's in the *History*, iii, ch. xiii.

rebellion forms the last stage in the development of the Council of the North.

The organized rebellion was brought to an end by the pacification at Doncaster, December 2, 1536, but the danger of a fresh outbreak was not passed until the execution of Aske in the following July. During these seven months the North was governed under martial law by the Duke of Norfolk and a council. Early in January (1537), Norfolk, who had gone home after the meeting at Doncaster, was again on his way northward.[1] A few members of the council which was to help him to restore order accompanied him; the rest were northern gentlemen who were appointed to join him at Doncaster. Norfolk's instructions show that the mission of a council and lieutenant at this time was a provisional measure. The king himself intended to go northward in the summer. Meanwhile, Norfolk and the council were to hear complaints, redress grievances and in general to pacify the North by exercising as much severity as could safely be applied. The part to be played by the council is also set forth in Norfolk's instructions: ' that things may be handled substantially, so that people may see the good of law and the evil of violence, his Majesty has joined with the said Duke an honourable council . . . whose advice the Duke shall in all things use.'[2] The rebels were required to sue out their pardons individually, and to facilitate this process Norfolk was directed to go from place to place, administering to those who sued for pardon the oath of allegiance under a special form. He had express instructions to keep all who asked for pardons ' dangling ' until the king's arrival.[3] The lieutenant and council were also instructed to promote the spreading of the new religion by official preachers, and to contrive if possible to remove the religious of suppressed houses who had returned to their former seats. The lieutenant and council had high judicial authority; they were to hold a bi-weekly session replacing the visits of the judges and the local courts, and to make progresses through the country taking cognizance of all commotions and

[1] *C.S.P.* XII, i, No. 86.   [2] *Ibid.* XII, i, no. 98.
[3] *Ibid.* At Doncaster Henry had promised a free pardon to all and this is the way the promise was redeemed. Froude, the apologist, does not boggle at this ; he says, ' Norfolk was instructed to respect literally the terms of the pardon '. *History* III, 188.

offences that had occurred since the granting of the pardon in December. Considerable allowance was made for Norfolk's inability to carry out these instructions, the whole tone of which is disingenuous[1] and indicates no intention on the part of the king ' to respect literally the terms of the pardon '.[2]

Norfolk reached Pontefract on February 2, 1537.[3] In the meantime the abortive rising of Bigod and Hallam had occurred and on February 12 riotous scenes, amounting to a fresh outbreak of rebellion, took place at Carlisle.[4] On February 14 the Council of the Marches—for so the body is styled in the contemporary endorsement of the letter—wrote to the king advising him to use greater severity in dealing with these troubles,[5] a suggestion which Henry was not slow to accept. The pacification of the North now began in earnest. The king was alarmed by the renewed outbreak of the rebellion, and Norfolk, at no time over nice, was ready to go to almost any extreme of harshness to redeem himself from the suspicion of disloyalty that he had incurred by his dealings with the insurgents at Doncaster.[6] On February 22 the king instructed Norfolk to proclaim martial law. ' You must cause such dreadful execution,' he wrote, ' upon a good number of the inhabitants, hanging them on trees, quartering them, and setting their heads and quarters in every town, as shall be a fearful warning, whereby shall ensue the preservation of a great multitude.'[7] Norfolk was diligent in carrying out these instructions. In Cumberland six thousand persons were arrested and brought before the council, for no convictions could be secured by

---

[1] If any one refused the oath of allegiance, ' the Duke, if he thinks himself able, shall use him as the king's rebel ; and if he may not proceed to that punishment without danger, he shall pretend to make light of such a fool '. Persons found guilty in the progresses of inquiry ' he shall afterwards cause to be apprehended and executed, if it may be done without danger . . . and if he may not do that without danger, he shall look through his fingers at their offences, and free them to continue till the King's Majesty's arrival in those parts '. *C.S.P.* XII i, no. 98.

[2] Froude, *History* III, 188.

[3] *State Papers* (Rec. Com.) I, ii, no. lxxix.

[4] Froude, *History* III, 182–190.

[5] *C.S.P.* XII, i, No. 421. This letter is signed by T. Clifford, W. Eure, J. Weddrington, R. Collingwood, L. Gray, C. Ratcliffe and J. Horslee, but the Earl of Northumberland and one of the Bowes were also members of the council ; *ibid.* XII, i, no. 86.

[6] See Norfolk's letter to Cromwell quoted in Froude, *History* III, 190.

[7] *C.S.P.* XII, i, no. 479.

jury. Seventy-four were executed, ' and, sir,' wrote Norfolk
to the king, ' though the number be nothing so great as their
deserts did require to have suffered, yet I think the like number
hath not be heard of put to execution at one time.'[1]

These measures produced the required result, and by the
middle of the summer the North was quiet. Whether it had
been effectually pacified or merely stunned may be judged from
the action of the next generation in 1569. For present purposes
it should be noticed that the lieutenant and council of the
marches were not regarded as a permanent institution. Some
enduring machinery of government had yet to be devised. The
discussion of this point is worth attention. A scheme of government submitted to the king early in March 1537 illustrates the
general principles upon which Norfolk and Cromwell were
agreed. These involved a permanent royal lieutenant and a
council with greatly increased authority. It was proposed that
some nobleman (who should also be a privy councillor) be
appointed lieutenant, ' with a discreet council commissioned
to hear all causes in Cumberland, Westmorland, Northumberland, the bishopric of Durham and Yorkshire, and that he
[the lieutenant] for the most part abide in those parts '.[2] The
march laws were to be reformed and the marches practically
incorporated with the adjacent counties, the authority of the
wardens passing to the lieutenant, who was to exercise some of
these functions by deputy. Finally, the king was, as far as
possible, to take into his own hands all lordships and special
jurisdictions.[3]

This proposition gave rise to a curious correspondence.
Norfolk and his council continued to urge their scheme while
Cromwell threw every difficulty in the way of its execution.
Norfolk was told that no suitable nobleman could be found to

---

[1] *C.S.P.* XII, i, no. 498. Froude calls this ' wholesome severity ' and
' not excessive ', *History* III, 190–192. But even Norfolk boggled at the
application of wholesome severity on this scale. Before undertaking the
punishment of the eastern counties he wrote to Cromwell asking how many
executions the King expected in that region, and adding ' folks think the
last justice at Carlisle great, and if more than 20 suff(er) at Durham and
York it will be talked about '. *C.S.P.* XII, i, no. 609.

[2] *C.S.P.* XII, i, no. 595.

[3] *Ibid.* All franchises and liberties had been much curtailed by act of
Parliament in 1536,—27 Henry VIII, cap. xiv, *Statutes of the Realm*
III, 555.

assume the office of lieutenant; Dacre and Cumberland were on bad terms, Northumberland exerted too powerful an influence in the North. Would not the duke's authority, it was asked, ' make even a mean man respected ? '[1] But Norfolk declined to take the responsibility of suggesting any candidate until in April he mentioned, ' for the king's ear only ', the names of Lord Rutland and the Earl of Westmorland. All through the negotiation, however, he insisted on the importance of the office being held by a nobleman. Early in May the king closed the discussion with a characteristic letter. He thanks Norfolk for his advice but feels sure that he will accept the decision which the king has reached, ' for we will not be bound to accept the services of none but lords.'[2] The explanation of this episode lies in the relations of Cromwell and Norfolk. As long as the plebeian minister remained in favour the king did not altogether trust Norfolk. The duke perfectly understood this and chafed at being kept in exile in the North. Cromwell's advantage lay in the fact that no one in England was better fitted for the office of lieutenant than Norfolk, ' whom all offenders in the North regarded as their scourge '.[3] By trying to force Norfolk to accept the task Cromwell was able at once to serve his own ends and his master's cause.

As far as concerned the selection of an agent the king carried through his plan, for the choice ultimately fell upon Cuthbert Tunstall, the pliable bishop of Durham, who became lord president of the council, the title of lieutenant having been abandoned. For the rest Norfolk had his will, but at the cost of some tergiversation. He was ill, afraid of the harsh northern winter and determined to come home. The pressure that he was able to exert on the king may be judged from a note in Cromwell's agenda for the privy council in June 1537 : ' If the king will recall him [Norfolk], that then a council be established there as in the Marches of Wales, and lands appointed for its support '.[4] On June 12 the king notified Norfolk of his intention of postponing for a year his projected visitation of the

---

[1] *C.S.P.* XII, i, no. 636.
[2] *Ibid.* XII, i, nos. 636, 651, 667, 916, 919, 1118.
[3] So wrote Sir Thomas Tempest to Cromwell in July 1537 ; *ibid.* XII, ii, no. 238.
[4] *Ibid.* XII, ii, No. 177.

D d 2

North.[1] Under these circumstances, and out of regard for the
duke's health, the king wrote, ' We doo purpose shortly to
revoke you, and to establishe a standing Counseill ther, for the
conservation of those Countreyes in quiete, and thadministra-
tion of commen justice : which, being ones sett in a frame, We
shall incontinently call you unto Us '.[2] Norfolk's answer
(June 15) shows that he was beginning to recede from his original position with regard to the necessity of having a nobleman
as lieutenant, for he accepts as an equivalent the appointment
of the bishop of Durham as president of the council.[3] On July
8 he wrote to Cromwell that with a council under a president,
and a minister of justice ' so usyng hymself that men may be
affrayed of hym, this contry is nowe in that sorte, that none of
the realme shalbe better governed than this '.[4]

Thus the question reached a final solution. There followed
some discussion about the membership of the new body, which
in the end included nearly all of those who had formed part of
Norfolk's temporary council.[5] Norfolk remained in the North
helping to set the new council ' in a frame,' until September,
when he was at length recalled.[6] The jurisdiction of the Council
of the North extended over the counties of Northumberland,
Cumberland, Westmorland, Durham and York. It had the
general administrative and judicial control of this district.
The council was authorized to maintain the peace and suppress
disturbances, either by regular process of law or otherwise
according to its discretion. It was enabled to take cognizance,
to the exclusion of the ordinary courts, of all pleas and contentious litigation where one of the parties was so poor, or of such
mean estate, as to be hampered in obtaining his remedy at the
common law.[7]

[1] The reasons generally given for this change are, the delicate state of
foreign relations, the queen's pregnancy and the king's own health, which
made travelling very hard for him. But it is scarcely likely that Henry
would have allowed any of these considerations to weigh with him if
Norfolk's vigorous policy had not been so successful in subduing the North.
C.S.P. xii, ii, no. 77.

[2] State Papers (Rec. Com.) i, ii, no. lxxxix.

[3] C.S.P. xii, ii, no. 100.

[4] State Papers (Rec. Com.) v, no. cccxxii.

[5] C.S.P. xii, ii, nos. 77, 100, 102, 249, 250 (2, iv).

[6] State Papers (Rec. Com.) v, nos. cccxxv, cccxxviii, cccxxx, cccxxxiii.

[7] Coke, Fourth Institute, ch. xlix ; Prothero, Statutes and Documents,
xc–xci. The important parts of the commission are printed by Coke.

The institution of the Council of the North contained no elements that had not been familiar, at least in a rudimentary form, since the fourteenth century. The novelty lay in the reorganization and development of these elements. The existence of the Council was later considered to be an infringement on the authority of parliament and the judiciary;[1] and no doubt in the seventeenth century it became at once an instrument of oppression and an obstacle to the normal development of government. But the institution must be judged by the conditions which brought it into being, not those under which it was abolished. To say that it impeded the progress of England in 1641 is to say that it had, at that time, no reason for existence; that it had made itself superfluous, resembling, in that respect at least, the ideal government. It has been the object of the present study to show that in the sixteenth century the Council of the North had a very urgent reason for existence.

[1] Coke, *Fourth Institute,* ch. xlix.

INDEX